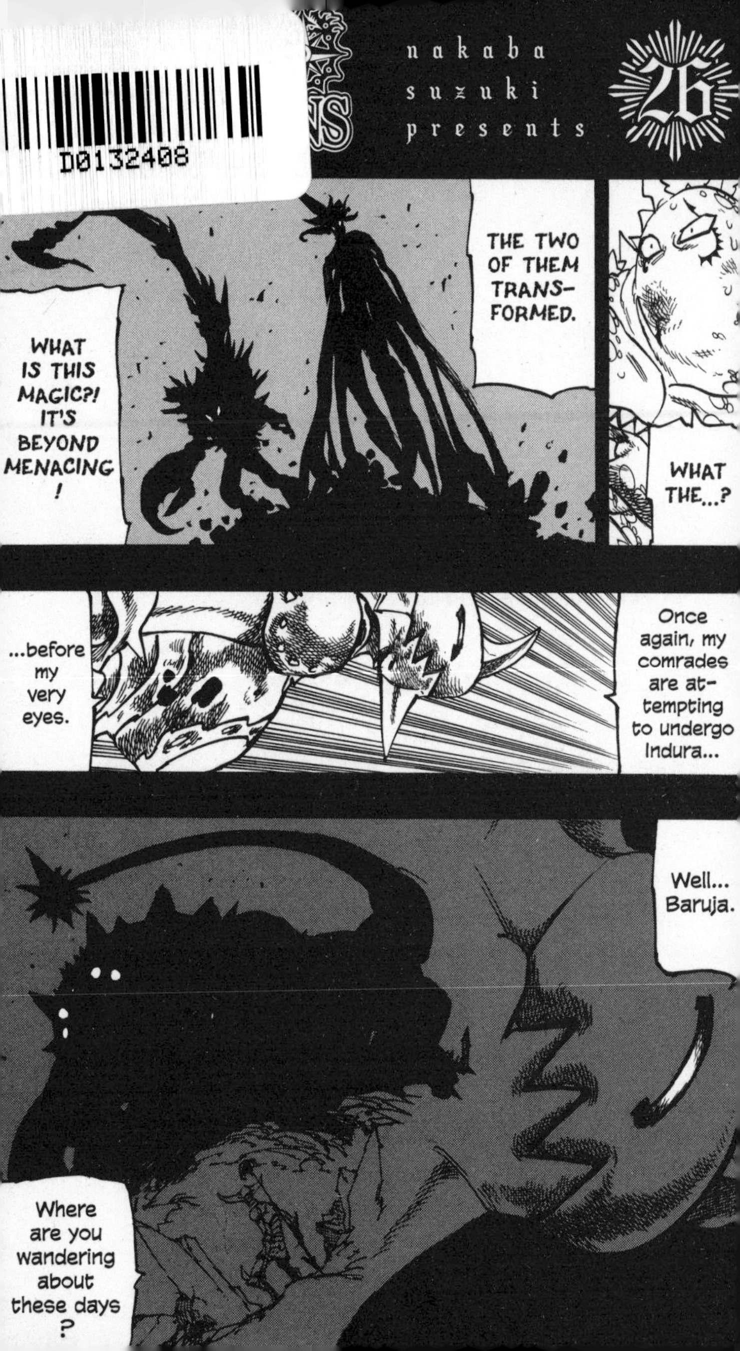
nakaba suzuki presents
26
WHAT THE...?
THE TWO OF THEM TRANSFORMED.
WHAT IS THIS MAGIC?! IT'S BEYOND MENACING!
Once again, my comrades are attempting to undergo Indura...
...before my very eyes.
Well... Baruja.
Where are you wandering about these days?

CONTENTS

BOAR HAT

The Seven Deadly Sins

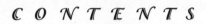

THE SEVEN DEADLY SINS

Chapter 207 - Indura, Creature of Destruction

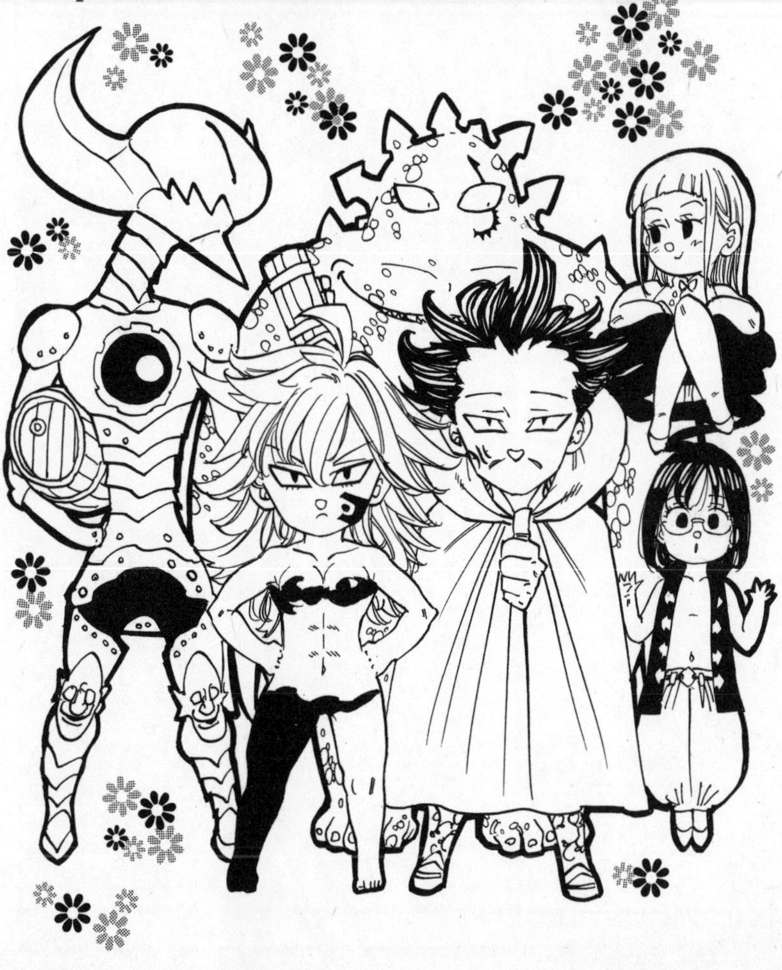

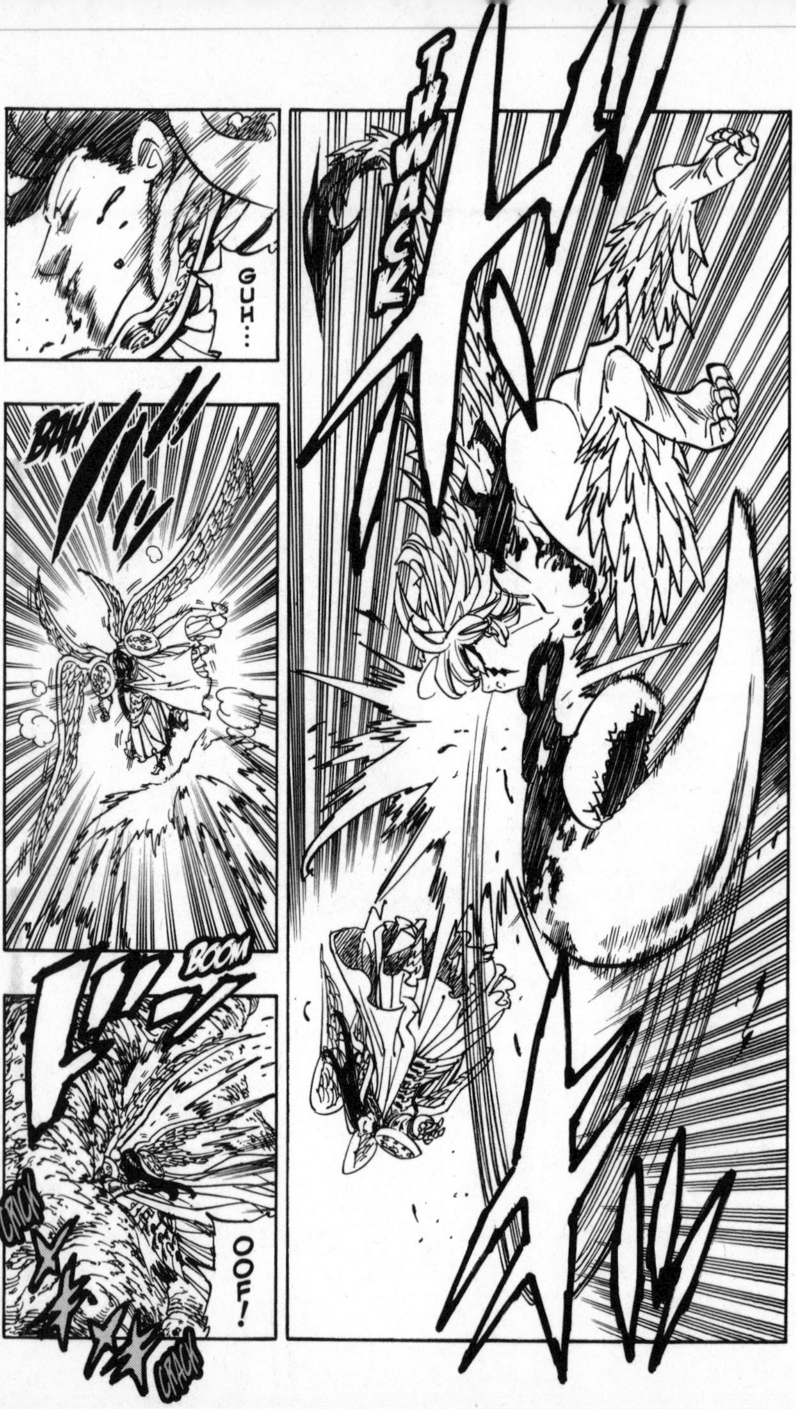
THWACK
GUH...
BAH
BOOM
OOF!
CRACK
CRACK

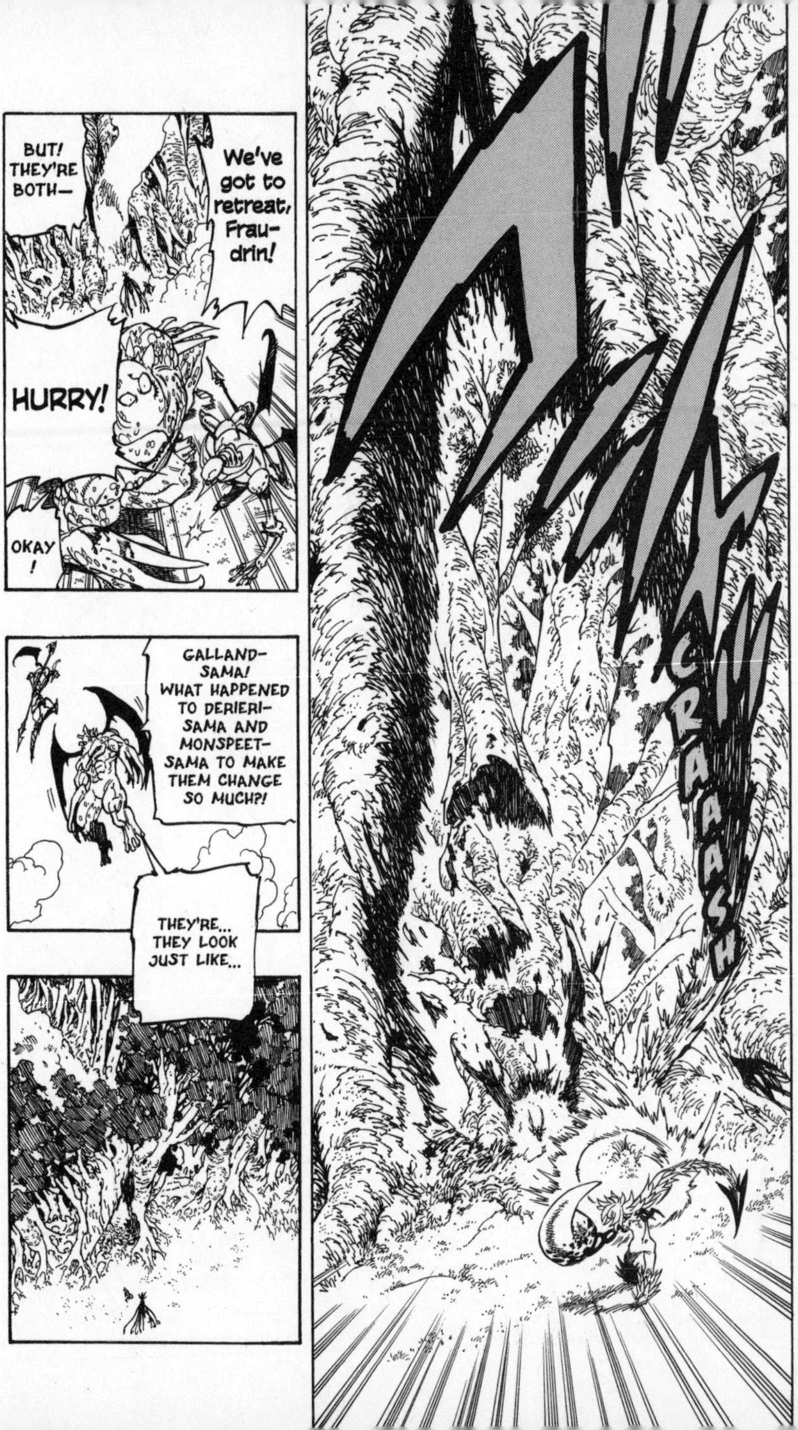
CRAAAASH
We've got to retreat, Fraudrin!
BUT! THEY'RE BOTH—
HURRY!
OKAY!
GALLAND-SAMA! WHAT HAPPENED TO DERIERI-SAMA AND MONSPEET-SAMA TO MAKE THEM CHANGE SO MUCH?!
THEY'RE... THEY LOOK JUST LIKE...

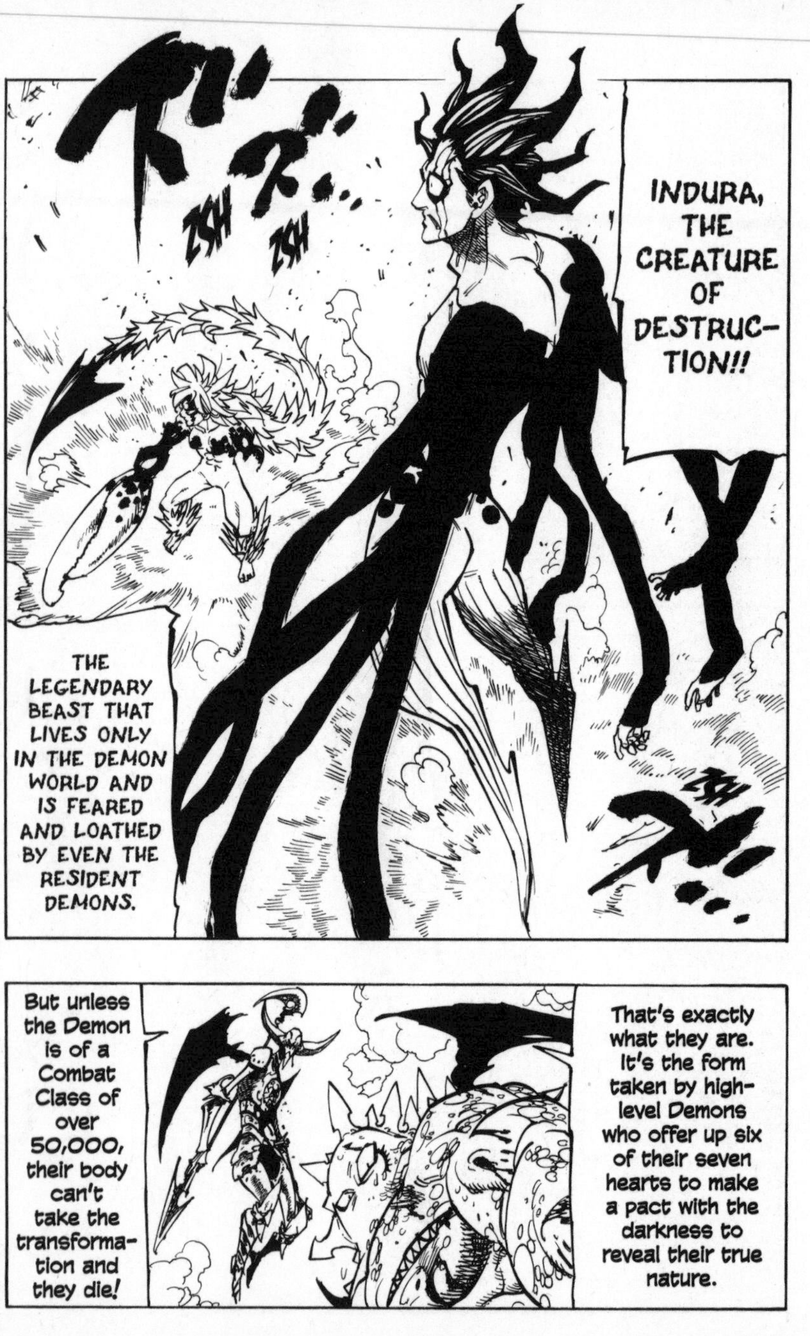
INDURA, THE CREATURE OF DESTRUCTION!!
ZSH
ZSH
THE LEGENDARY BEAST THAT LIVES ONLY IN THE DEMON WORLD AND IS FEARED AND LOATHED BY EVEN THE RESIDENT DEMONS.
ZSH
That's exactly what they are. It's the form taken by high-level Demons who offer up six of their seven hearts to make a pact with the darkness to reveal their true nature.
But unless the Demon is of a Combat Class of over 50,000, their body can't take the transformation and they die!

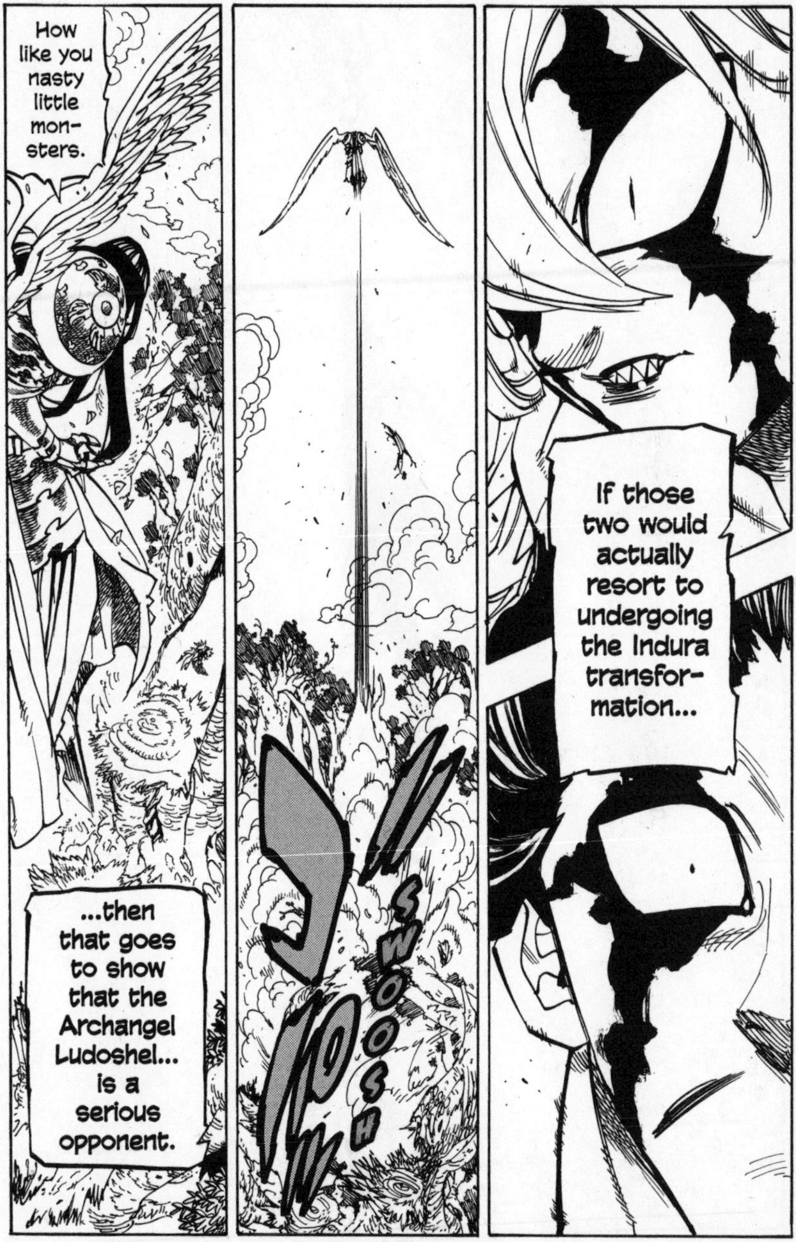
If those two would actually resort to undergoing the Indura transformation...
SWOOSH
How like you nasty little monsters.
...then that goes to show that the Archangel Ludoshel... is a serious opponent.

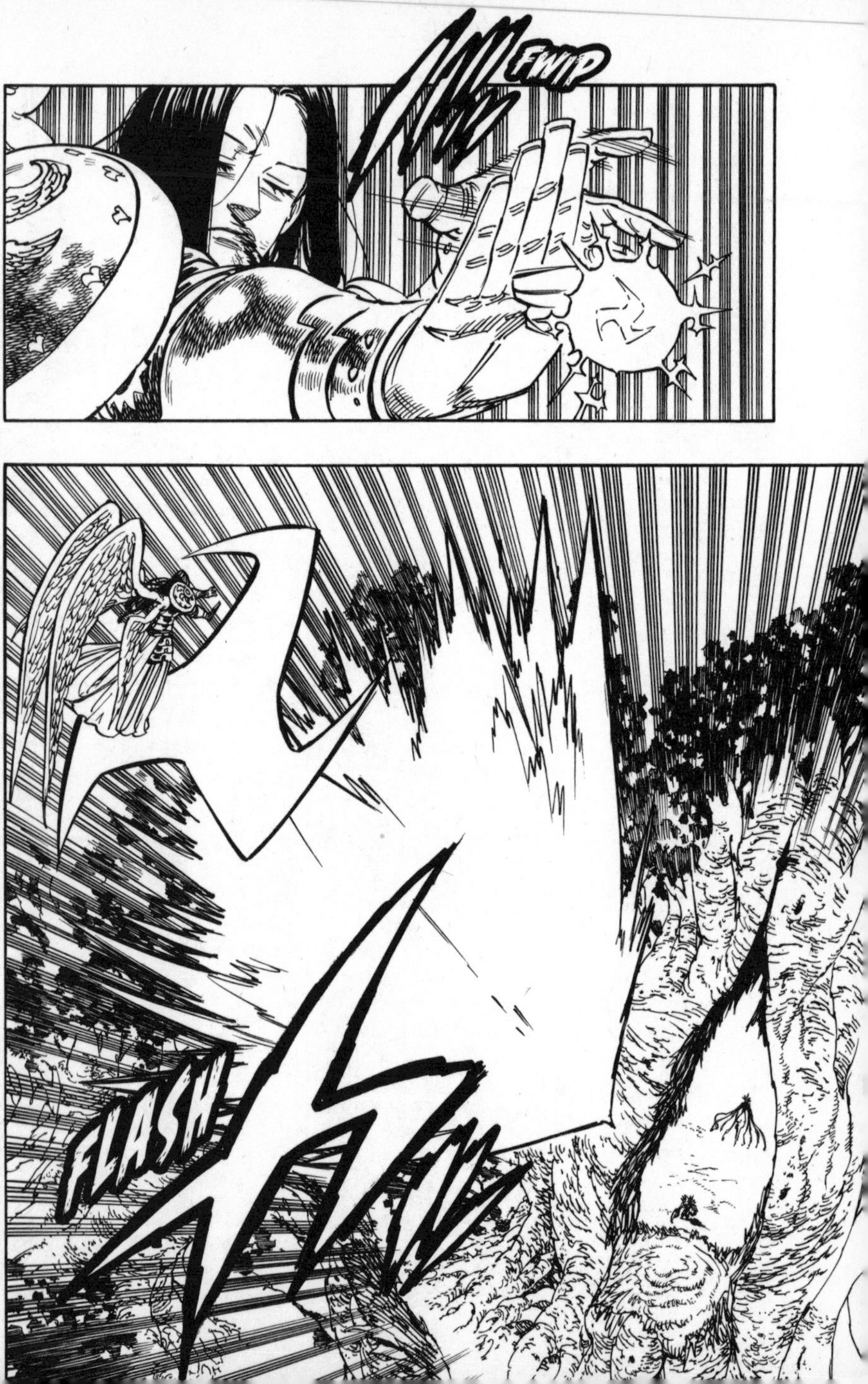
FWIP
FLASH

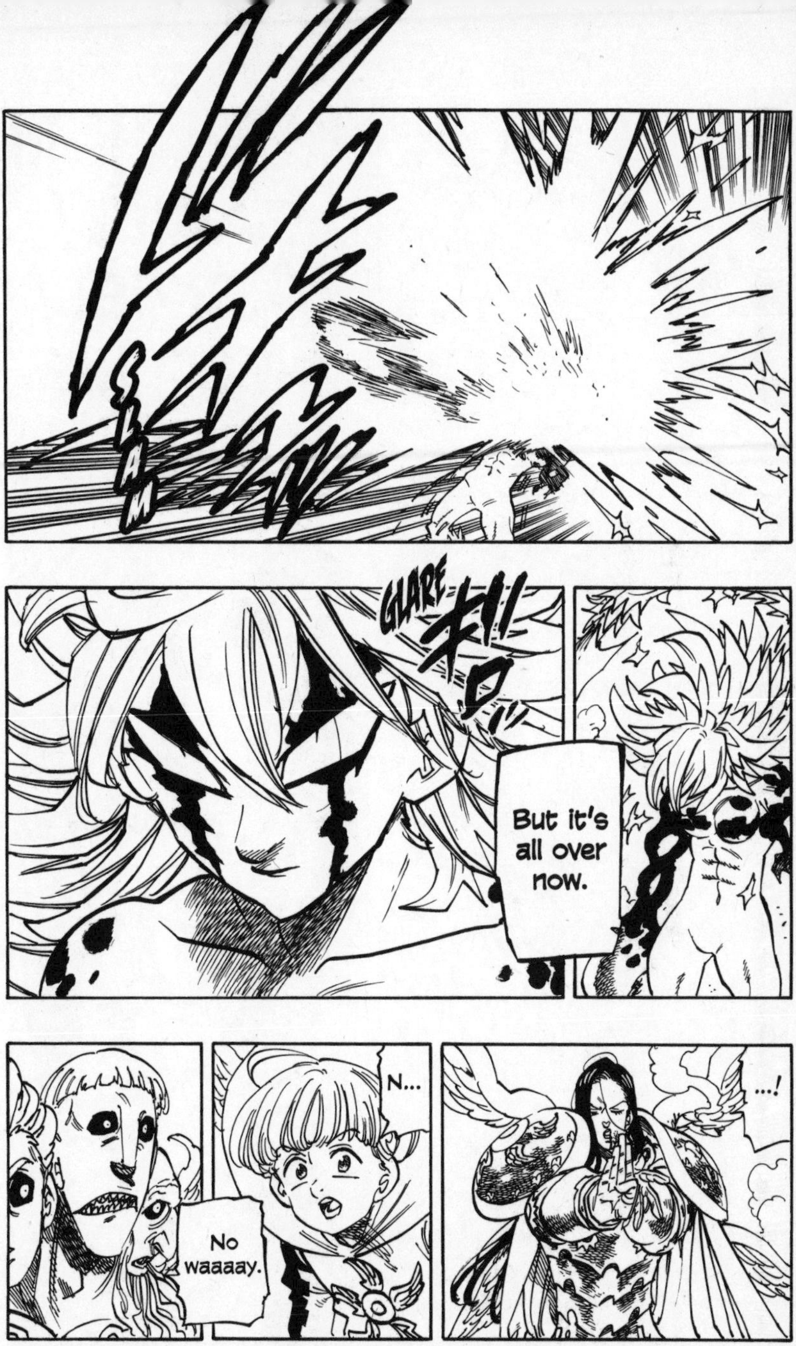
SLAM
But it's all over now.
GLARE
...!
N...
No waaaay.

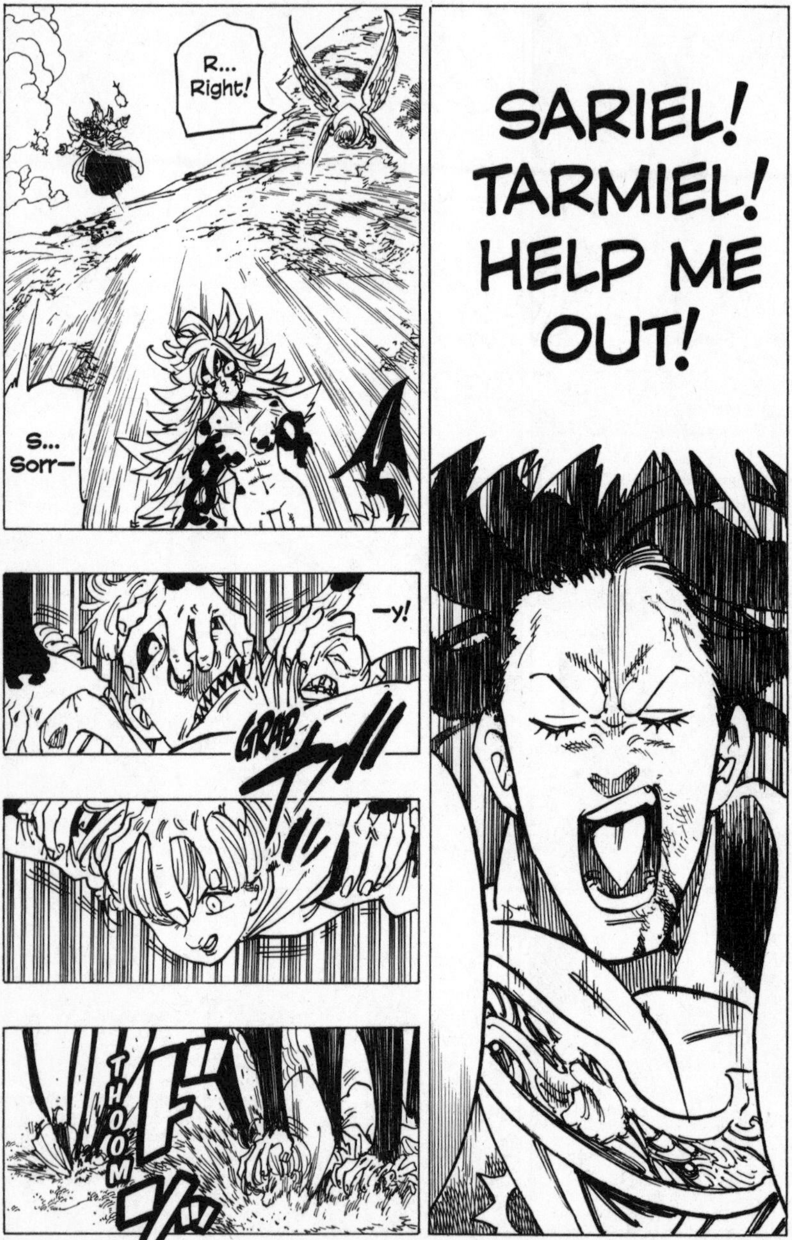
SARIEL! TARMIEL! HELP ME OUT!
R... Right!
S... Sorr—
—y!
GRAB
THOOM

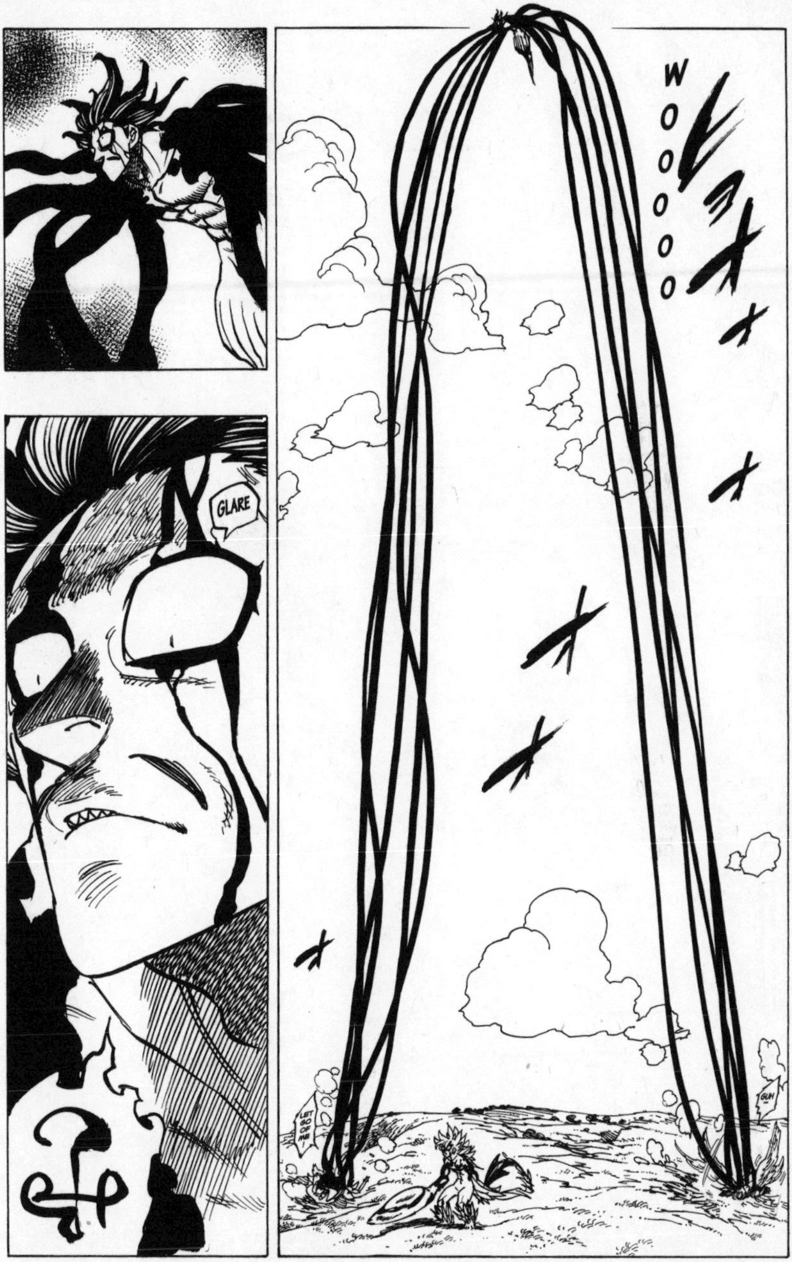
WOOOOOO
LET GO OF ME!
GUH–
GLARE

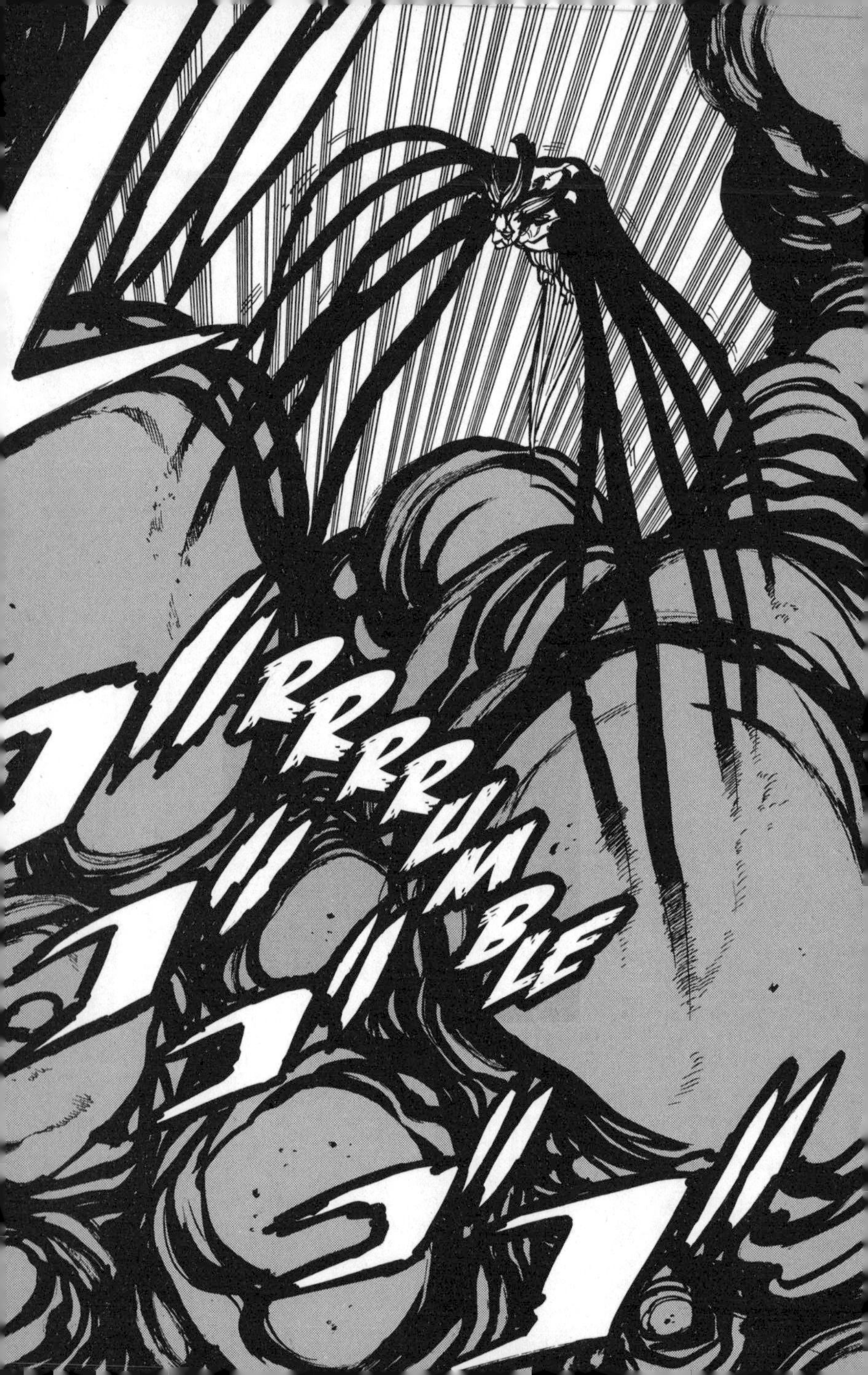
RRRUMBLE

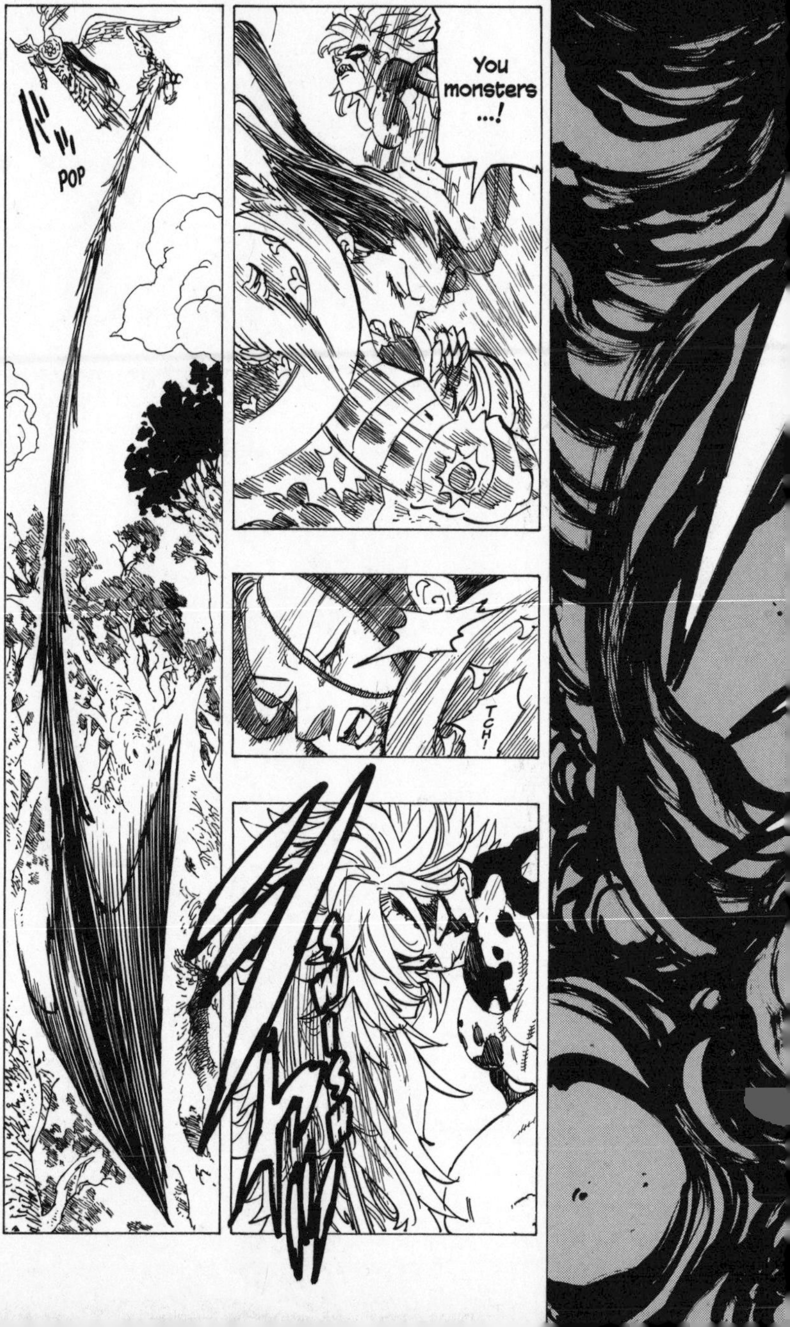

You monsters ...!
TCH!
SWISH
ドッ
POP

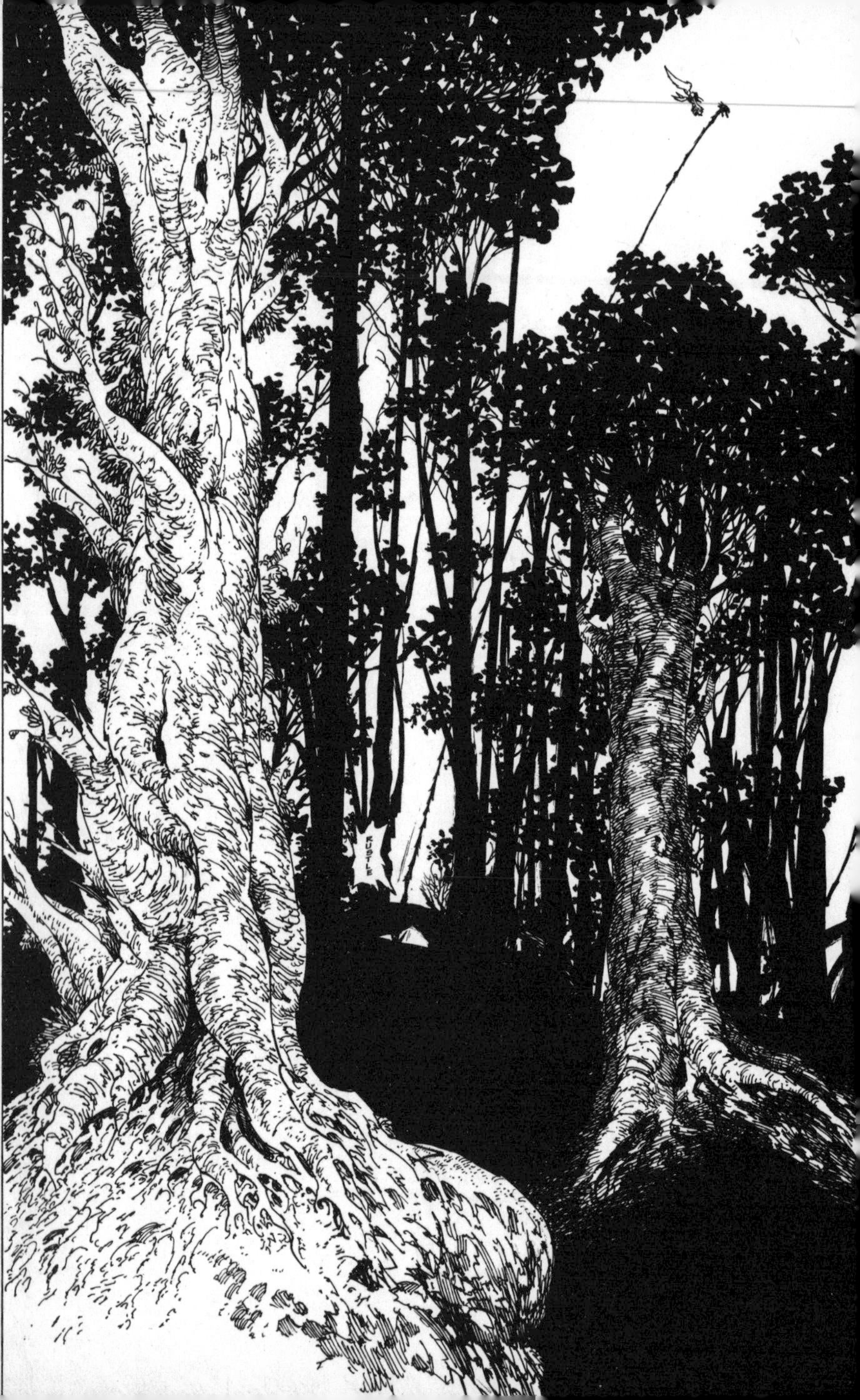
RUSTLE

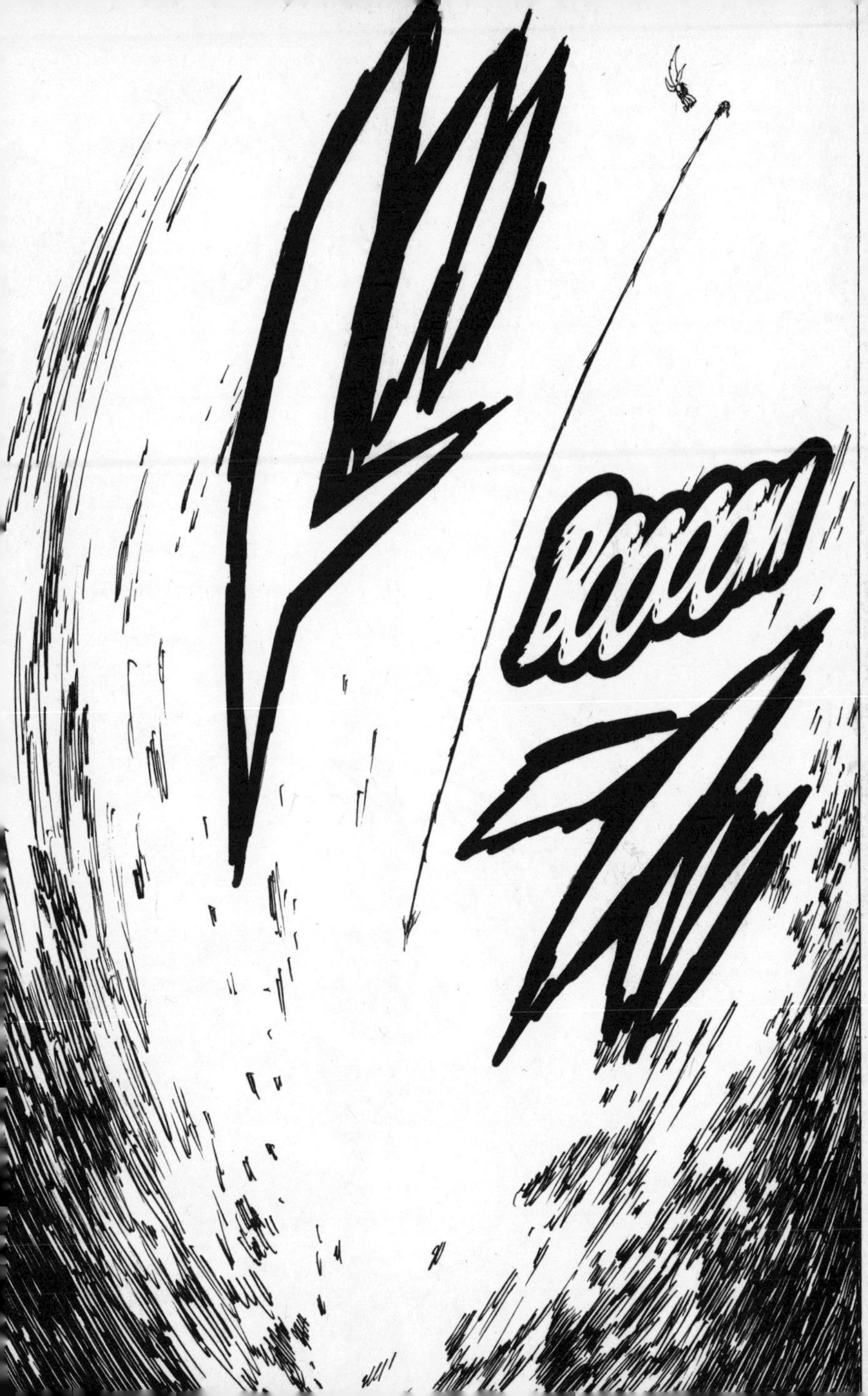

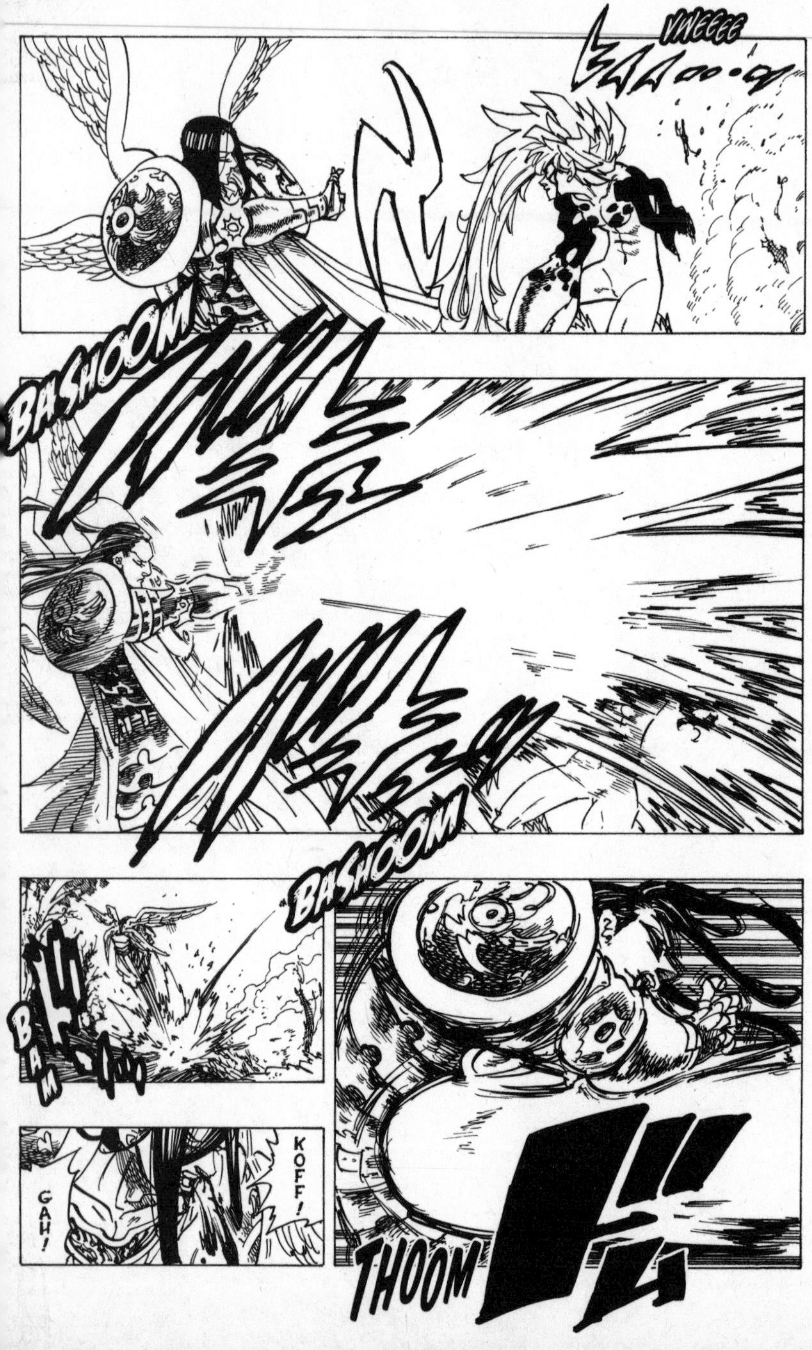
VWEEEE
BASHOOM
BASHOOM
THOOM
BAM
KOFF!
GAH!

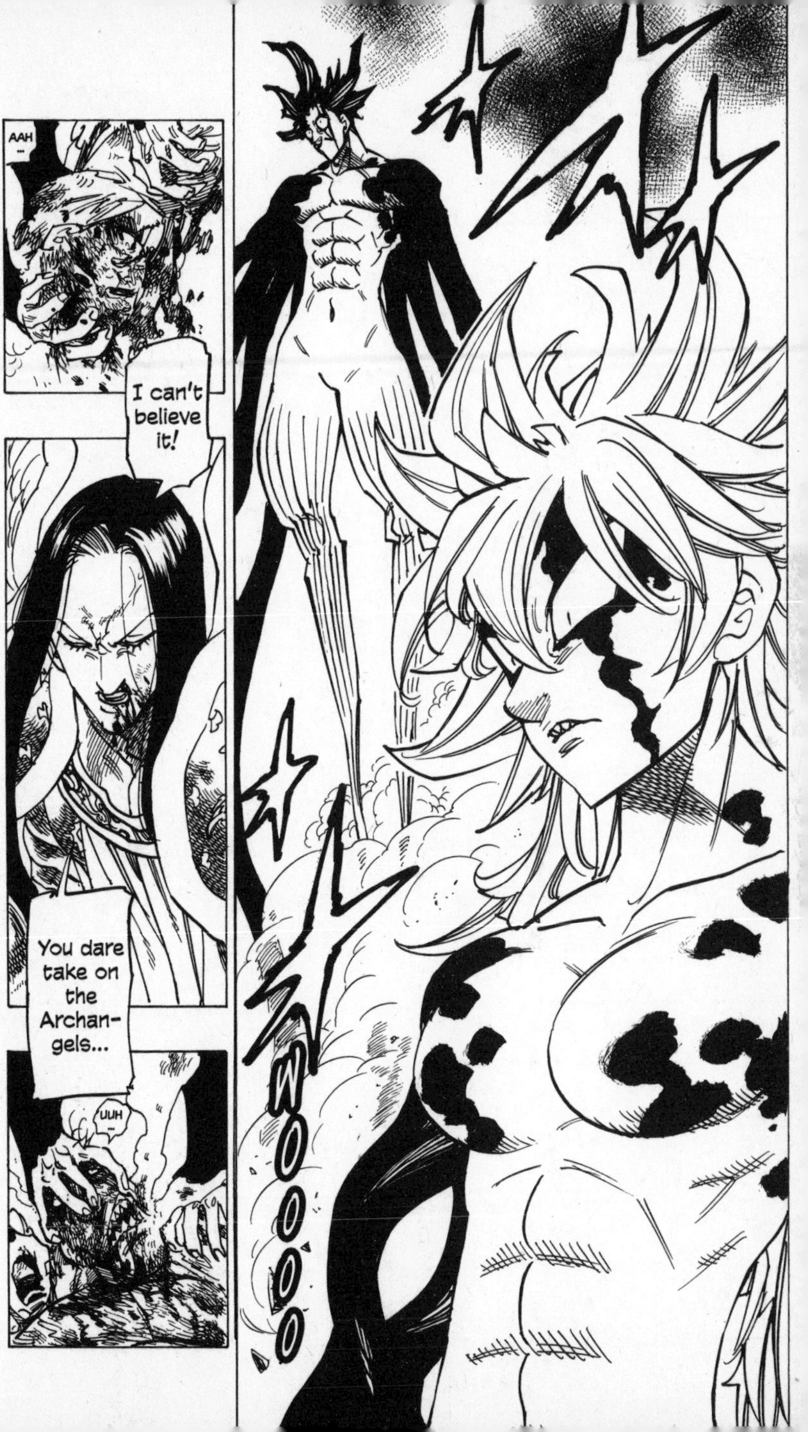
WOOOOO
AAH...
I can't believe it!
You dare take on the Archangels...
UUH...

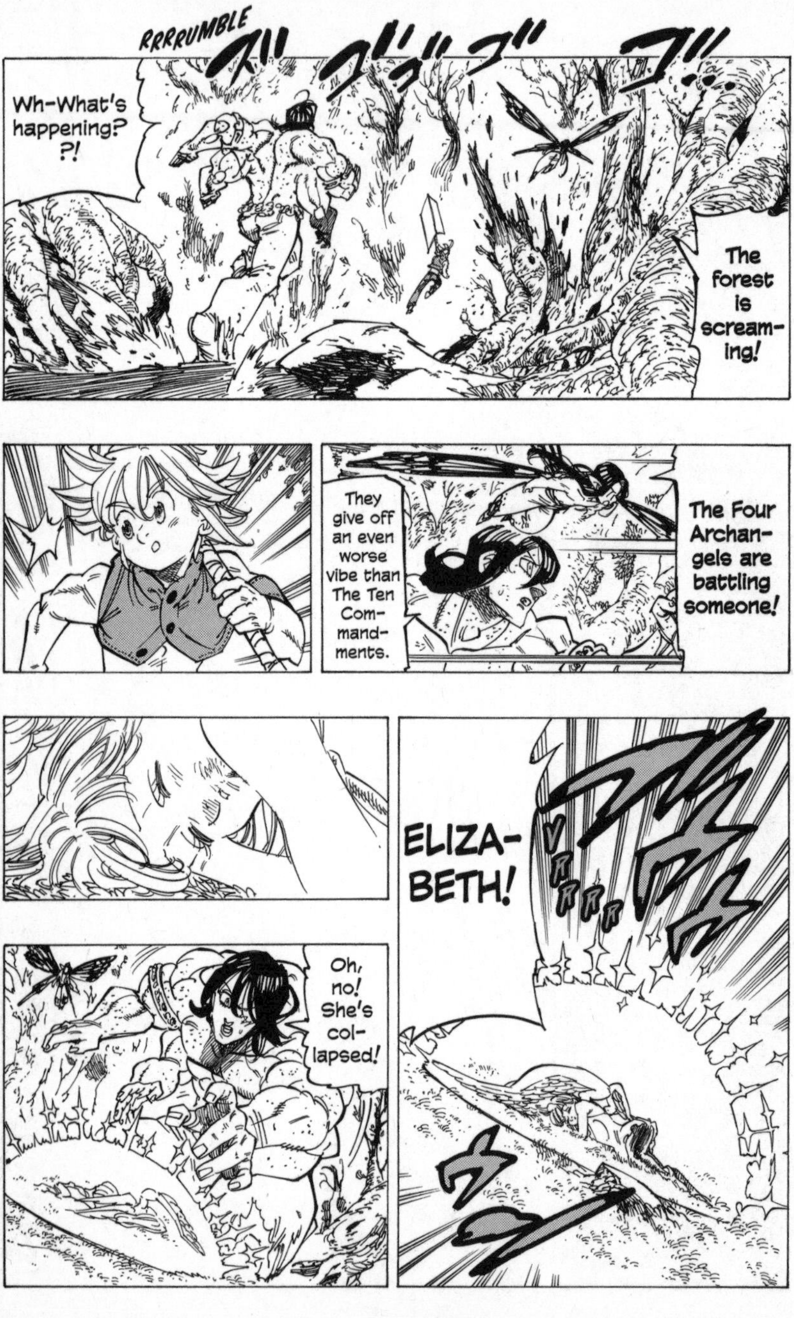
RRRUMBLE
The forest is scream-ing!
Wh-What's happening??!
The Four Archan-gels are battling someone!
They give off an even worse vibe than The Ten Com-mand-ments.
ELIZA-BETH!
VRRRRR
Oh, no! She's col-lapsed!

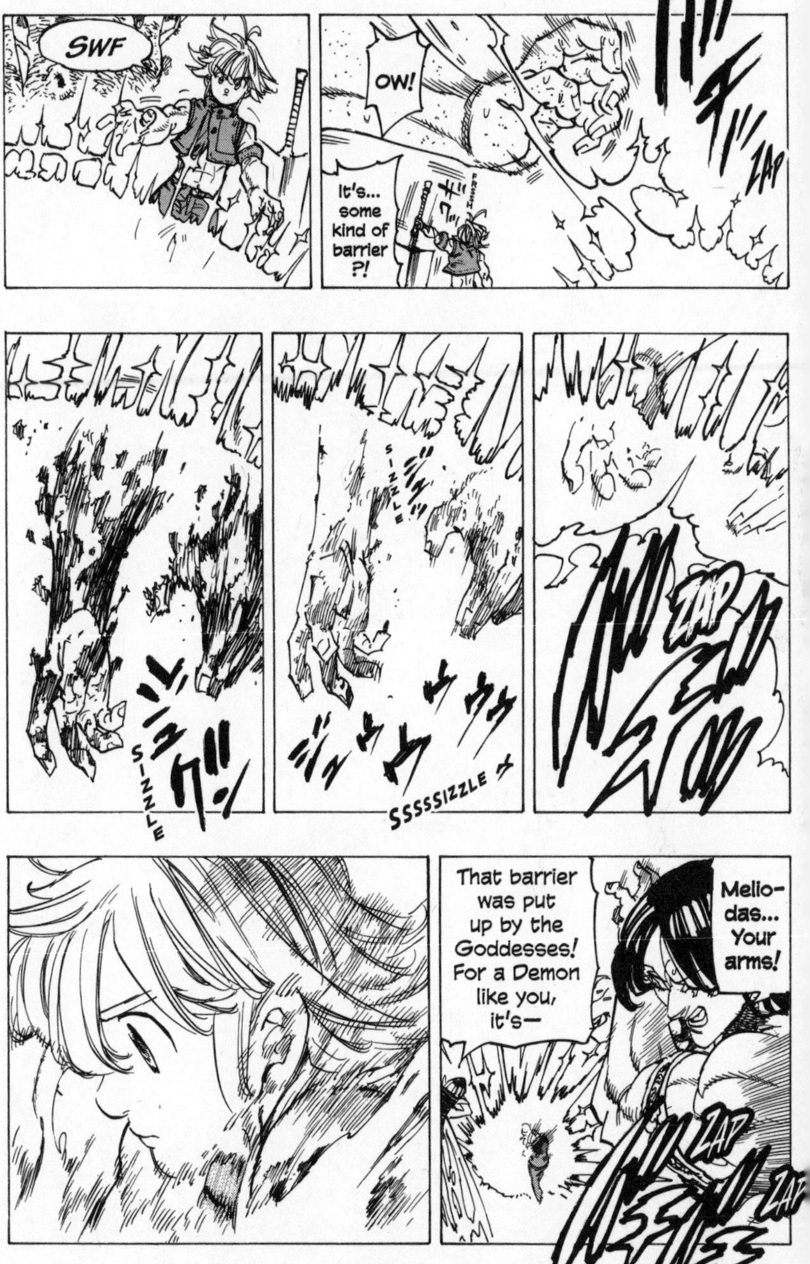
OW!
ZAP
It's... some kind of barrier ?!
SWF
ZAP
SIZZLE
SSSSSIZZLE
SIZZLE
Melio-das... Your arms!
That barrier was put up by the Goddesses! For a Demon like you, it's—
ZAP
ZAP

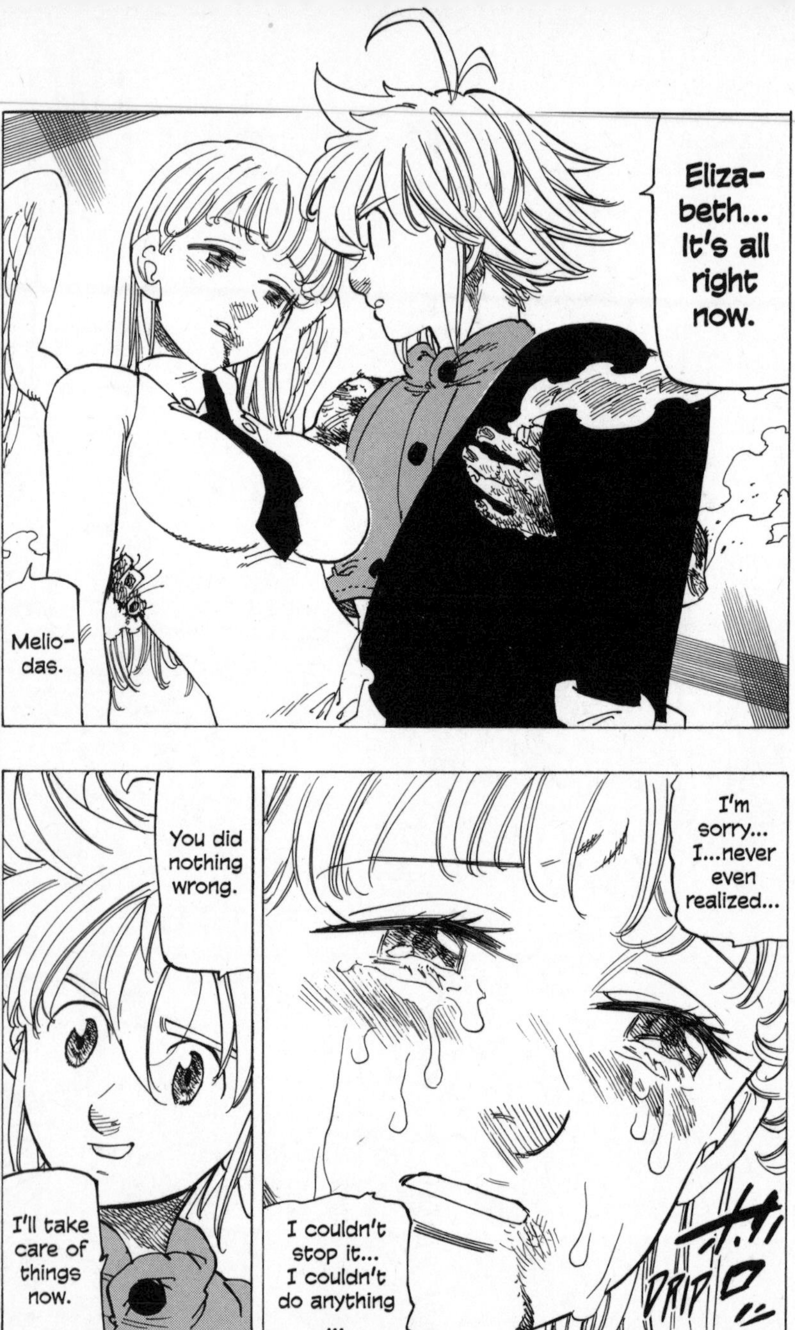
Eliza-beth... It's all right now.
Melio-das.
I'm sorry... I...never even realized...
I couldn't stop it... I couldn't do anything ...
DRIP
You did nothing wrong.
I'll take care of things now.

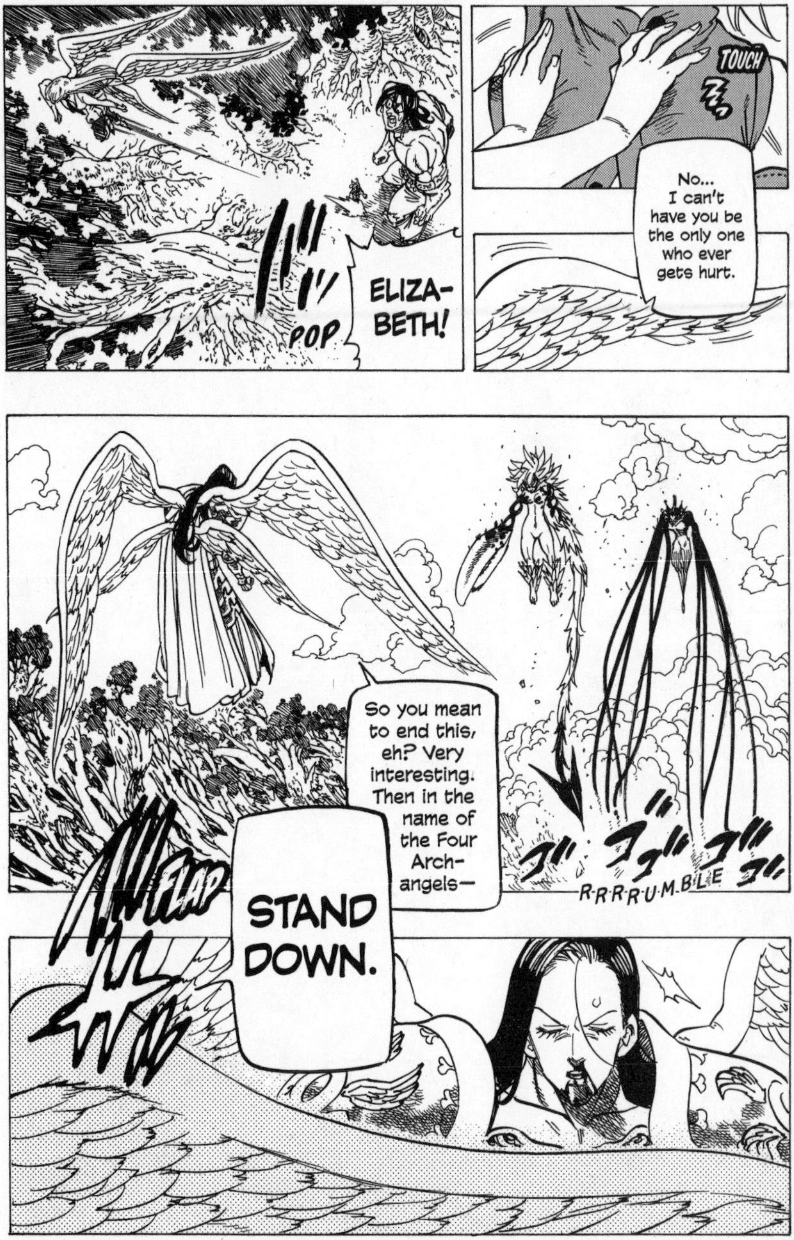
TOUCH
No... I can't have you be the only one who ever gets hurt.
ELIZA-BETH!
POP
R-R-R-R-U-M-B-L-E
So you mean to end this, eh? Very interesting. Then in the name of the Four Arch-angels—
FLAP
STAND DOWN.

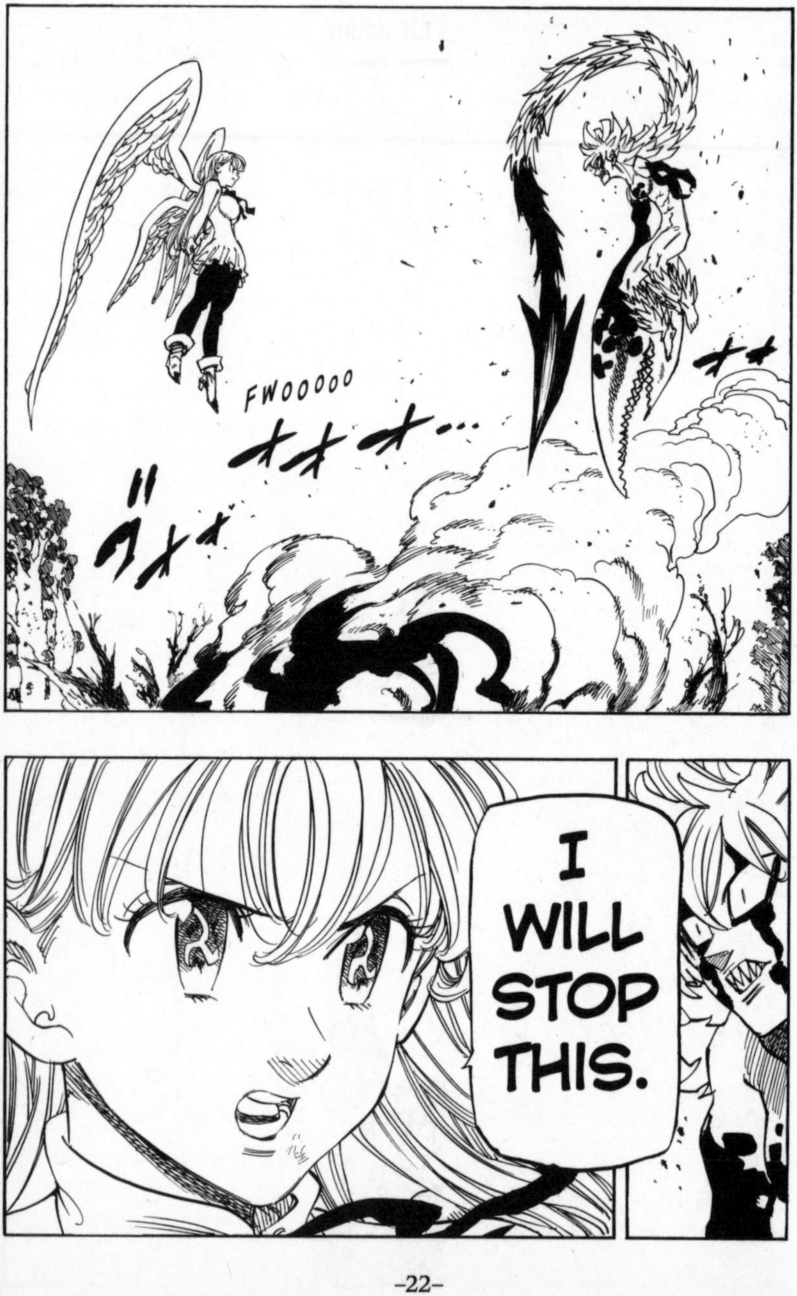
FWOOOOO
ヴォォオオオ…
I WILL STOP THIS.

Chapter 208 - Elizabeth vs. Indura

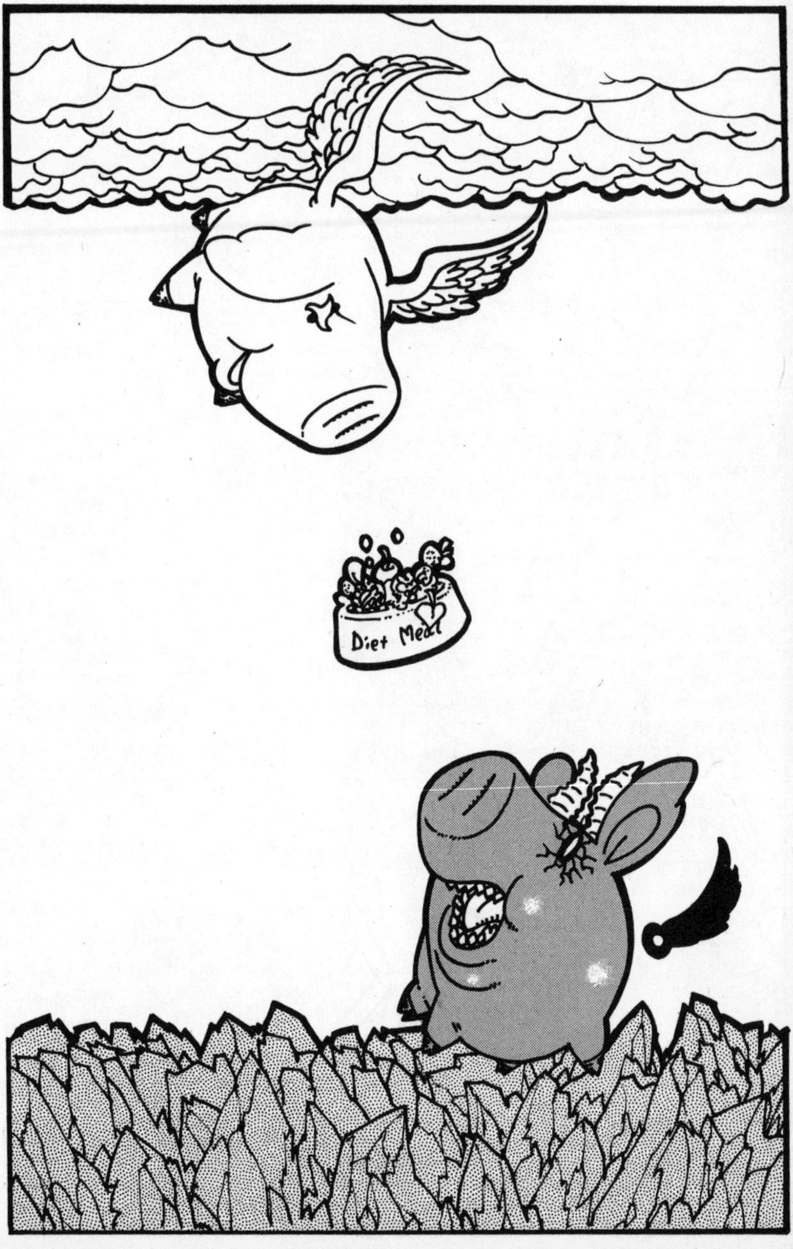
Diet Meal

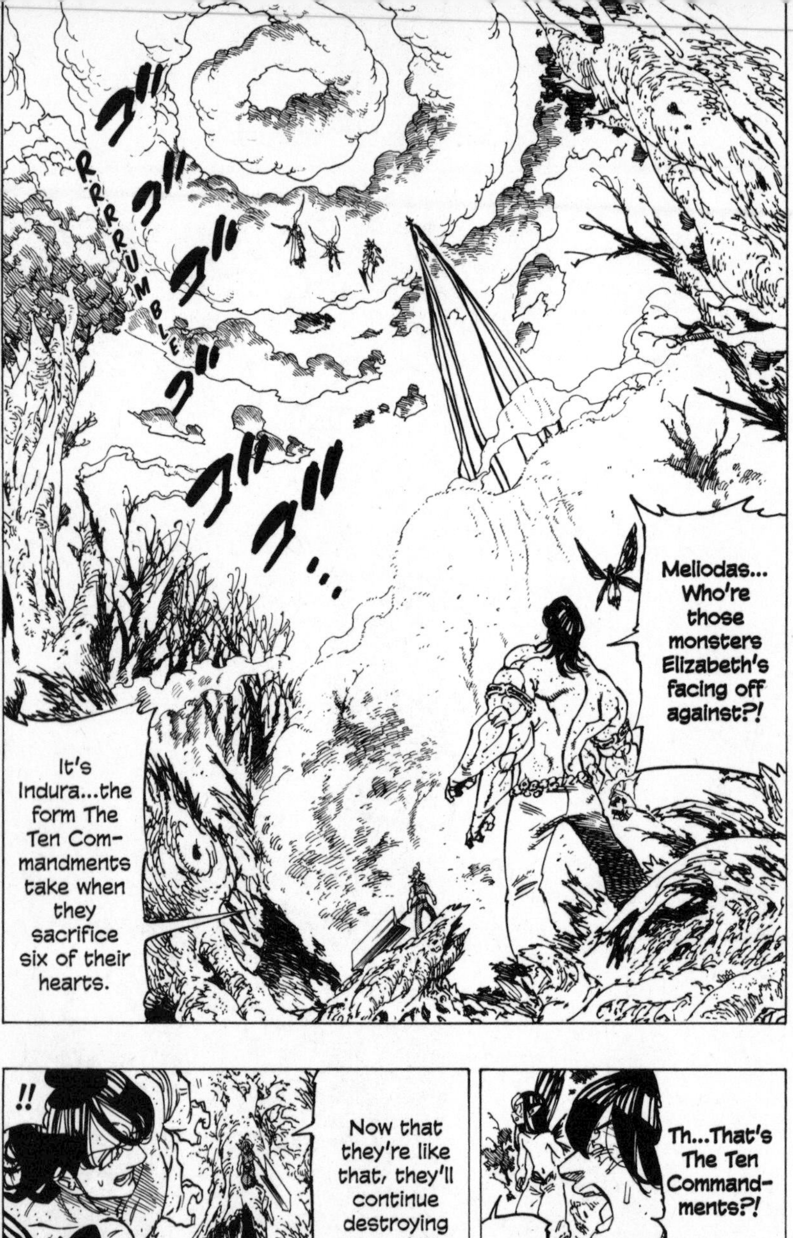
RRRRUMBLE
Meliodas... Who're those monsters Elizabeth's facing off against?!
It's Indura...the form The Ten Commandments take when they sacrifice six of their hearts.
Th...That's The Ten Commandments?!
Indura ...?!
!!
Now that they're like that, they'll continue destroying everything until they die!

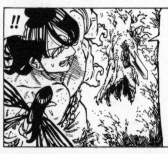

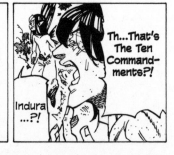

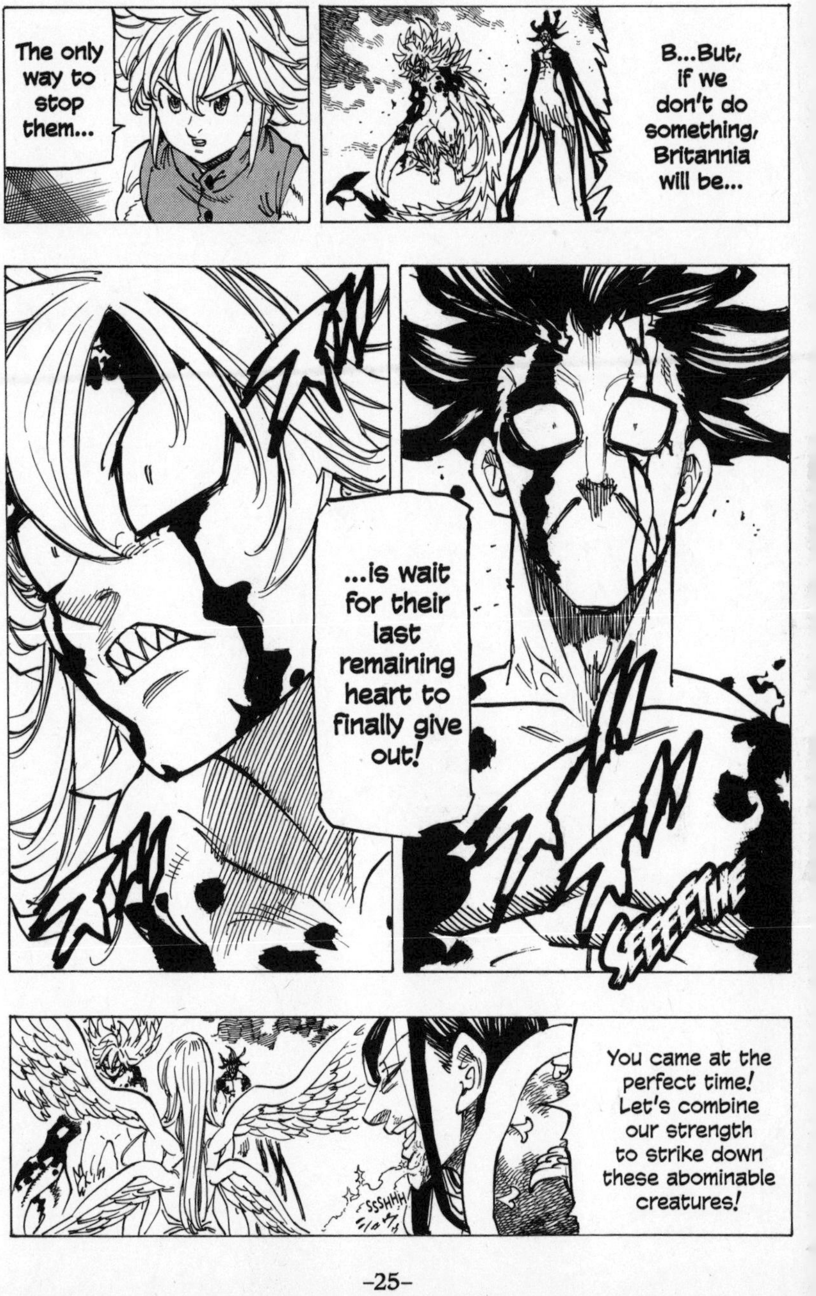
B...But, if we don't do something, Britannia will be...
The only way to stop them...
...is wait for their last remaining heart to finally give out!
SEEEETHE
You came at the perfect time! Let's combine our strength to strike down these abominable creatures!
SSSHHH

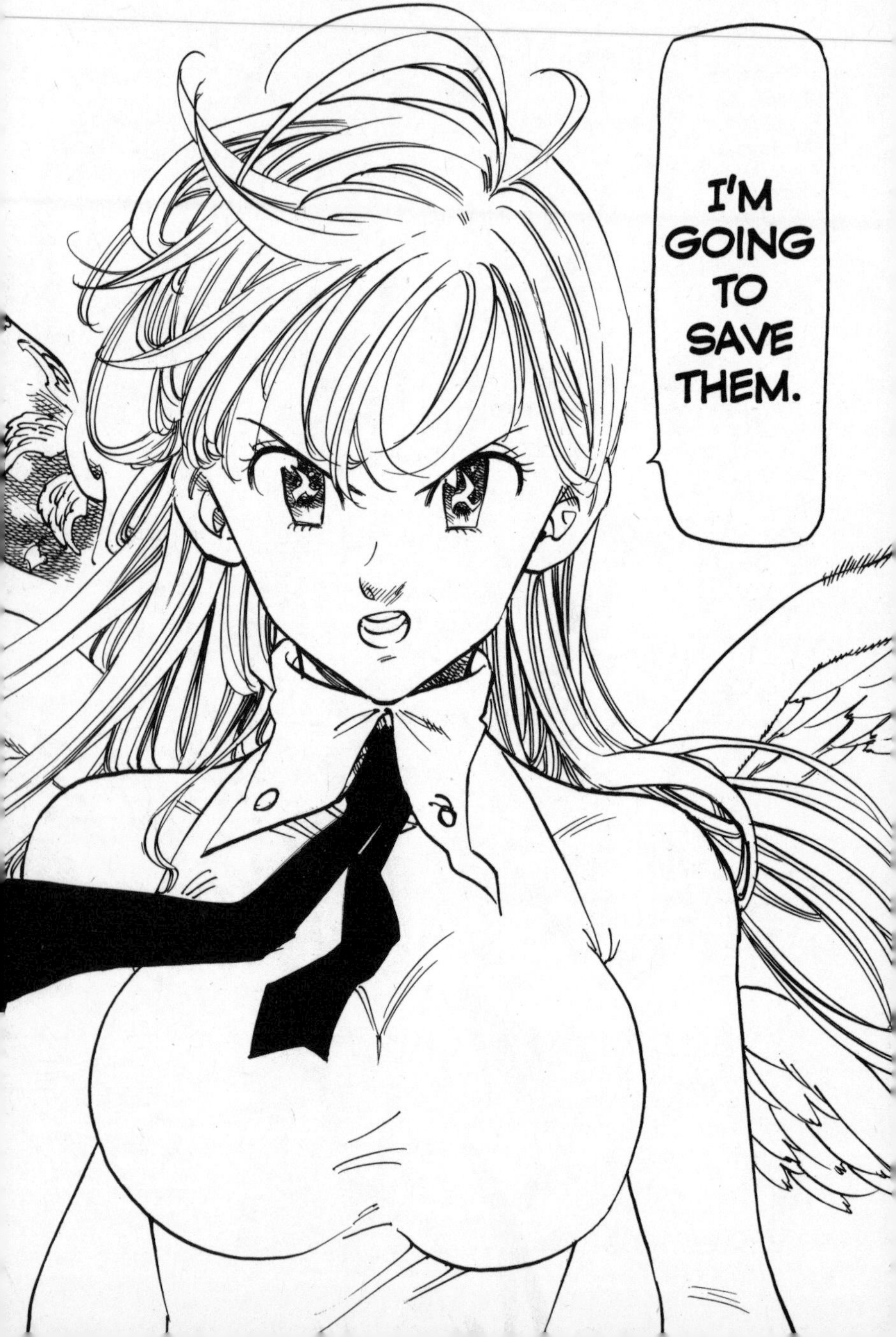
I'M GOING TO SAVE THEM.

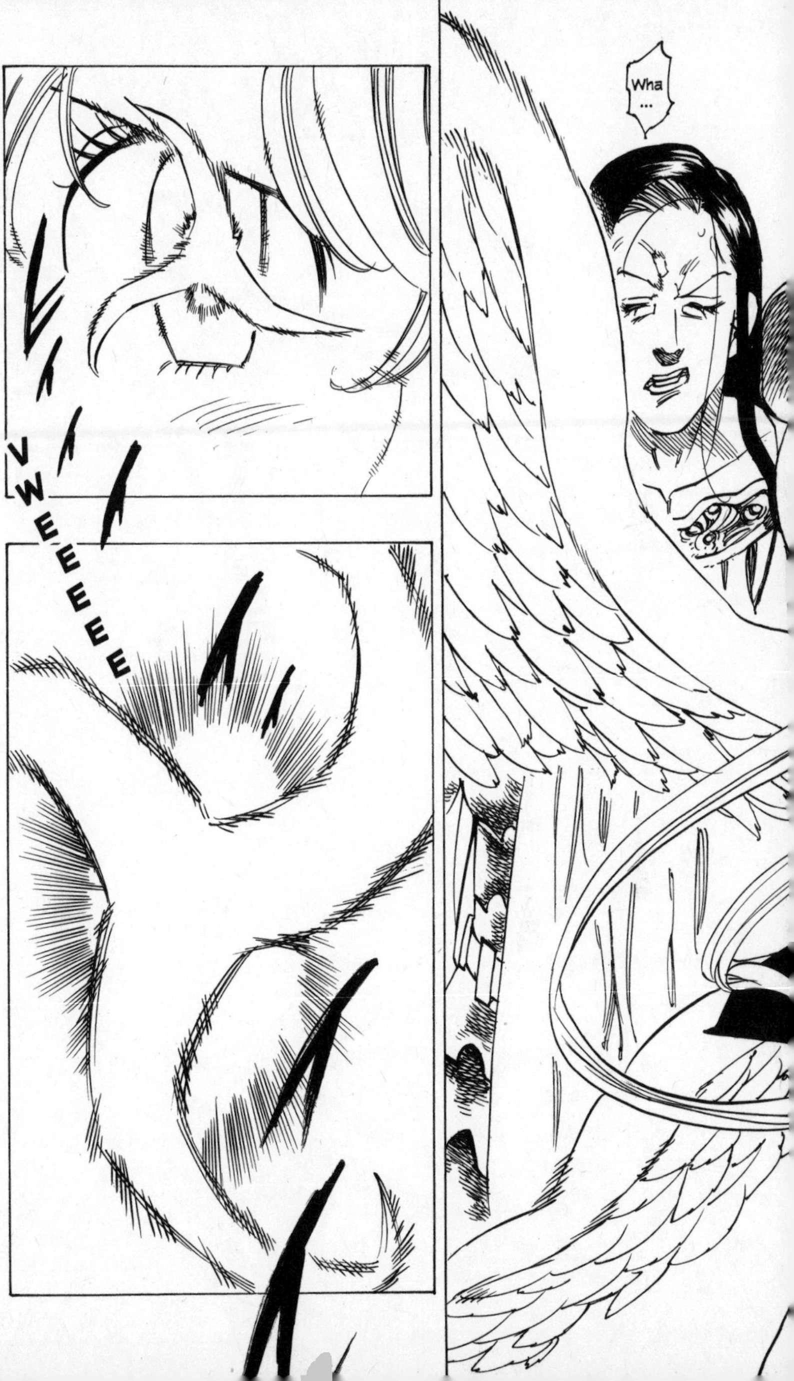
Wha
...
VWEEEEE

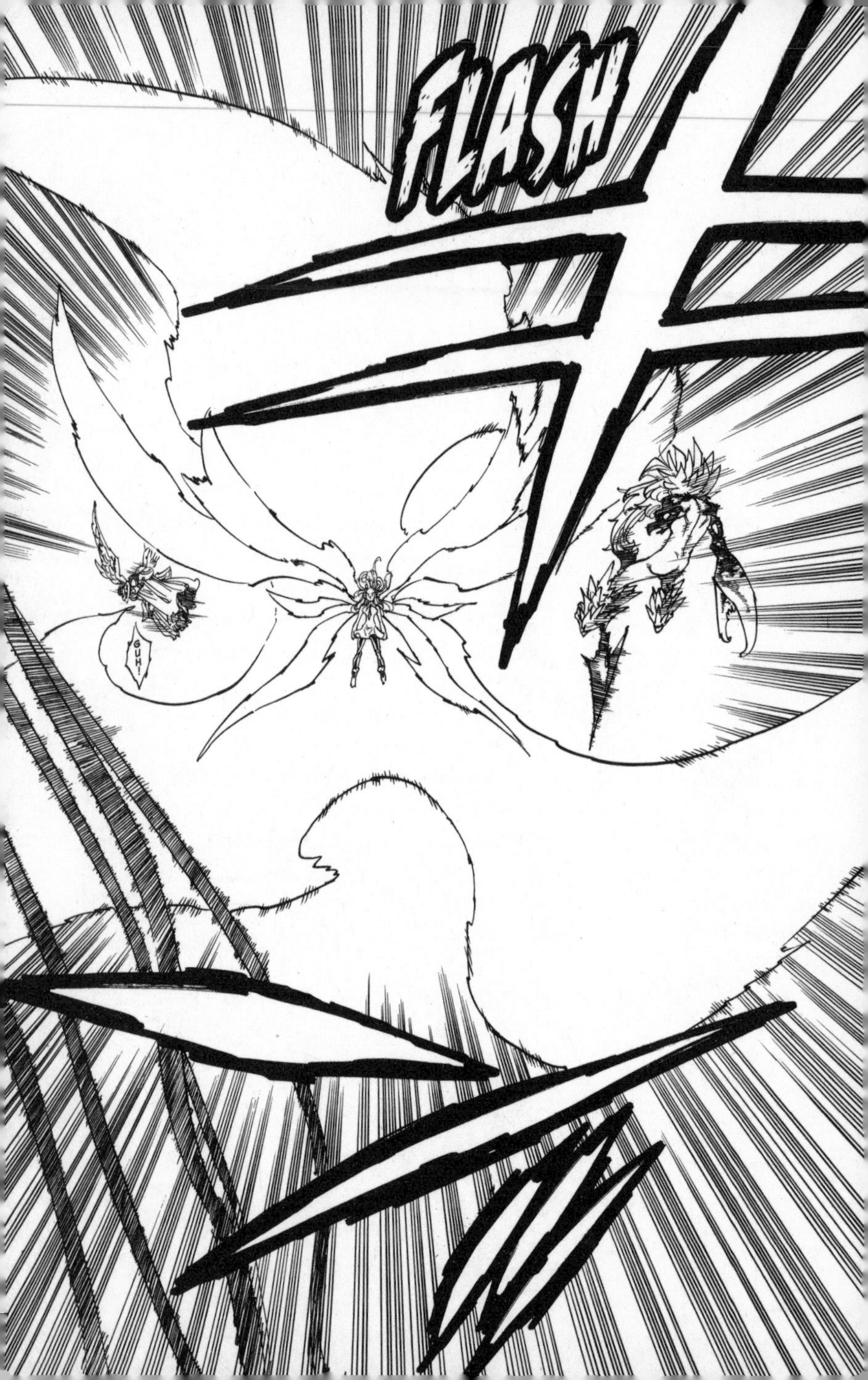
FLASH
GUH!

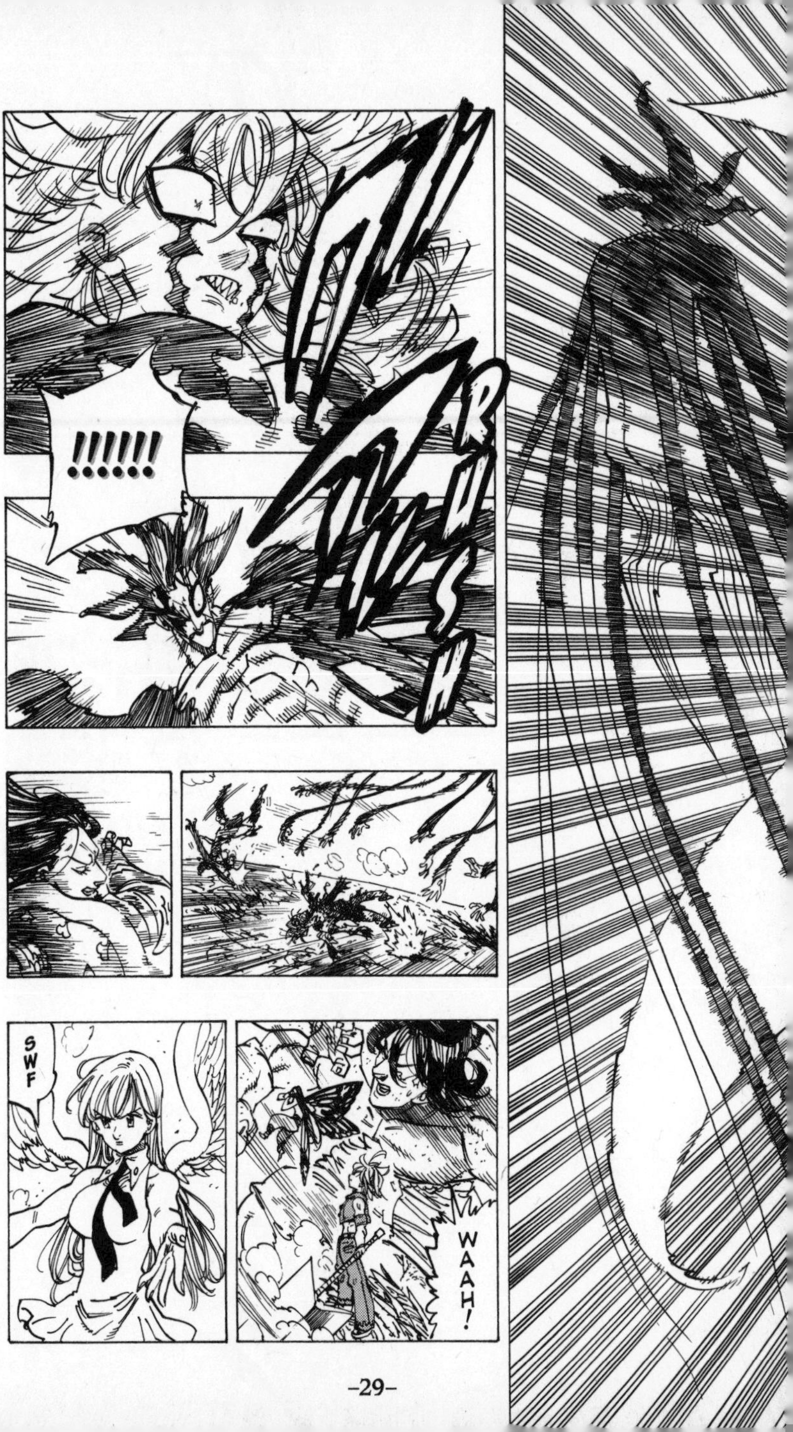

RUSH
!!!!!!
WAAH!
SWF

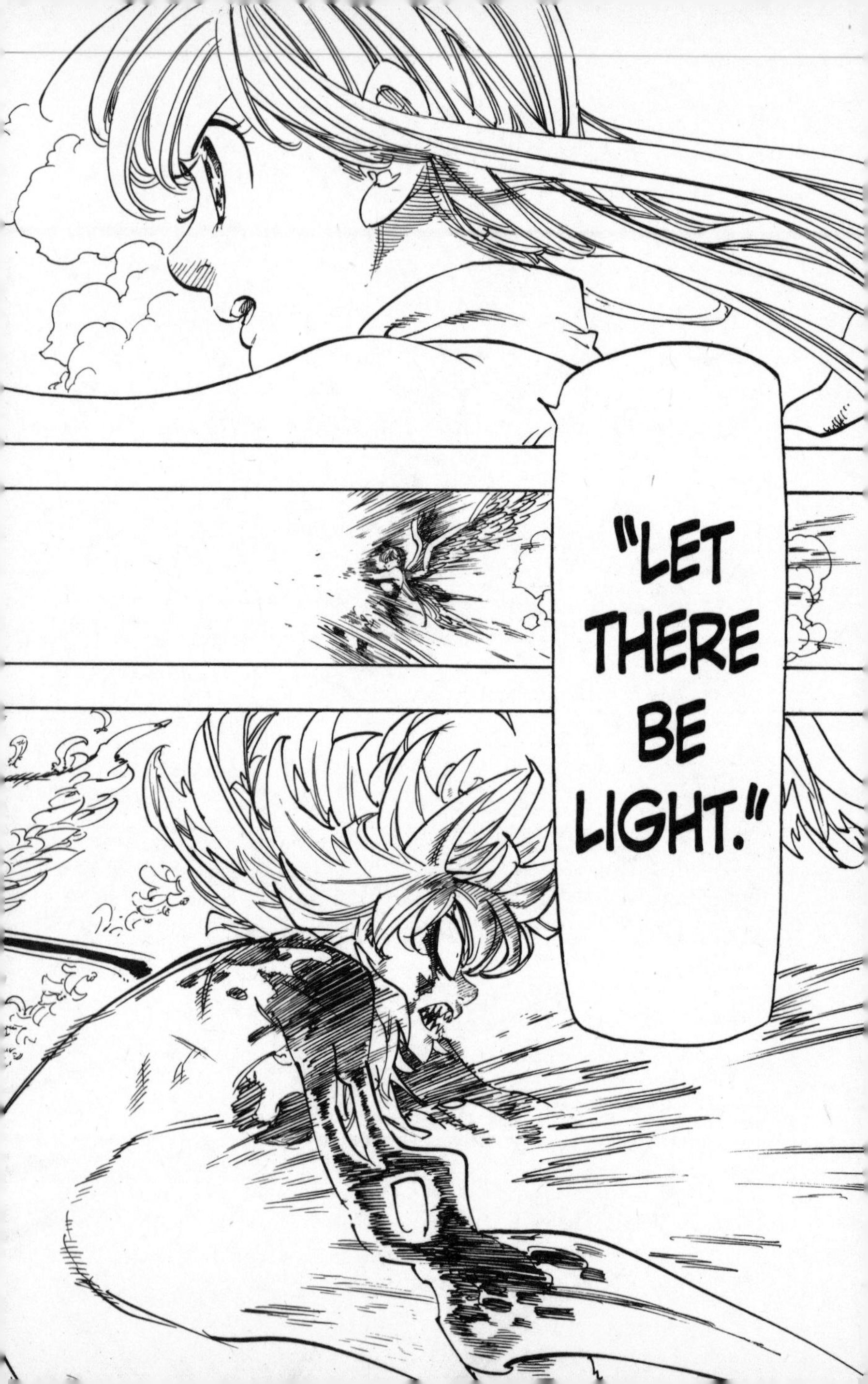
"LET THERE BE LIGHT."

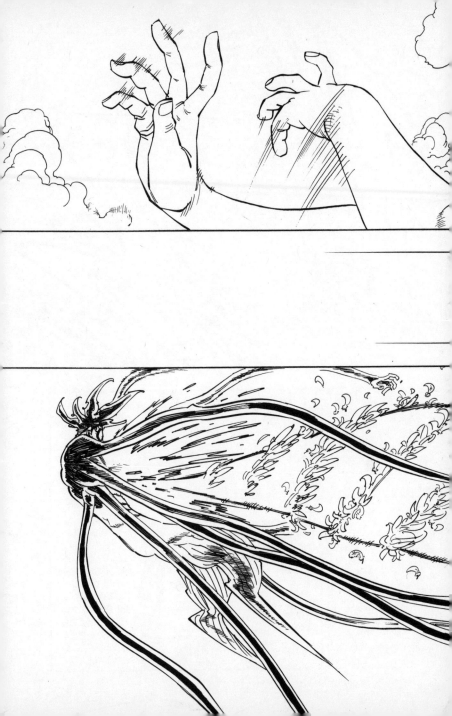

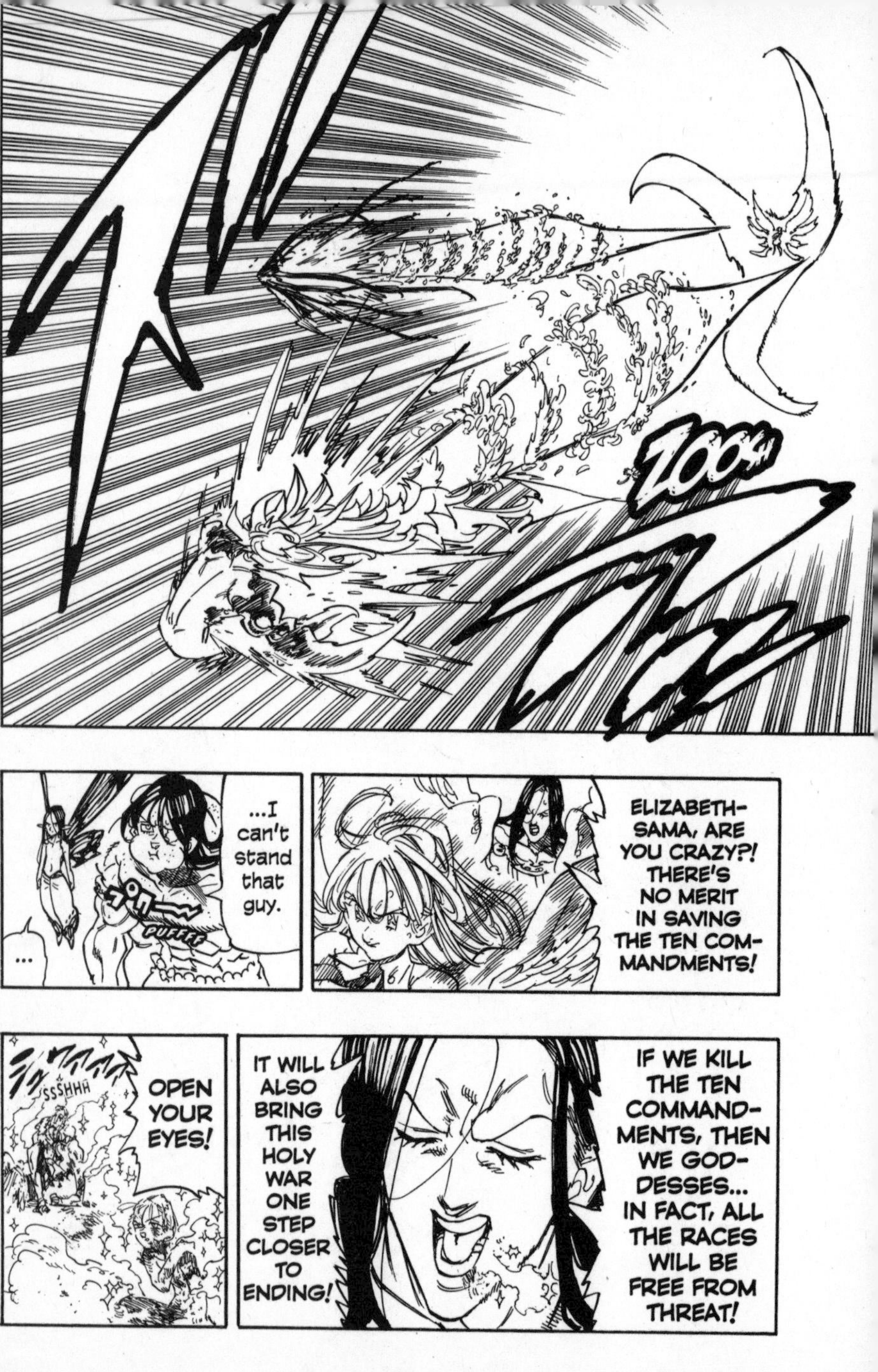
ZOO
ELIZABETH-SAMA, ARE YOU CRAZY?! THERE'S NO MERIT IN SAVING THE TEN COMMANDMENTS!
...I can't stand that guy.
PUFFFF
...
IF WE KILL THE TEN COMMANDMENTS, THEN WE GODDESSES... IN FACT, ALL THE RACES WILL BE FREE FROM THREAT!
IT WILL ALSO BRING THIS HOLY WAR ONE STEP CLOSER TO ENDING!
OPEN YOUR EYES!
SSSHHH

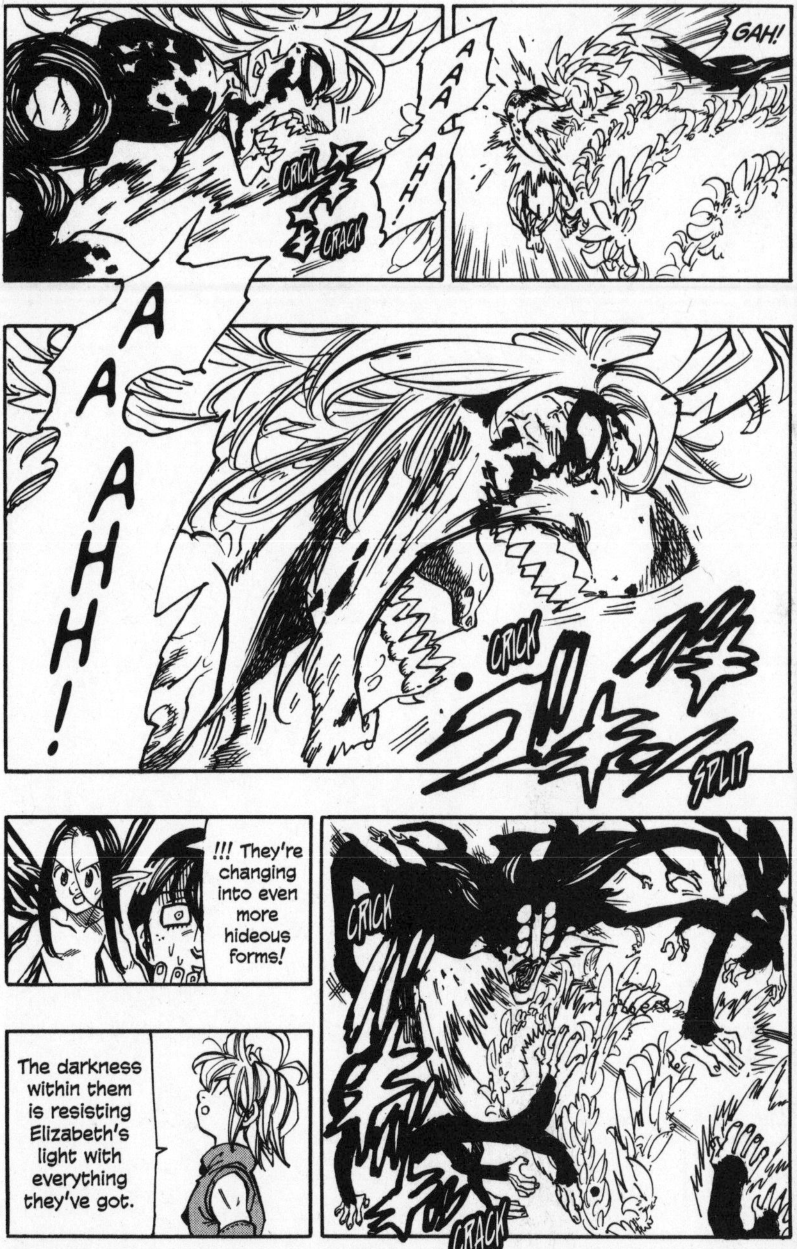
GAH!
AAAAHH!
CRICK
CRACK
AAAAHH!
CRICK
SPLIT
CRICK
CRACK
!!! They're changing into even more hideous forms!
The darkness within them is resisting Elizabeth's light with everything they've got.

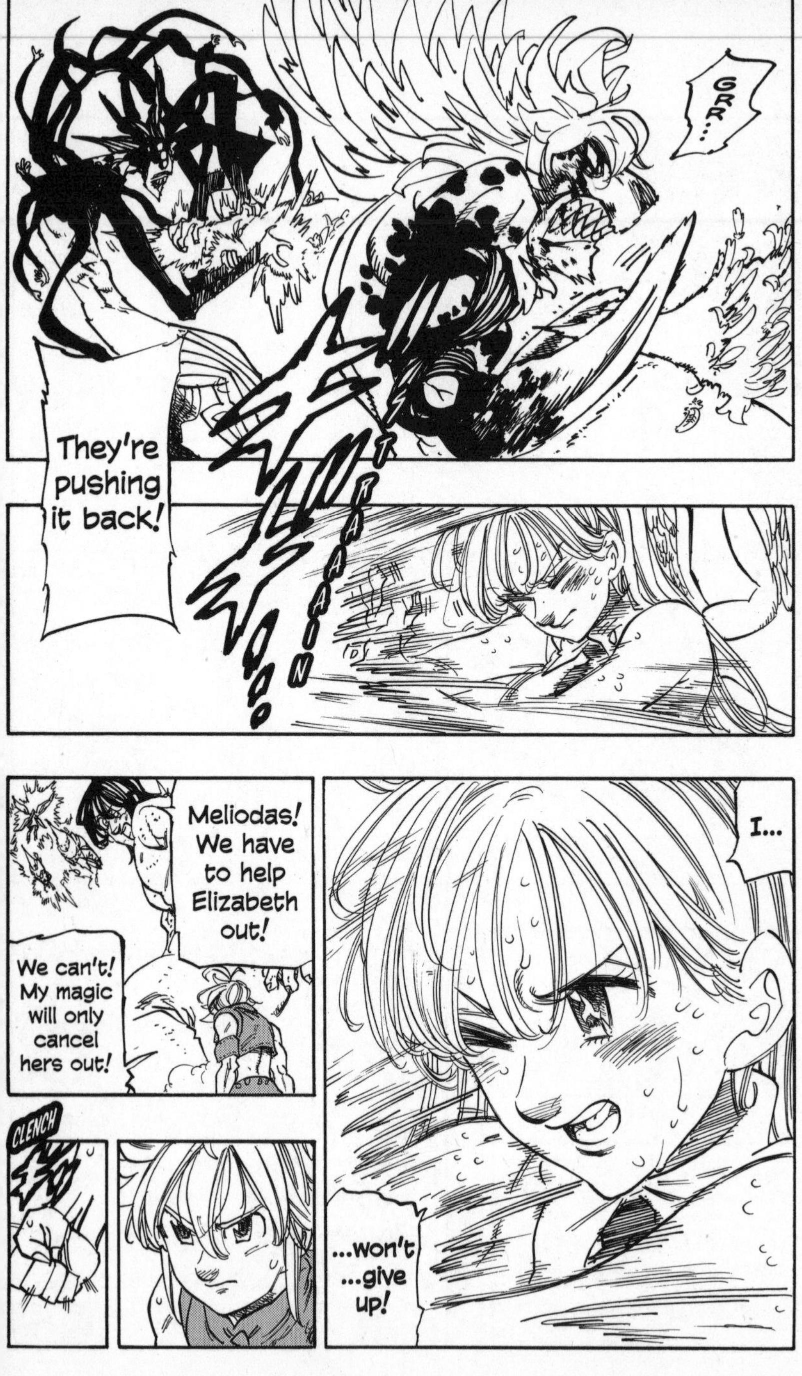
GRR...
They're pushing it back!
STRAAAIN
I...
...won't ...give up!
Meliodas! We have to help Elizabeth out!
We can't! My magic will only cancel hers out!
CLENCH

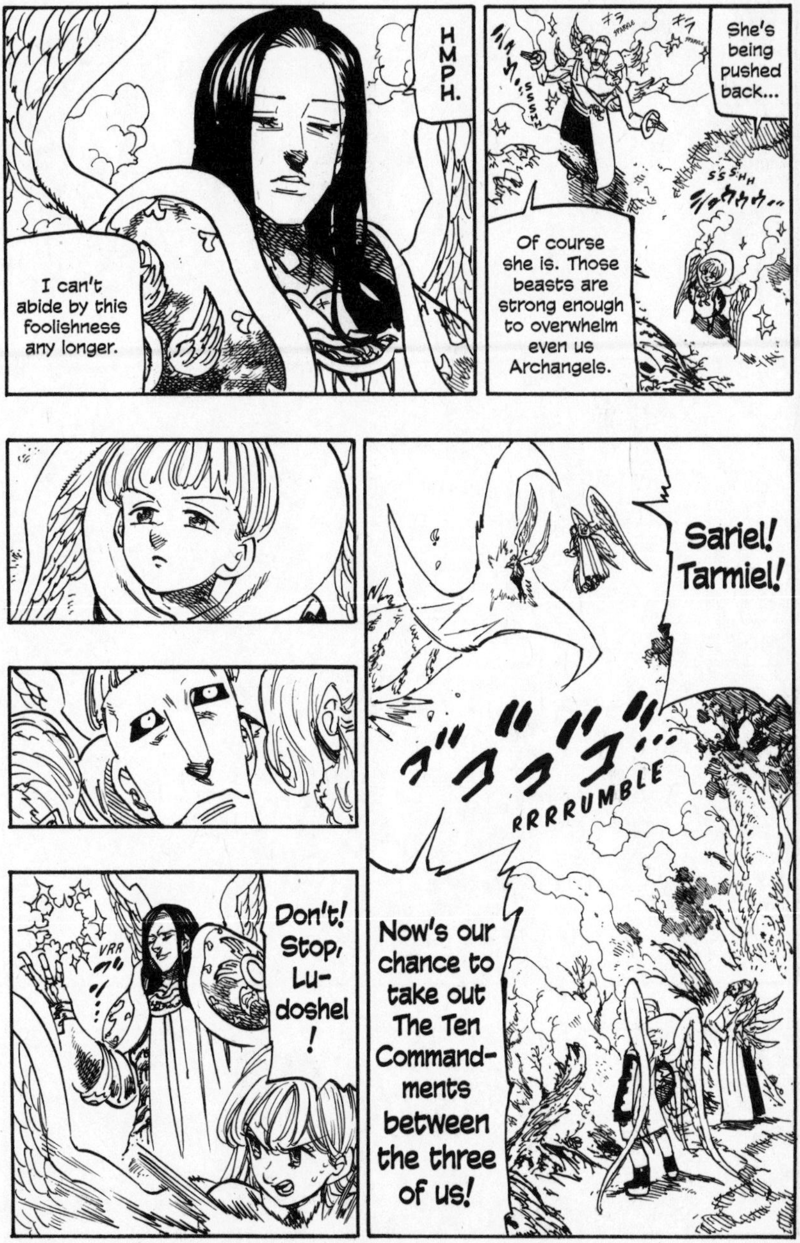

She's being pushed back...
SSHH
Of course she is. Those beasts are strong enough to overwhelm even us Archangels.
HMPH.
I can't abide by this foolishness any longer.
Sariel! Tarmiel!
RRRRUMBLE
Now's our chance to take out The Ten Command-ments between the three of us!
VRR
Don't! Stop, Lu-doshel!

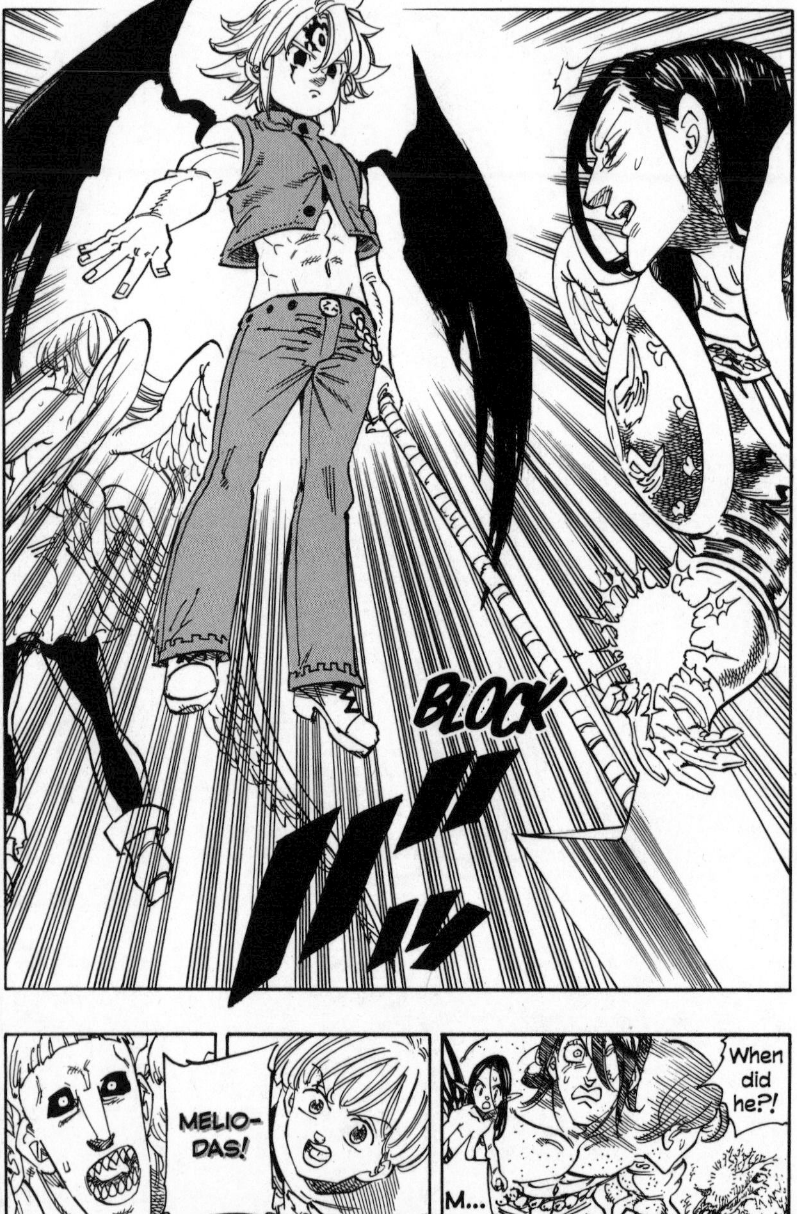
BLOCK
When did he?!
M...
MELIO-DAS!

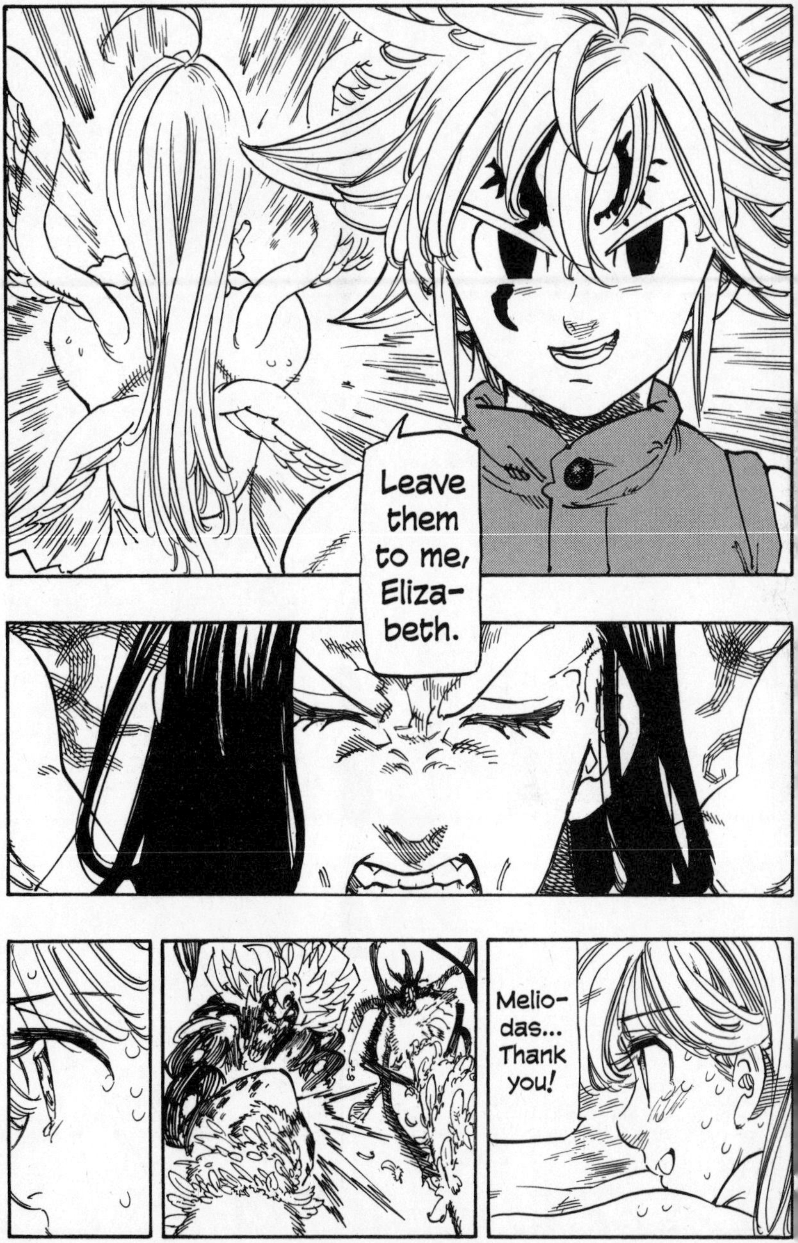
Leave them to me, Elizabeth.
Melio-das... Thank you!

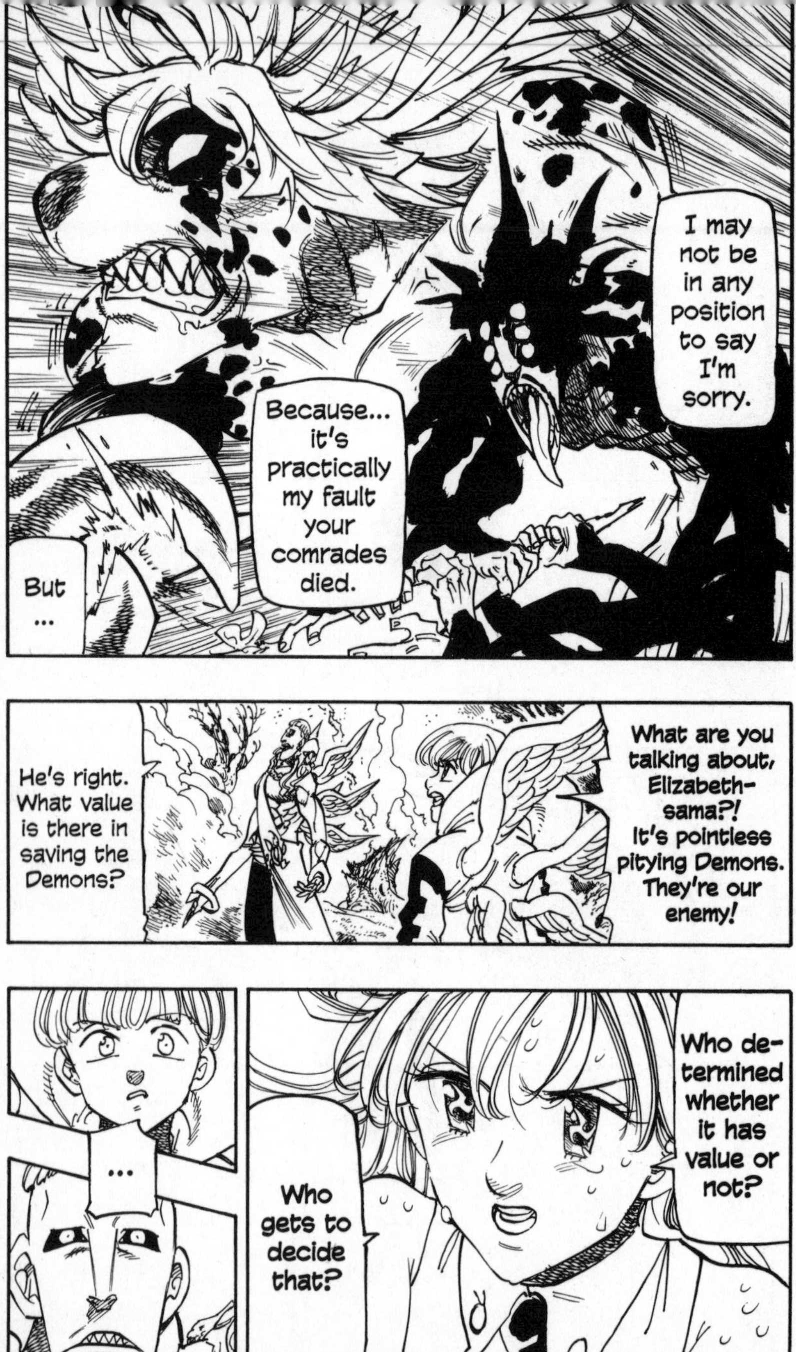
I may not be in any position to say I'm sorry.
Because... it's practically my fault your comrades died.
But ...
What are you talking about, Elizabeth-sama?! It's pointless pitying Demons. They're our enemy!
He's right. What value is there in saving the Demons?
Who determined whether it has value or not?
Who gets to decide that?
...

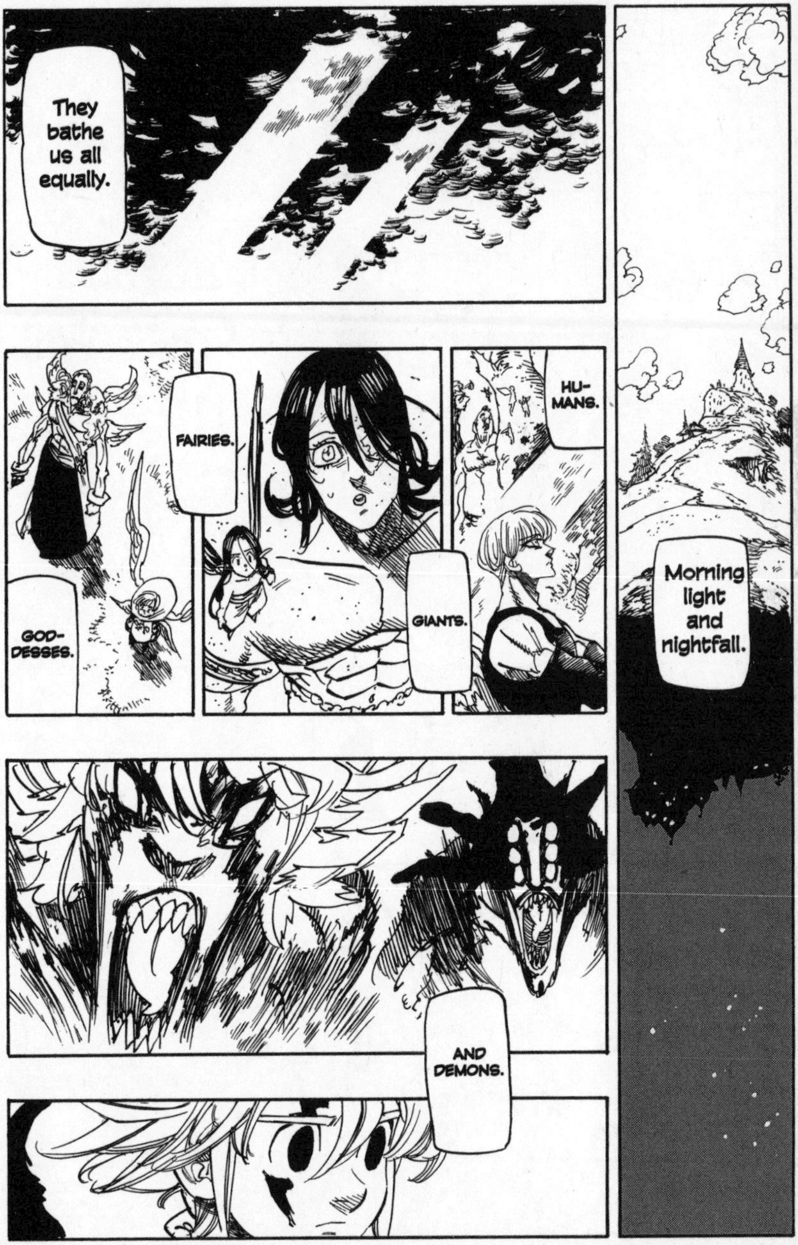
Morning light and nightfall.
They bathe us all equally.
HU-MANS.
FAIRIES.
GIANTS.
GOD-DESSES.
AND DEMONS.

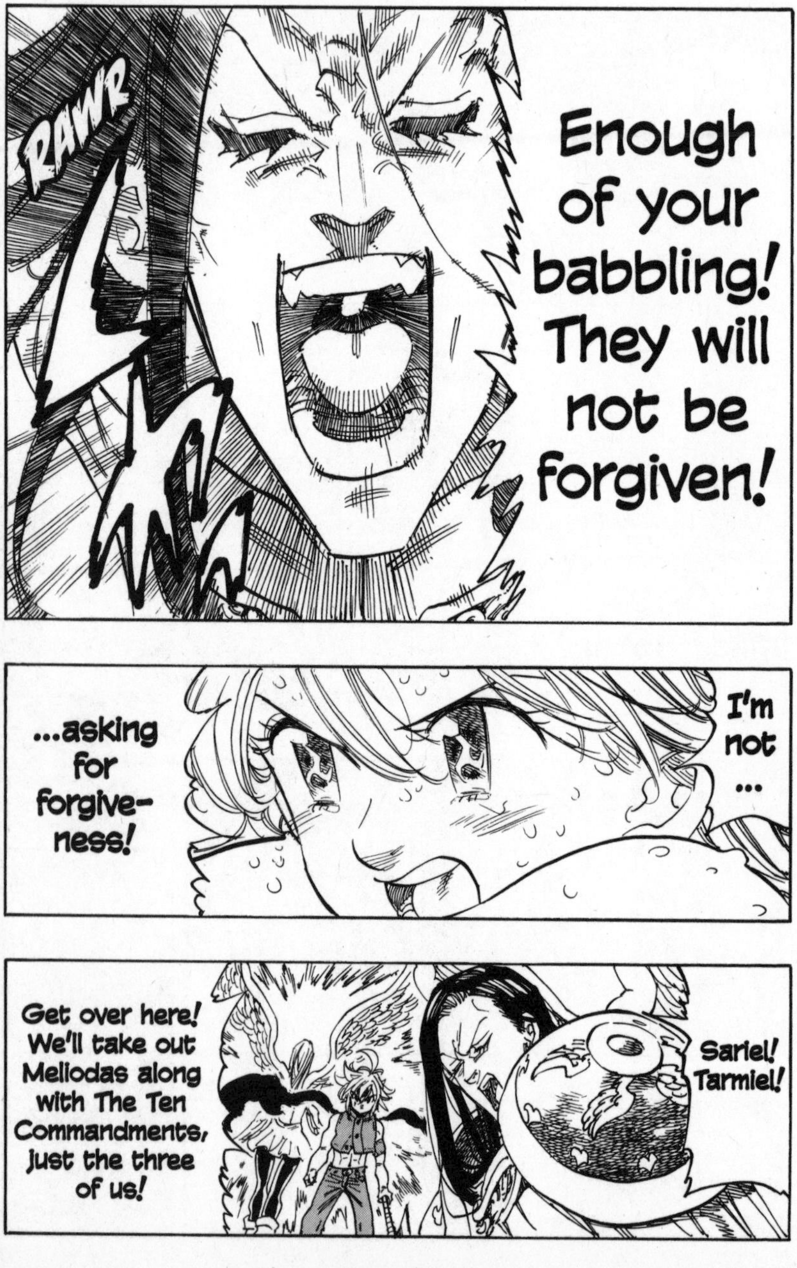
Enough of your babbling! They will not be forgiven!
RAWR
I'm not ...
...asking for forgive-ness!
Sariel! Tarmiel!
Get over here! We'll take out Meliodas along with The Ten Commandments, just the three of us!

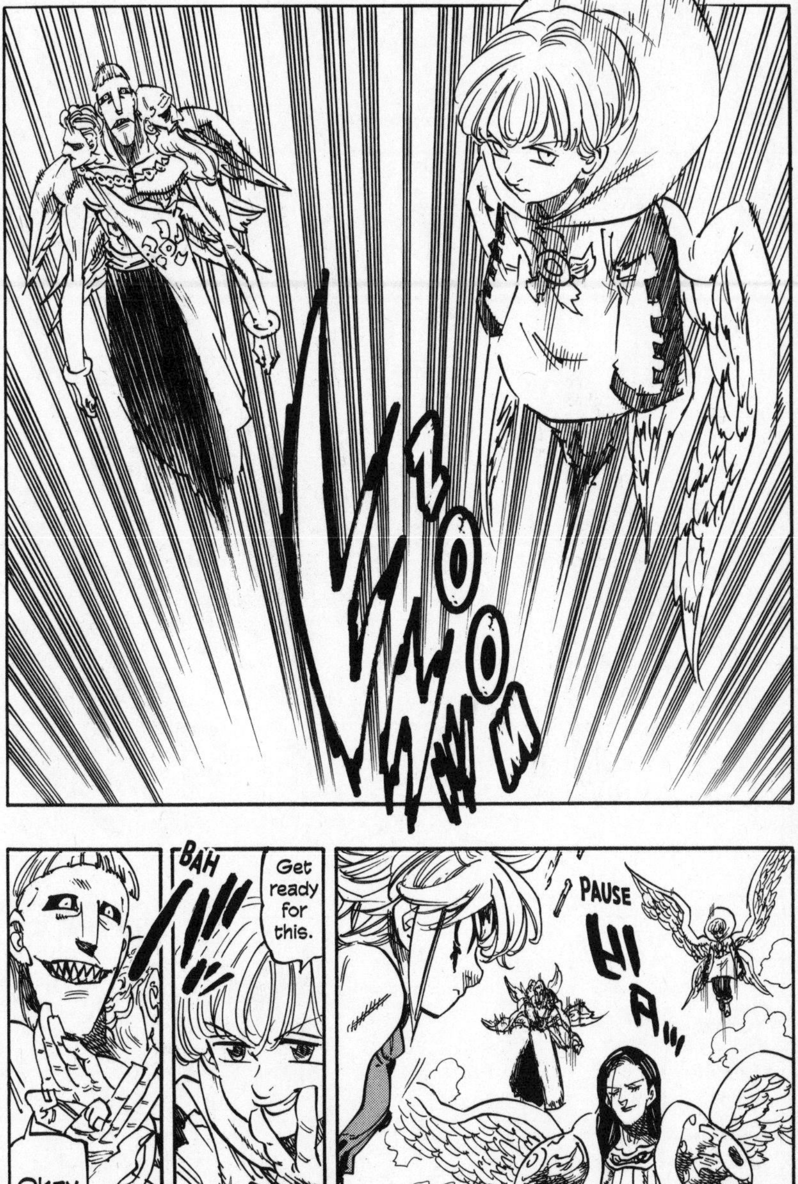
ZOOM
PAUSE
Get ready for this.
BAH
Okay.

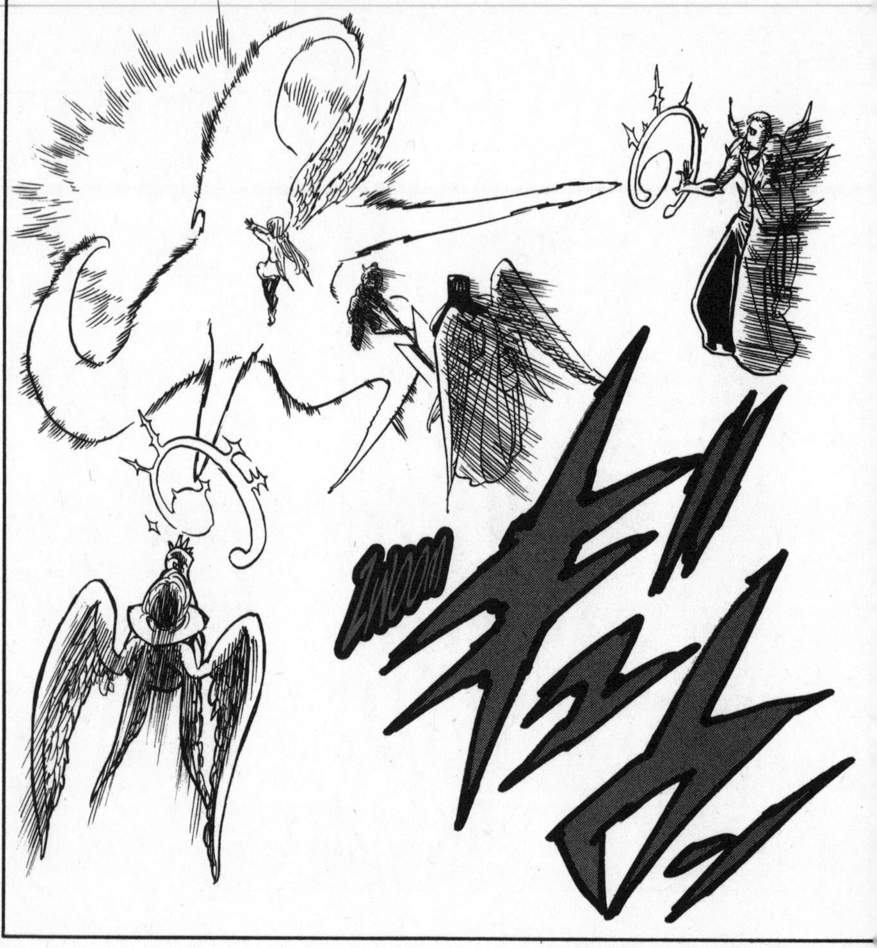
ZWOOM

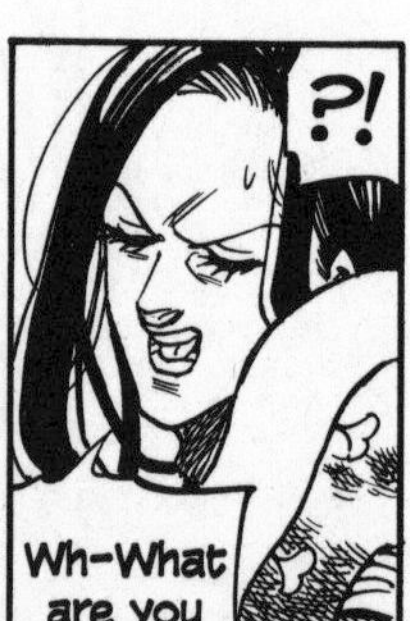
?!
Wh-What are you doing?!

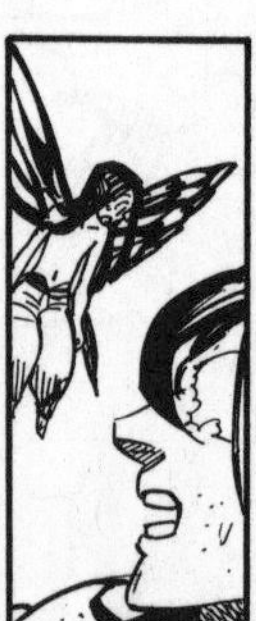

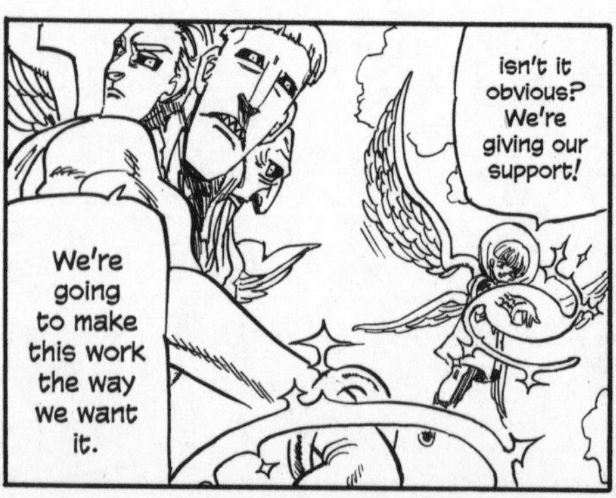
isn't it obvious? We're giving our support!
We're going to make this work the way we want it.

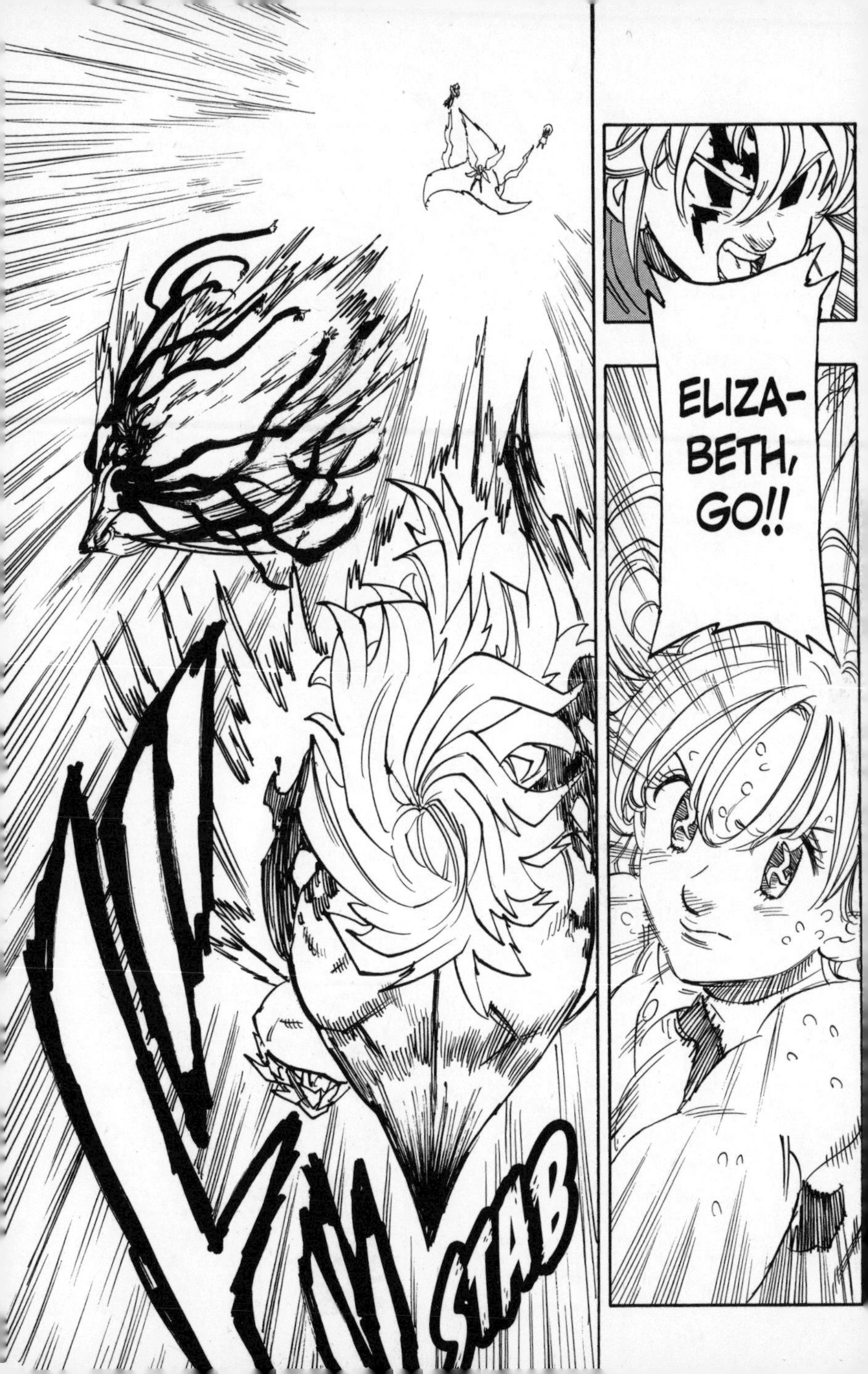
ELIZA-BETH, GO!!
STAB

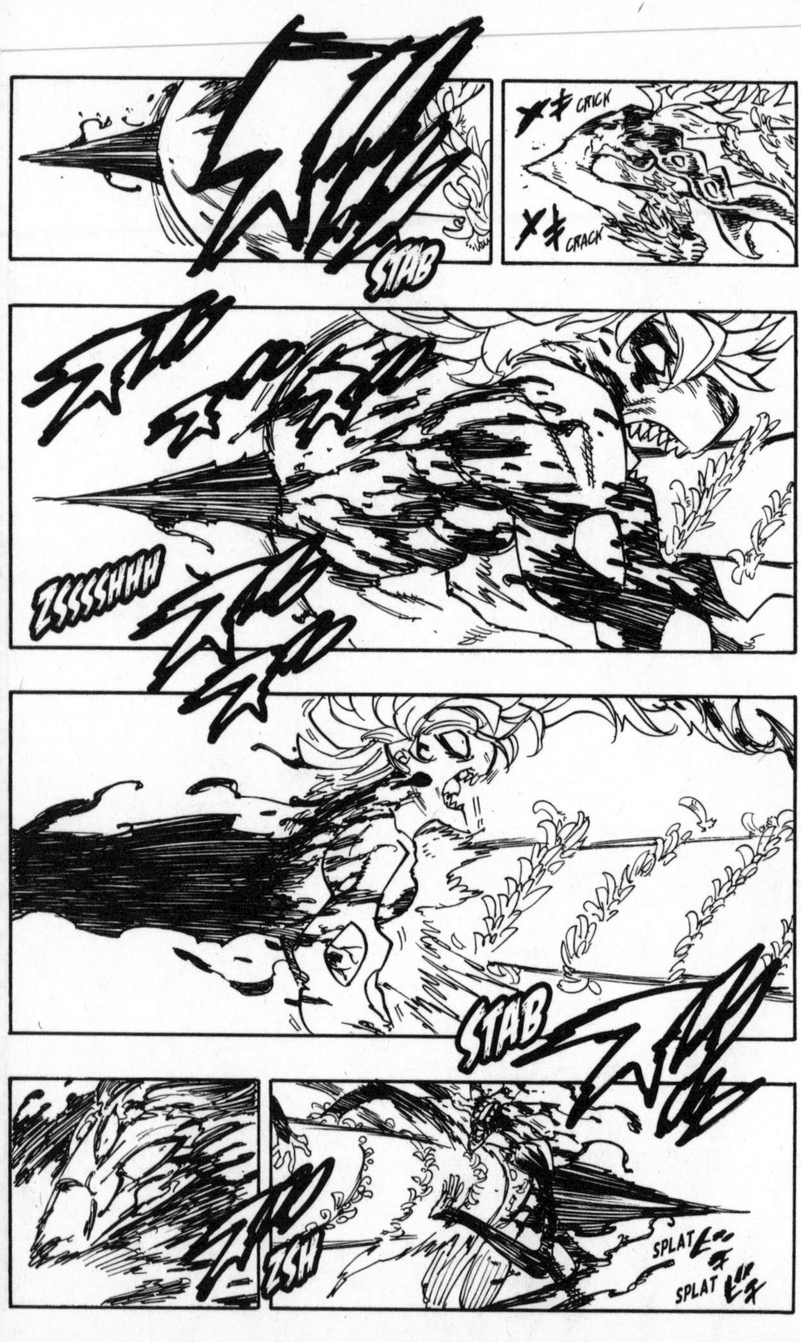
メキ CRICK
メキ CRACK
STAB
ZSSSSHHH
STAB
SPLAT ビチ
SPLAT ビチ
ZSH

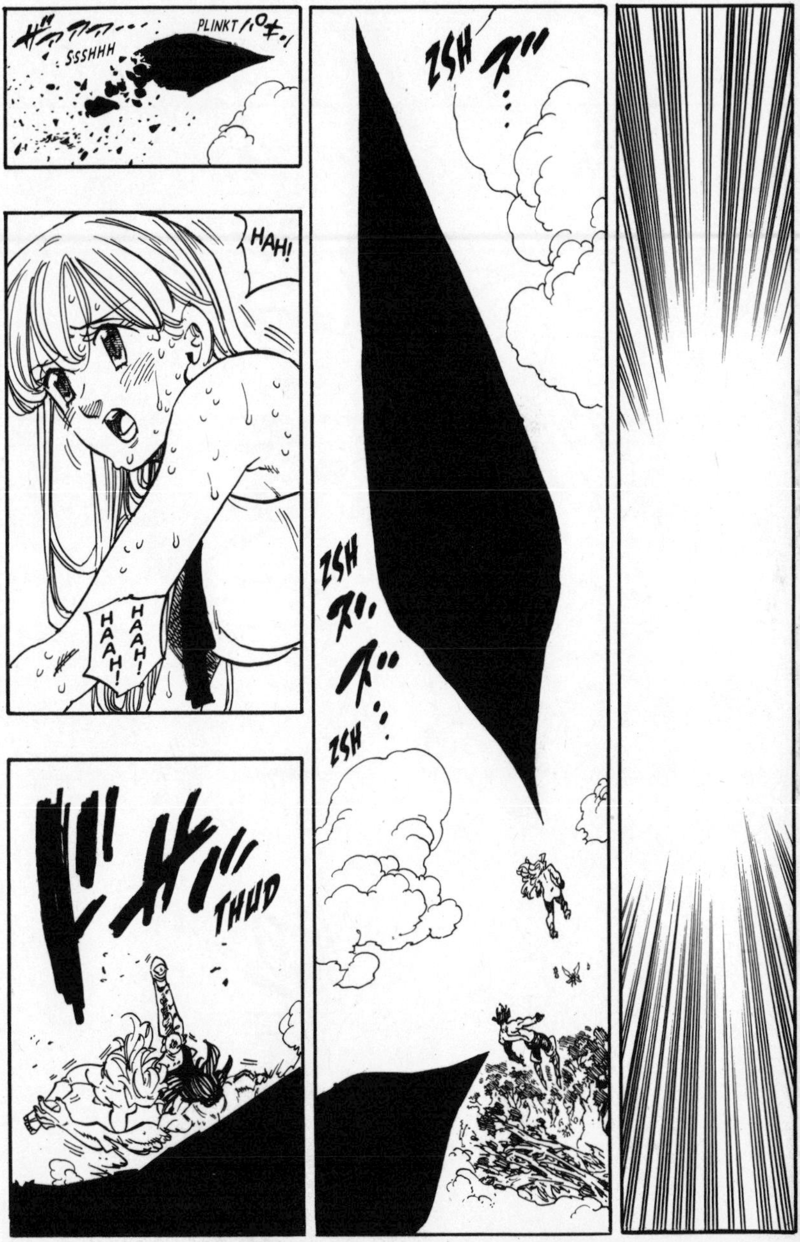
ZSH
ZSH
ZSH
SSSHHH
PLINKT
HAH!
HAAAH! HAAAH!
THUD

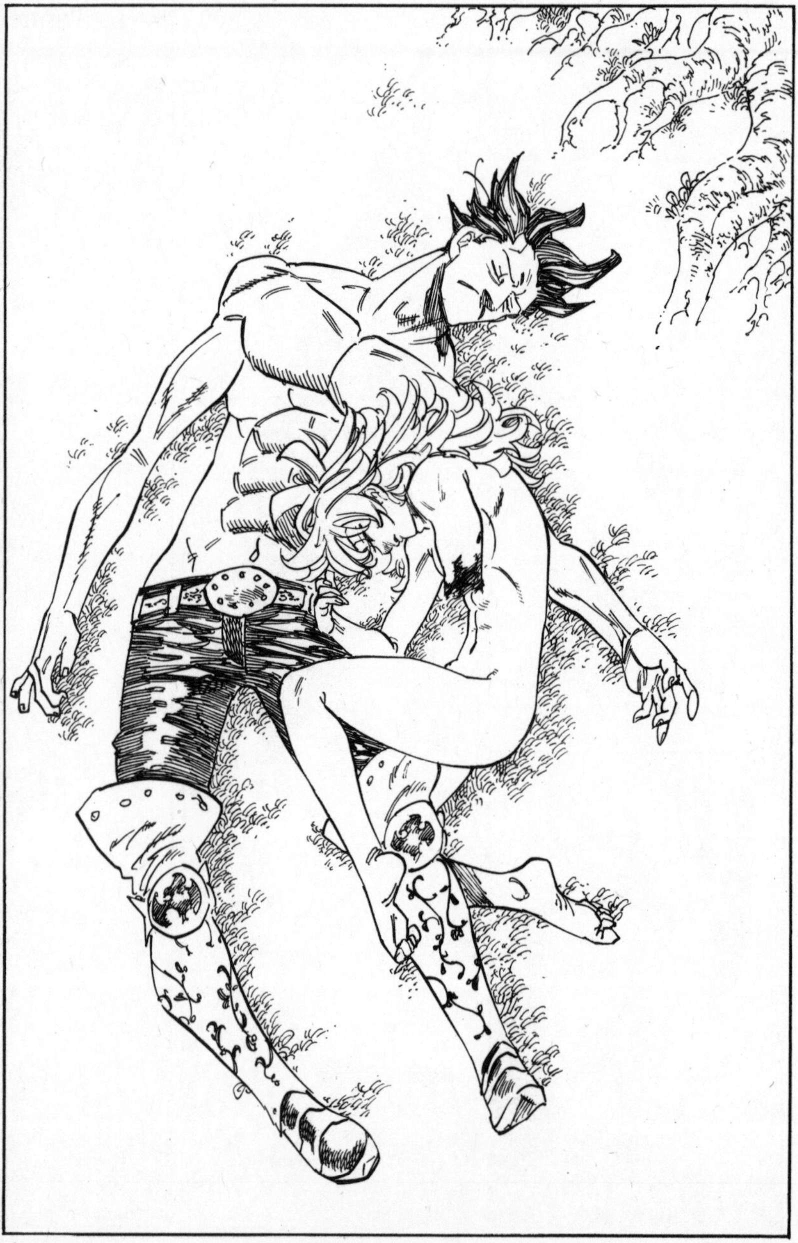

Chapter 209 - Into the Future

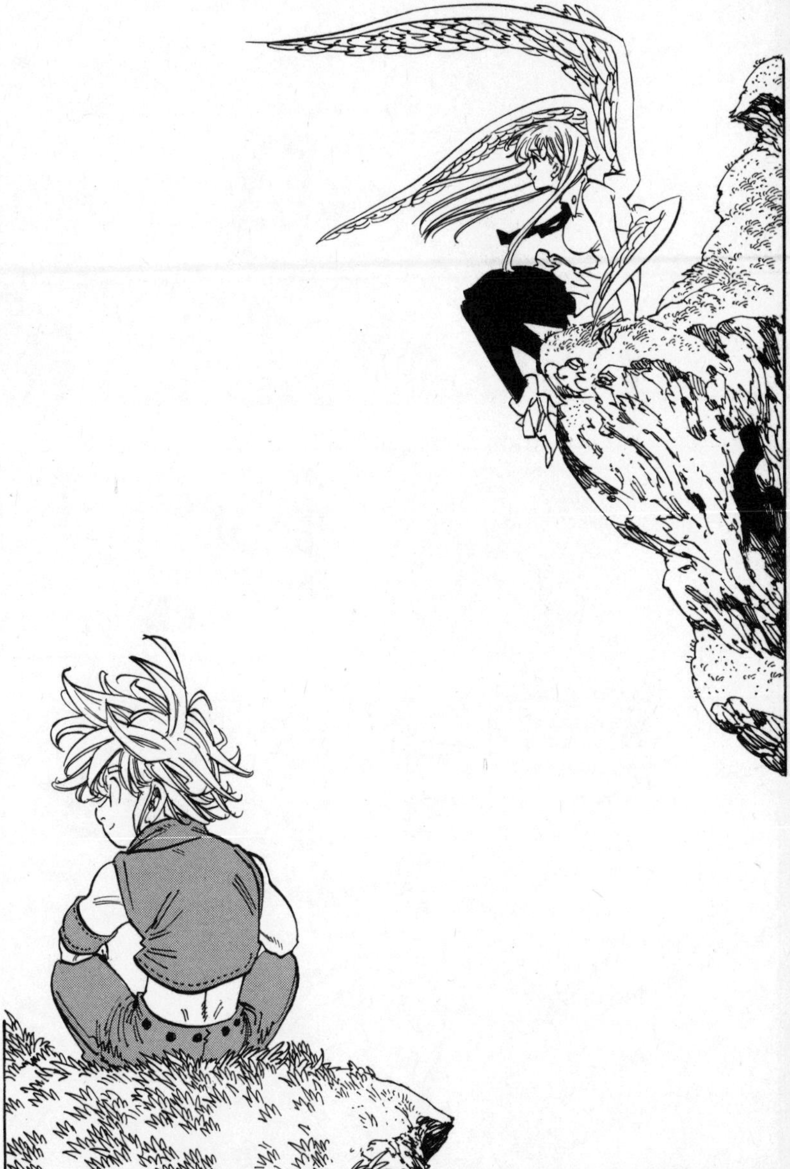

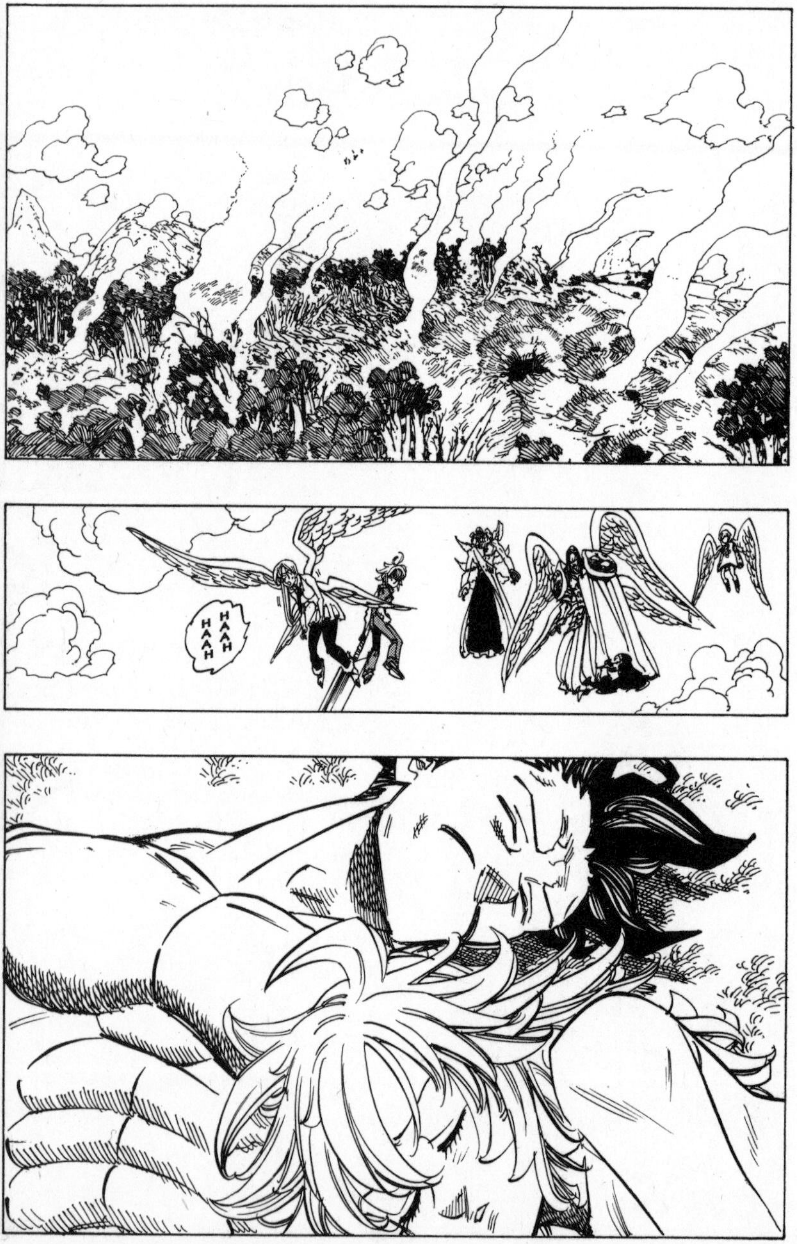
HAAH HAAH

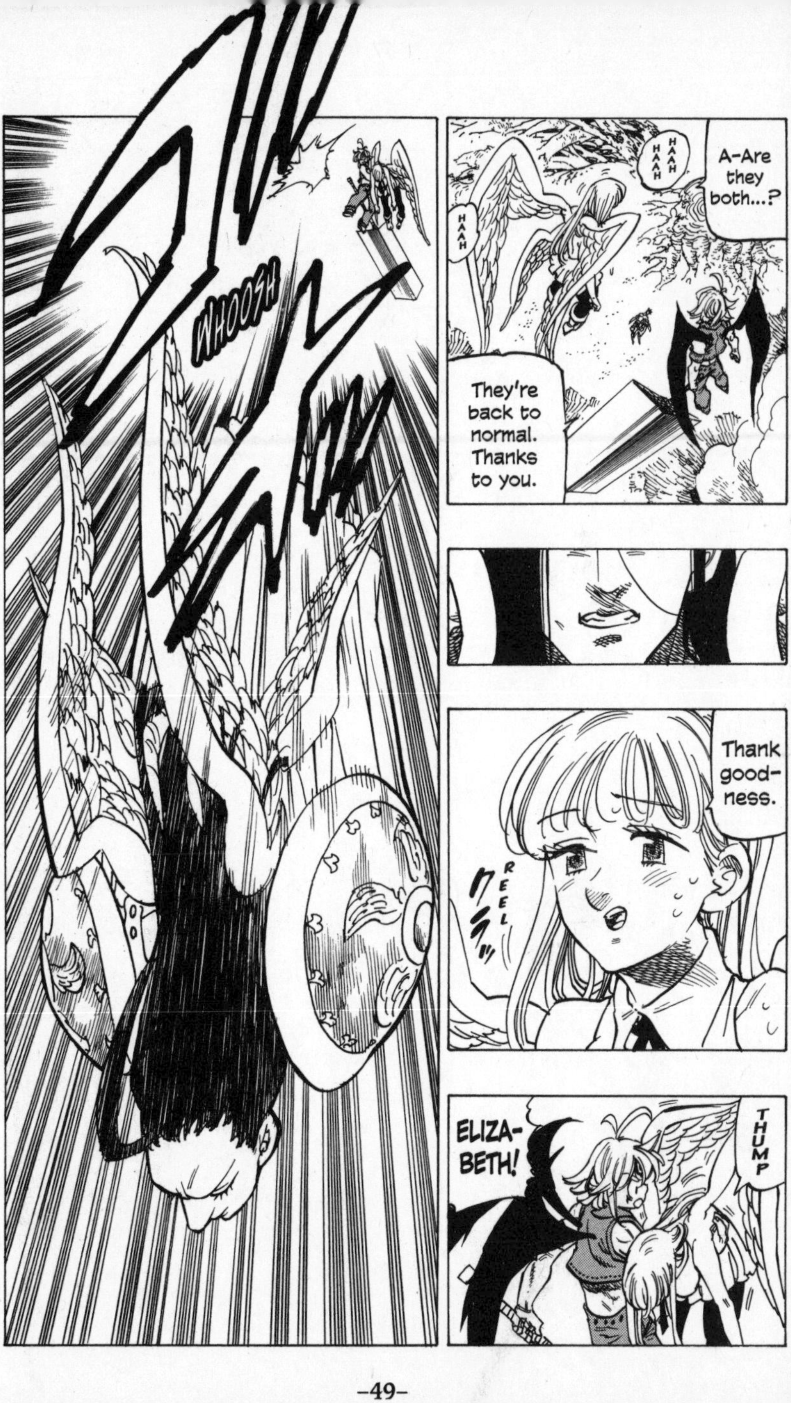
A-Are they both...?
HAAH HAAH
HAAH
They're back to normal. Thanks to you.
Thank goodness.
REEL
THUMP
ELIZA-BETH!
WHOOSH

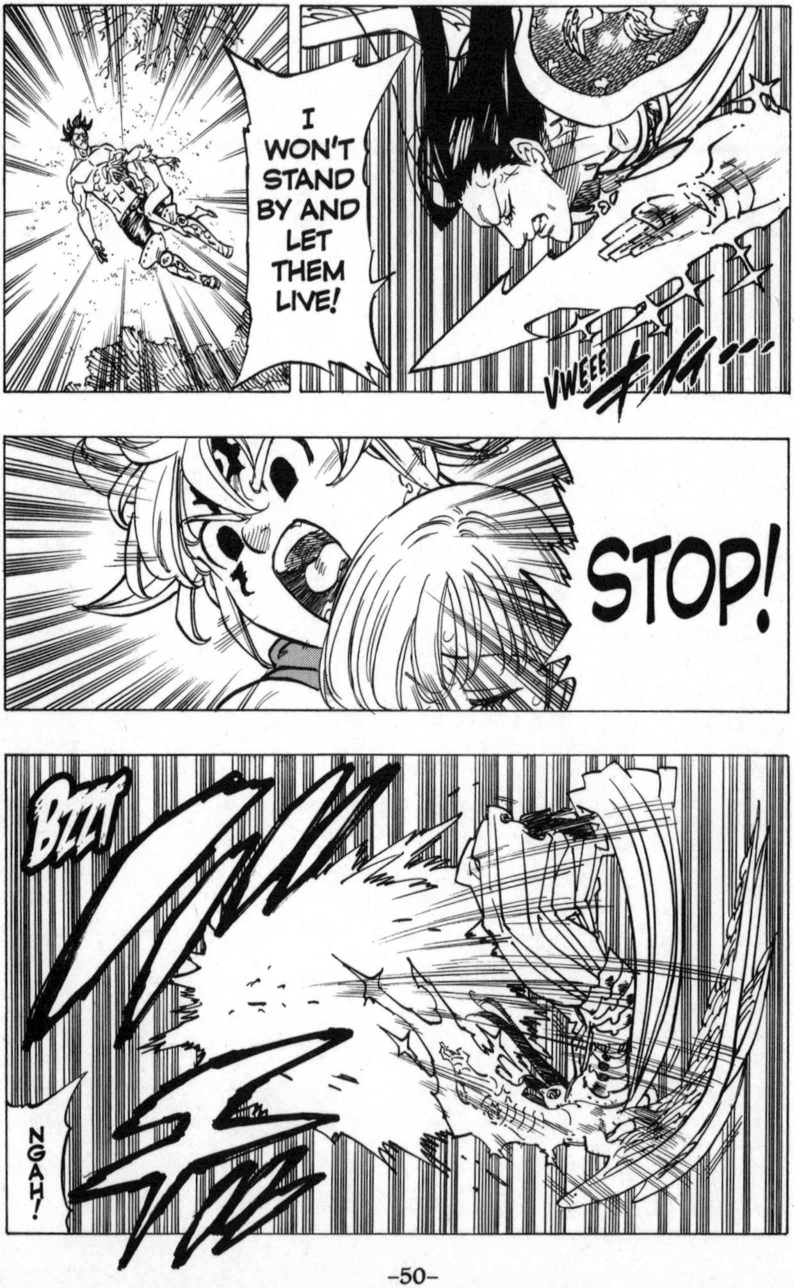
I WON'T STAND BY AND LET THEM LIVE!
VWEEE
STOP!
BZZT
NGAH!

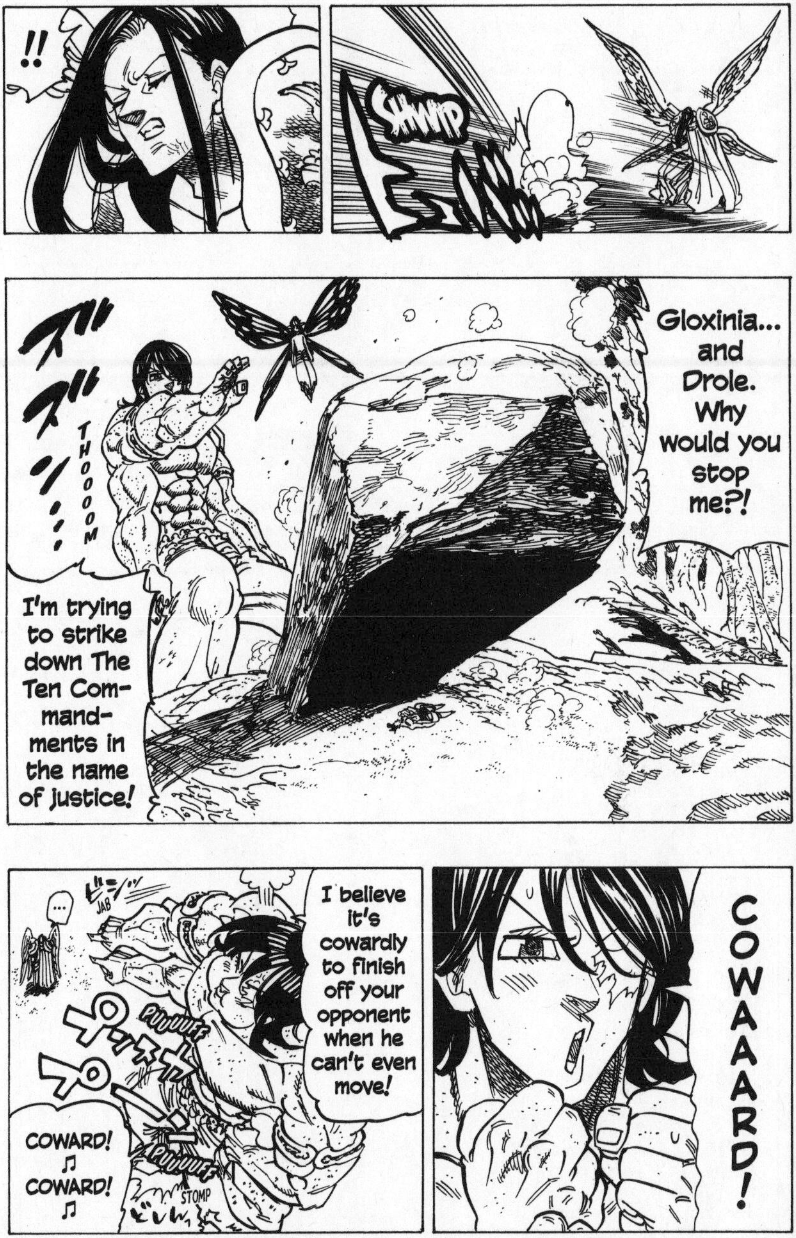

SHWIP
!!
Gloxinia... and Drole. Why would you stop me?!
THOOOOM
I'm trying to strike down The Ten Commandments in the name of justice!
COWAAARD!
I believe it's cowardly to finish off your opponent when he can't even move!
JAB
...
PUUUFF
PUUUFF
COWARD! ♫ COWARD! ♫
STOMP

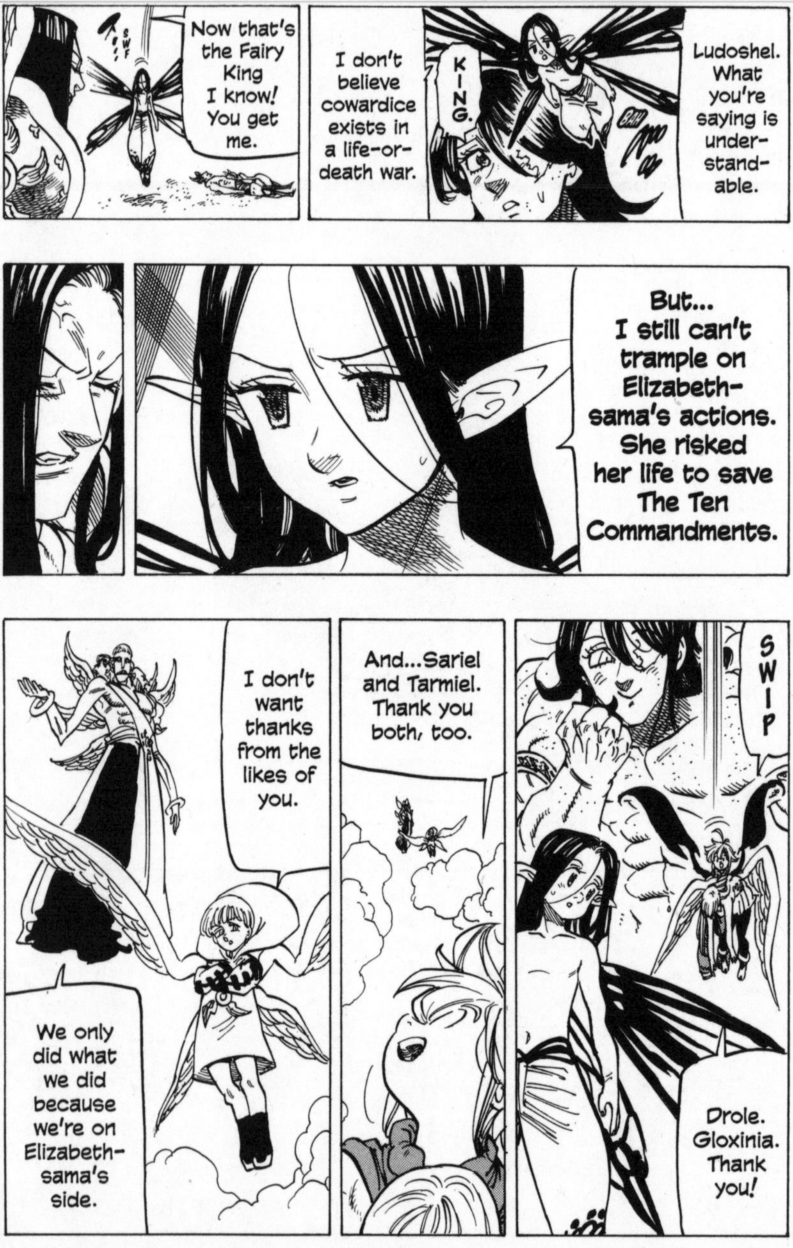
Ludoshel. What you're saying is understandable.
KING.
I don't believe cowardice exists in a life-or-death war.
SWF
Now that's the Fairy King I know! You get me.
But... I still can't trample on Elizabeth-sama's actions. She risked her life to save The Ten Commandments.
SWIP
Drole. Gloxinia. Thank you!
And...Sariel and Tarmiel. Thank you both, too.
I don't want thanks from the likes of you.
We only did what we did because we're on Elizabeth-sama's side.

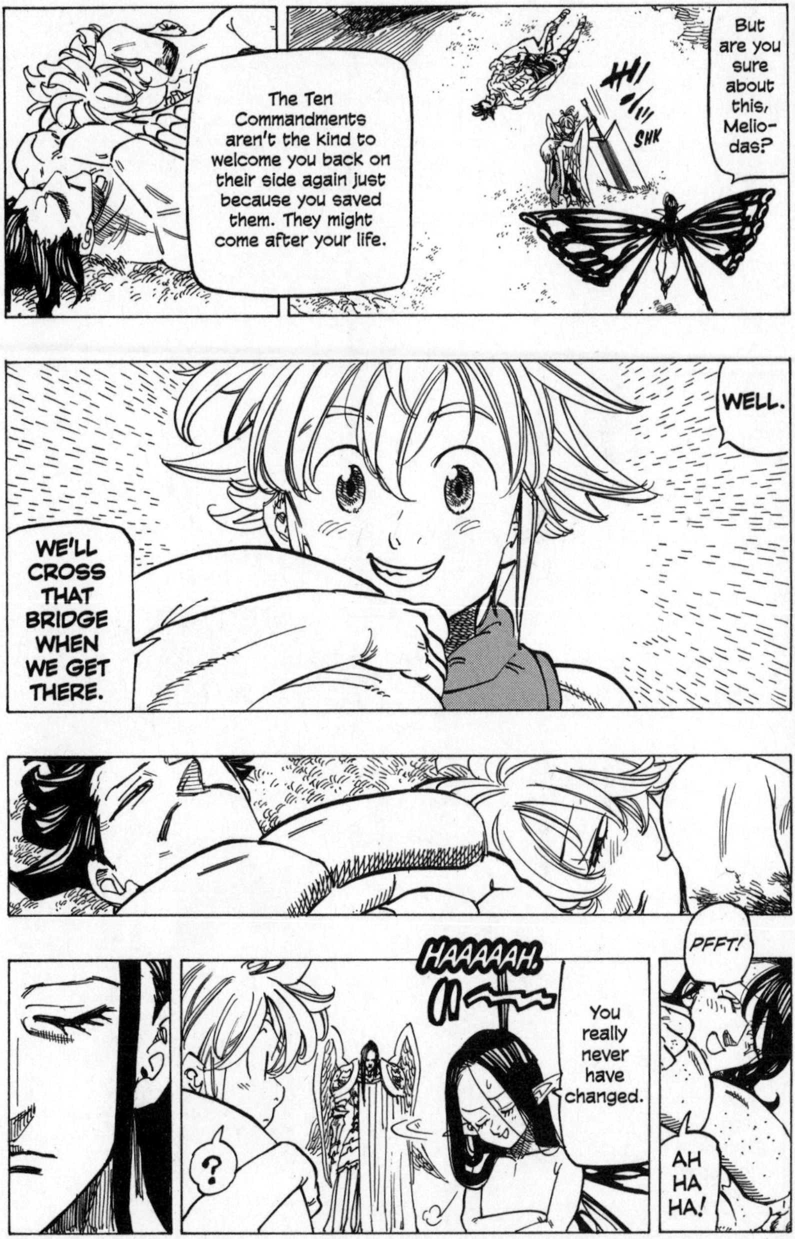
But are you sure about this, Melio-das?
HH!
SHK
The Ten Commandments aren't the kind to welcome you back on their side again just because you saved them. They might come after your life.
WELL.
WE'LL CROSS THAT BRIDGE WHEN WE GET THERE.
PFFT!
AH HA HA!
HAAAAAH.
You really never have changed.
?

High-ranking Demons who possess seven hearts, a Combat Class of over 50,000, and who sacrifice six of their hearts will become the legendary beast Indura. By making a pact with darkness and showing their true colors, they lose control of themselves, and their form becomes more and more sinister as time passes. Of all their iterations, The Ten Commandments who were bestowed commandments by the Demon Lord transform into what's called the "favored" Indura. There are other types of Induras who have been given such titles of "Ashes," "Years," "Distant Thunder," and "Retribution," among others, and who still roam the Demon World to this day.

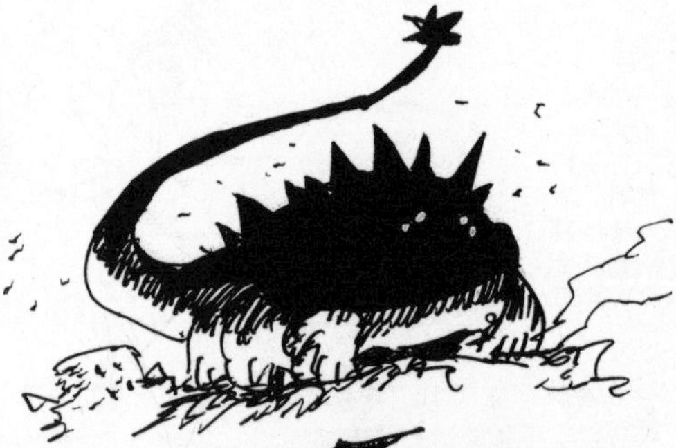

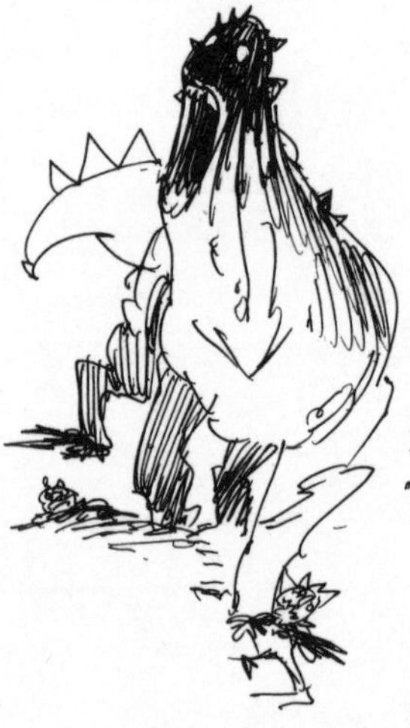

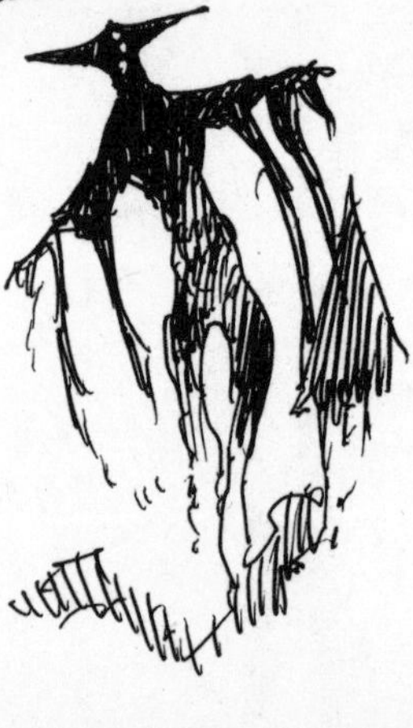

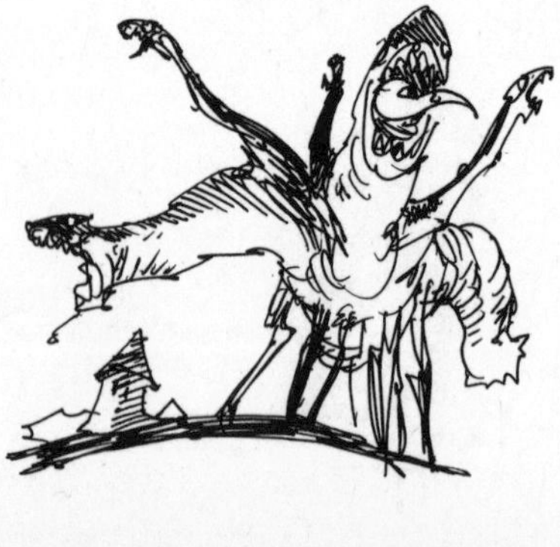

Chapter 210 - Emotional Maelstrom

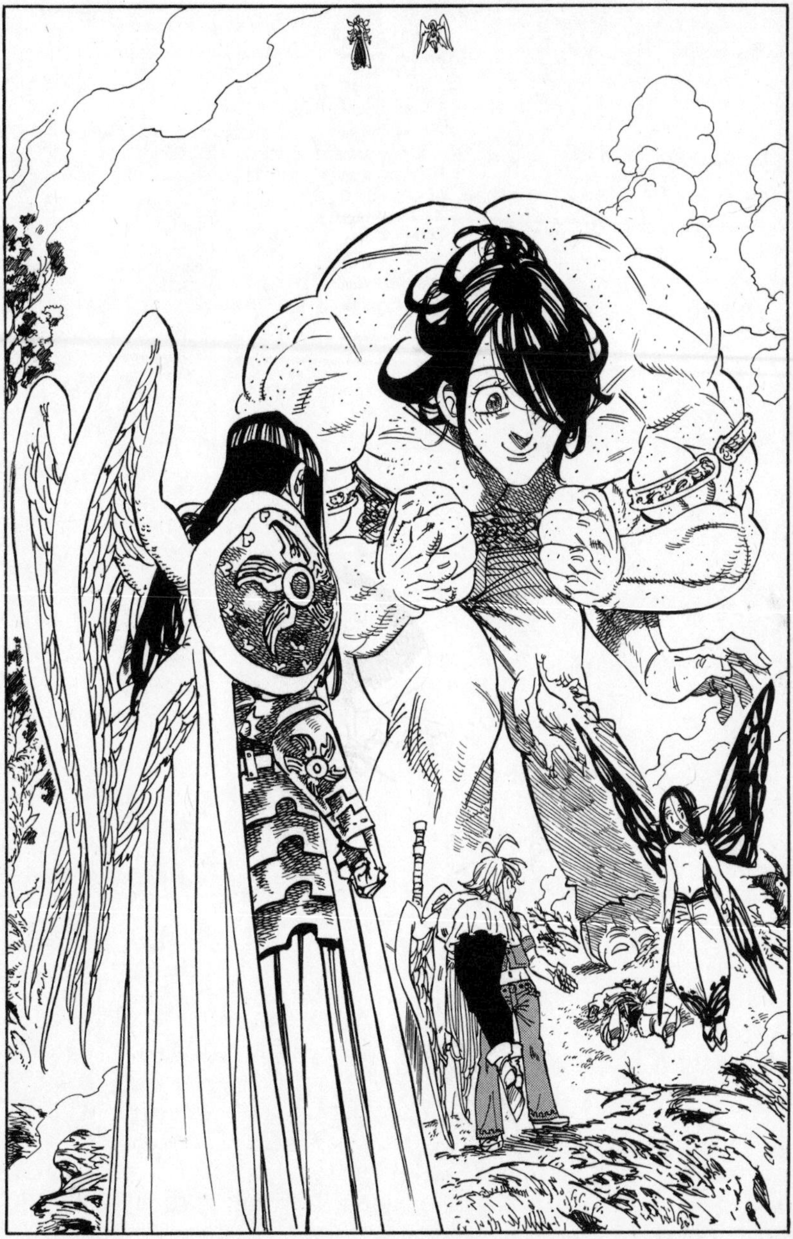

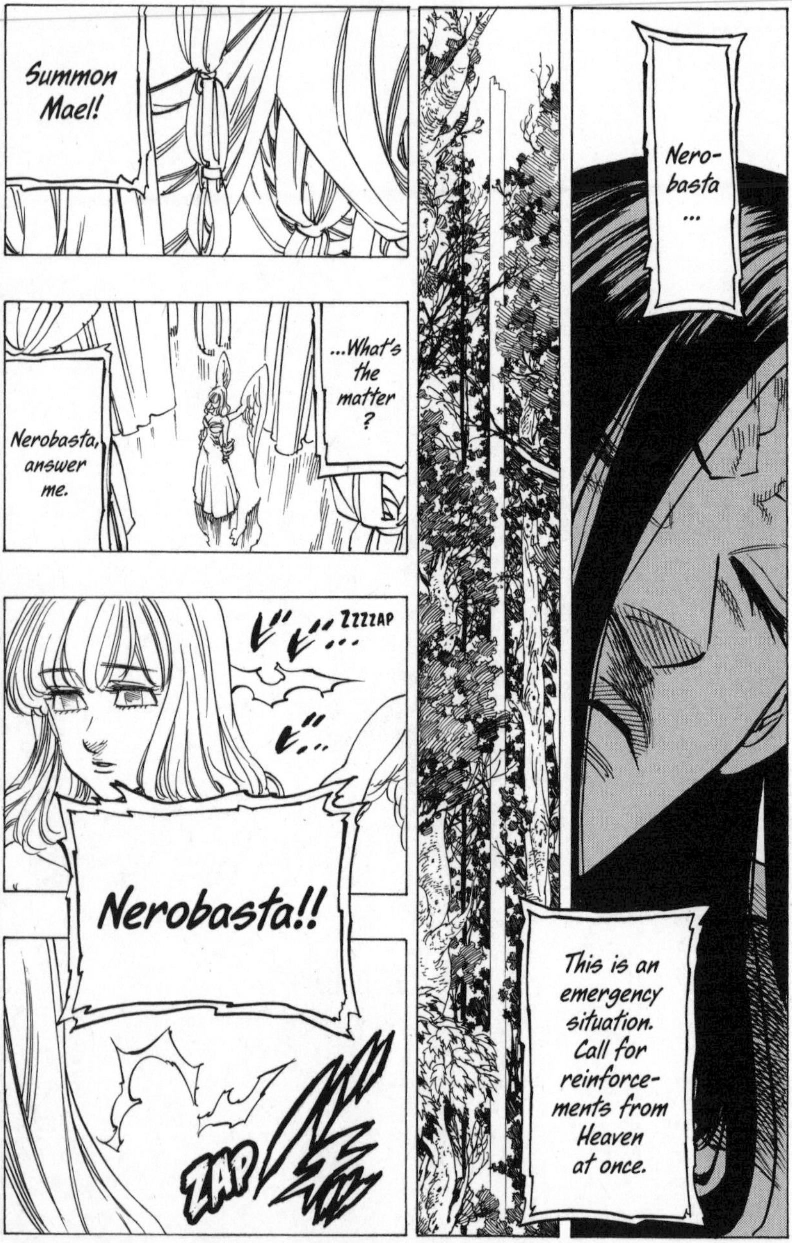
Nero-basta...
This is an emergency situation. Call for reinforcements from Heaven at once.
Summon Mael!
...What's the matter?
Nerobasta, answer me.
ZZZZAP
Nerobasta!!
ZAP

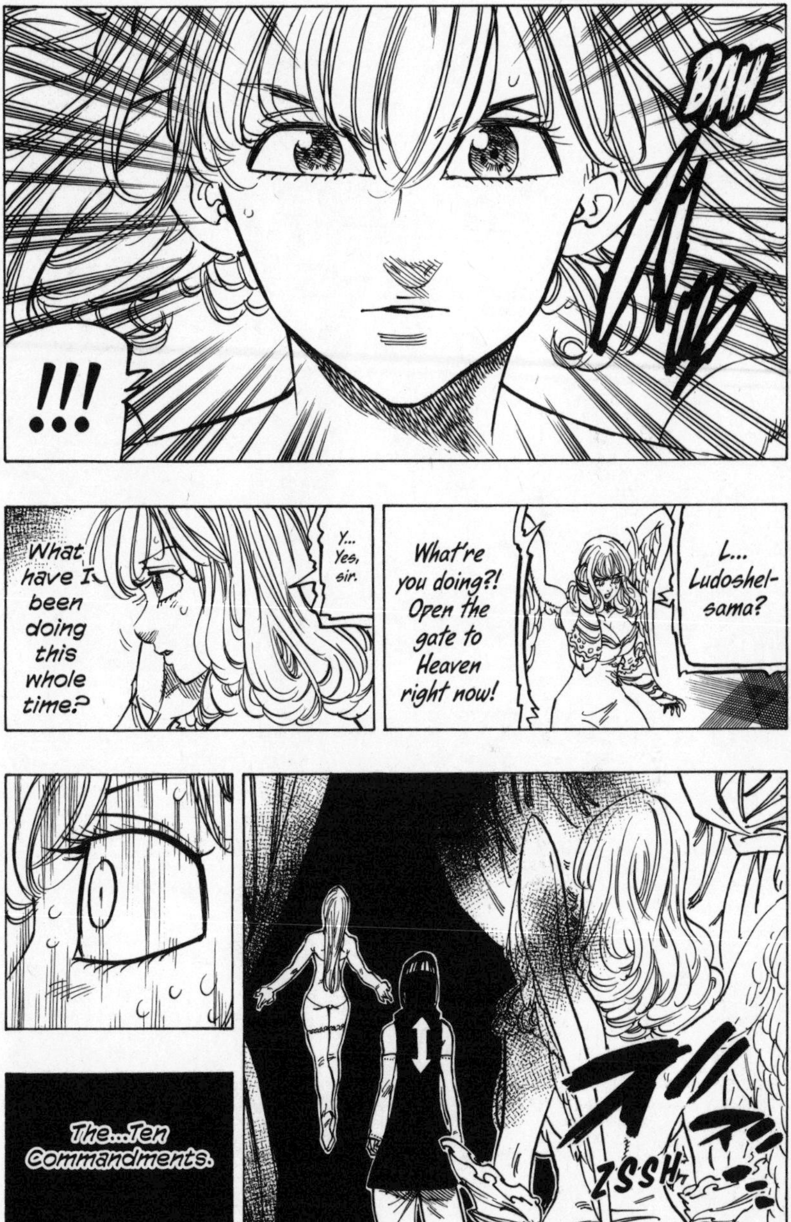
BAH
!!!
L... Ludoshel-sama?
What're you doing?! Open the gate to Heaven right now!
Y... Yes, sir.
What have I been doing this whole time?
ZSSH
The...Ten Commandments.

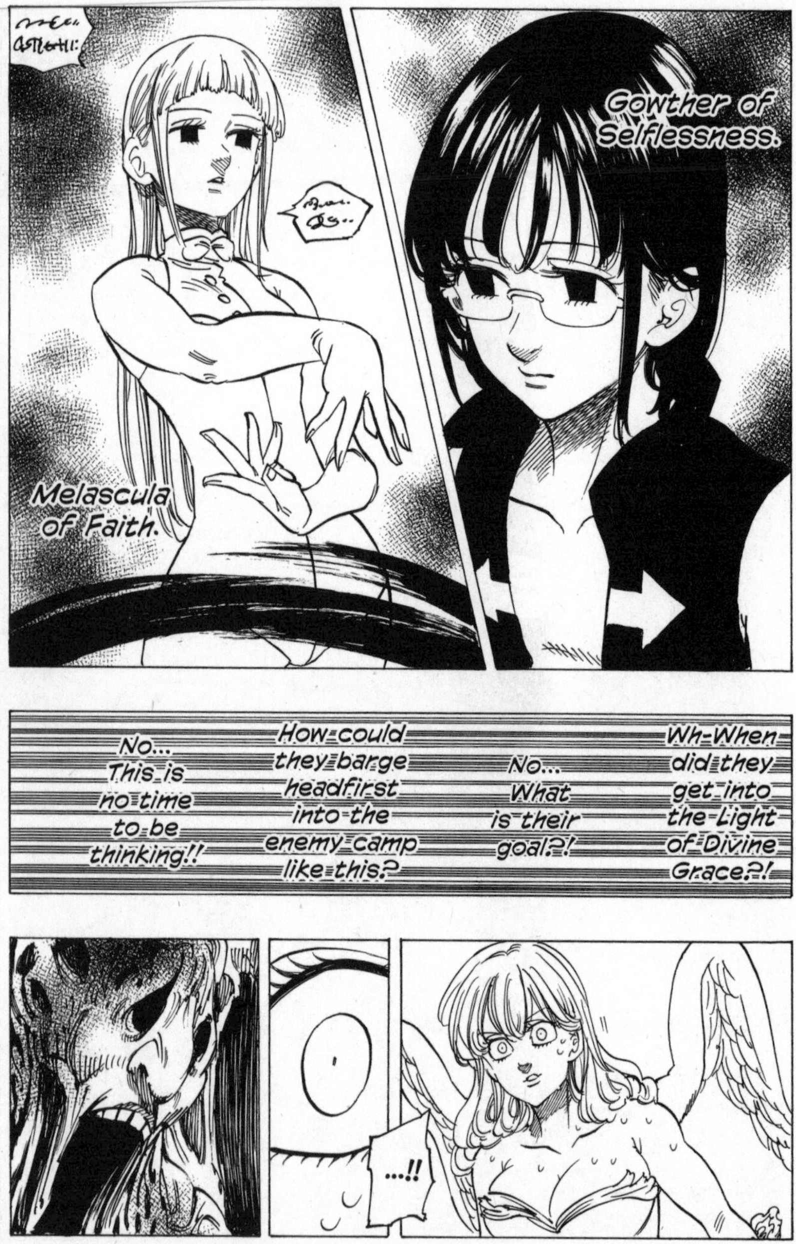
Gowther of Selflessness.
Melascula of Faith.
Wh-When did they get into the Light of Divine Grace?!
No... What is their goal?!
How could they barge headfirst into the enemy camp like this?
No... This is no time to be thinking!!
...!!

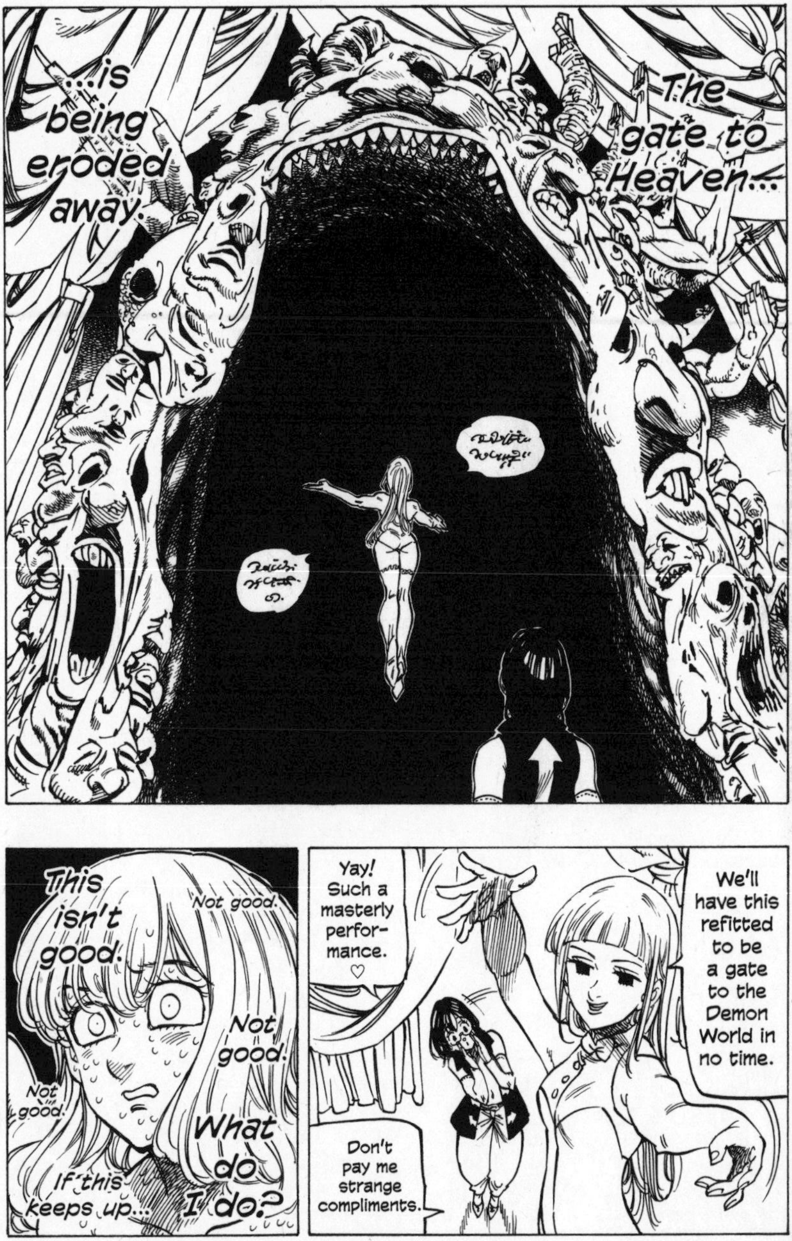
The gate to Heaven...
...is being eroded away.
We'll have this refitted to be a gate to the Demon World in no time.
Yay! Such a masterly performance. ♡
Don't pay me strange compliments.
This isn't good.
Not good.
Not good.
What do I do?
Not good.
If this keeps up...

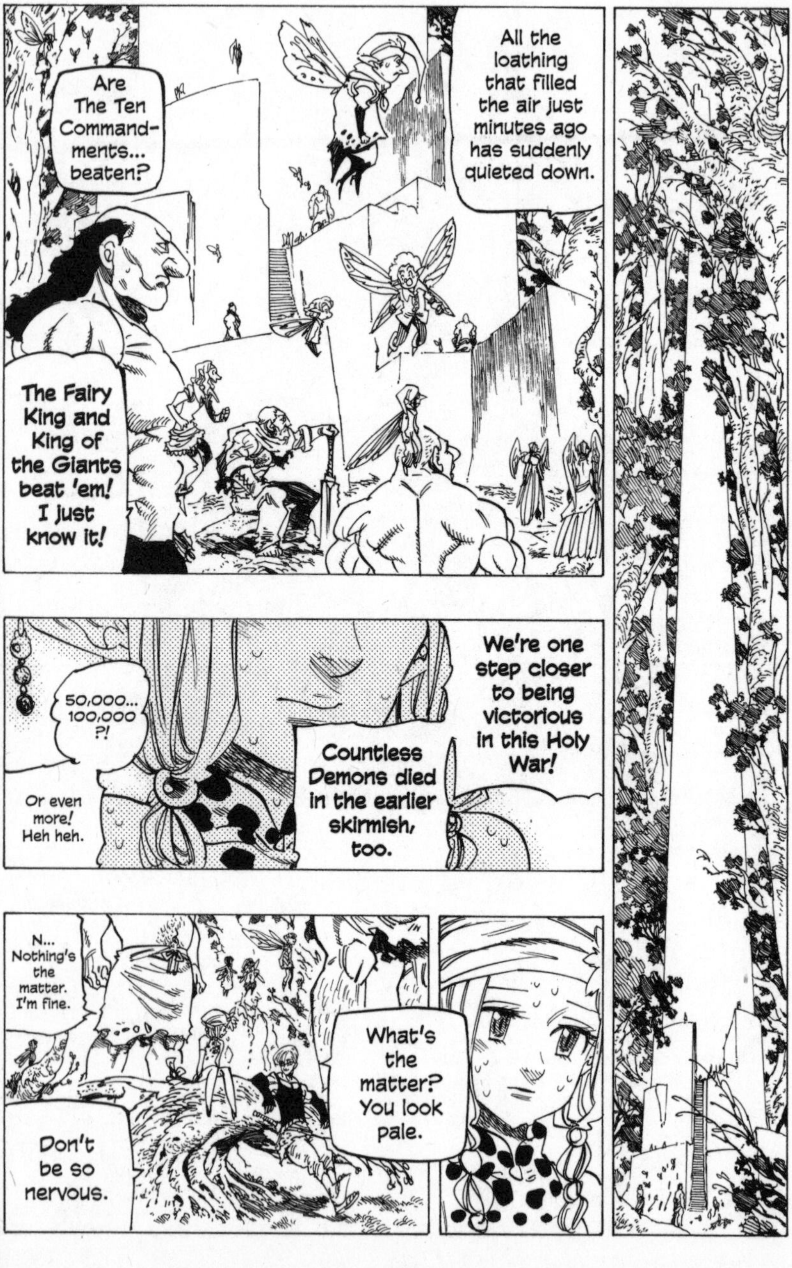
All the loathing that filled the air just minutes ago has suddenly quieted down.
Are The Ten Commandments... beaten?
The Fairy King and King of the Giants beat 'em! I just know it!
We're one step closer to being victorious in this Holy War!
Countless Demons died in the earlier skirmish, too.
50,000... 100,000?!
Or even more! Heh heh.
What's the matter? You look pale.
N... Nothing's the matter. I'm fine.
Don't be so nervous.

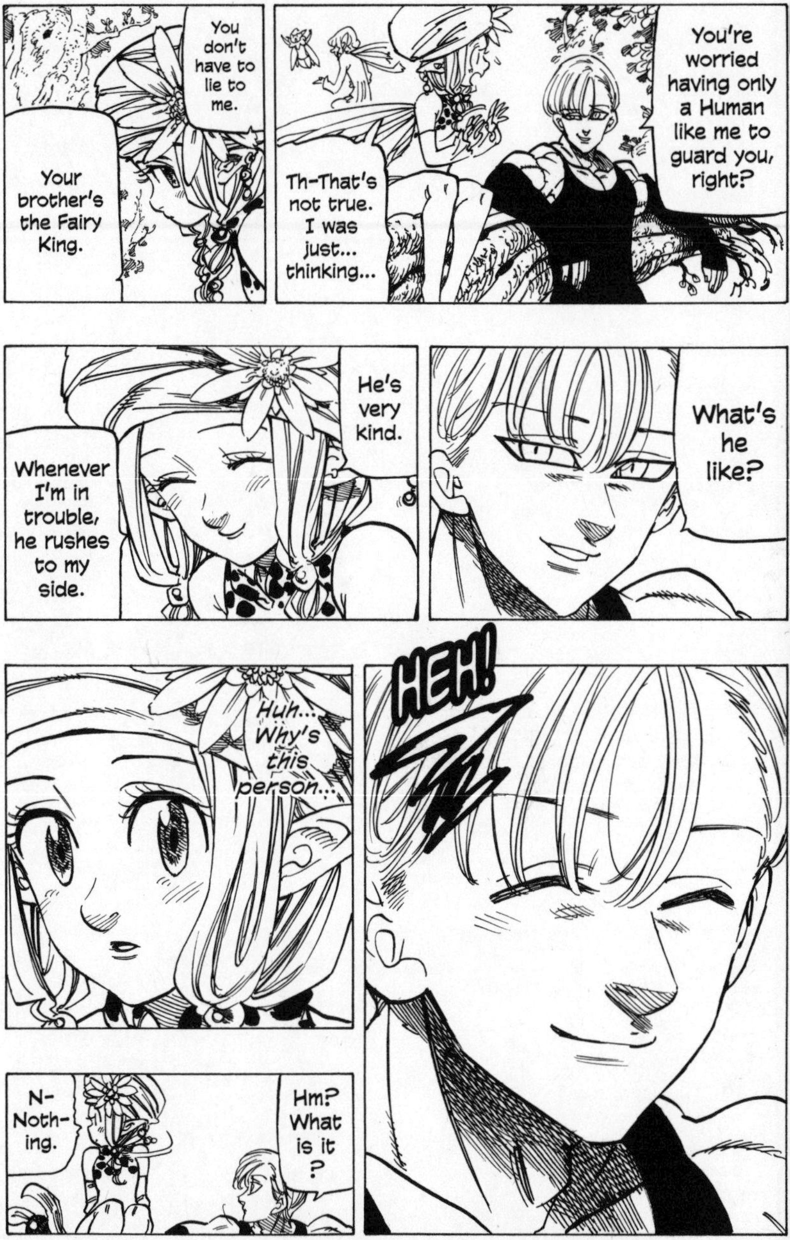
You're worried having only a Human like me to guard you, right?
Th-That's not true. I was just... thinking...
You don't have to lie to me.
Your brother's the Fairy King.
What's he like?
He's very kind.
Whenever I'm in trouble, he rushes to my side.
HEH!
Huh... Why's this person...
Hm? What is it?
N-Nothing.

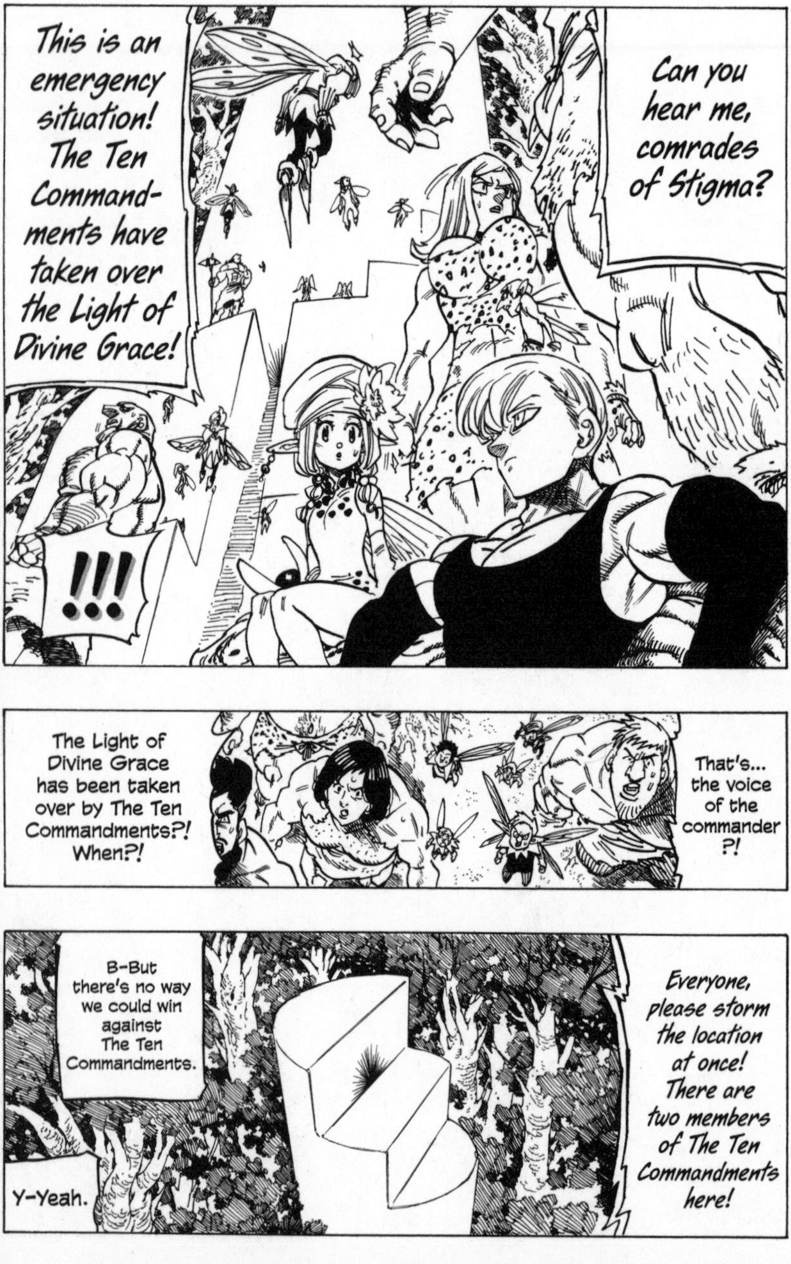
Can you hear me, comrades of Stigma?
This is an emergency situation! The Ten Command-ments have taken over the Light of Divine Grace!
!!!
That's... the voice of the commander ?!
The Light of Divine Grace has been taken over by The Ten Commandments?! When?!
Everyone, please storm the location at once! There are two members of The Ten Commandments here!
B-But there's no way we could win against The Ten Commandments.
Y-Yeah.

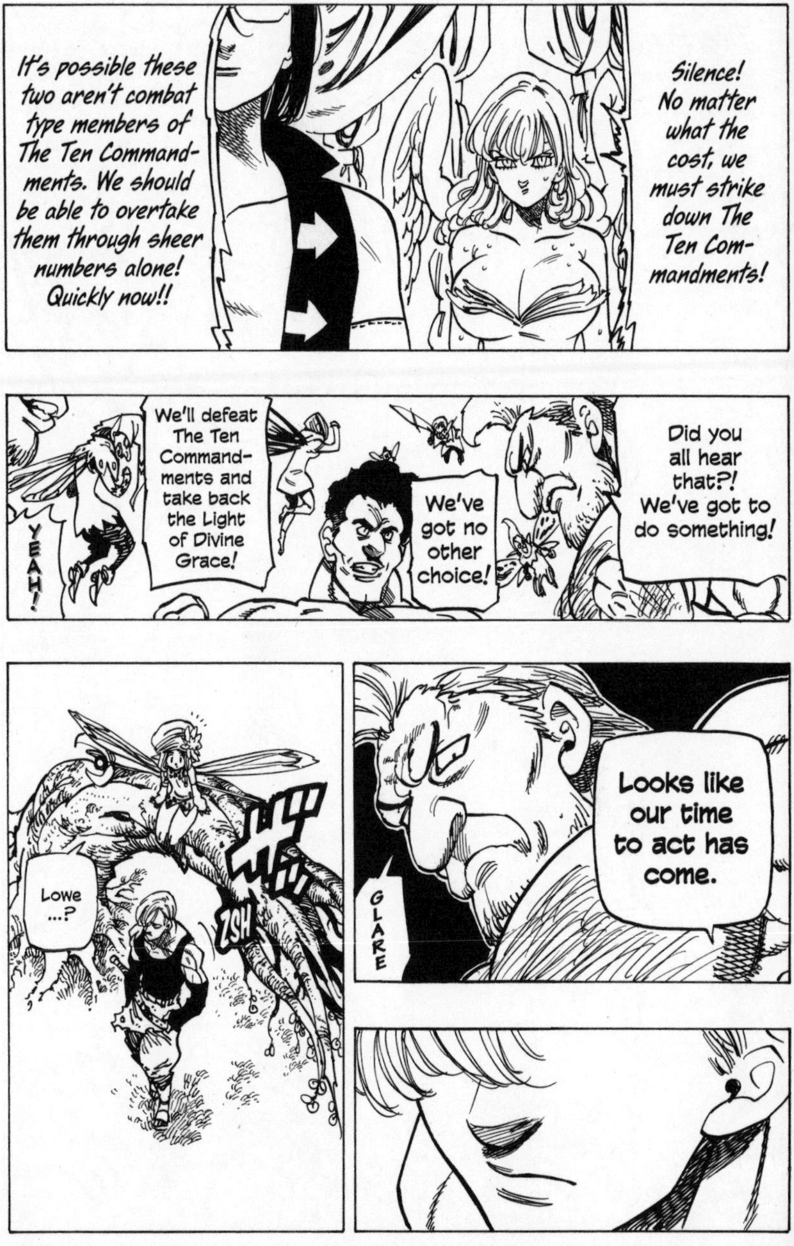
Silence! No matter what the cost, we must strike down The Ten Commandments!
It's possible these two aren't combat type members of The Ten Commandments. We should be able to overtake them through sheer numbers alone! Quickly now!!
Did you all hear that?! We've got to do something!
We've got no other choice!
We'll defeat The Ten Commandments and take back the Light of Divine Grace!
YEAH!
Looks like our time to act has come.
GLARE
ZSH
Lowe ...?

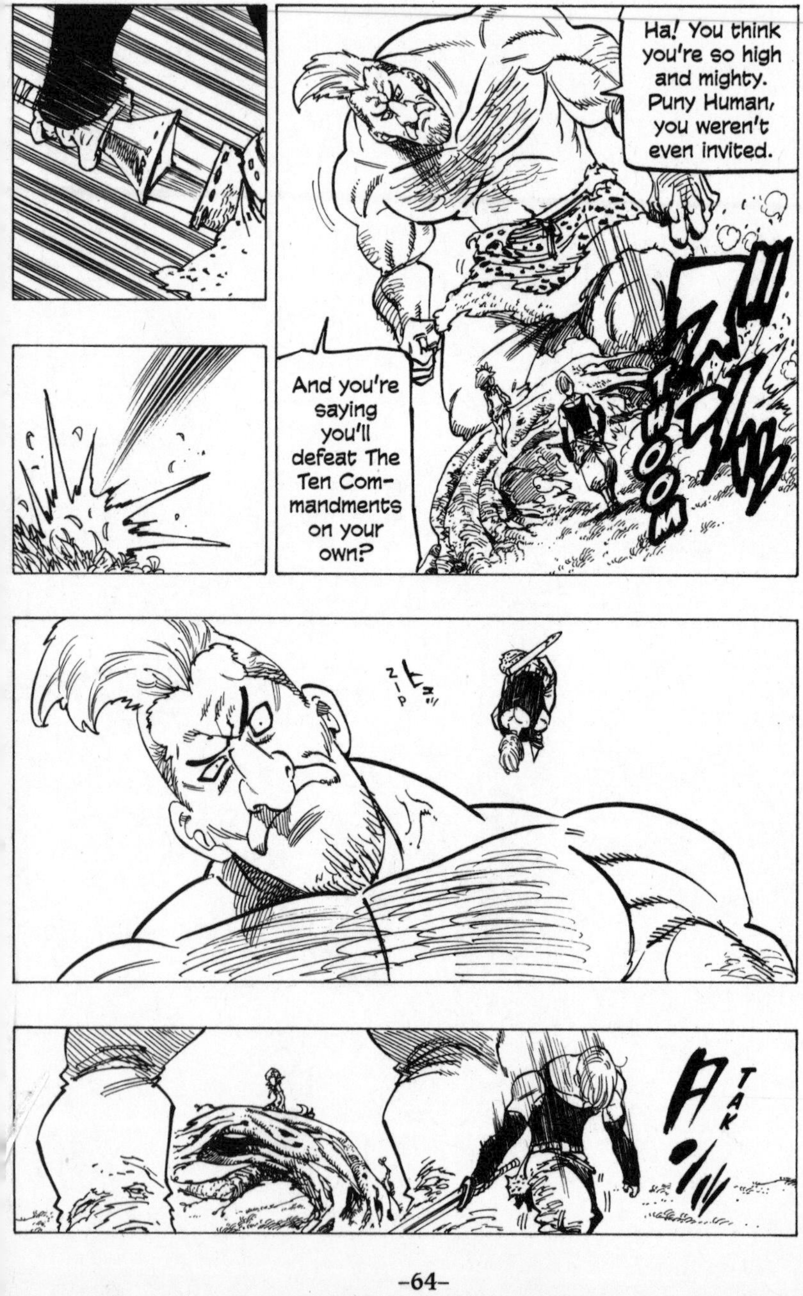
Ha! You think you're so high and mighty. Puny Human, you weren't even invited.
THOOOM
And you're saying you'll defeat The Ten Commandments on your own?
ZIP
TAK

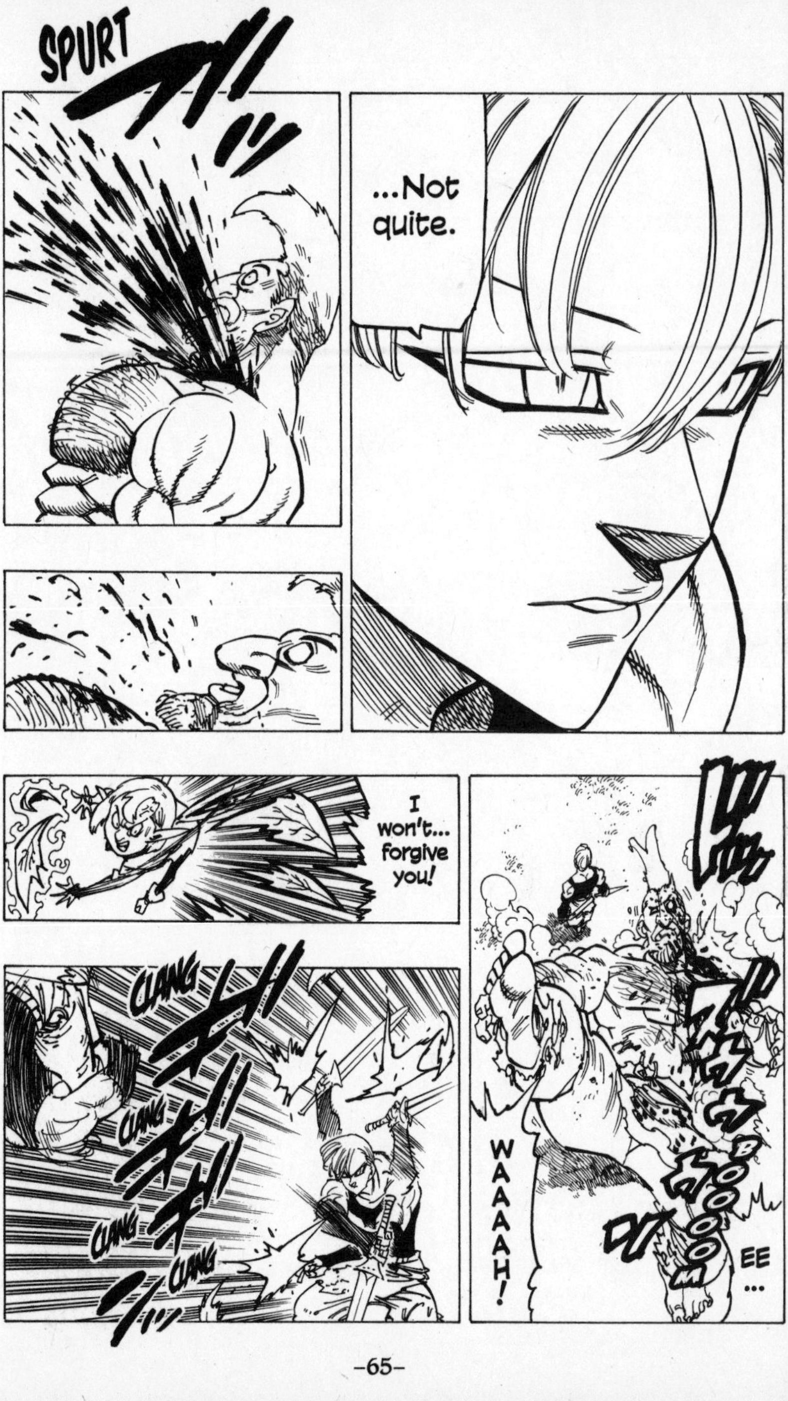
...Not quite.
SPURT
BOOOOM
EE...
WAAAAH!
I won't... forgive you!
CLANG
CLANG
CLANG
CLANG

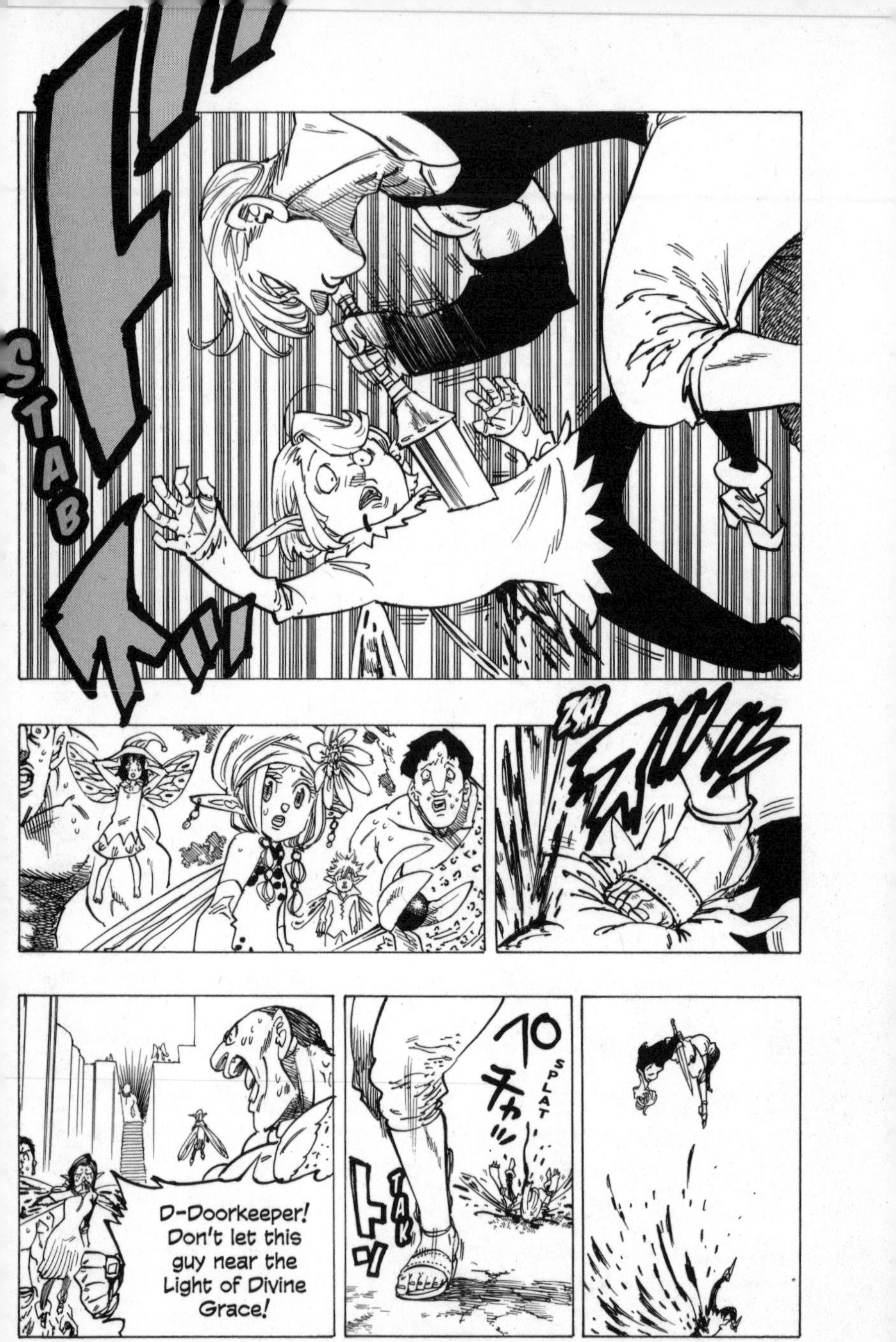
STAB
ZSH
SPLAT
TAK
D-Doorkeeper! Don't let this guy near the Light of Divine Grace!

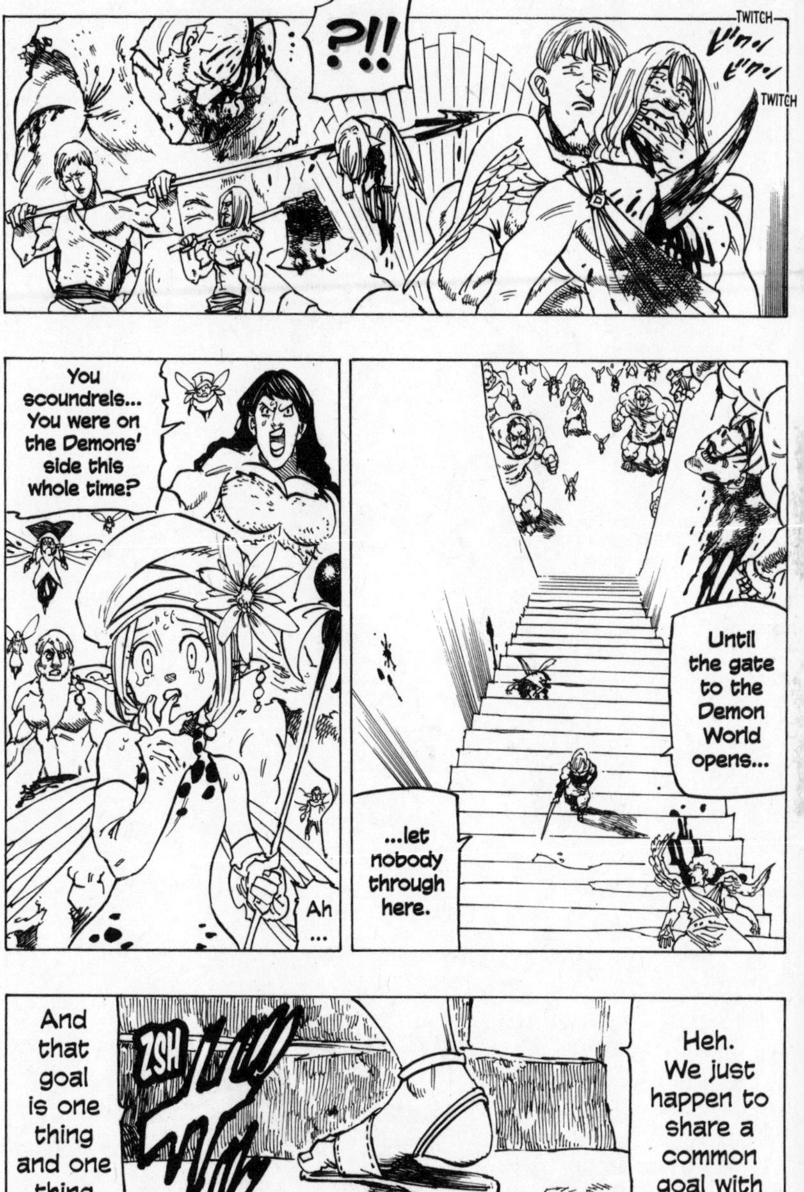
TWITCH
TWITCH
?!!
Until the gate to the Demon World opens...
...let nobody through here.
You scoundrels... You were on the Demons' side this whole time?
Ah ...
Heh. We just happen to share a common goal with them.
ZSH
And that goal is one thing and one thing alone.

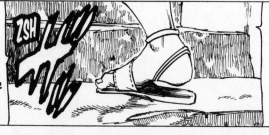

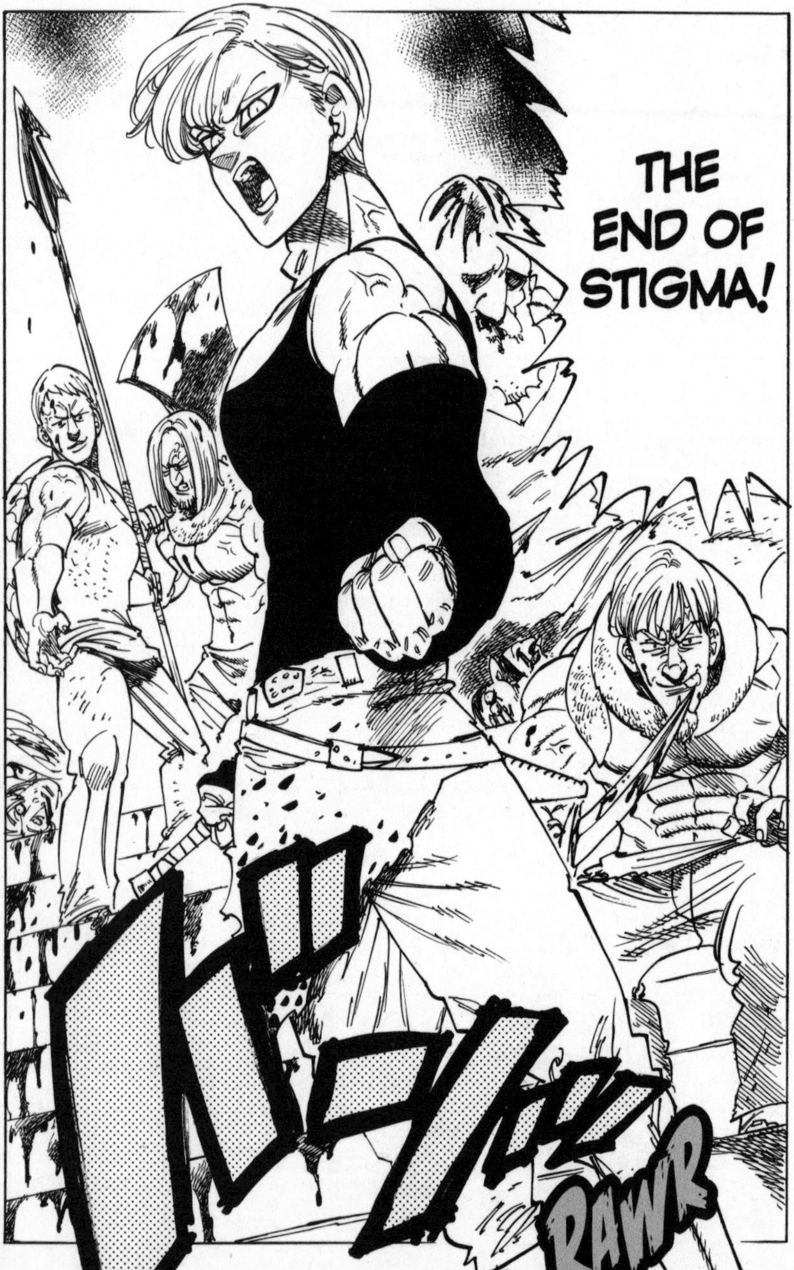
THE END OF STIGMA!
RAWR

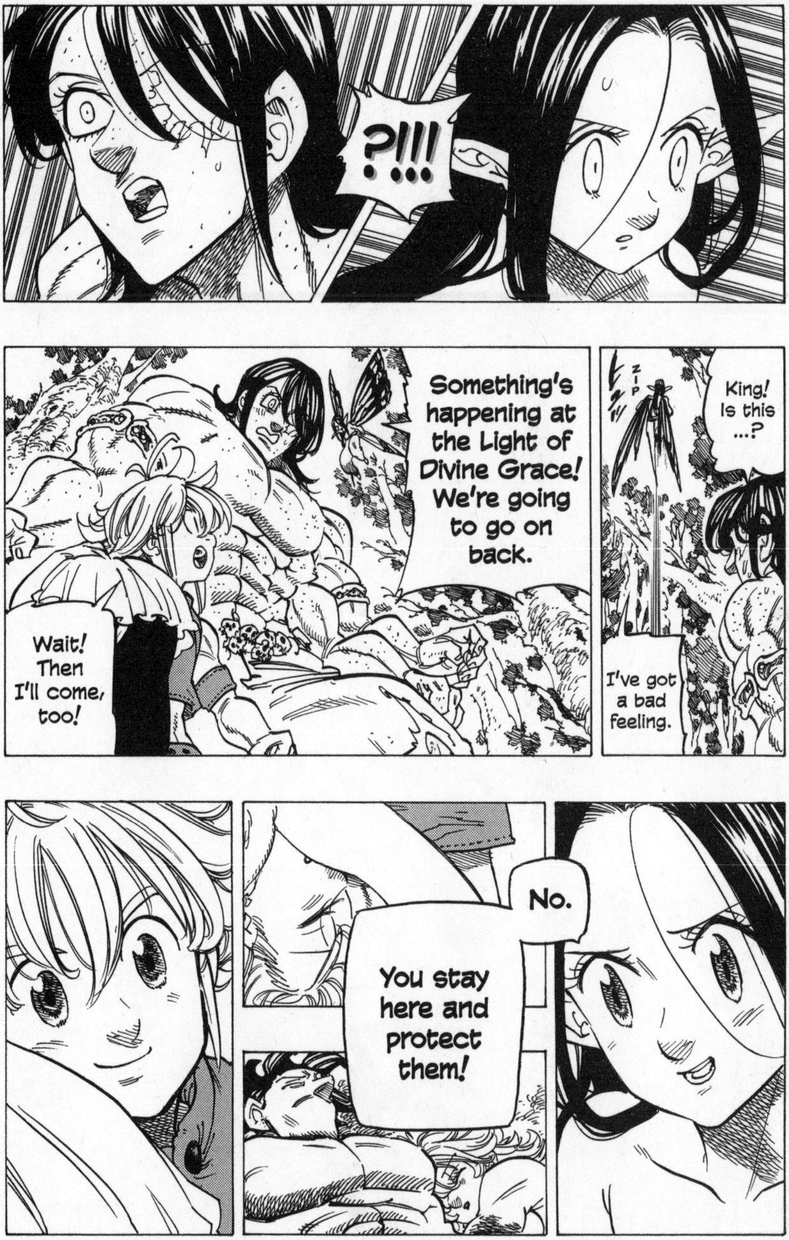
?!!!
ZIP
King! Is this ...?
I've got a bad feeling.
Something's happening at the Light of Divine Grace! We're going to go on back.
Wait! Then I'll come, too!
No.
You stay here and protect them!

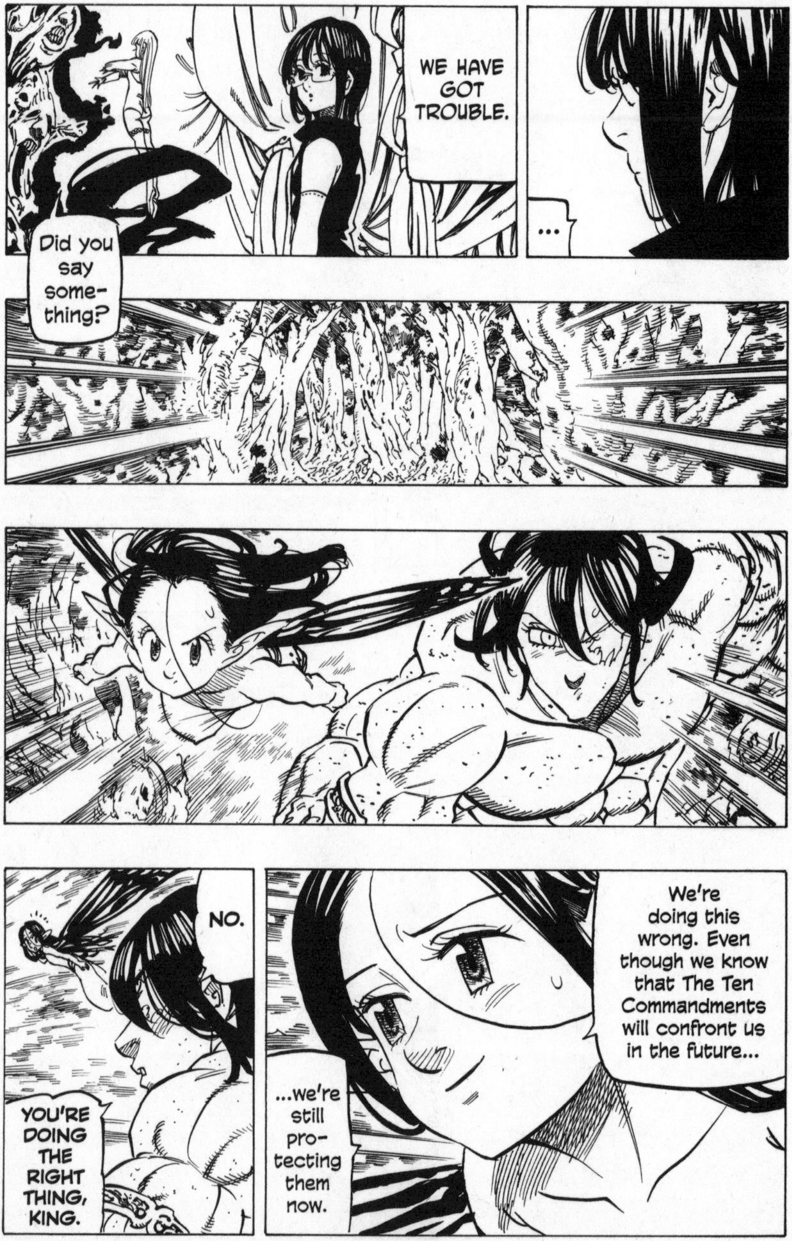
...
WE HAVE GOT TROUBLE.
Did you say some-thing?
We're doing this wrong. Even though we know that The Ten Commandments will confront us in the future...
...we're still pro-tecting them now.
NO.
YOU'RE DOING THE RIGHT THING, KING.

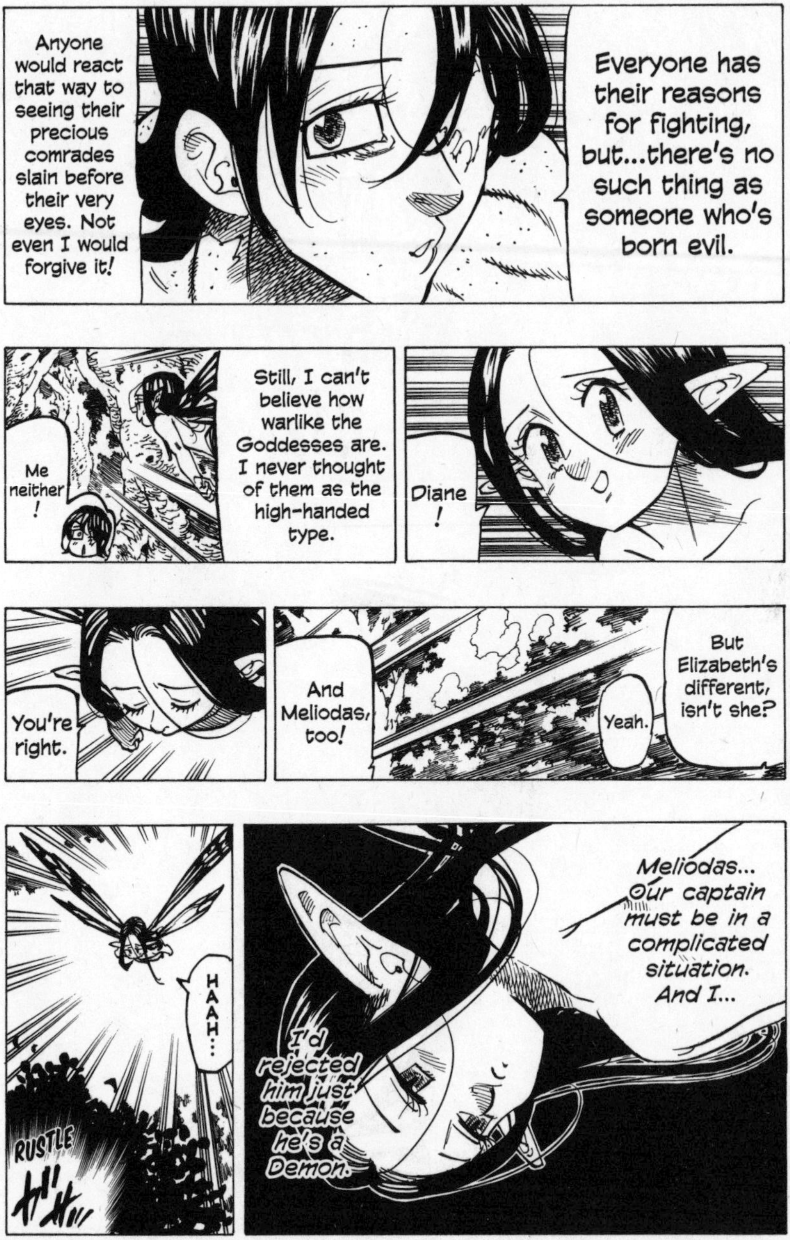
Everyone has their reasons for fighting, but...there's no such thing as someone who's born evil.
Anyone would react that way to seeing their precious comrades slain before their very eyes. Not even I would forgive it!
Diane!
Still, I can't believe how warlike the Goddesses are. I never thought of them as the high-handed type.
Me neither!
But Elizabeth's different, isn't she?
Yeah.
And Meliodas, too!
You're right.
Meliodas... Our captain must be in a complicated situation. And I...
I'd rejected him just because he's a Demon.
HAAH...
RUSTLE

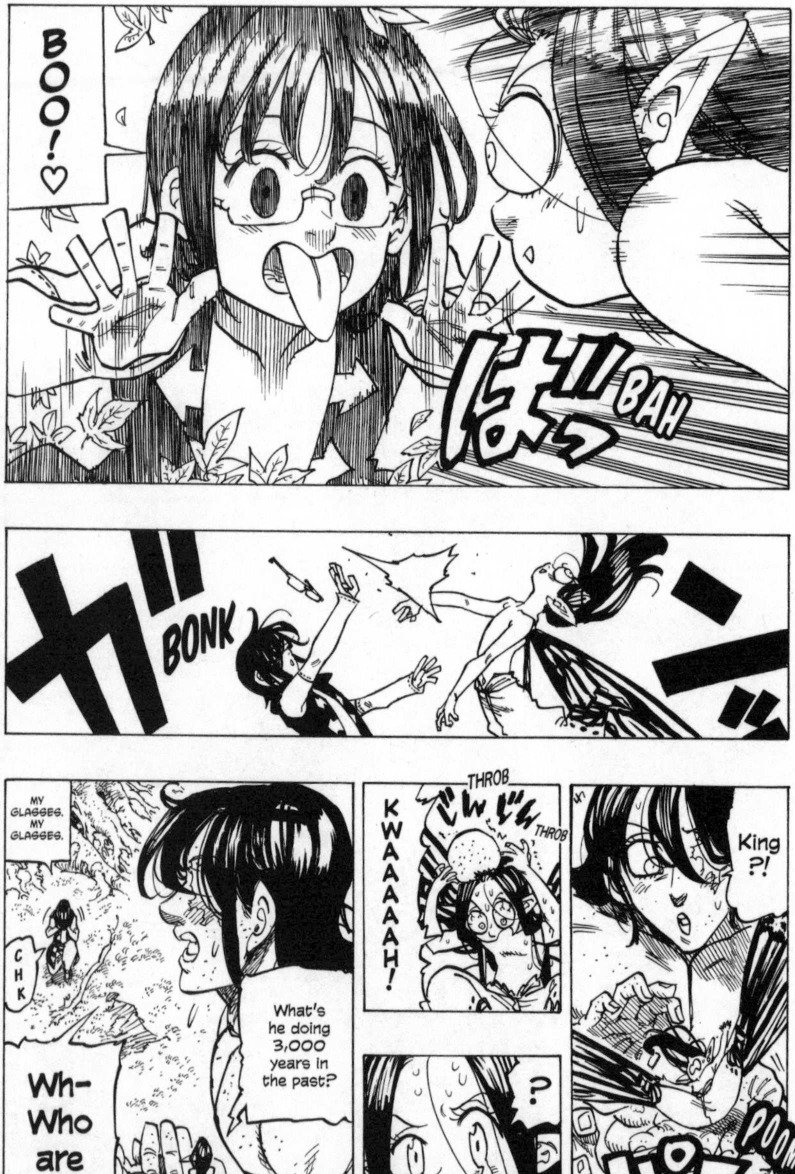
BOO!♡
ばっ
BAH
ガッ
BONK
King ?!
パフッ
POOMF
THROB
じんじん
THROB
KWAAAAAAH!
?
MY GLASSES. MY GLASSES.
CHK
What's he doing 3,000 years in the past?
Wh- Who are you?

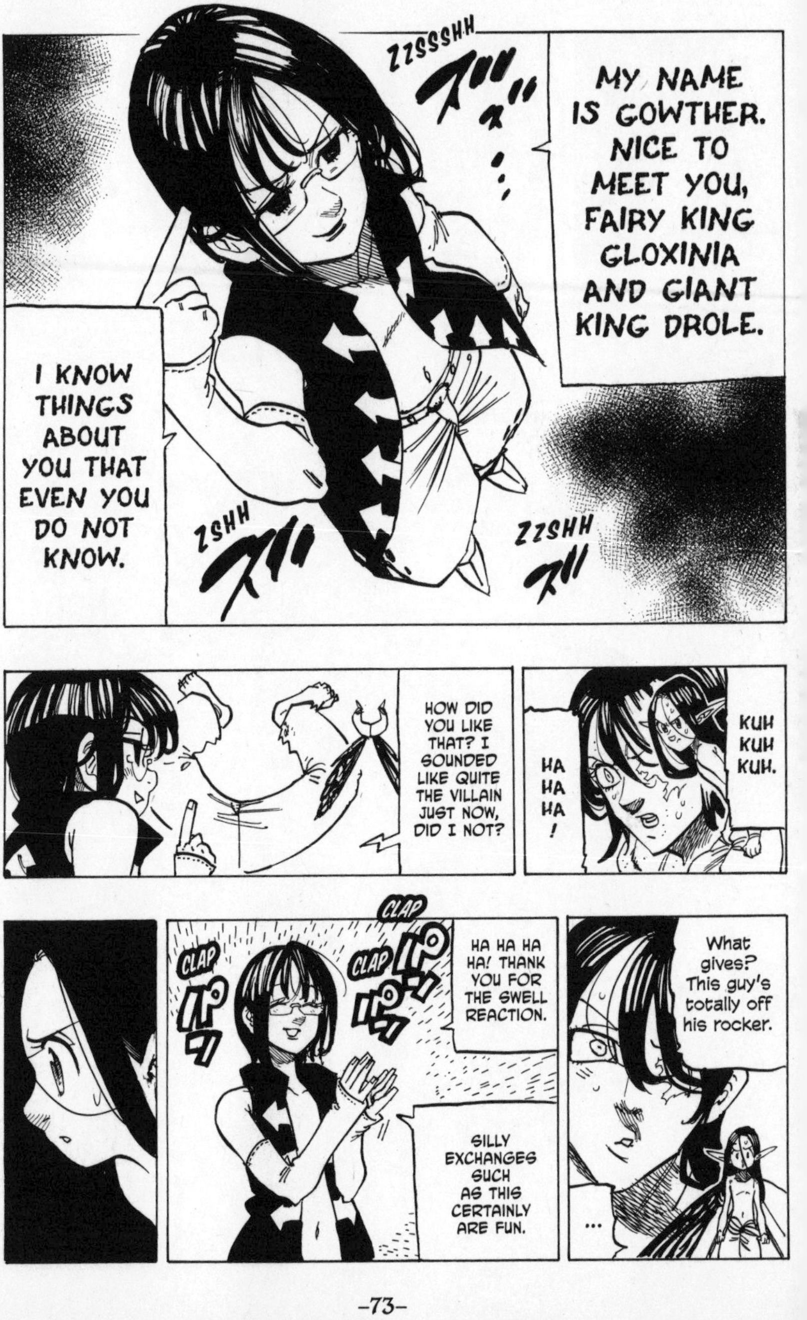
MY NAME IS GOWTHER. NICE TO MEET YOU, FAIRY KING GLOXINIA AND GIANT KING DROLE.
ZZSSSHH
I KNOW THINGS ABOUT YOU THAT EVEN YOU DO NOT KNOW.
ZZSHH
ZSHH
KUH KUH KUH.
HA HA HA!
HOW DID YOU LIKE THAT? I SOUNDED LIKE QUITE THE VILLAIN JUST NOW, DID I NOT?
What gives? This guy's totally off his rocker.
...
CLAP
HA HA HA HA! THANK YOU FOR THE SWELL REACTION.
CLAP
CLAP
SILLY EXCHANGES SUCH AS THIS CERTAINLY ARE FUN.

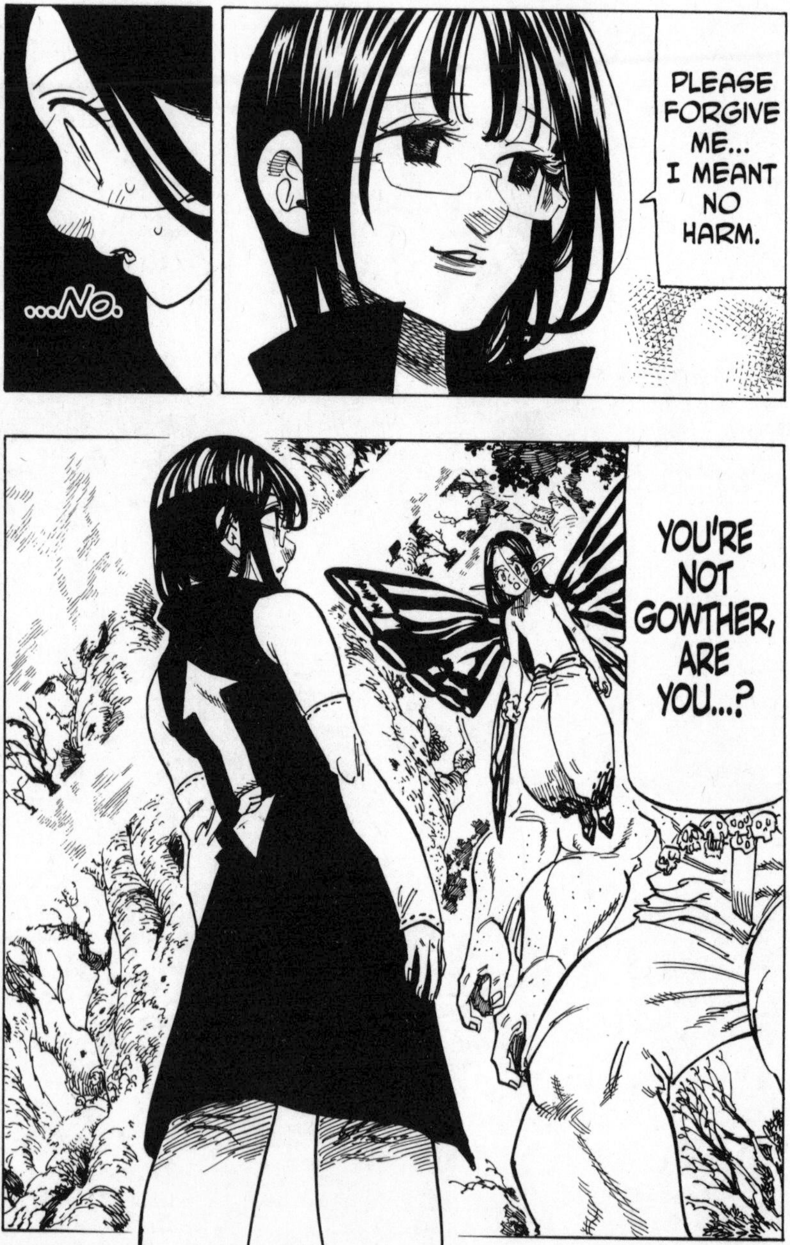
PLEASE FORGIVE ME... I MEANT NO HARM.
...No.
YOU'RE NOT GOWTHER, ARE YOU...?

Chapter 211 - He Who Says Goodbye

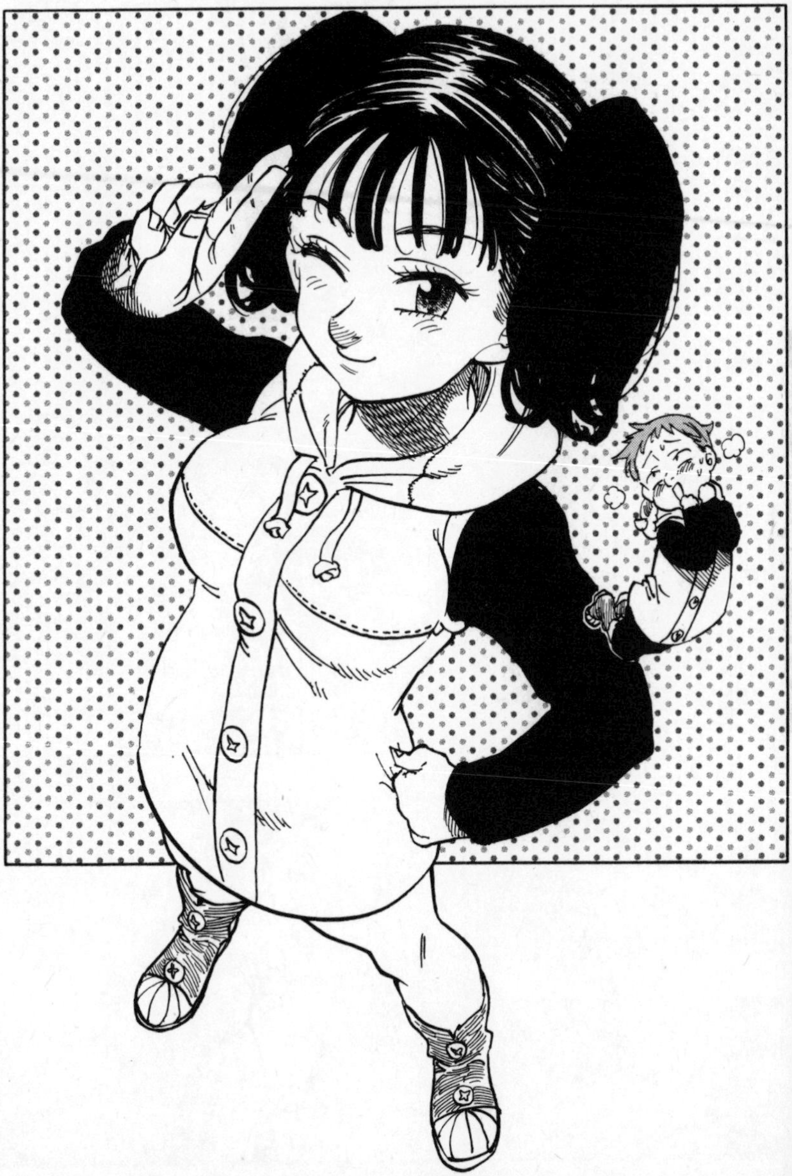

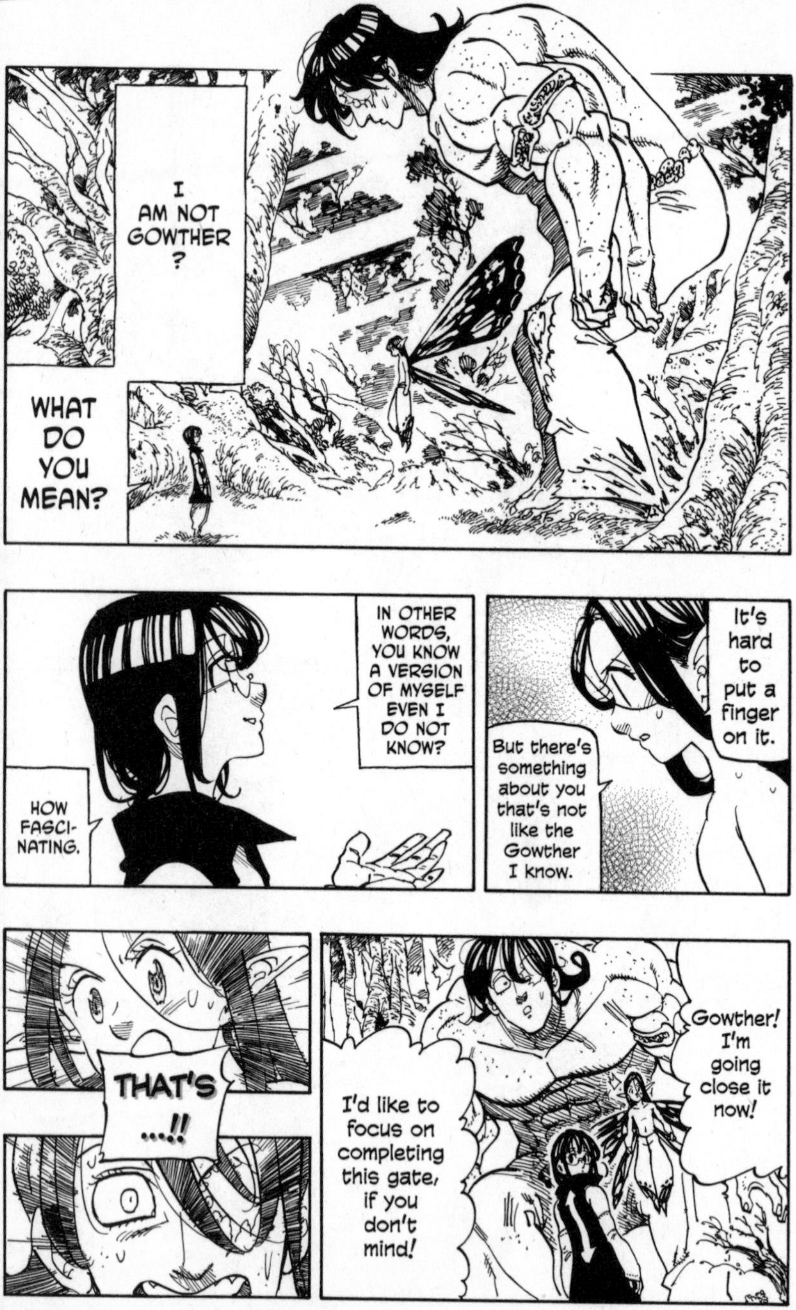
I AM NOT GOWTHER ?
WHAT DO YOU MEAN?
It's hard to put a finger on it.
But there's something about you that's not like the Gowther I know.
IN OTHER WORDS, YOU KNOW A VERSION OF MYSELF EVEN I DO NOT KNOW?
HOW FASCINATING.
Gowther! I'm going close it now!
I'd like to focus on completing this gate, if you don't mind!
THAT'S ...!!

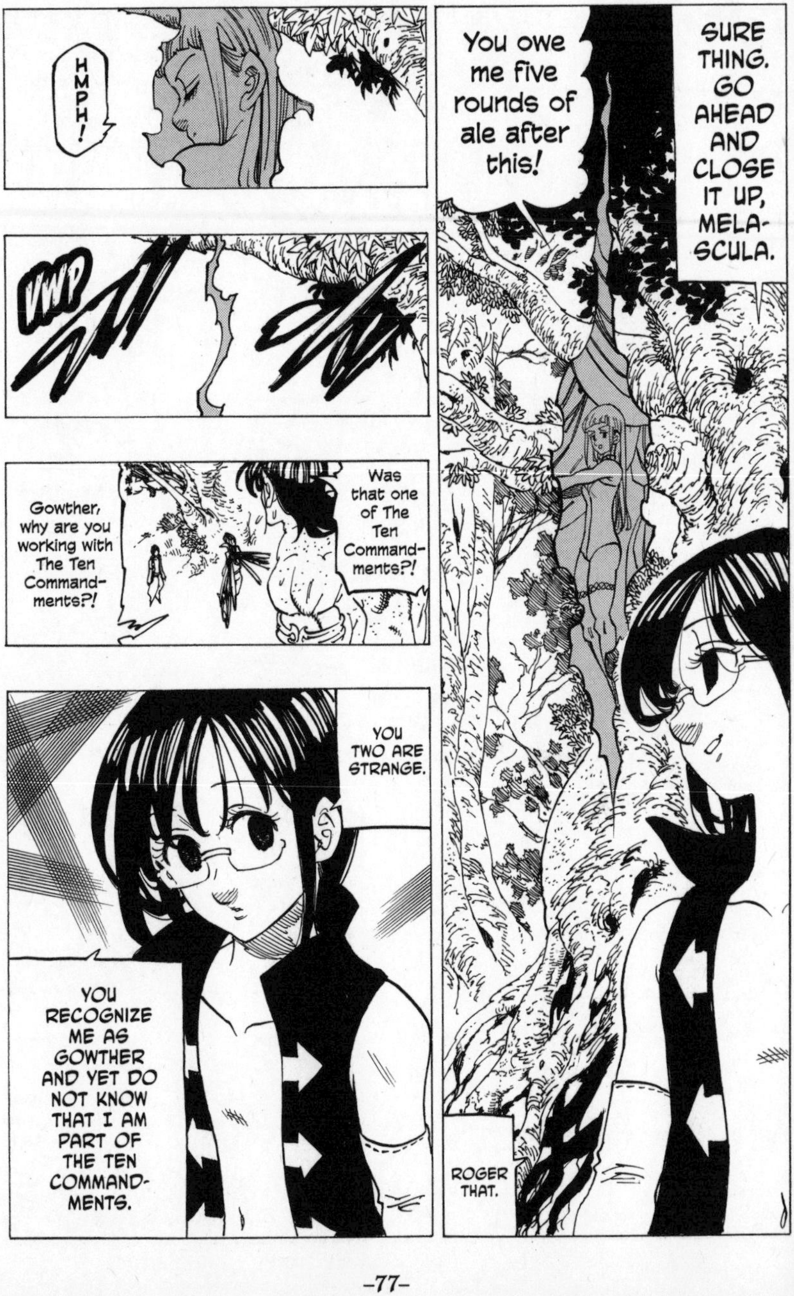
You owe me five rounds of ale after this!
SURE THING. GO AHEAD AND CLOSE IT UP, MELA-SCULA.
ROGER THAT.
HMPH!
VWP
Was that one of The Ten Command-ments?!
Gowther, why are you working with The Ten Command-ments?!
YOU TWO ARE STRANGE.
YOU RECOGNIZE ME AS GOWTHER AND YET DO NOT KNOW THAT I AM PART OF THE TEN COMMAND-MENTS.

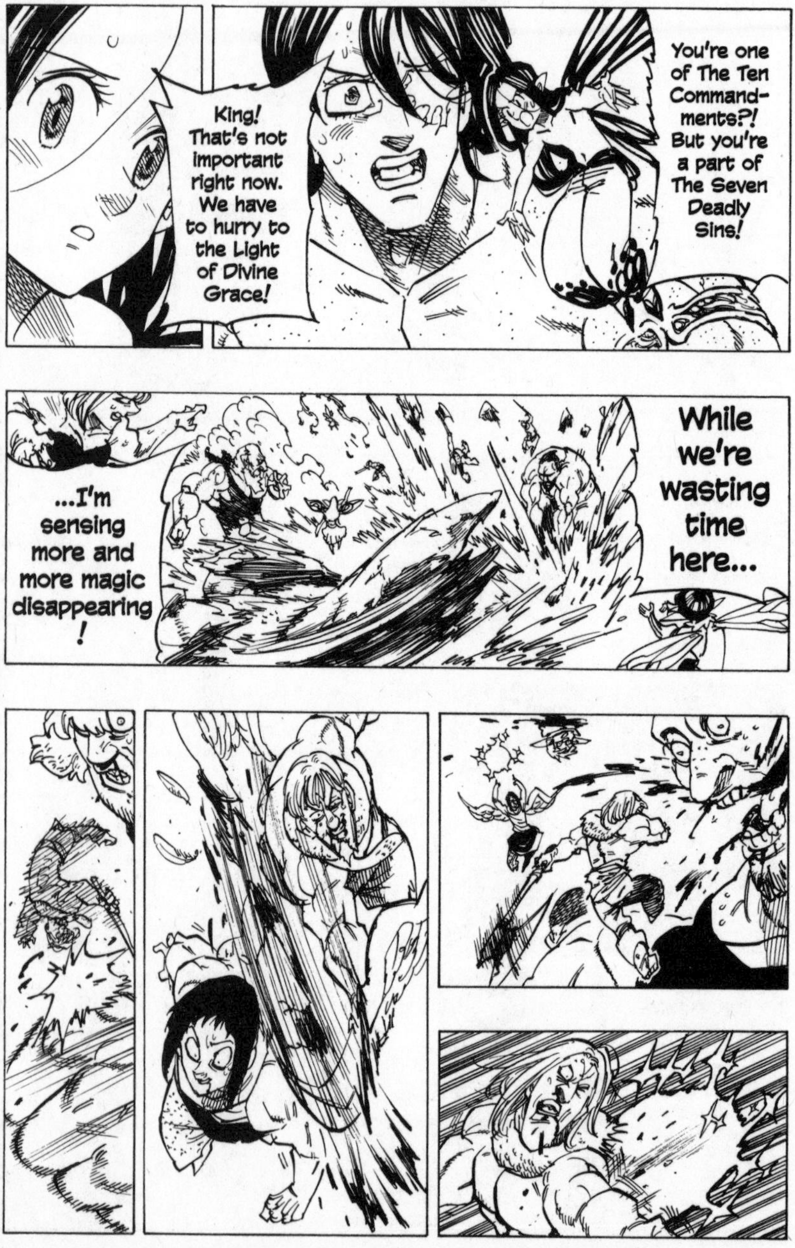
You're one of The Ten Commandments?! But you're a part of The Seven Deadly Sins!
King! That's not important right now. We have to hurry to the Light of Divine Grace!
While we're wasting time here...
...I'm sensing more and more magic disappearing!

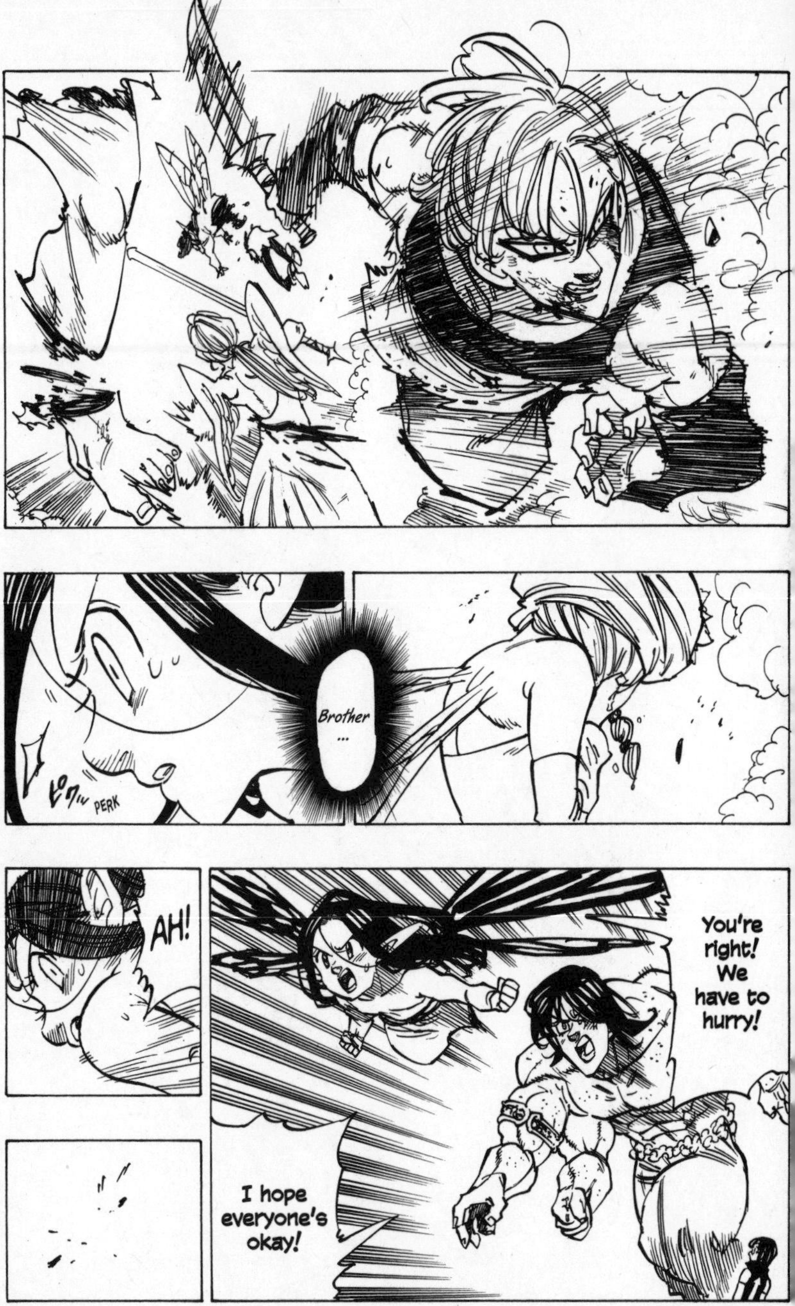
Brother ...
ピクッ
PERK
You're right! We have to hurry!
I hope everyone's okay!
AH!

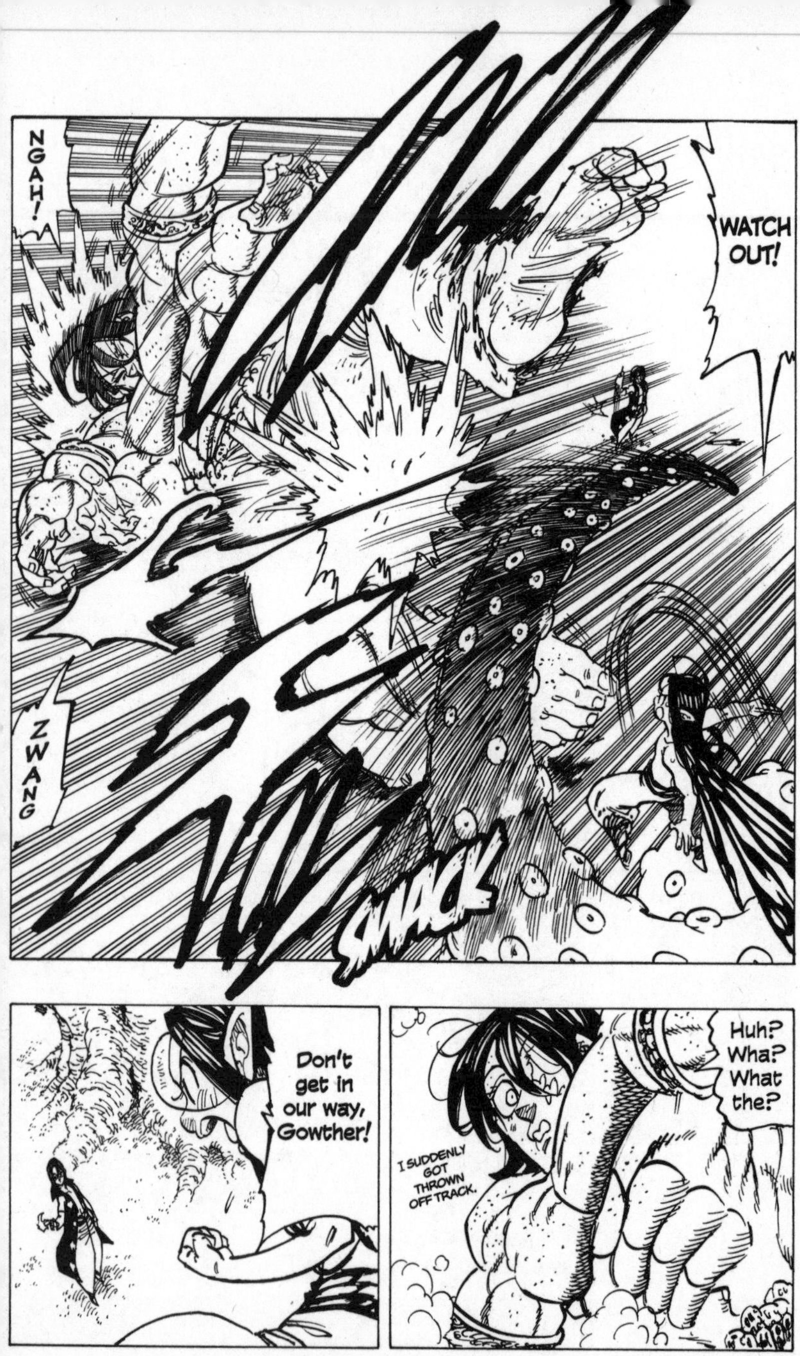
WATCH OUT!
NGAH!
ZWANG
SMACK
Huh? Wha? What the?
I SUDDENLY GOT THROWN OFF TRACK.
Don't get in our way, Gowther!

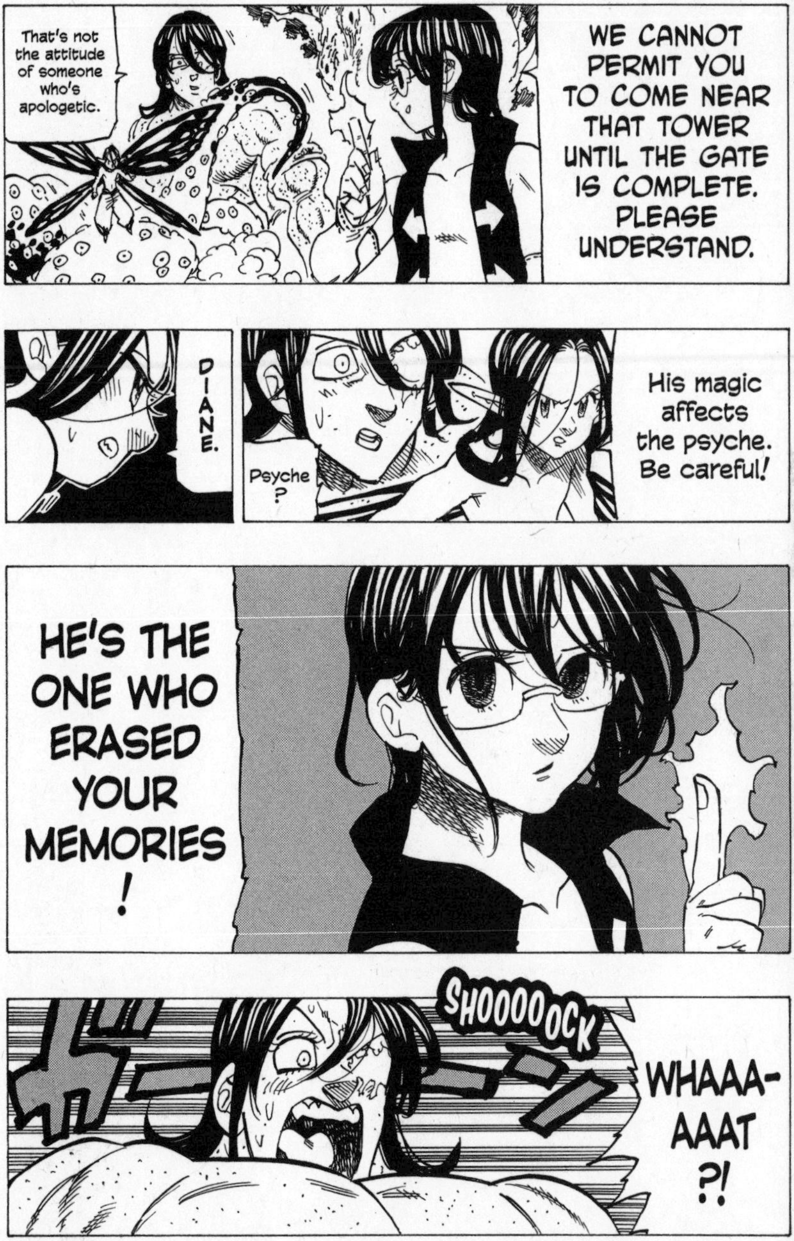
WE CANNOT PERMIT YOU TO COME NEAR THAT TOWER UNTIL THE GATE IS COMPLETE. PLEASE UNDERSTAND.
That's not the attitude of someone who's apologetic.
His magic affects the psyche. Be careful!
Psyche?
DIANE.
HE'S THE ONE WHO ERASED YOUR MEMORIES!
SHOOOOOCK
WHAAA-AAAT?!

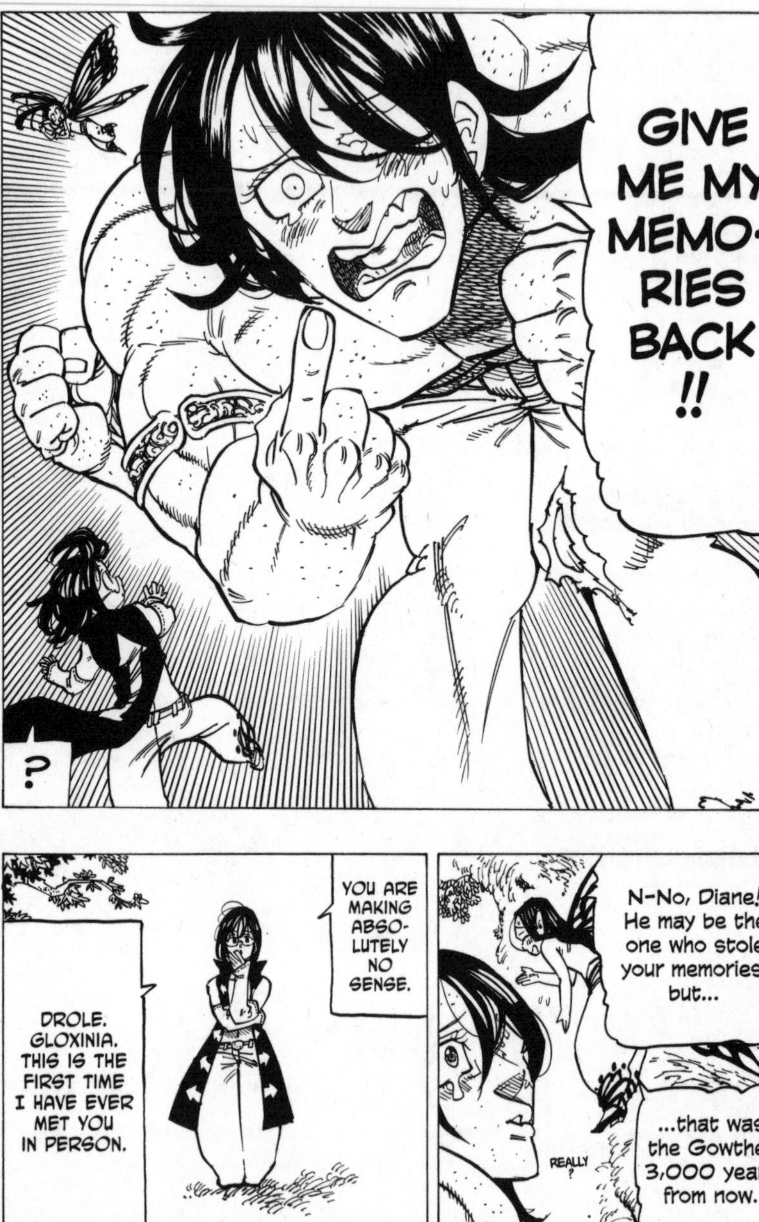
GIVE ME MY MEMO-RIES BACK !!
?
N-No, Diane! He may be the one who stole your memories, but...
...that was the Gowther 3,000 years from now.
REALLY ?
YOU ARE MAKING ABSO-LUTELY NO SENSE.
DROLE. GLOXINIA. THIS IS THE FIRST TIME I HAVE EVER MET YOU IN PERSON.

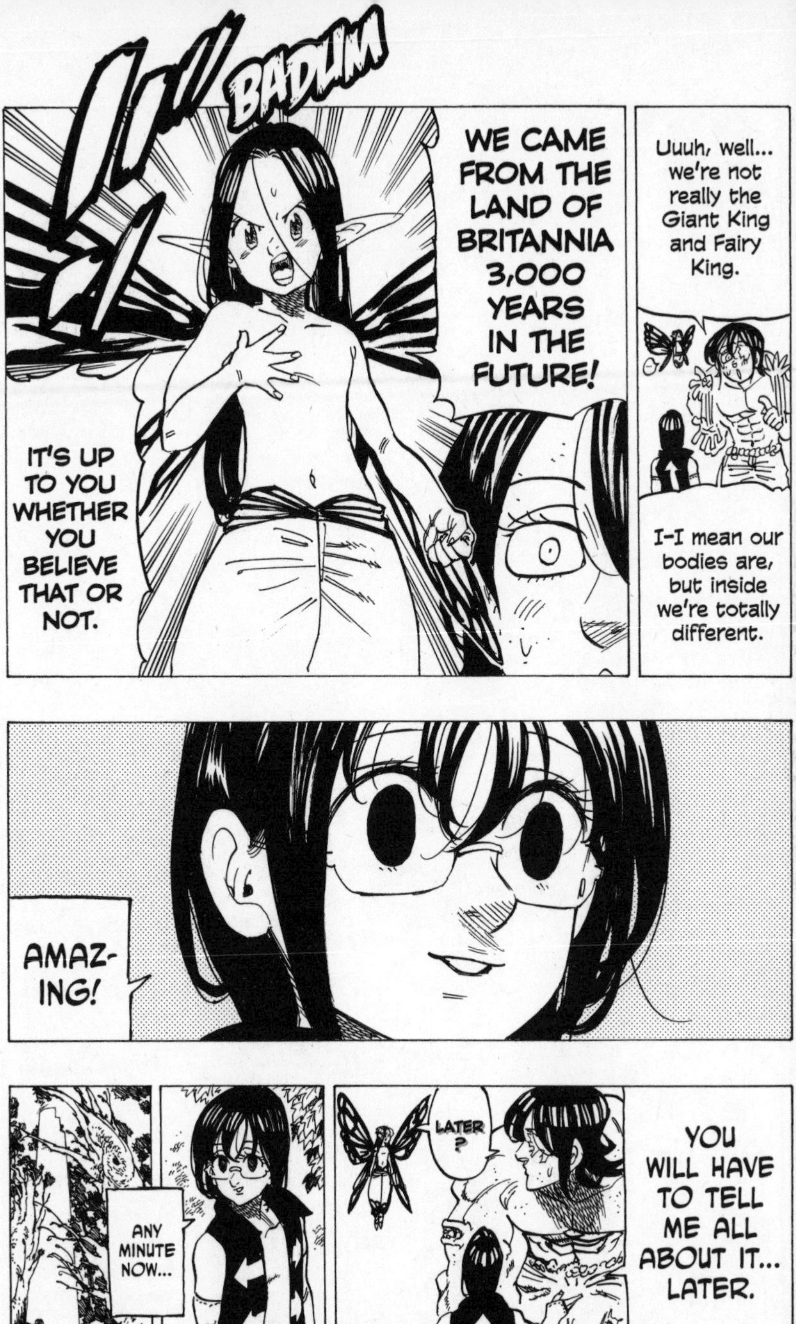
Uuuh, well... we're not really the Giant King and Fairy King.
I-I mean our bodies are, but inside we're totally different.
BADUM
WE CAME FROM THE LAND OF BRITANNIA 3,000 YEARS IN THE FUTURE!
IT'S UP TO YOU WHETHER YOU BELIEVE THAT OR NOT.
AMAZ-ING!
YOU WILL HAVE TO TELL ME ALL ABOUT IT... LATER.
LATER?
ANY MINUTE NOW...

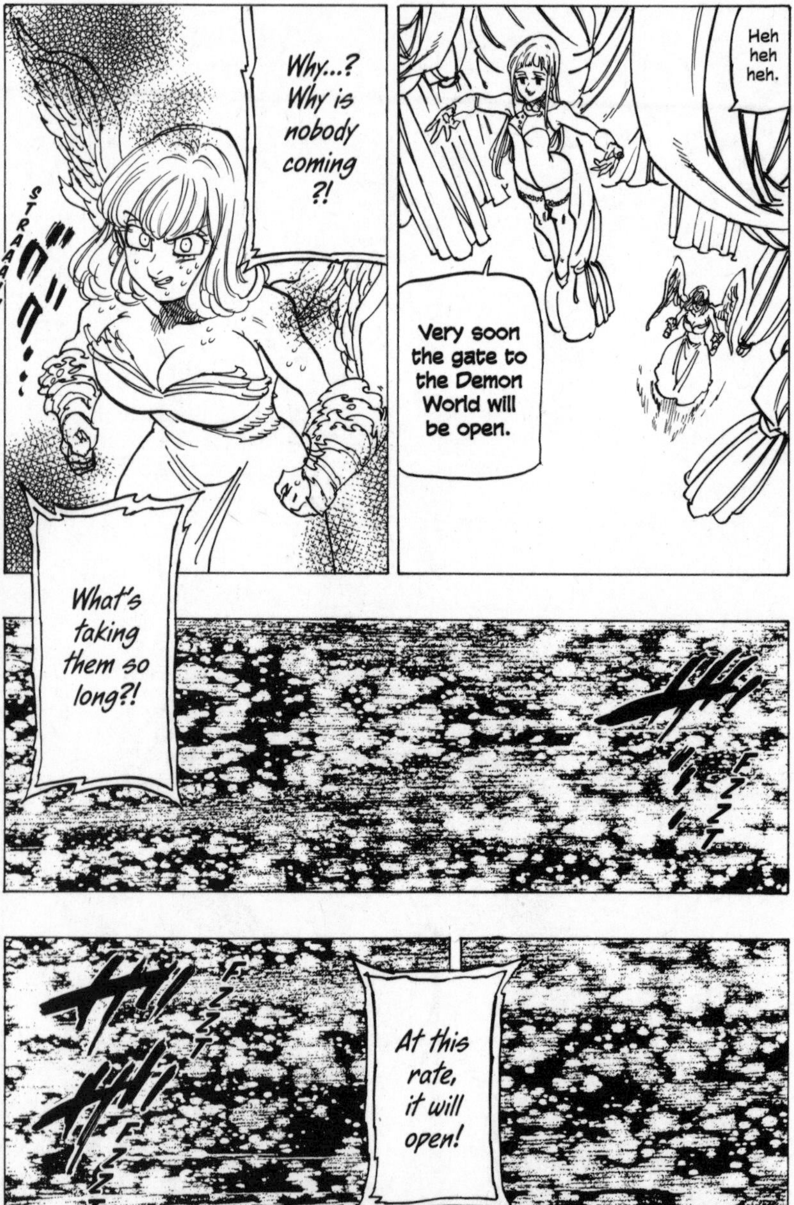
Heh heh heh.
Very soon the gate to the Demon World will be open.
Why...? Why is nobody coming ?!
STRAAAIN
What's taking them so long?!
FZZZT
At this rate, it will open!
FZZZT
FZZZT

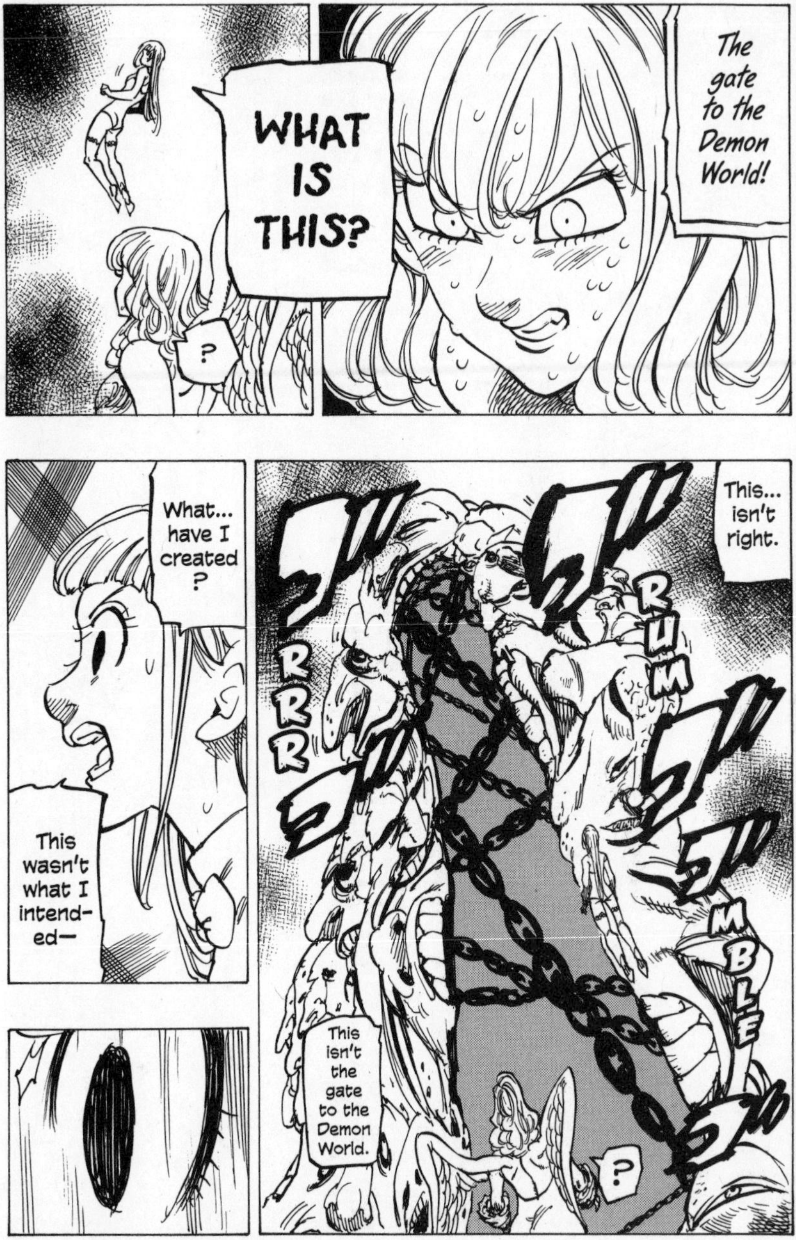
The gate to the Demon World!
WHAT IS THIS?
?
This... isn't right.
RUM
MBLE
RRRR
This isn't the gate to the Demon World.
?
What... have I created?
This wasn't what I intended—

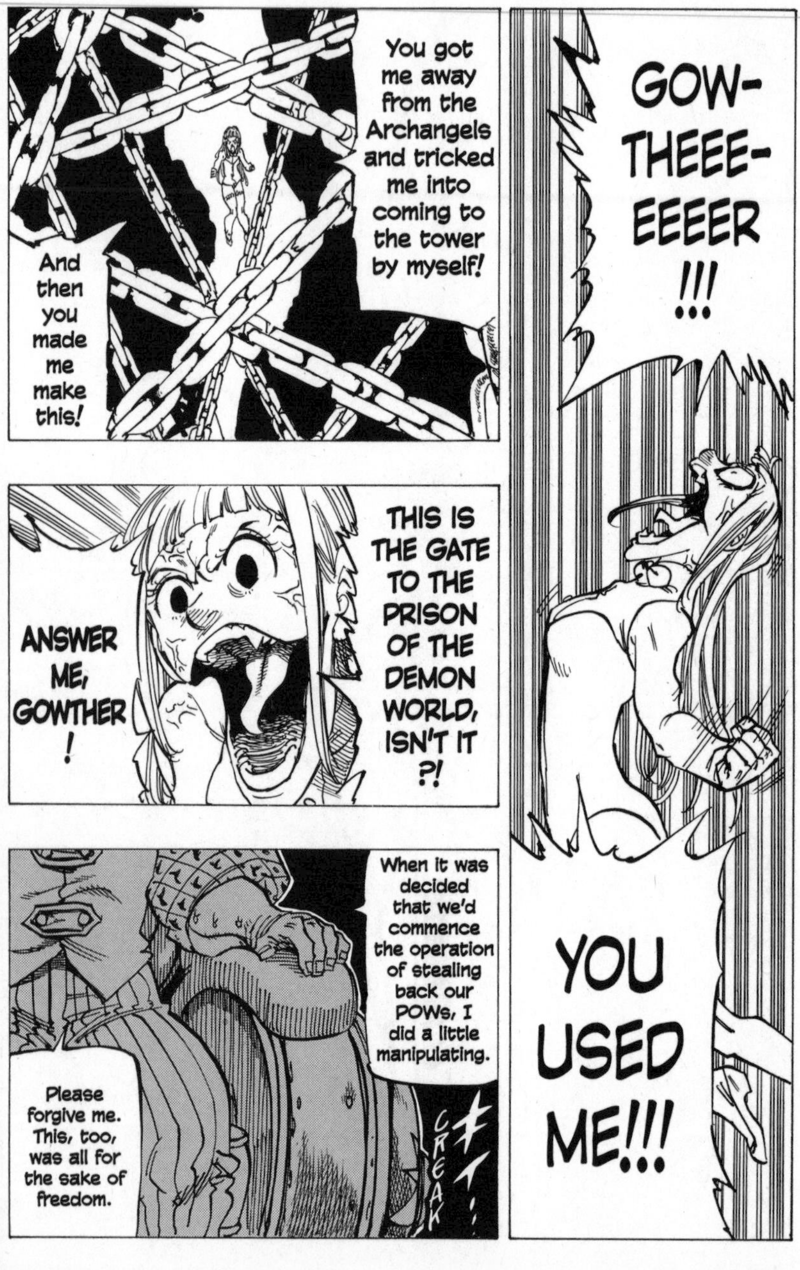
GOW-THEEE-EEEER!!!
YOU USED ME!!!
You got me away from the Archangels and tricked me into coming to the tower by myself!
And then you made me make this!
THIS IS THE GATE TO THE PRISON OF THE DEMON WORLD, ISN'T IT?!
ANSWER ME, GOWTHER!
When it was decided that we'd commence the operation of stealing back our POWs, I did a little manipulating.
CREAK
Please forgive me. This, too, was all for the sake of freedom.

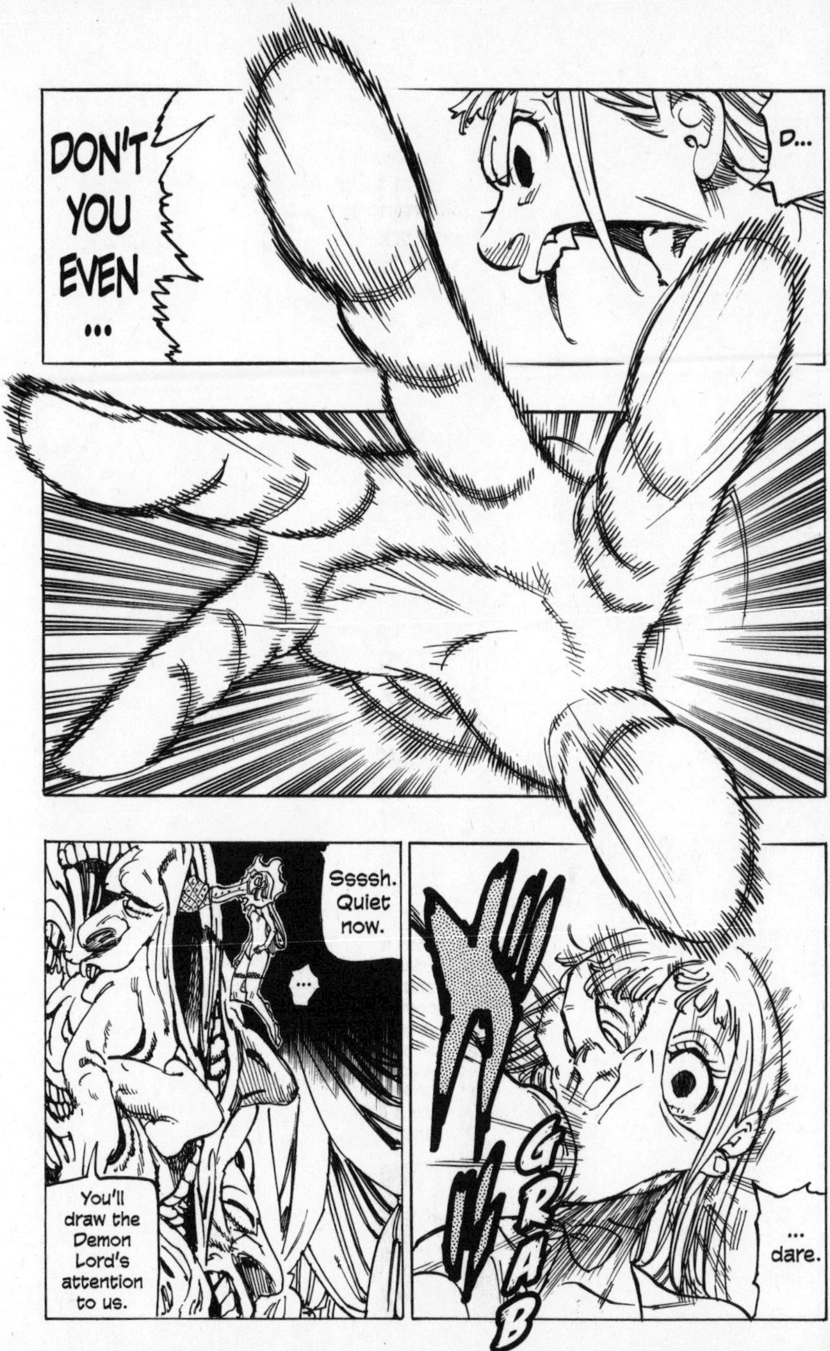
D...
DON'T YOU EVEN ...
GRAB
... dare.
Ssssh. Quiet now.
...
You'll draw the Demon Lord's attention to us.

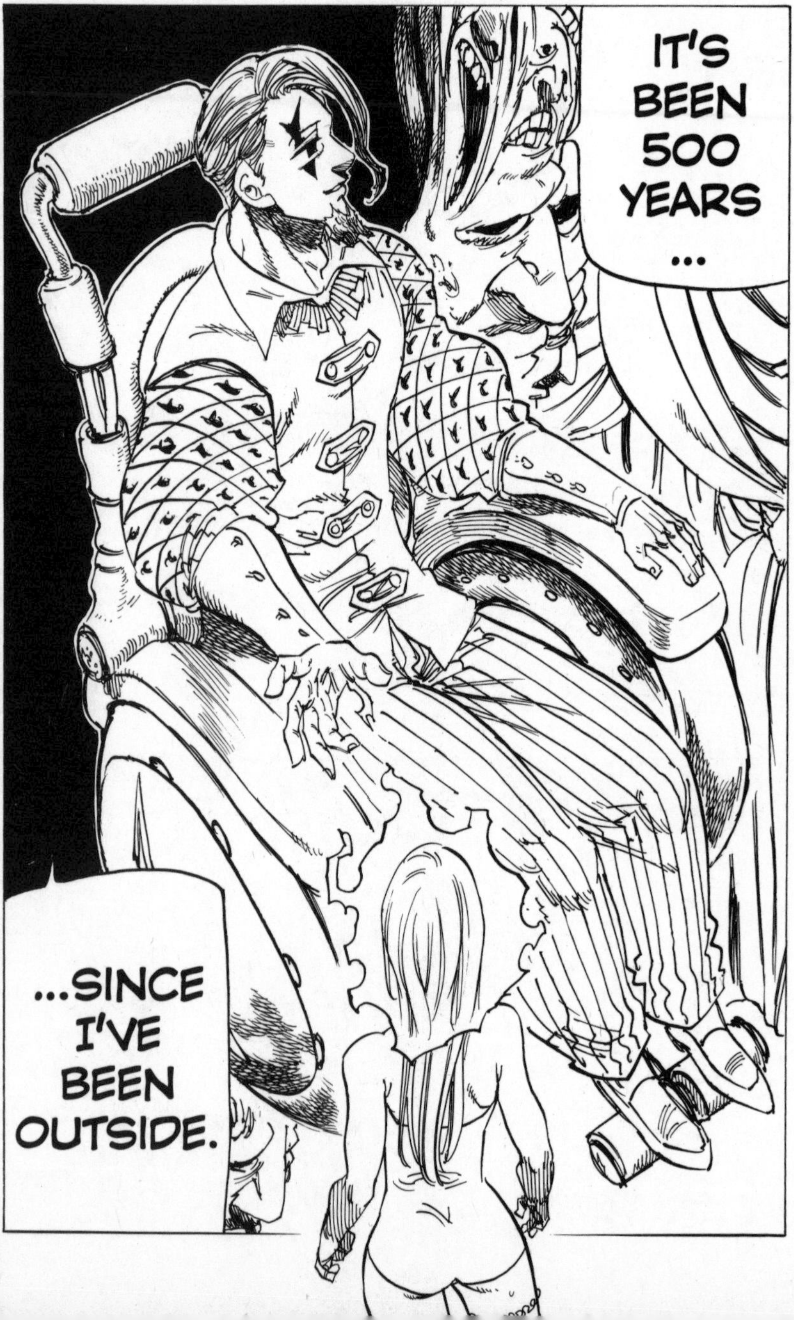
IT'S BEEN 500 YEARS ...
...SINCE I'VE BEEN OUTSIDE.

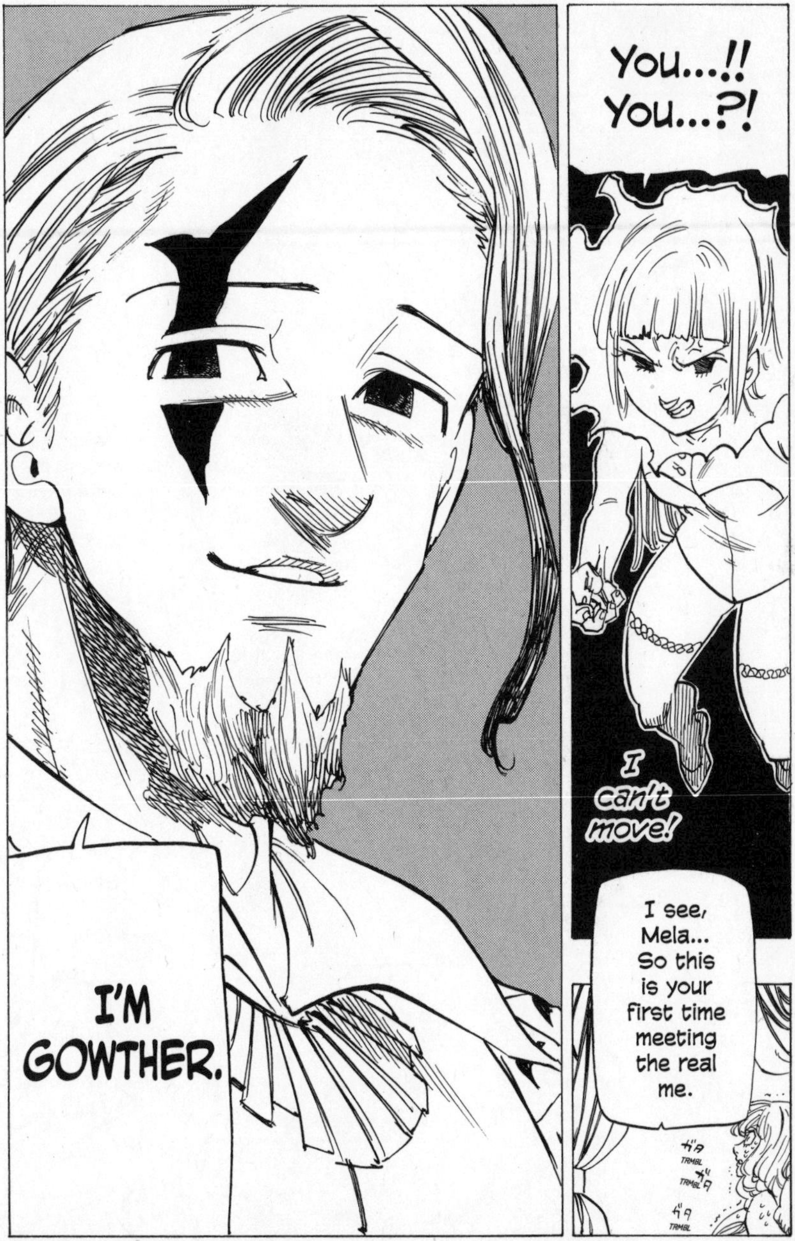
You...!!
You...?!
I can't move!
I see, Mela... So this is your first time meeting the real me.
TRMBL
TRMBL
TRMBL
I'M GOWTHER.

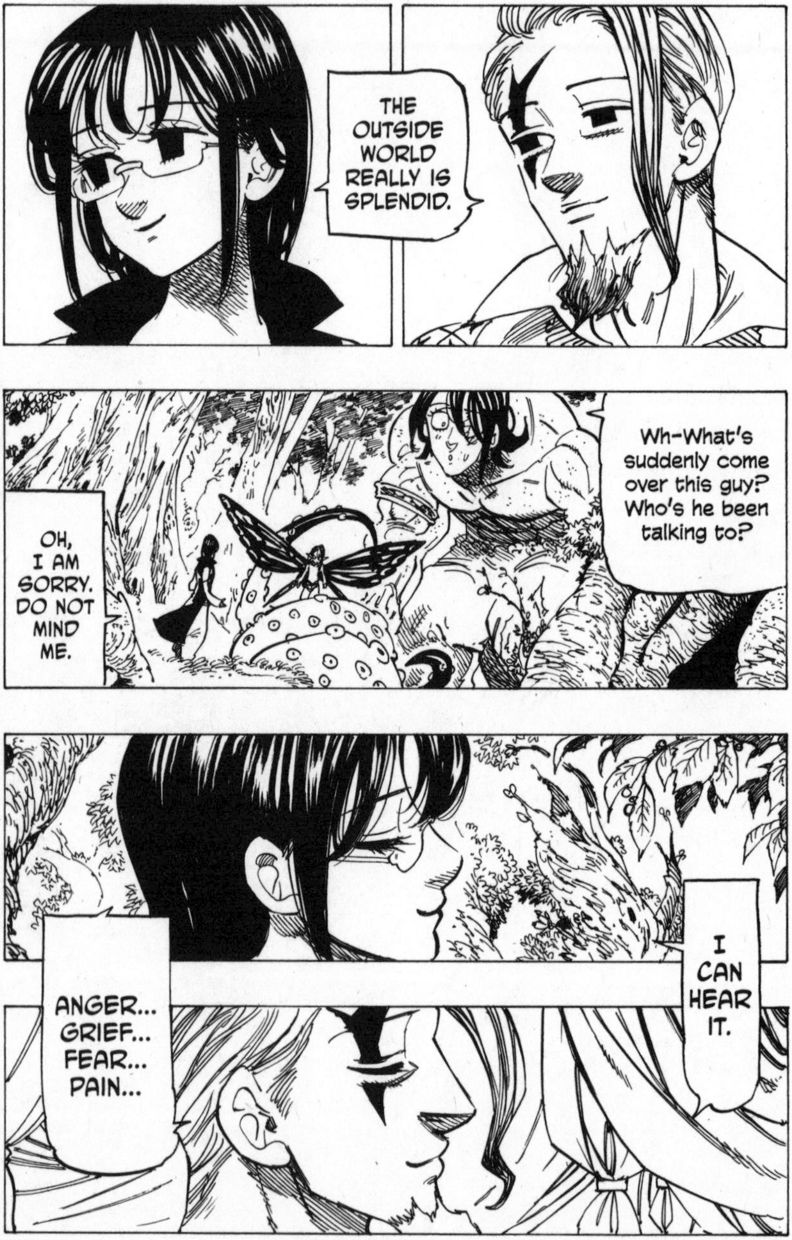
THE OUTSIDE WORLD REALLY IS SPLENDID.
Wh-What's suddenly come over this guy? Who's he been talking to?
OH, I AM SORRY. DO NOT MIND ME.
I CAN HEAR IT.
ANGER... GRIEF... FEAR... PAIN...

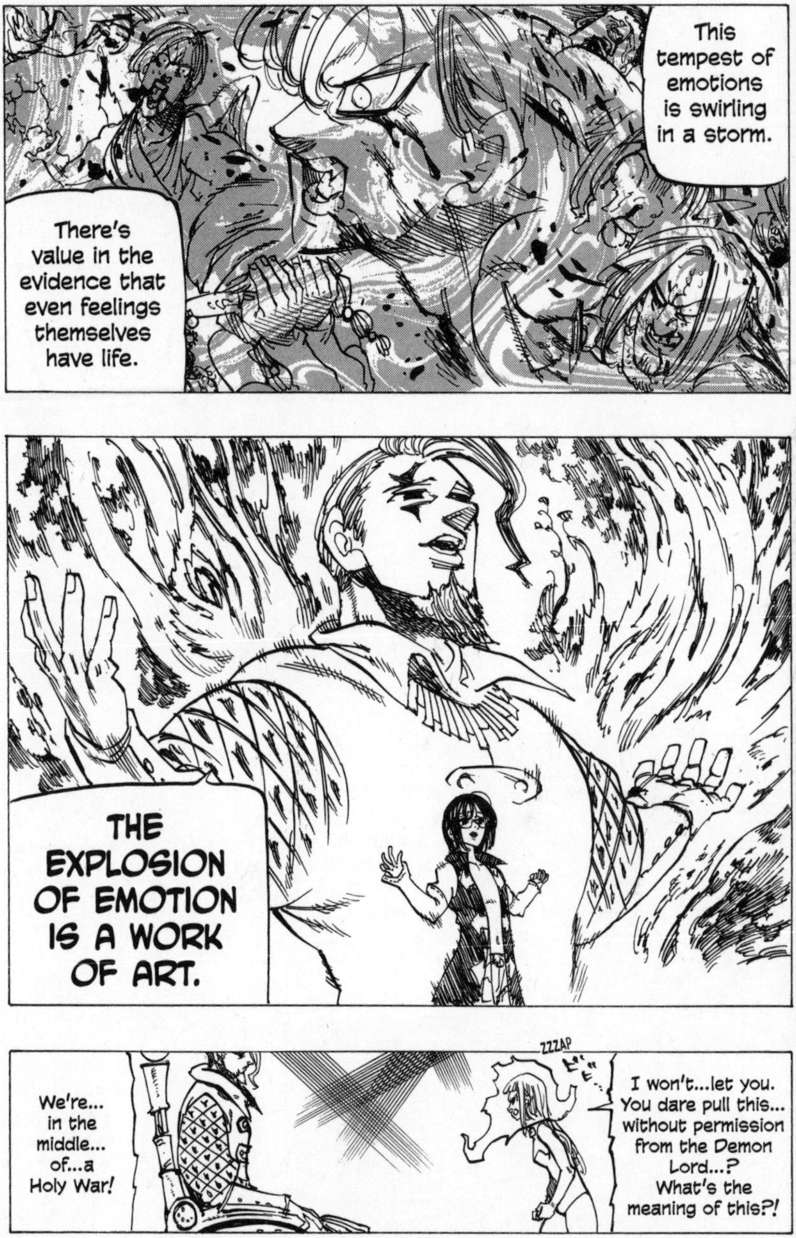
This tempest of emotions is swirling in a storm.
There's value in the evidence that even feelings themselves have life.
THE EXPLOSION OF EMOTION IS A WORK OF ART.
ZZZAP
I won't...let you. You dare pull this... without permission from the Demon Lord...? What's the meaning of this?!
We're... in the middle... of...a Holy War!

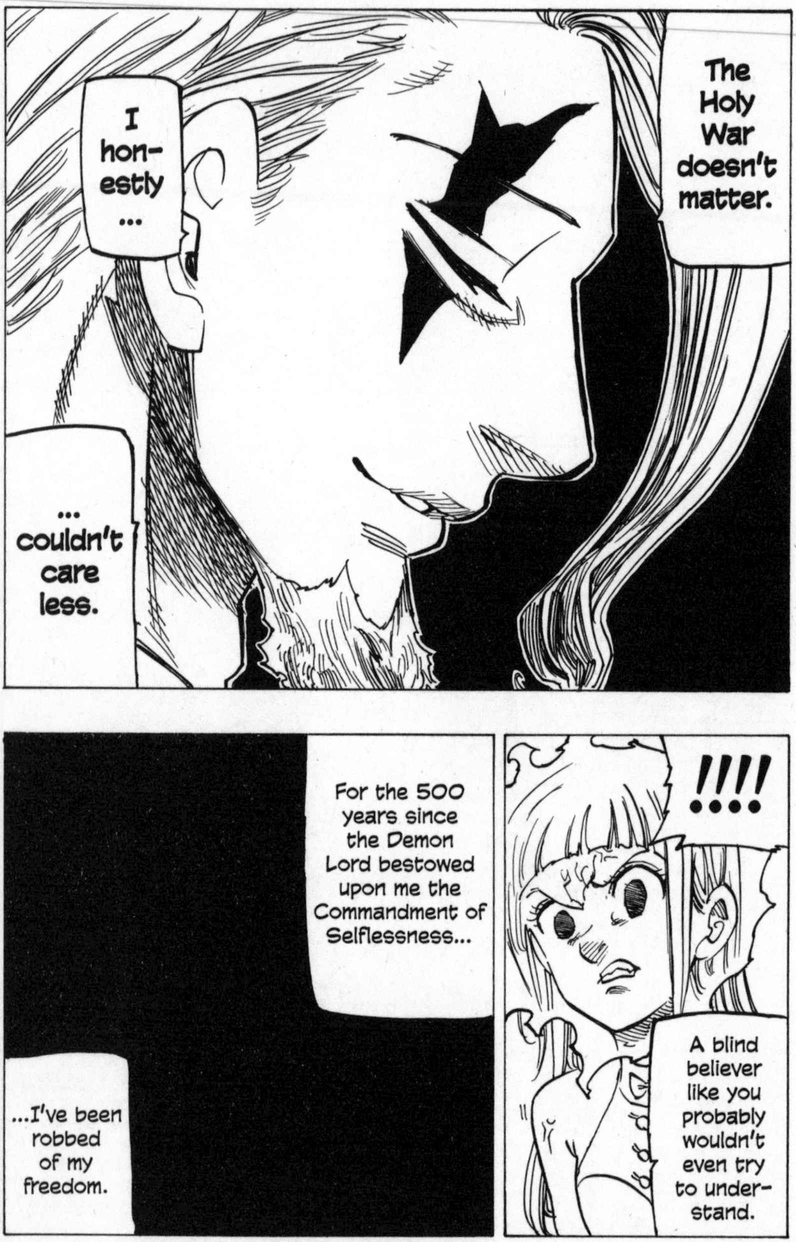
The Holy War doesn't matter.
I hon-estly ...
... couldn't care less.
!!!!
A blind believer like you probably wouldn't even try to under-stand.
For the 500 years since the Demon Lord bestowed upon me the Commandment of Selflessness...
...I've been robbed of my freedom.

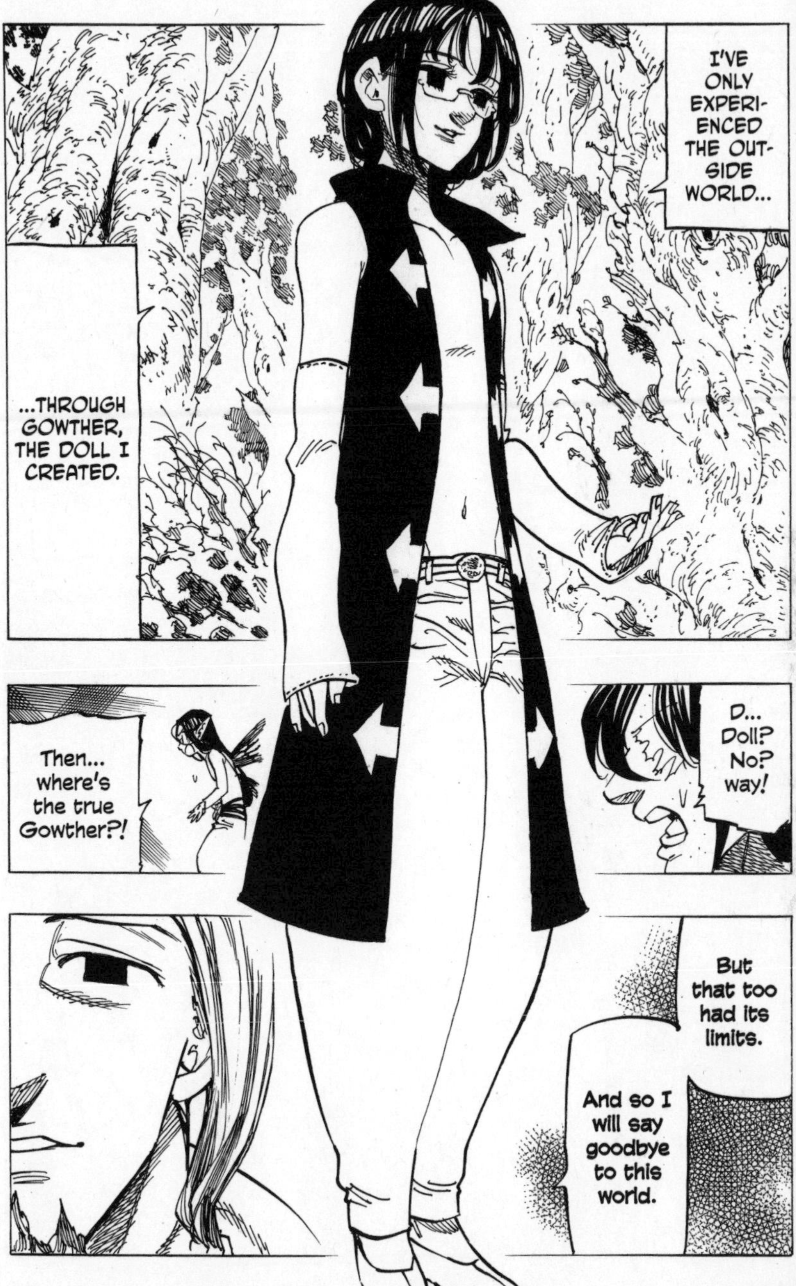
I'VE ONLY EXPERIENCED THE OUTSIDE WORLD...
...THROUGH GOWTHER, THE DOLL I CREATED.
D... Doll? No? way!
Then... where's the true Gowther?!
But that too had its limits.
And so I will say goodbye to this world.

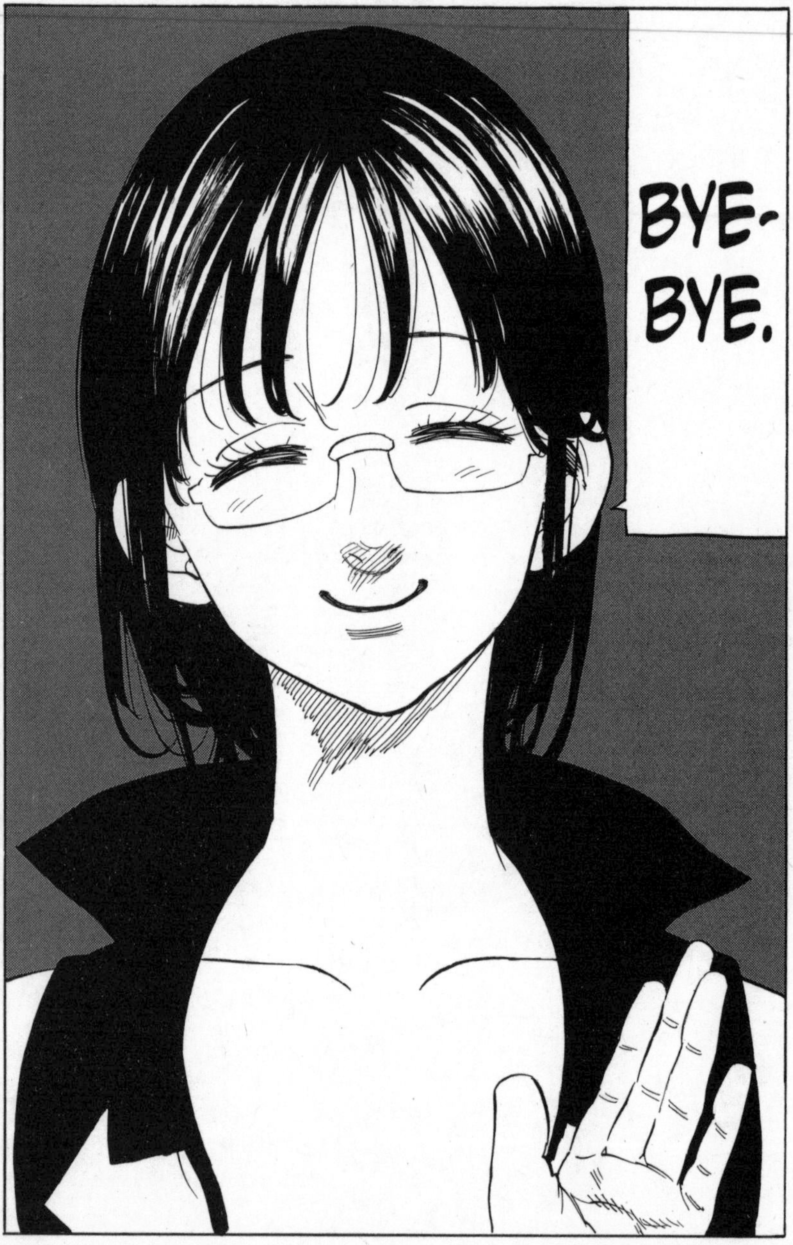
BYE-BYE.

The member of The Ten Commandments who possesses the command of Selflessness is the birth parent of The Seven Deadly Sins' Goat Sin of Lust, Gowther. His commandment could curse anyone with self-interest or ambition...and could even affect Demons in the Demon World, so the Demon Lord who gifted him the Commandment imprisoned him for 500 years.

Even though his design was based on D, I added the elements of the wheelchair and white hair from C, to make him a somewhat elderly wizard. He was Fraudrin's direct supervisor, so he trusts in both him and Gowther (one and the same.)

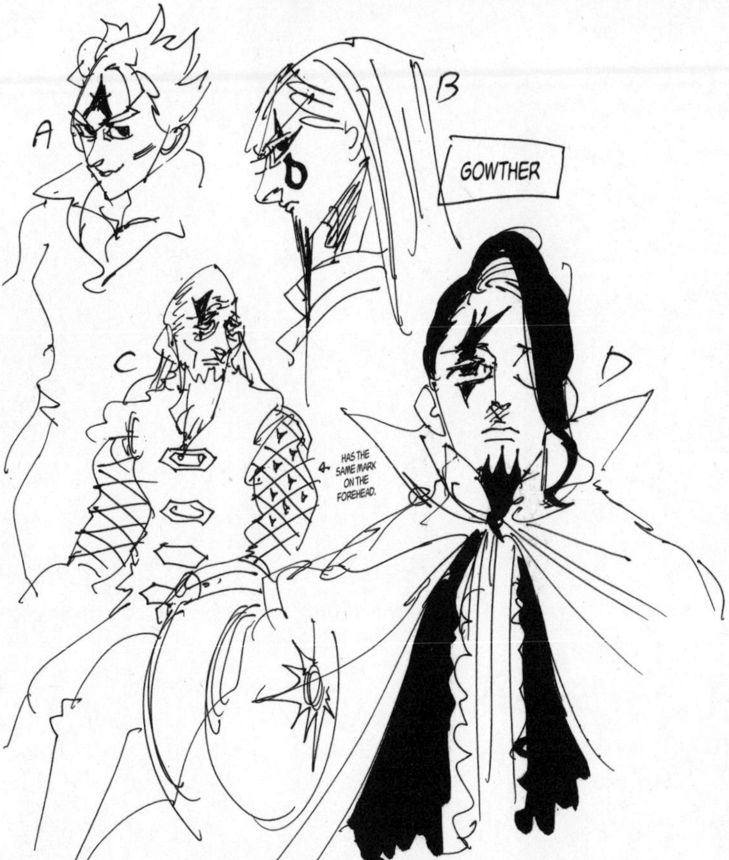
A
B
GOWTHER
C
D
HAS THE SAME MARK ON THE FOREHEAD.

THE SEVEN DEADLY SINS

Side Story - The Doll Seeks Love

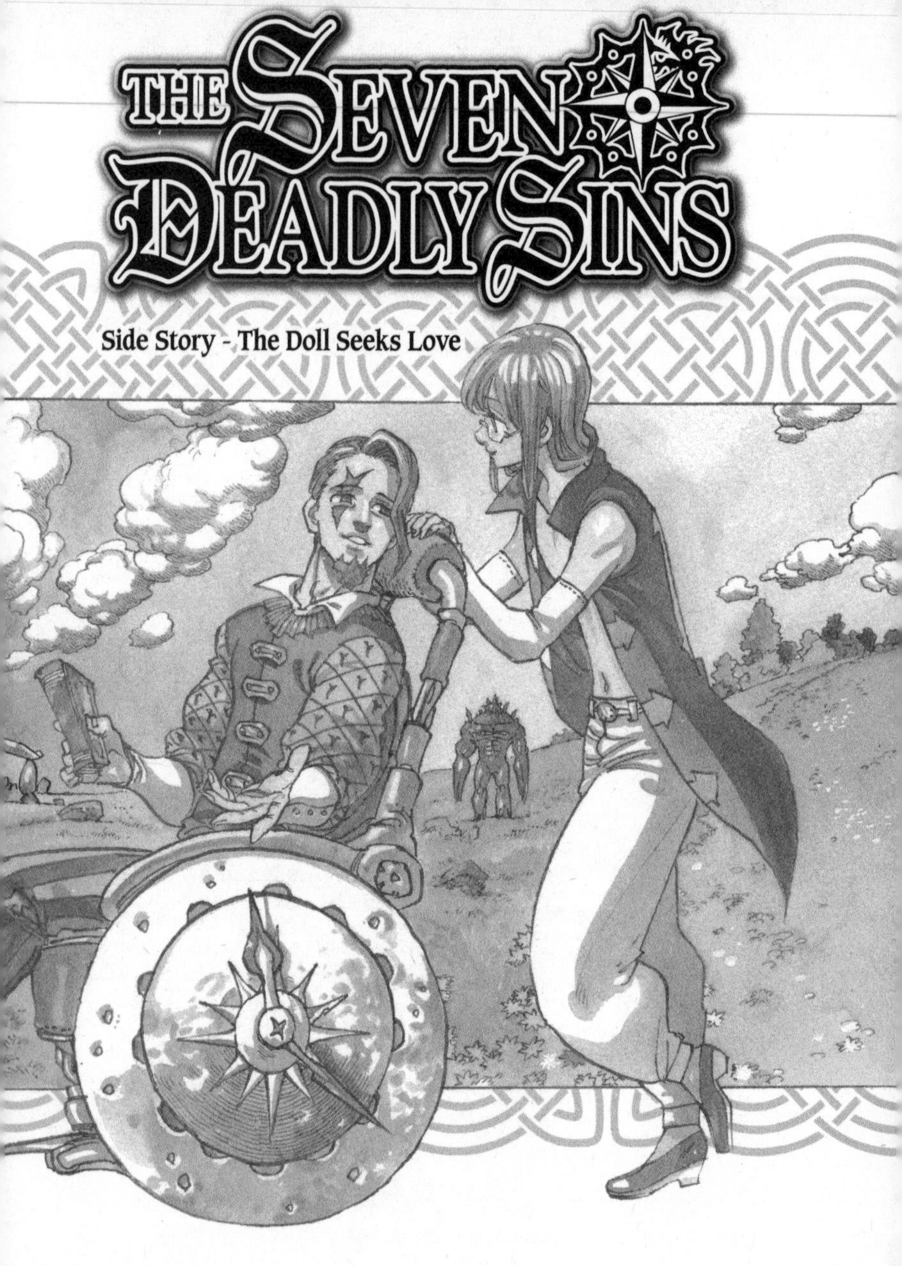

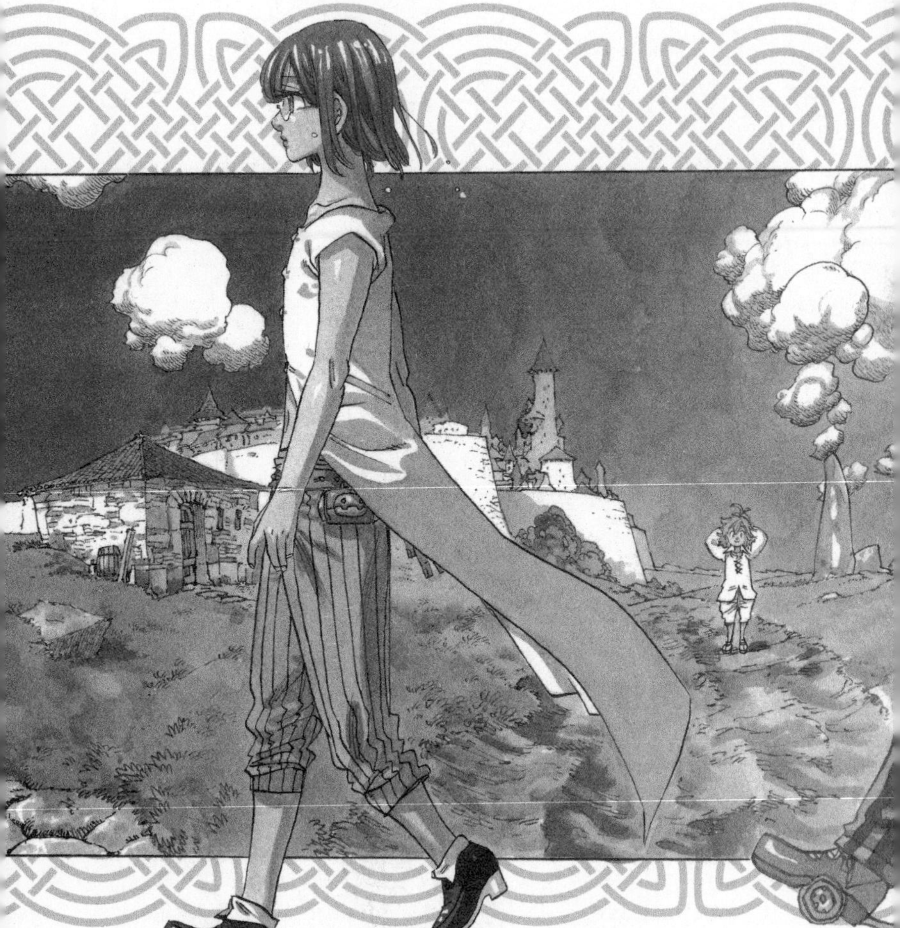

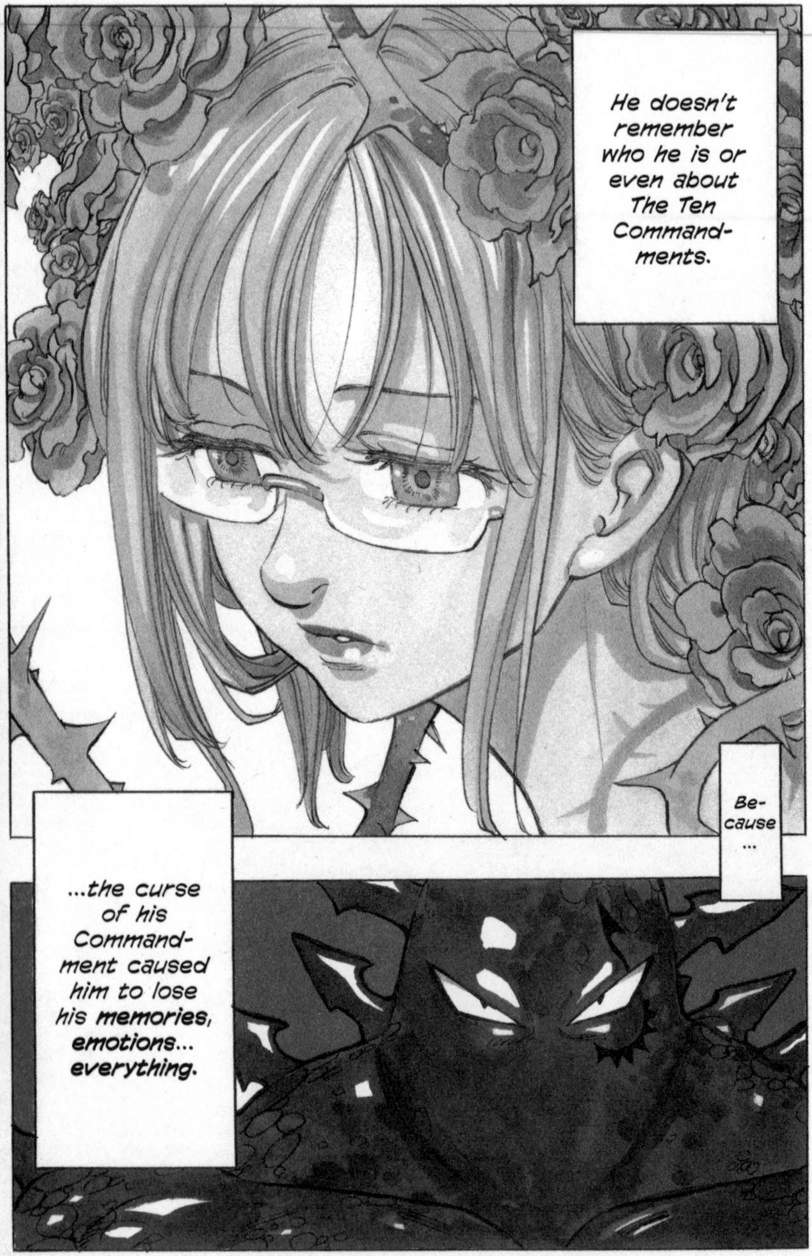
He doesn't remember who he is or even about The Ten Command-ments.
Be-cause ...
...the curse of his Command-ment caused him to lose his **memories, emotions... everything**.

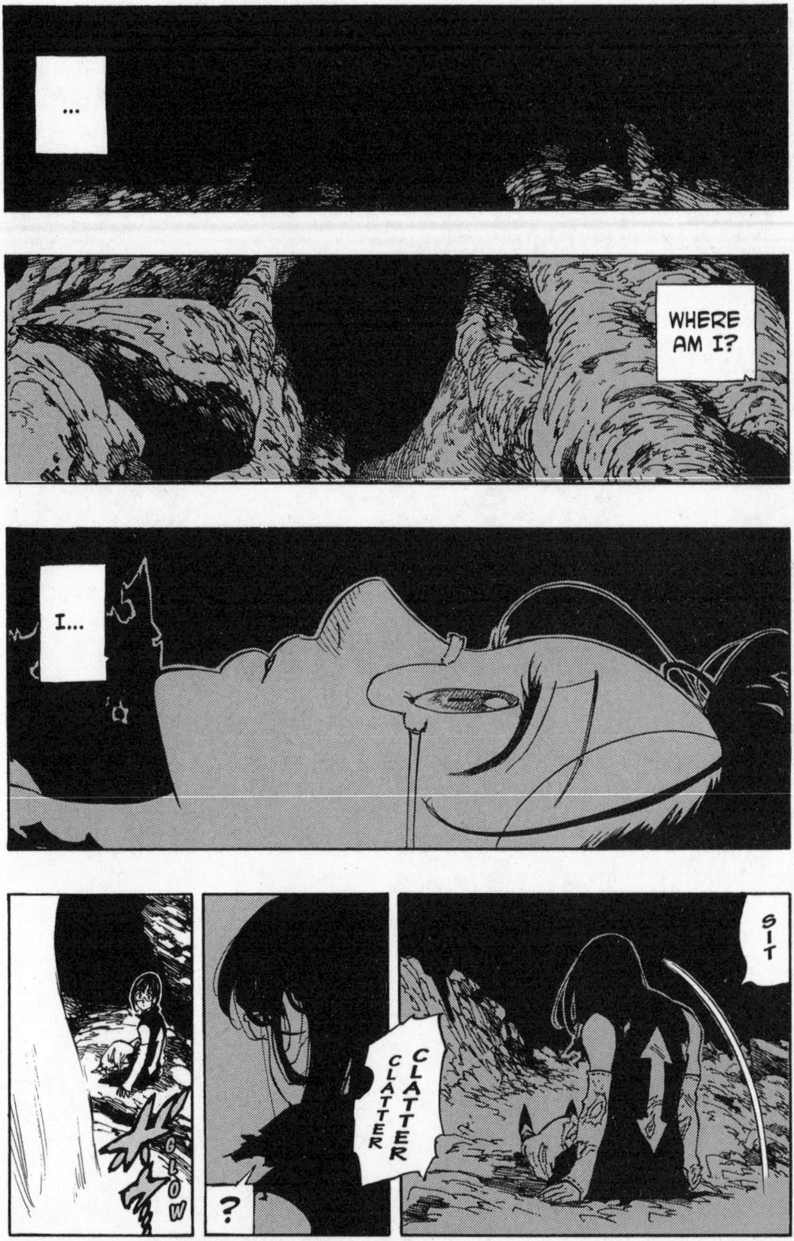
...
WHERE AM I?
I...
SIT
CLATTER CLATTER
?
GLOW

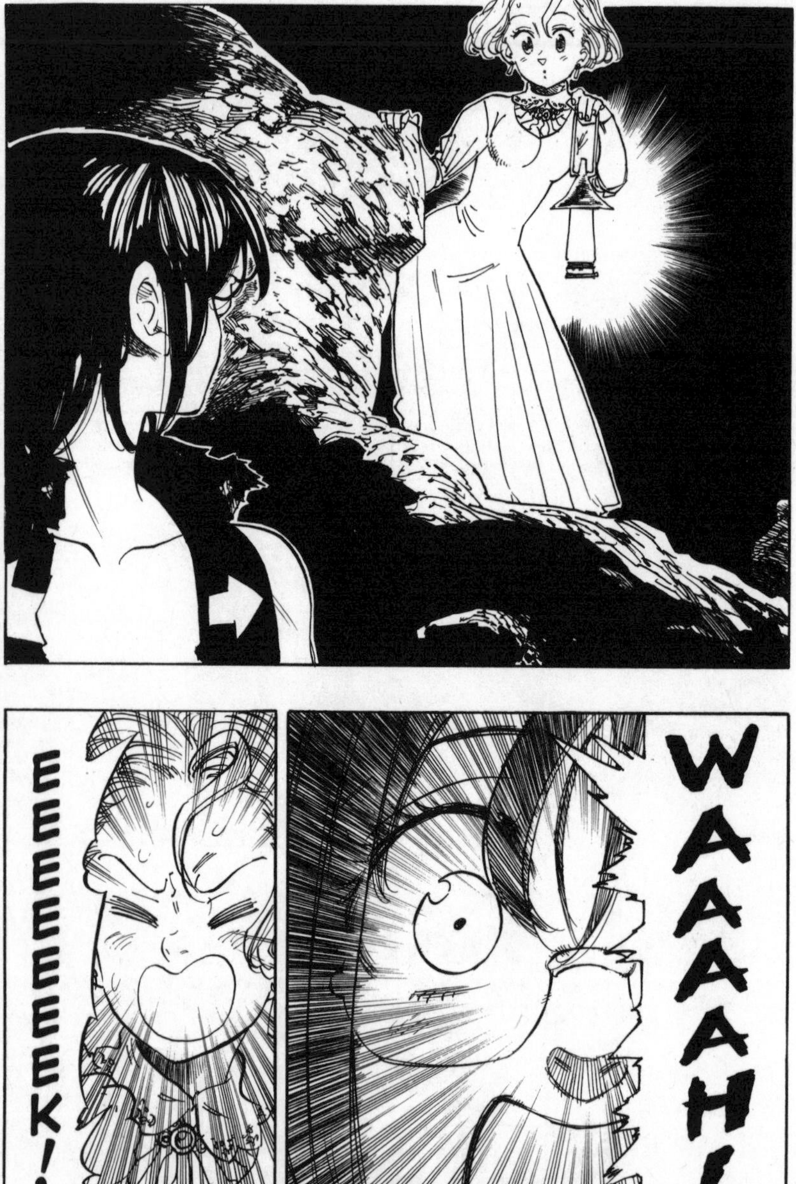
WAAAH!
EEEEEEEK!

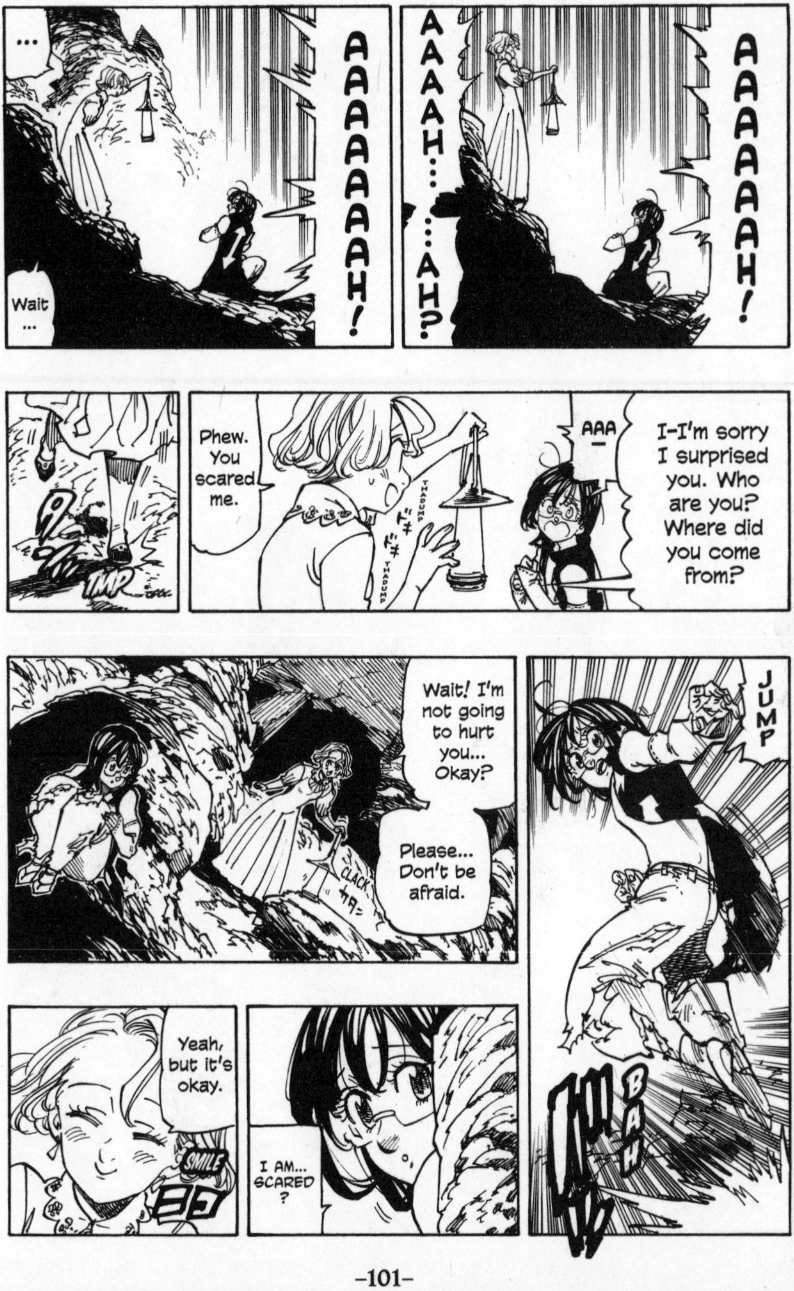
AAAAAAAH!
AAAAH... ...AH?
...
AAAAAAAAAH!
Wait ...
I-I'm sorry I surprised you. Who are you? Where did you come from?
AAA—
Phew. You scared me.
THADUMP ドキ
ドキ THADUMP
TMP
JUMP
BAH
Wait! I'm not going to hurt you... Okay?
Please... Don't be afraid.
CLACK カラ
I AM... SCARED ?
Yeah, but it's okay.
SMILE

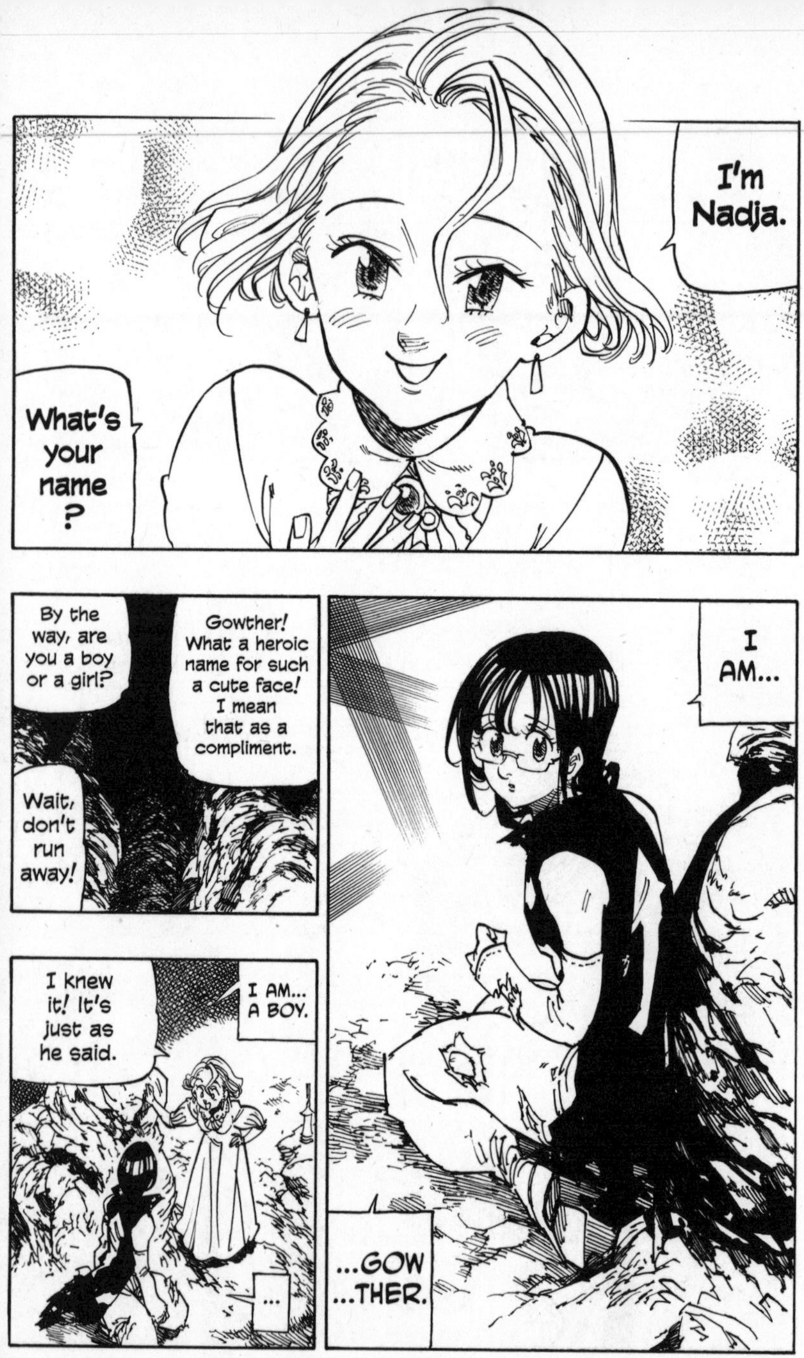
I'm Nadja.
What's your name?
I AM...
...GOW ...THER.
Gowther! What a heroic name for such a cute face! I mean that as a compliment.
By the way, are you a boy or a girl?
Wait, don't run away!
I AM... A BOY.
I knew it! It's just as he said.
...

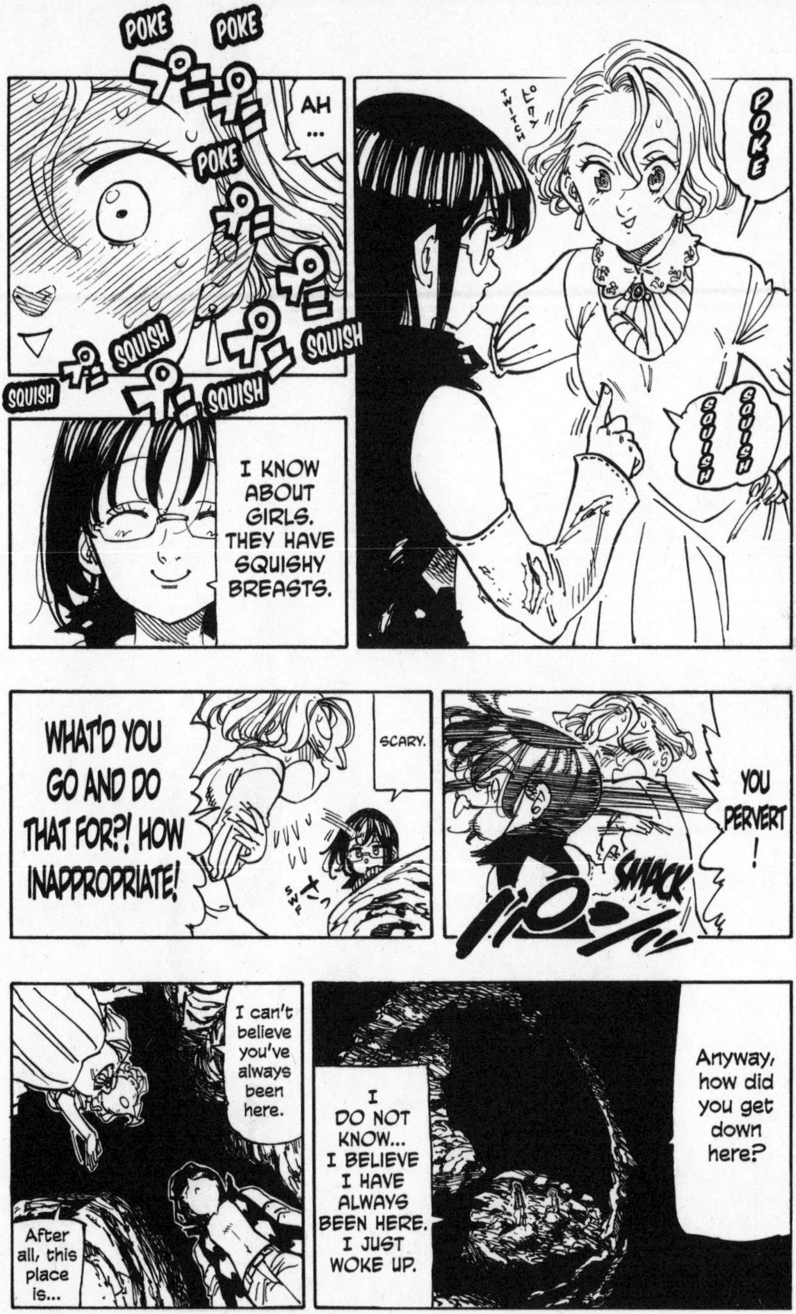

TWITCH
POKE
SQUISH SQUISH
POKE POKE
AH ...
POKE
SQUISH
SQUISH
SQUISH
SQUISH
I KNOW ABOUT GIRLS. THEY HAVE SQUISHY BREASTS.
YOU PERVERT!
SMACK
SCARY.
WHAT'D YOU GO AND DO THAT FOR?! HOW INAPPROPRIATE!
SWF
Anyway, how did you get down here?
I DO NOT KNOW... I BELIEVE I HAVE ALWAYS BEEN HERE. I JUST WOKE UP.
I can't believe you've always been here.
After all, this place is...

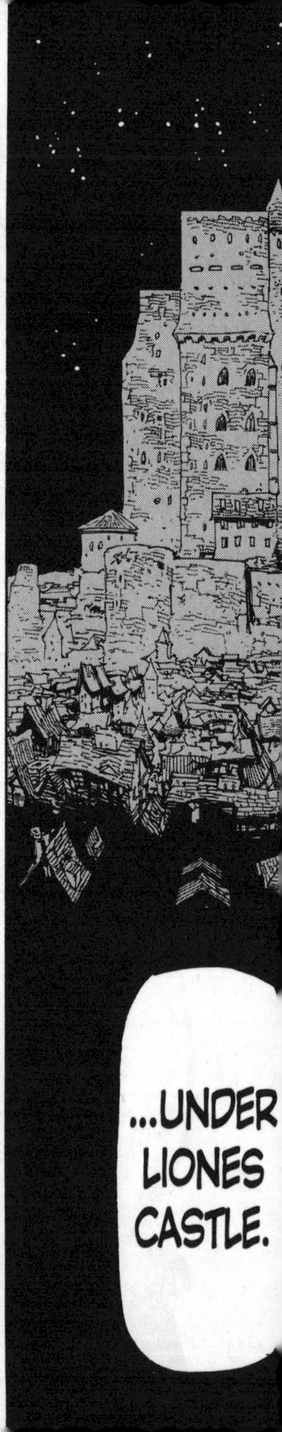
...UNDER LIONES CASTLE.

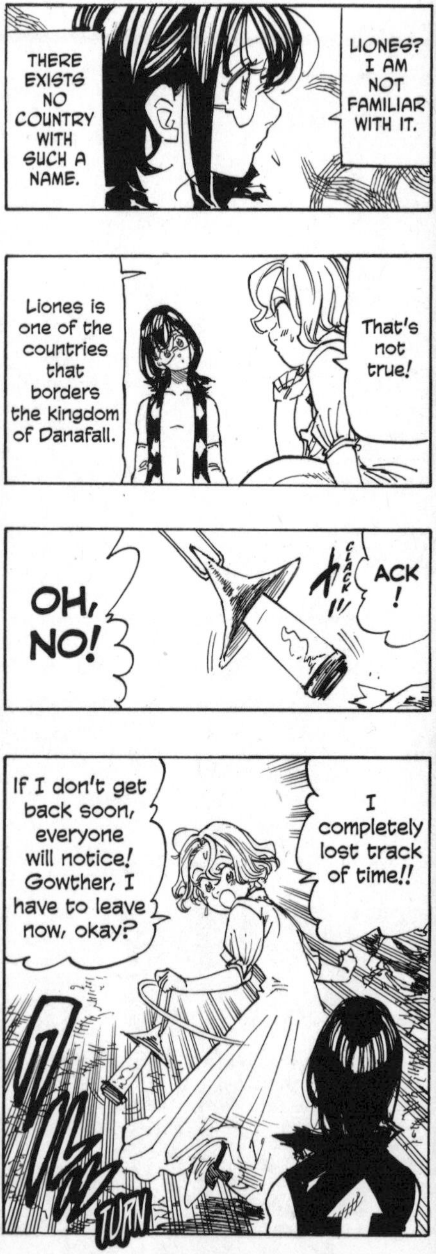
LIONES? I AM NOT FAMILIAR WITH IT.
THERE EXISTS NO COUNTRY WITH SUCH A NAME.
That's not true!
Liones is one of the countries that borders the kingdom of Danafall.
ACK!
CLACK
OH, NO!
I completely lost track of time!!
If I don't get back soon, everyone will notice! Gowther, I have to leave now, okay?
TURN

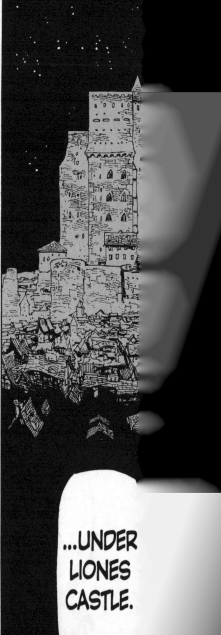

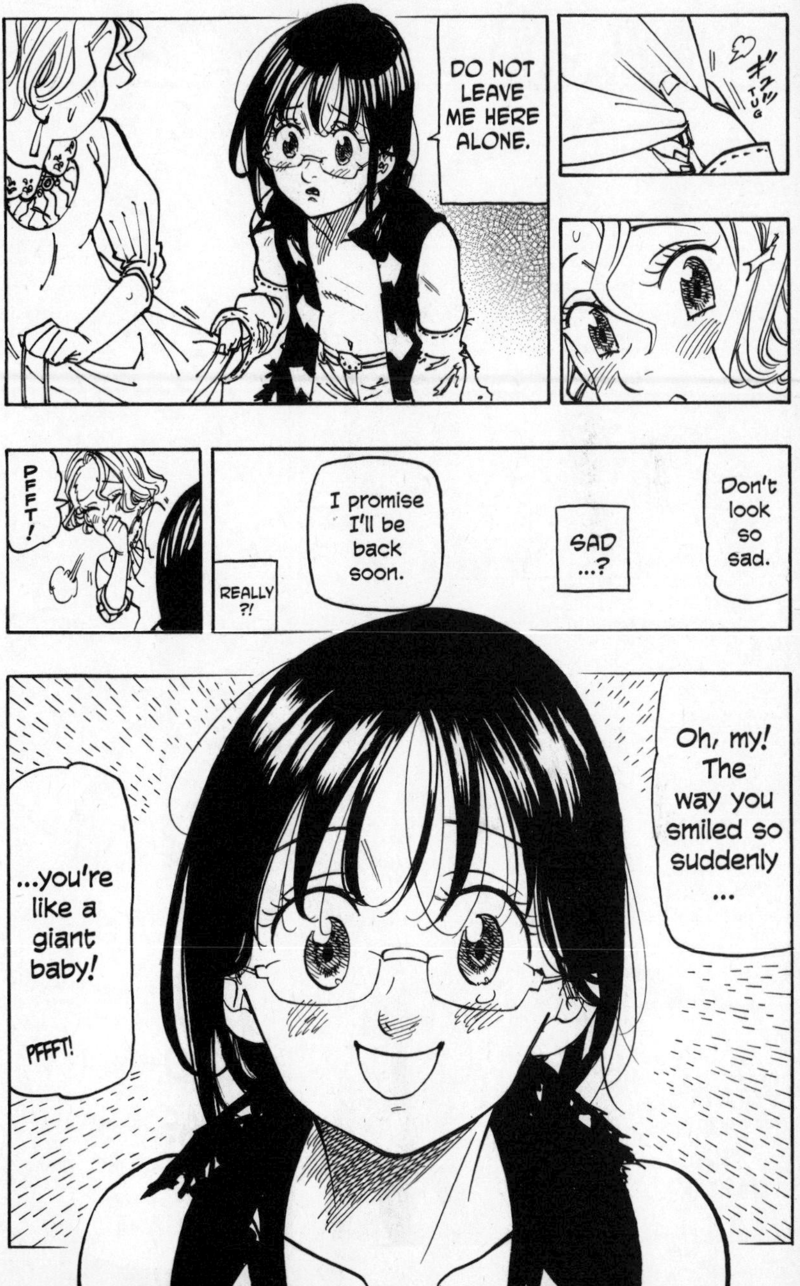
TUG
DO NOT LEAVE ME HERE ALONE.
Don't look so sad.
SAD ...?
I promise I'll be back soon.
REALLY ?!
PFFT!
Oh, my! The way you smiled so suddenly ...
...you're like a giant baby!
PFFFT!

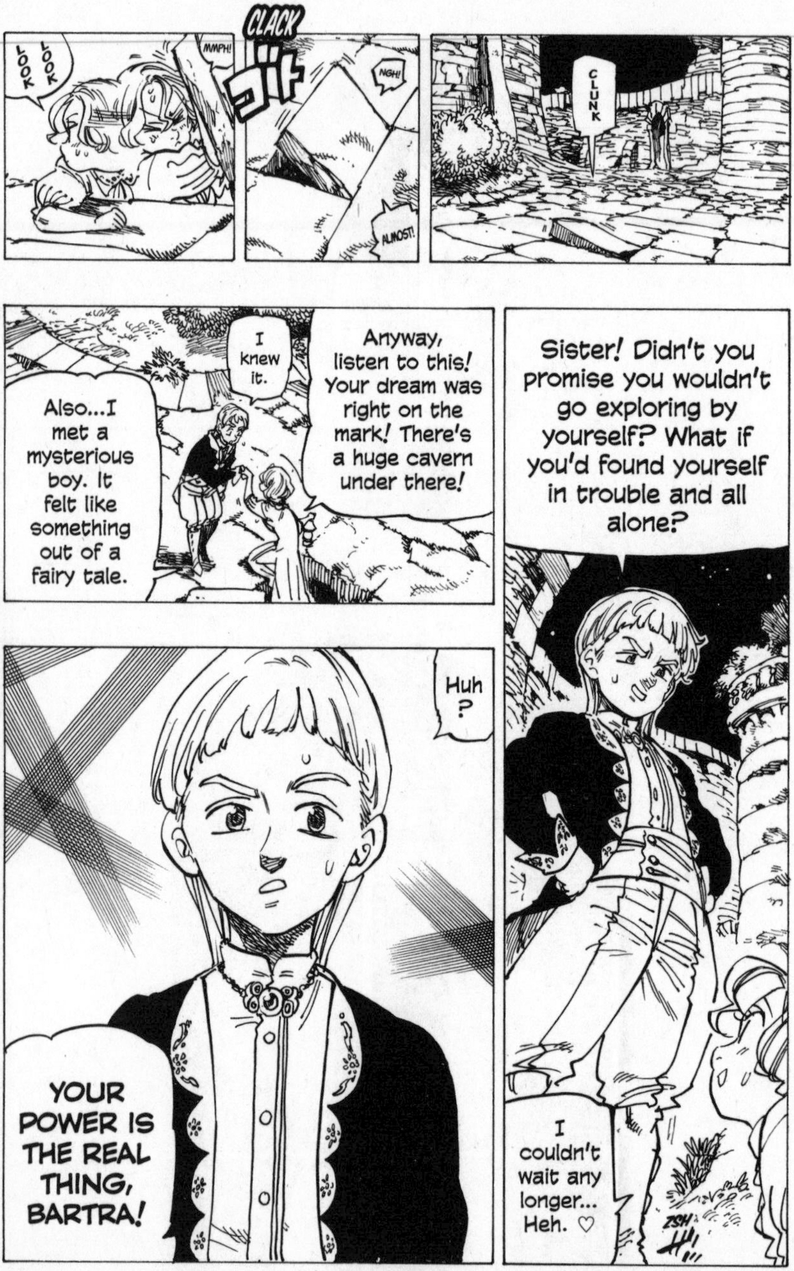
CLUNK
NGH!
CLACK
ゴト
ALMOST!
MMPH!
LOOK LOOK
Sister! Didn't you promise you wouldn't go exploring by yourself? What if you'd found yourself in trouble and all alone?
I couldn't wait any longer... Heh. ♡
ZSH
Anyway, listen to this! Your dream was right on the mark! There's a huge cavern under there!
I knew it.
Also...I met a mysterious boy. It felt like something out of a fairy tale.
Huh?
YOUR POWER IS THE REAL THING, BARTRA!

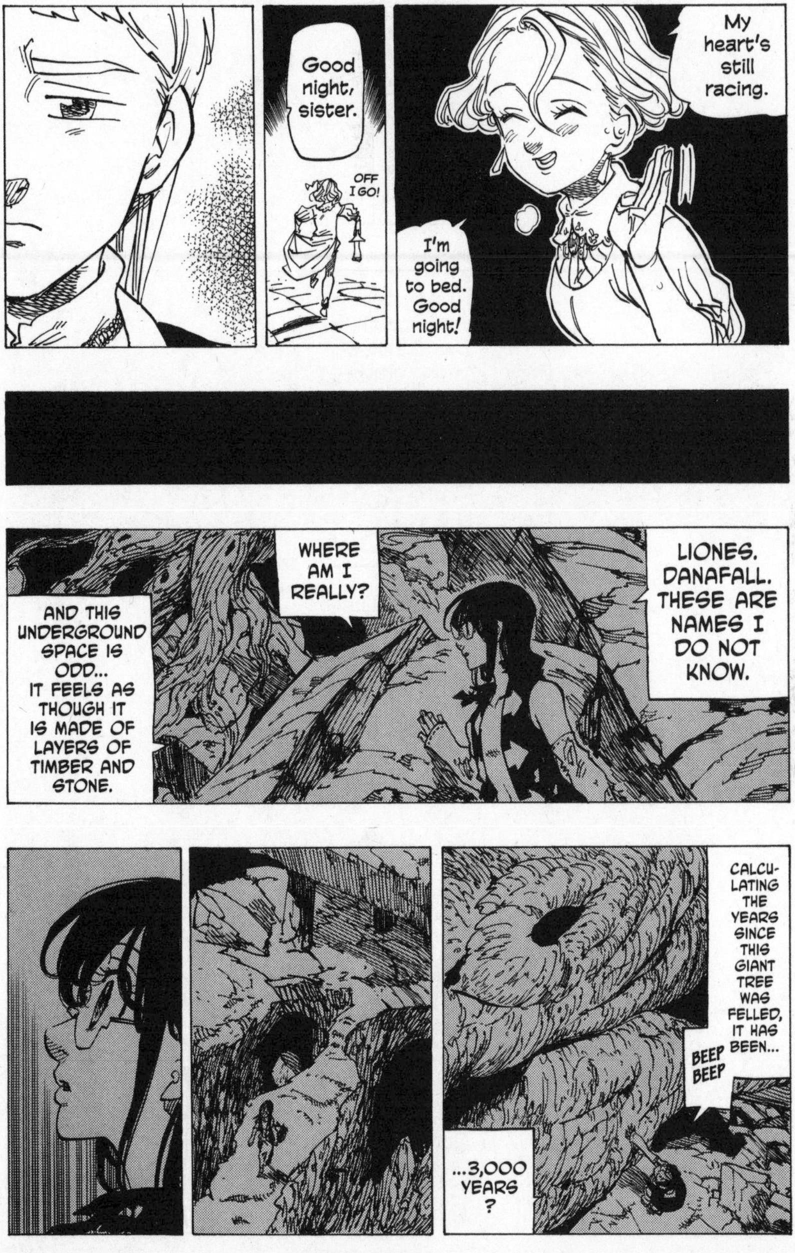
My heart's still racing.
I'm going to bed. Good night!
Good night, sister.
OFF I GO!
LIONES. DANAFALL. THESE ARE NAMES I DO NOT KNOW.
WHERE AM I REALLY?
AND THIS UNDERGROUND SPACE IS ODD... IT FEELS AS THOUGH IT IS MADE OF LAYERS OF TIMBER AND STONE.
CALCULATING THE YEARS SINCE THIS GIANT TREE WAS FELLED, IT HAS BEEN...
BEEP BEEP
...3,000 YEARS?

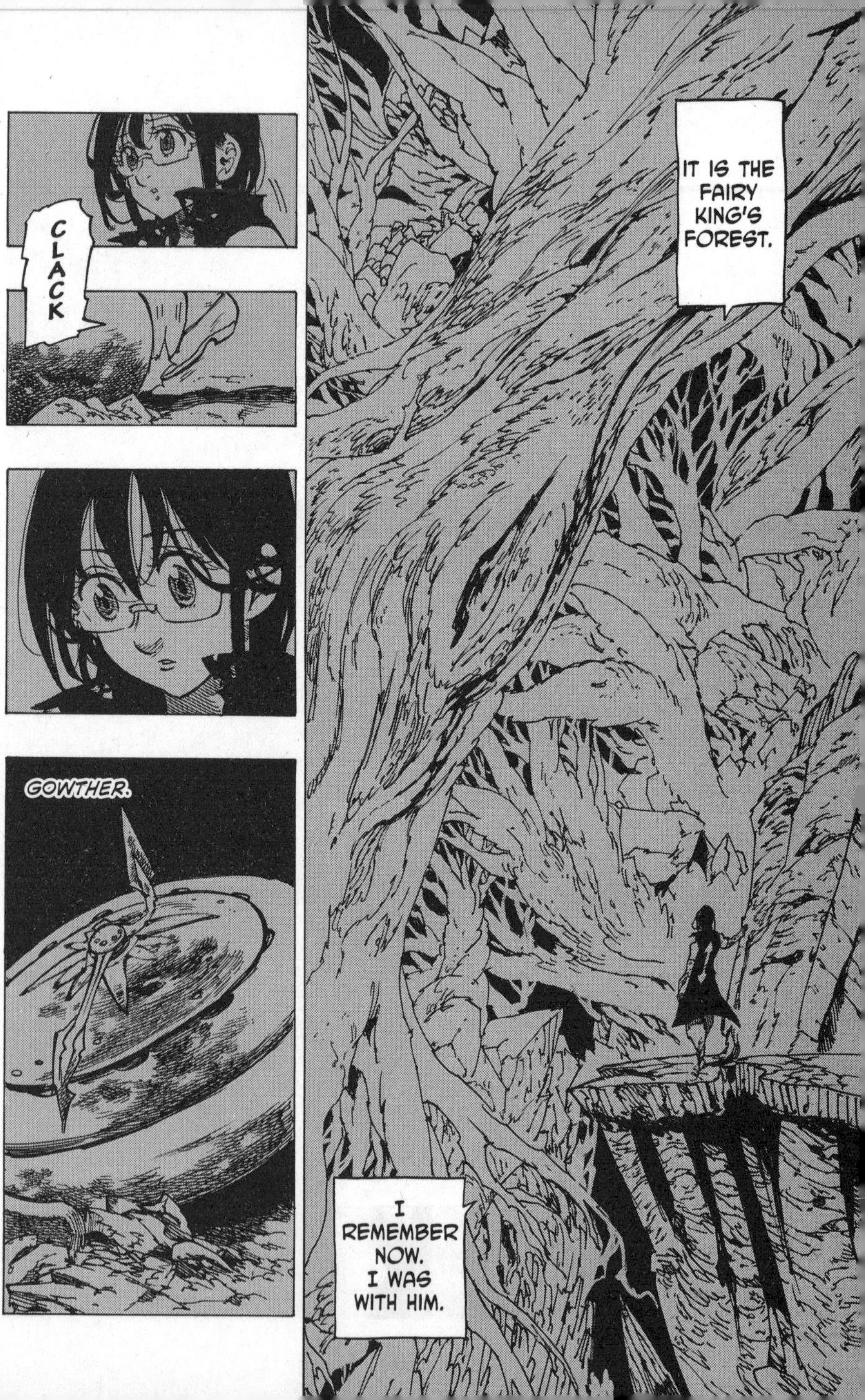
IT IS THE FAIRY KING'S FOREST.
I REMEMBER NOW. I WAS WITH HIM.
CLACK
GOWTHER.

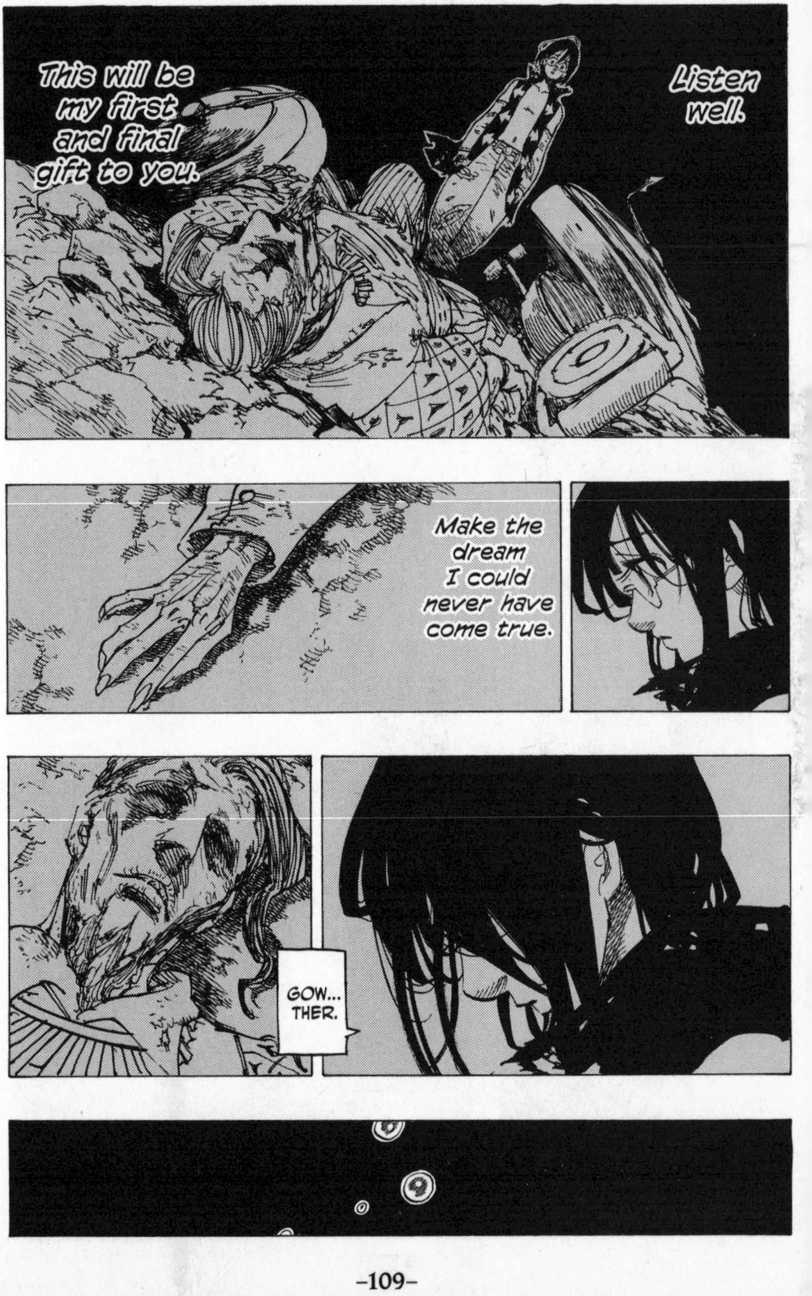
Listen well.
This will be my first and final gift to you.
Make the dream I could never have come true.
GOW... THER.

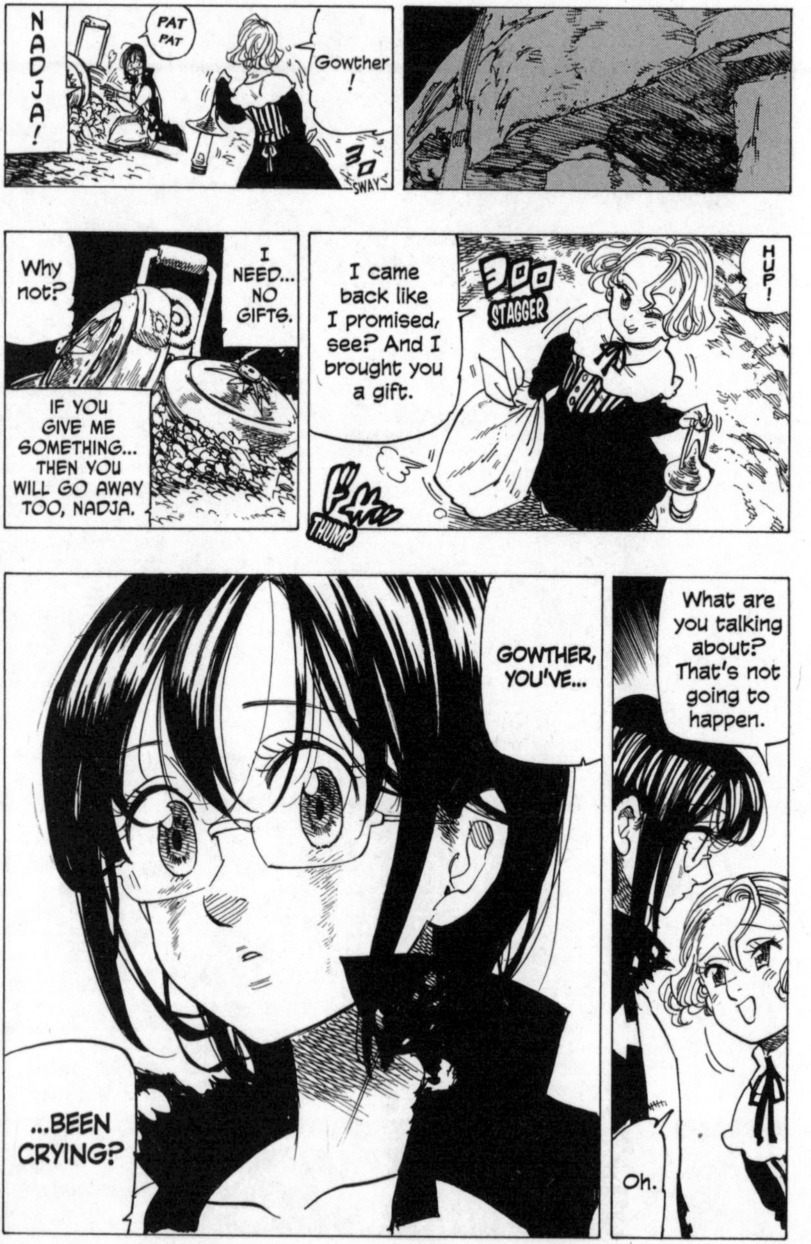
Gowther!
PAT PAT
NADJA!
ヨロ
SWAY
HUP!
ヨロロ
STAGGER
I came back like I promised, see? And I brought you a gift.
THUMP
I NEED... NO GIFTS.
Why not?
IF YOU GIVE ME SOMETHING... THEN YOU WILL GO AWAY TOO, NADJA.
What are you talking about? That's not going to happen.
Oh.
GOWTHER, YOU'VE...
...BEEN CRYING?

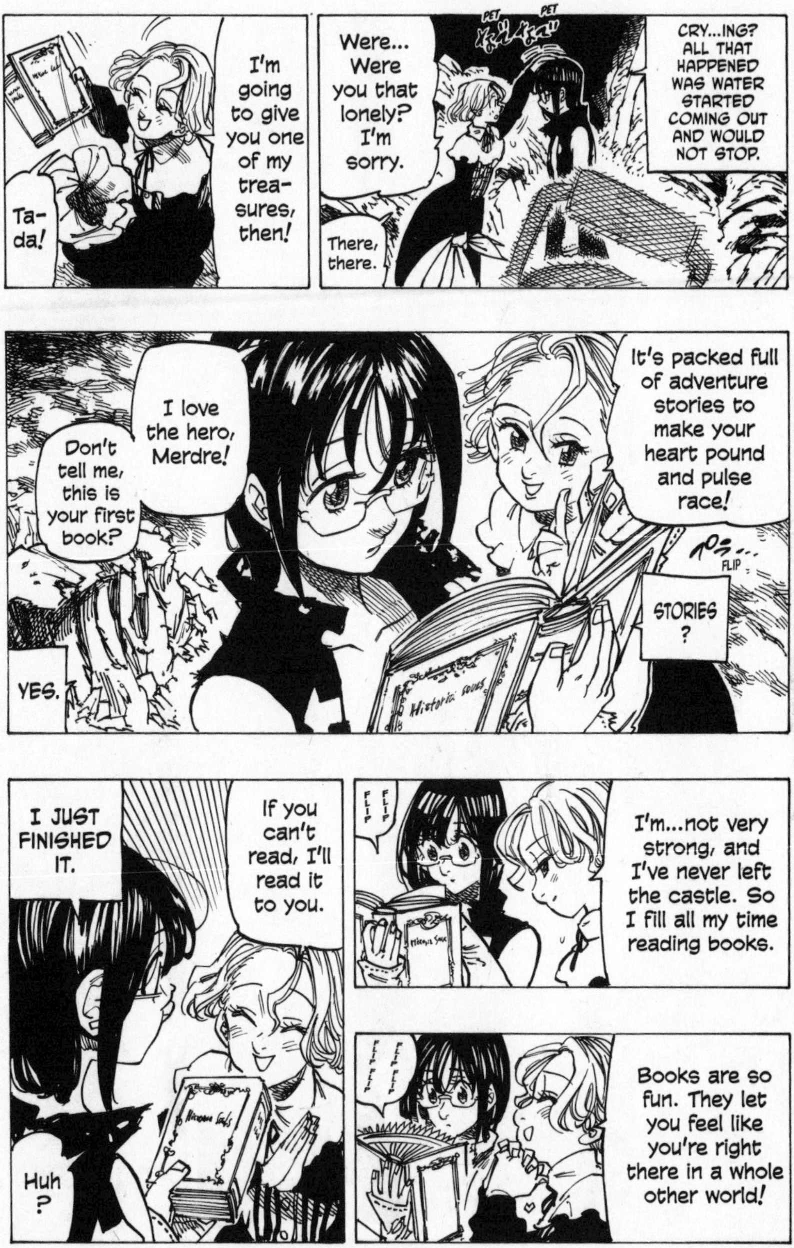
CRY...ING? ALL THAT HAPPENED WAS WATER STARTED COMING OUT AND WOULD NOT STOP.
PET PET
Were... Were you that lonely? I'm sorry.
There, there.
I'm going to give you one of my trea-sures, then!
Ta-da!
It's packed full of adventure stories to make your heart pound and pulse race!
FLIP
STORIES?
I love the hero, Merdre!
Don't tell me, this is your first book?
YES.
I'm...not very strong, and I've never left the castle. So I fill all my time reading books.
FLIP FLIP
Books are so fun. They let you feel like you're right there in a whole other world!
FLIP FLIP FLIP FLIP
If you can't read, I'll read it to you.
I JUST FINISHED IT.
Huh?

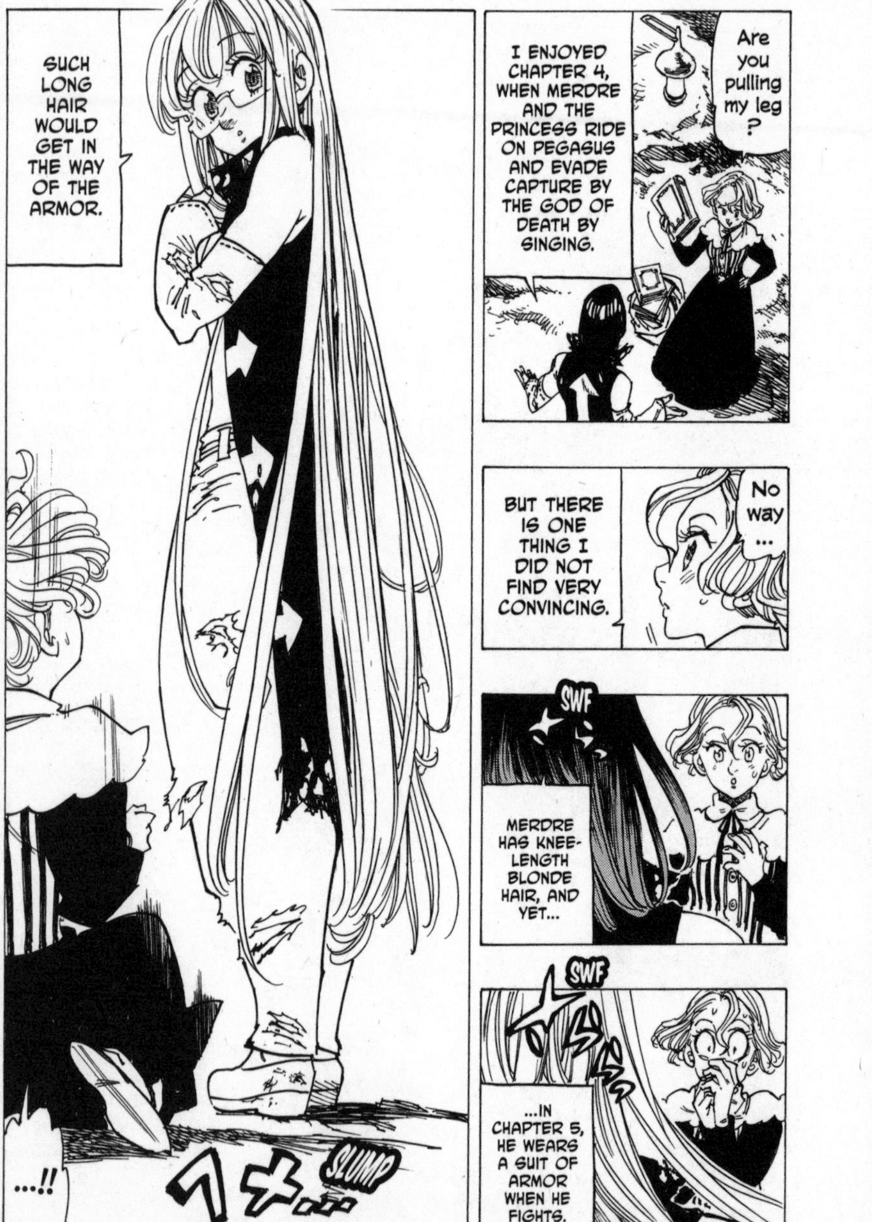
Are you pulling my leg?
I ENJOYED CHAPTER 4, WHEN MERDRE AND THE PRINCESS RIDE ON PEGASUS AND EVADE CAPTURE BY THE GOD OF DEATH BY SINGING.
No way...
BUT THERE IS ONE THING I DID NOT FIND VERY CONVINCING.
SWF
MERDRE HAS KNEE-LENGTH BLONDE HAIR, AND YET...
SWF
...IN CHAPTER 5, HE WEARS A SUIT OF ARMOR WHEN HE FIGHTS.
SUCH LONG HAIR WOULD GET IN THE WAY OF THE ARMOR.
SLUMP
...!!

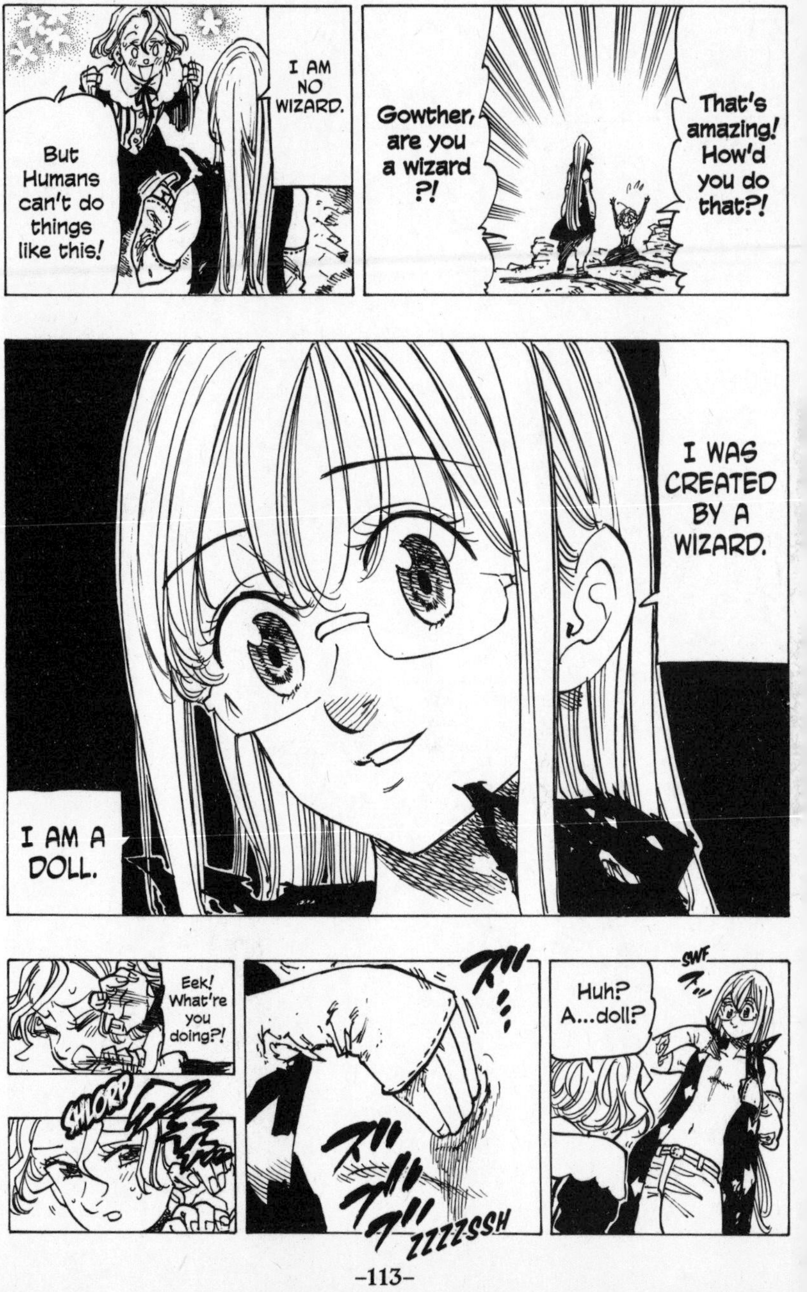
That's amazing! How'd you do that?!
Gowther, are you a wizard ?!
I AM NO WIZARD.
But Humans can't do things like this!
I WAS CREATED BY A WIZARD.
I AM A DOLL.
SWF
Huh? A...doll?
ZZZZ-SSH
Eek! What're you doing?!
SHLORP

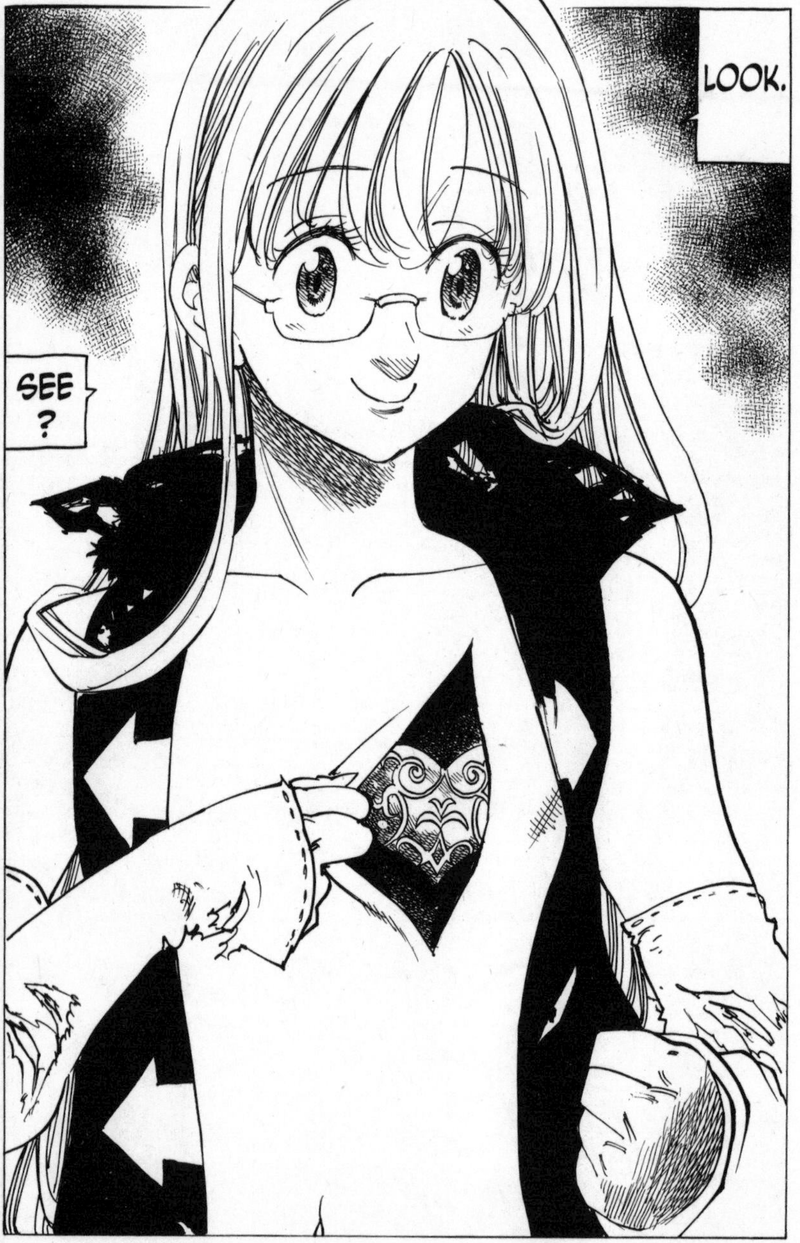
LOOK.
SEE ?

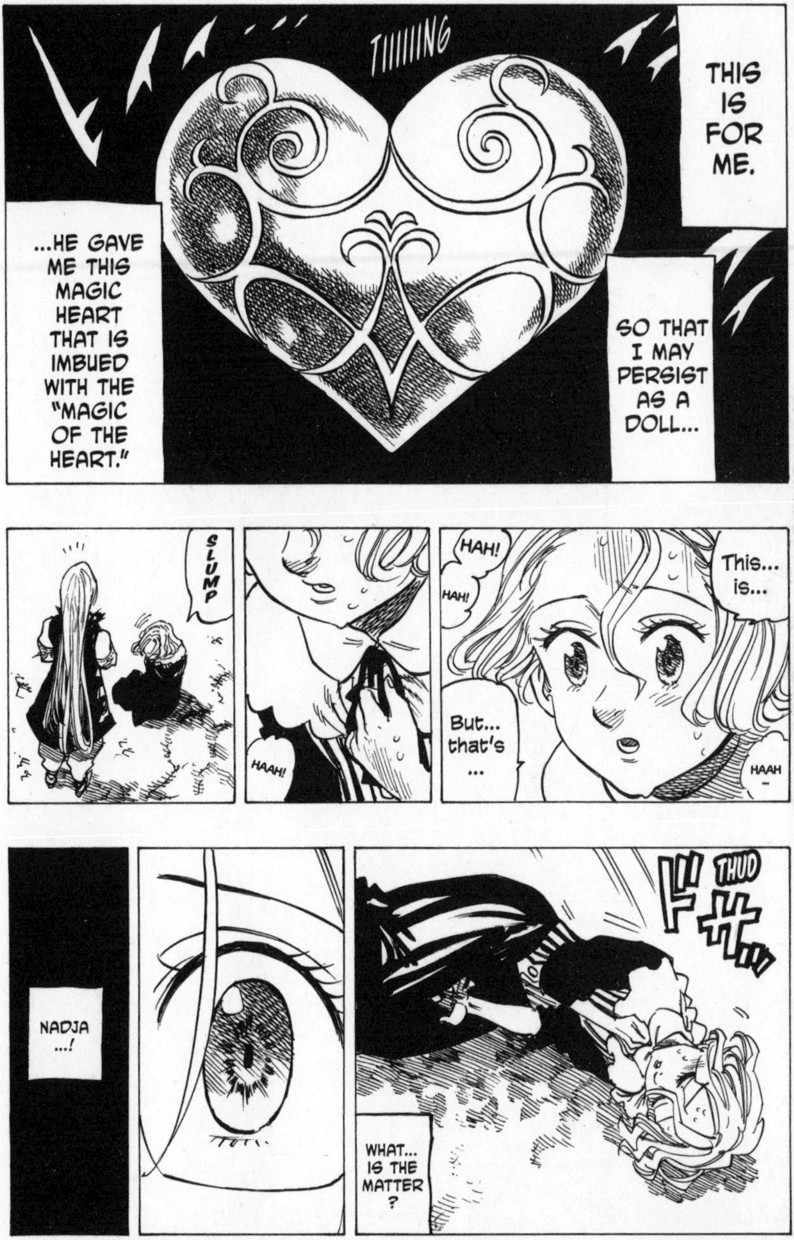
THIS IS FOR ME.
TIIIIIING
SO THAT I MAY PERSIST AS A DOLL...
...HE GAVE ME THIS MAGIC HEART THAT IS IMBUED WITH THE "MAGIC OF THE HEART."
This... is...
HAH!
HAH!
But... that's ...
HAAH ...
HAAH!
SLUMP
THUD
WHAT... IS THE MATTER ?
NADJA ...!

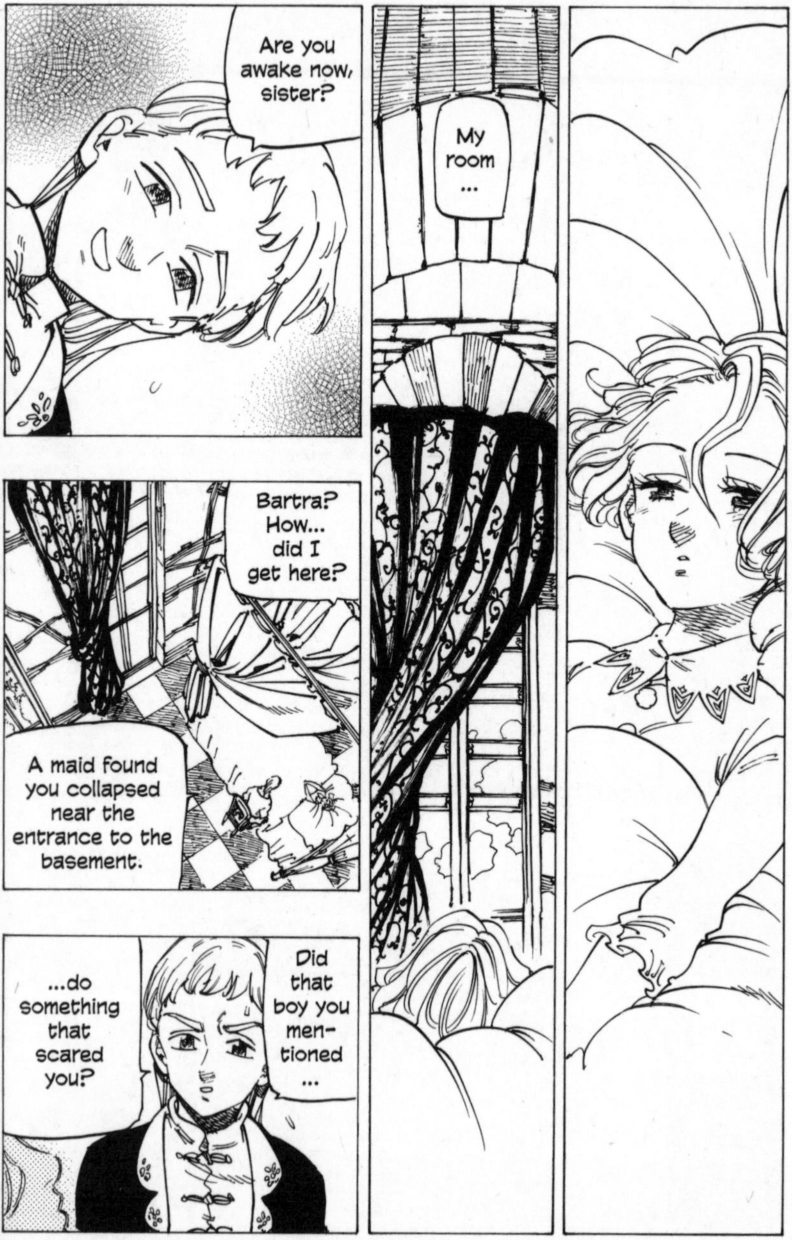
My room ...
Are you awake now, sister?
Bartra? How... did I get here?
A maid found you collapsed near the entrance to the basement.
Did that boy you mentioned ...
...do something that scared you?

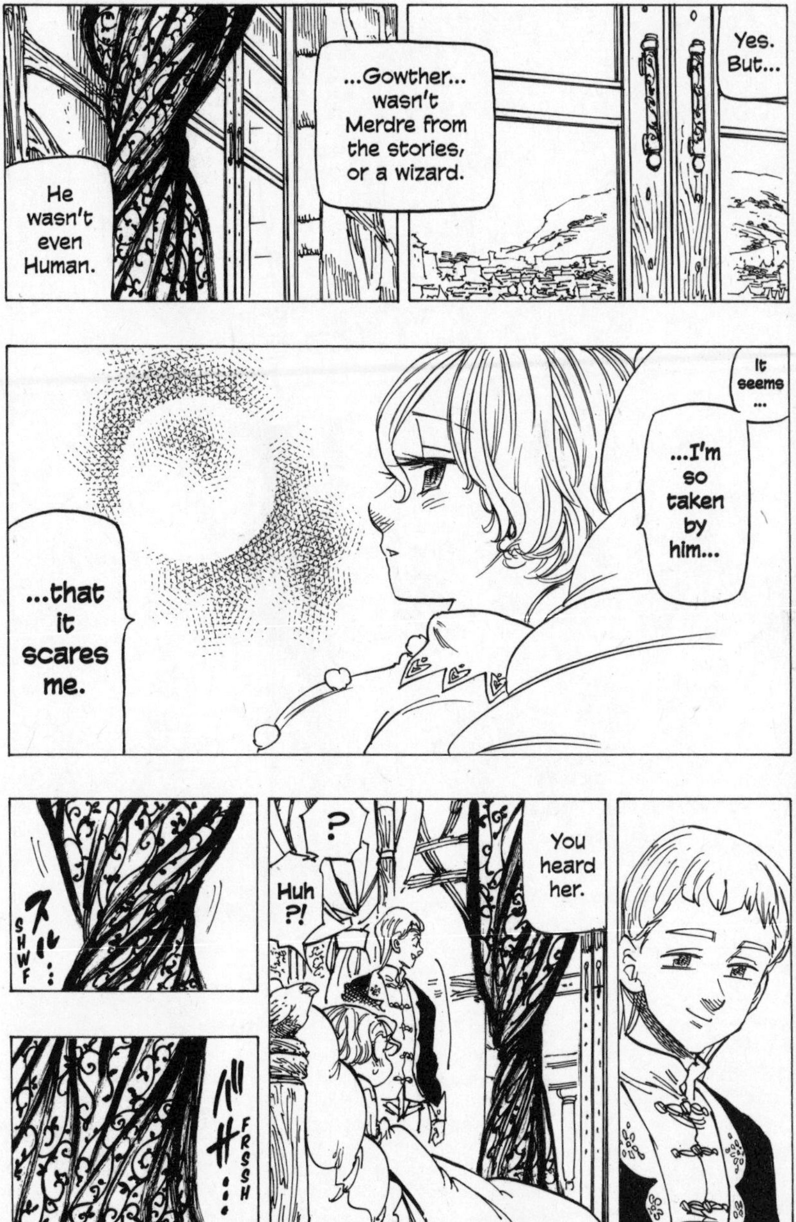
Yes. But...
...Gowther... wasn't Merdre from the stories, or a wizard.
He wasn't even Human.
It seems...
...I'm so taken by him...
...that it scares me.
You heard her.
?
Huh?!
SHWF
FRSSH

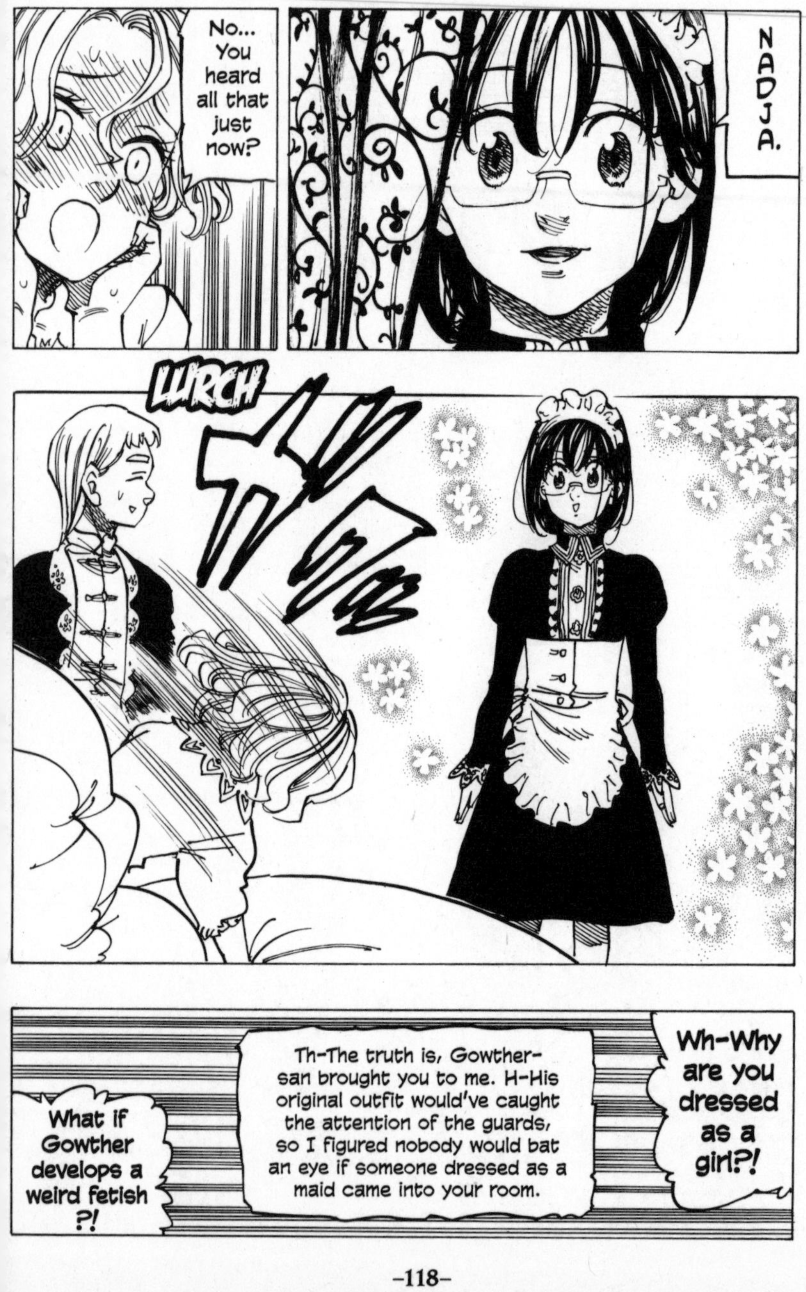
NADJA.
No... You heard all that just now?
LURCH
Wh-Why are you dressed as a girl?!
Th-The truth is, Gowther-san brought you to me. H-His original outfit would've caught the attention of the guards, so I figured nobody would bat an eye if someone dressed as a maid came into your room.
What if Gowther develops a weird fetish?!

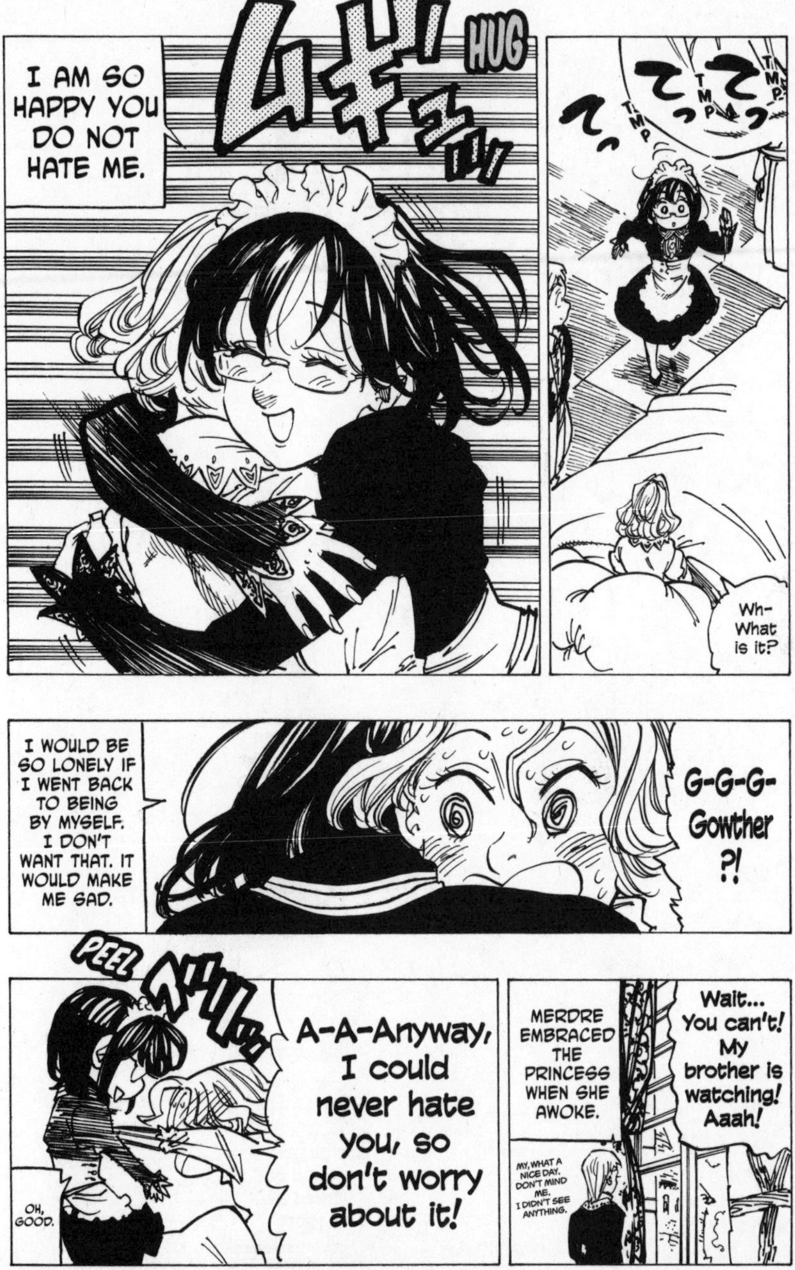

TMP
TMP
TMP
TMP
Wh- What is it?
HUG
I AM SO HAPPY YOU DO NOT HATE ME.
G-G-G-Gowther?!
I WOULD BE SO LONELY IF I WENT BACK TO BEING BY MYSELF. I DON'T WANT THAT. IT WOULD MAKE ME SAD.
Wait... You can't! My brother is watching! Aaah!
MERDRE EMBRACED THE PRINCESS WHEN SHE AWOKE.
MY, WHAT A NICE DAY. DON'T MIND ME. I DIDN'T SEE ANYTHING.
PEEL
A-A-Anyway, I could never hate you, so don't worry about it!
OH, GOOD.

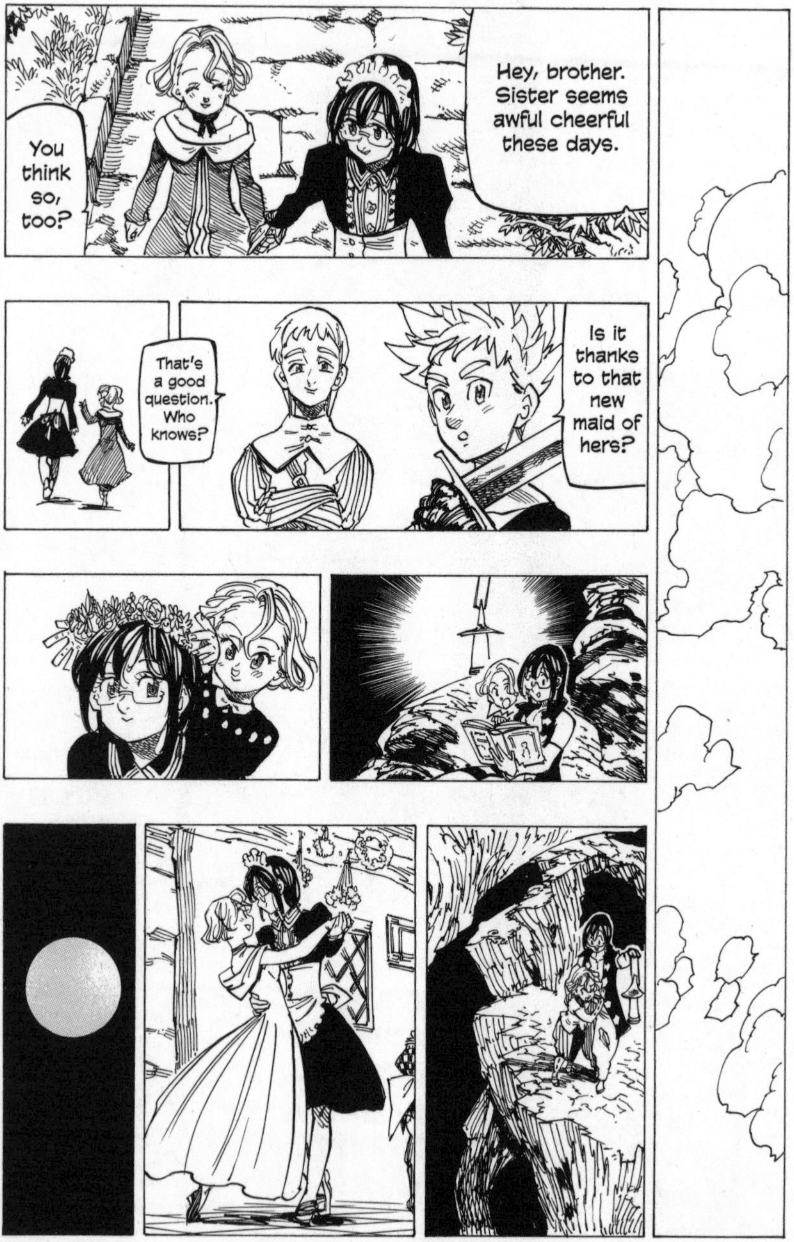
Hey, brother. Sister seems awful cheerful these days.
You think so, too?
Is it thanks to that new maid of hers?
That's a good question. Who knows?

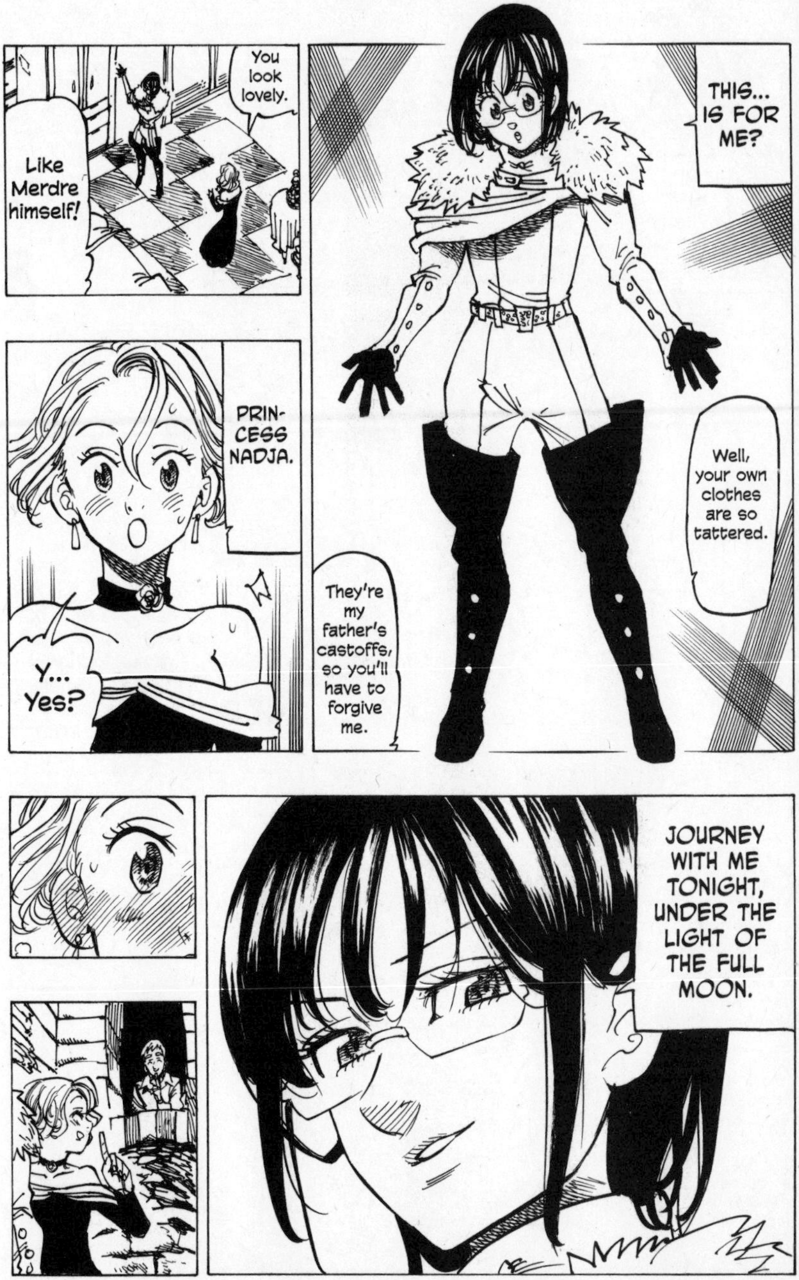
THIS... IS FOR ME?
Well, your own clothes are so tattered.
They're my father's castoffs, so you'll have to forgive me.
You look lovely.
Like Merdre himself!
PRINCESS NADJA.
Y... Yes?
JOURNEY WITH ME TONIGHT, UNDER THE LIGHT OF THE FULL MOON.

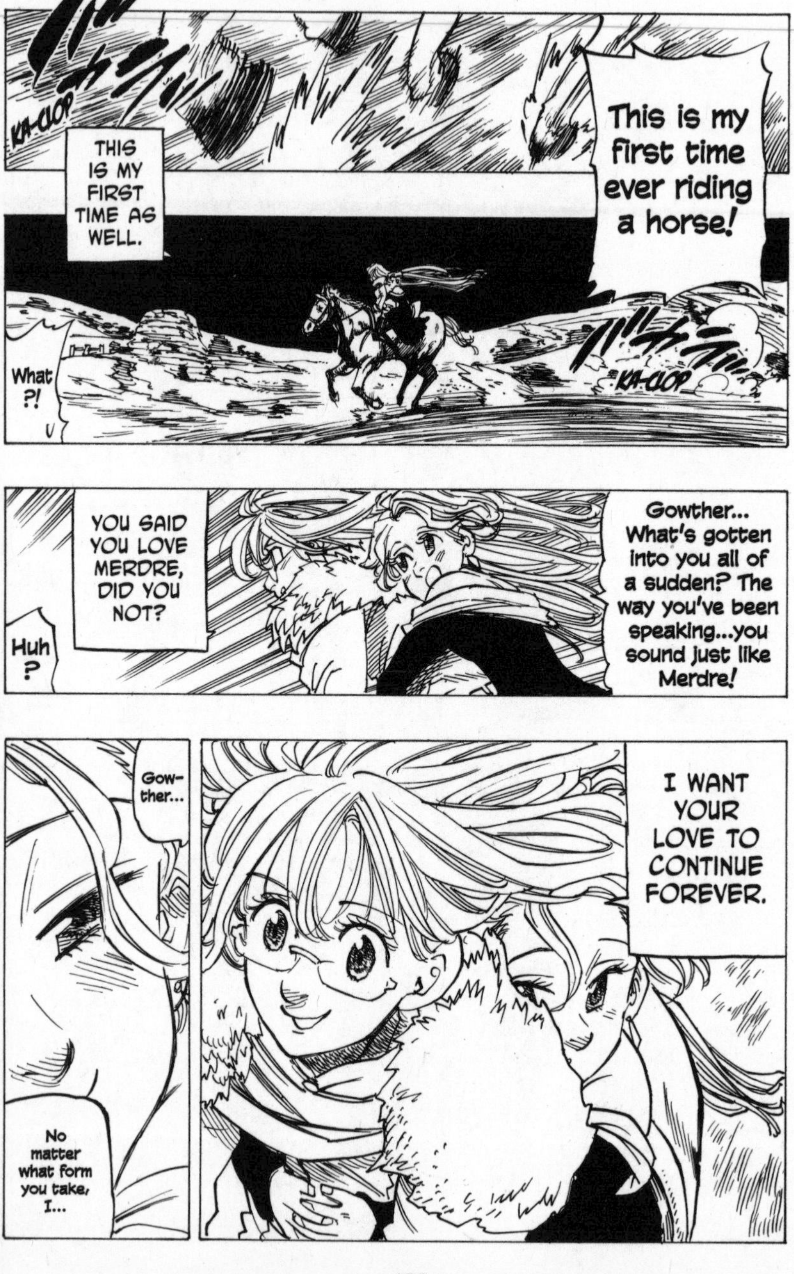
This is my first time ever riding a horse!
KA-CLOP
THIS IS MY FIRST TIME AS WELL.
KA-CLOP
What?!
Gowther... What's gotten into you all of a sudden? The way you've been speaking...you sound just like Merdre!
YOU SAID YOU LOVE MERDRE, DID YOU NOT?
Huh?
I WANT YOUR LOVE TO CONTINUE FOREVER.
Gow-ther...
No matter what form you take, I...

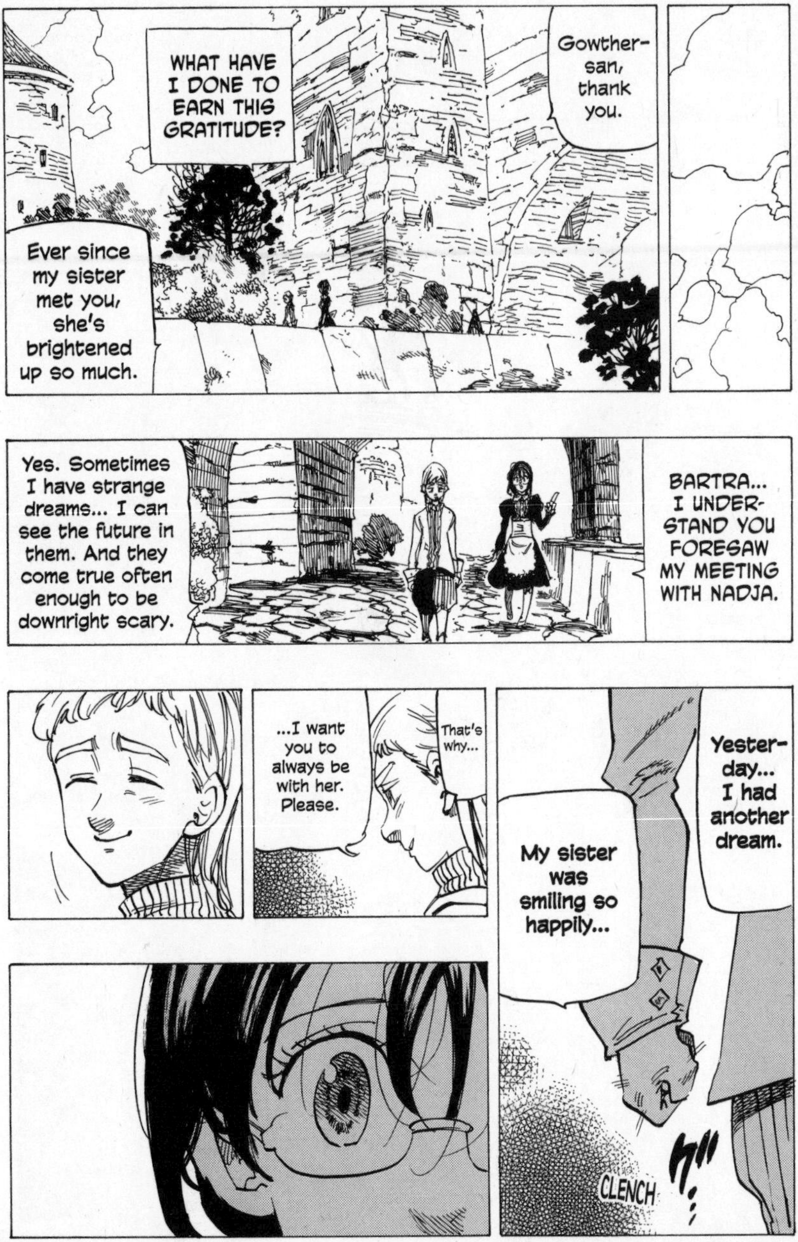
Gowther-san, thank you.
WHAT HAVE I DONE TO EARN THIS GRATITUDE?
Ever since my sister met you, she's brightened up so much.
BARTRA... I UNDERSTAND YOU FORESAW MY MEETING WITH NADJA.
Yes. Sometimes I have strange dreams... I can see the future in them. And they come true often enough to be downright scary.
Yesterday... I had another dream.
My sister was smiling so happily...
CLENCH
That's why...
...I want you to always be with her. Please.

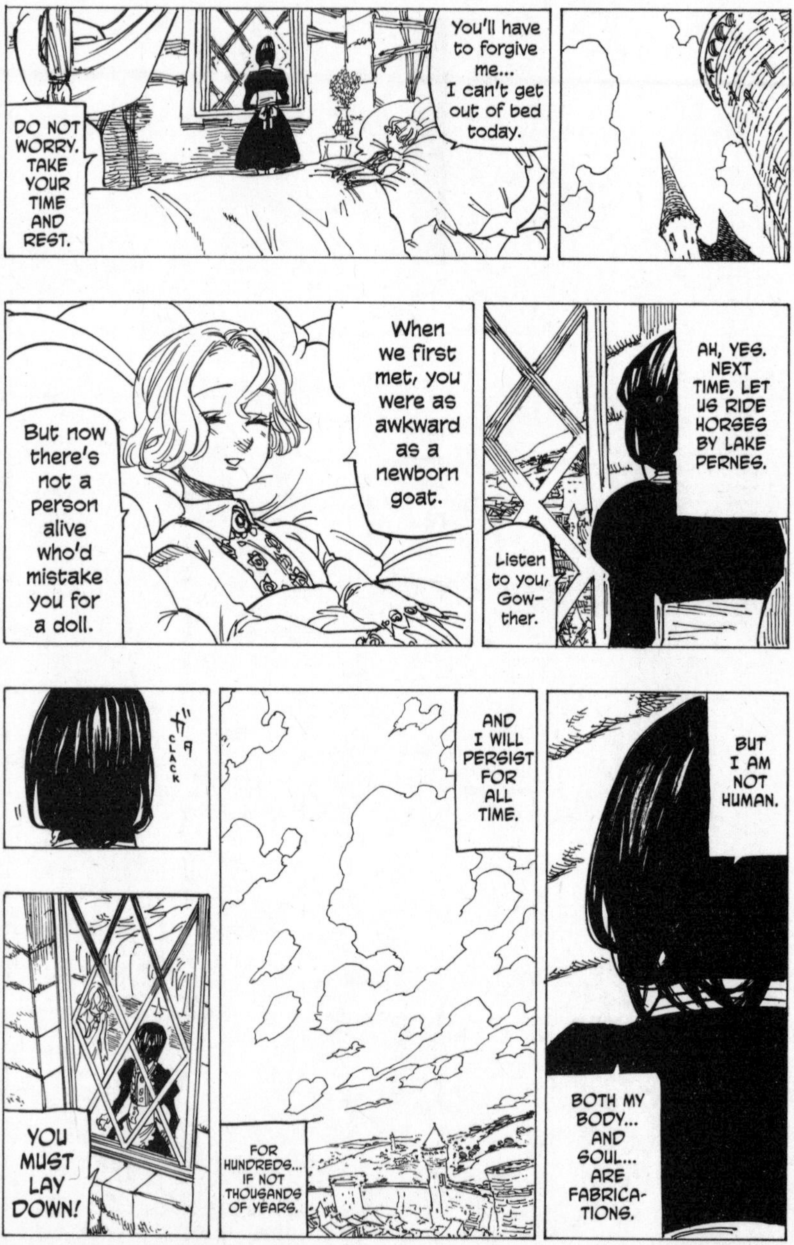

You'll have to forgive me... I can't get out of bed today.
DO NOT WORRY. TAKE YOUR TIME AND REST.
AH, YES. NEXT TIME, LET US RIDE HORSES BY LAKE PERNES.
Listen to you, Gow-ther.
When we first met, you were as awkward as a newborn goat.
But now there's not a person alive who'd mistake you for a doll.
BUT I AM NOT HUMAN.
BOTH MY BODY... AND SOUL... ARE FABRICA-TIONS.
AND I WILL PERSIST FOR ALL TIME.
FOR HUNDREDS... IF NOT THOUSANDS OF YEARS.
ガタ
CLACK
YOU MUST LAY DOWN!

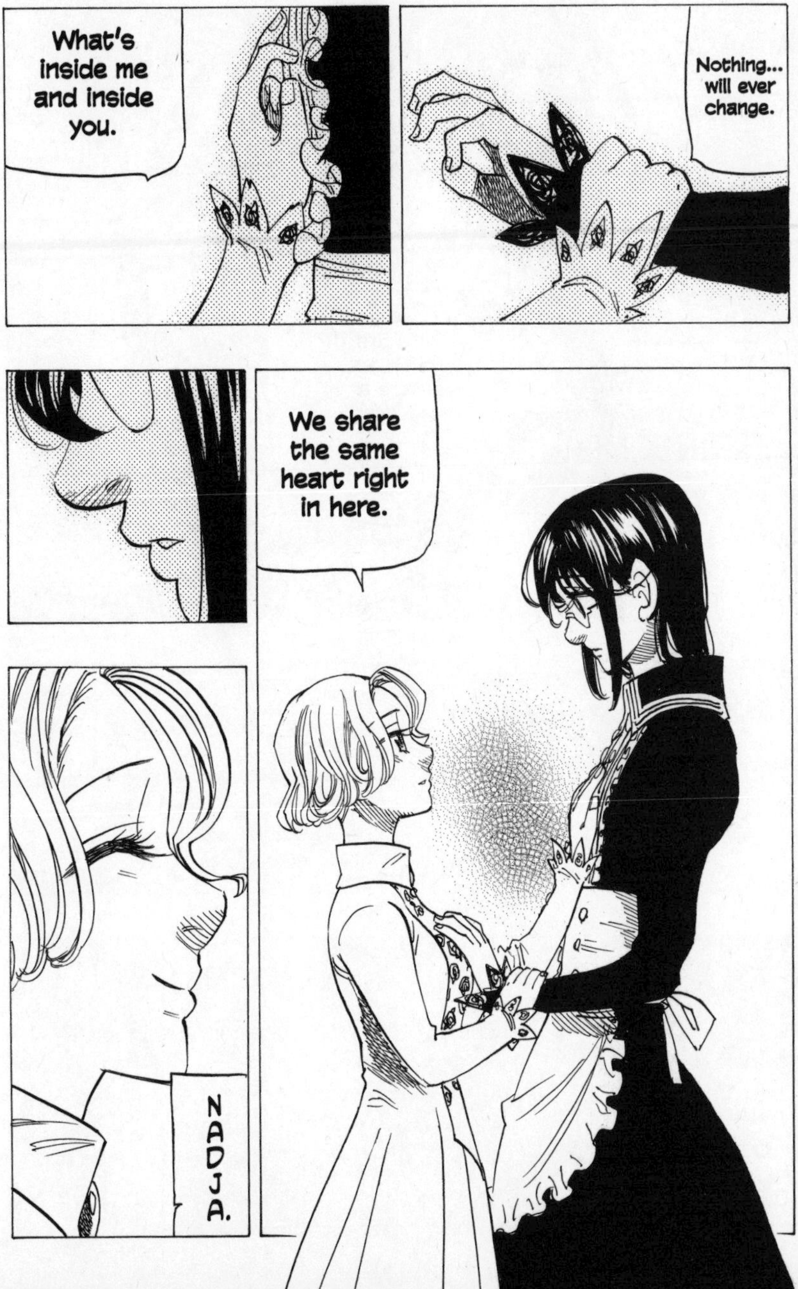
Nothing... will ever change.
What's inside me and inside you.
We share the same heart right in here.
NADJA.

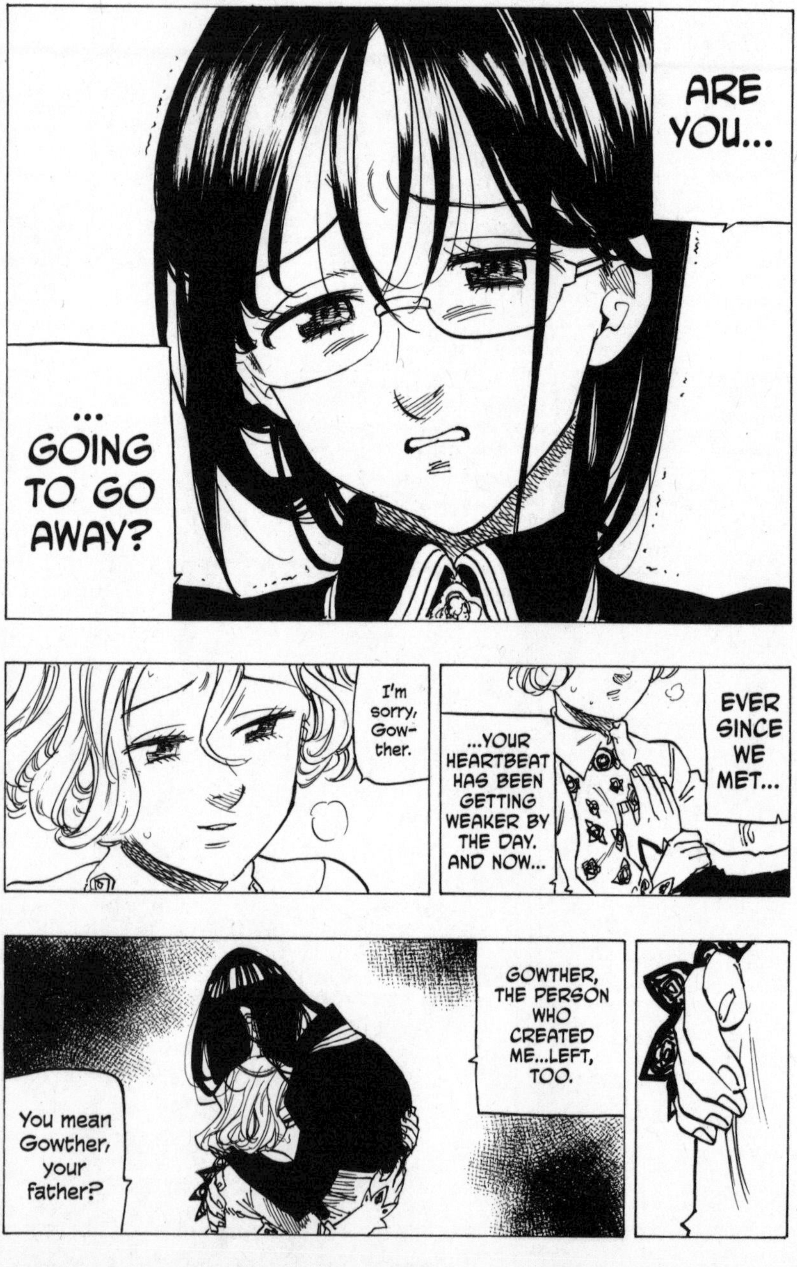
ARE YOU...
...GOING TO GO AWAY?
EVER SINCE WE MET...
...YOUR HEARTBEAT HAS BEEN GETTING WEAKER BY THE DAY. AND NOW...
I'm sorry, Gowther.
GOWTHER, THE PERSON WHO CREATED ME...LEFT, TOO.
You mean Gowther, your father?

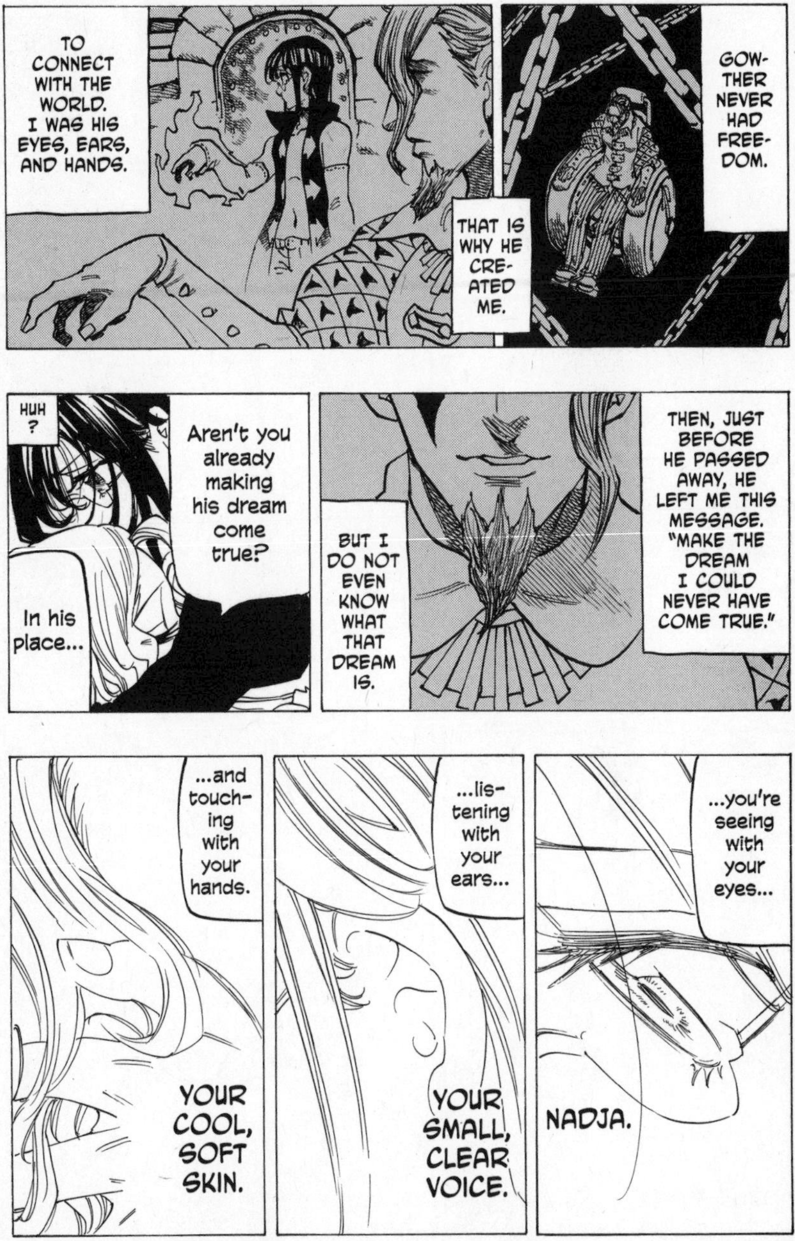
GOWTHER NEVER HAD FREEDOM.
THAT IS WHY HE CREATED ME.
TO CONNECT WITH THE WORLD. I WAS HIS EYES, EARS, AND HANDS.
THEN, JUST BEFORE HE PASSED AWAY, HE LEFT ME THIS MESSAGE. "MAKE THE DREAM I COULD NEVER HAVE COME TRUE."
BUT I DO NOT EVEN KNOW WHAT THAT DREAM IS.
Aren't you already making his dream come true?
HUH?
In his place...
...you're seeing with your eyes...
NADJA.
...listening with your ears...
YOUR SMALL, CLEAR VOICE.
...and touching with your hands.
YOUR COOL, SOFT SKIN.

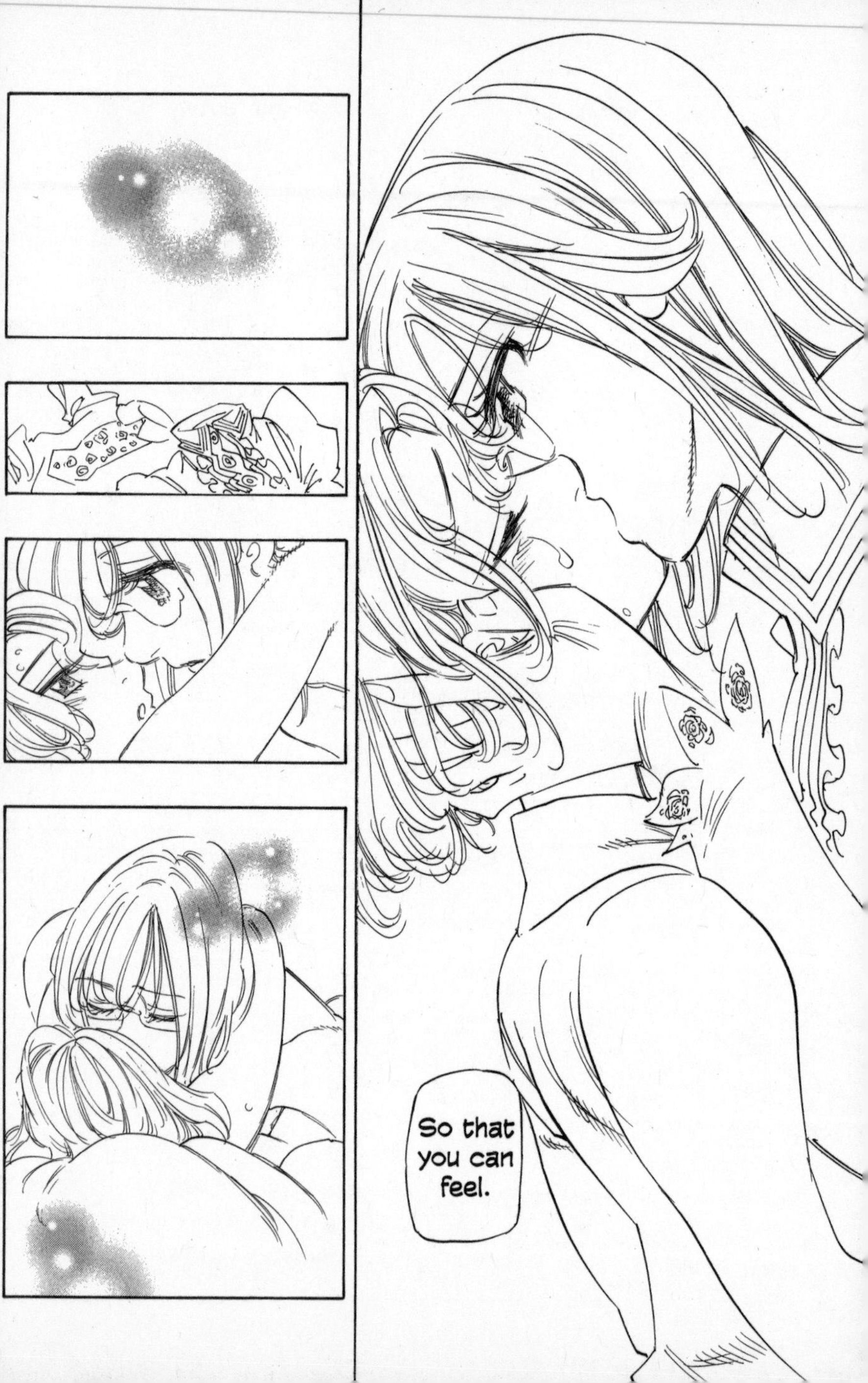
So that you can feel.

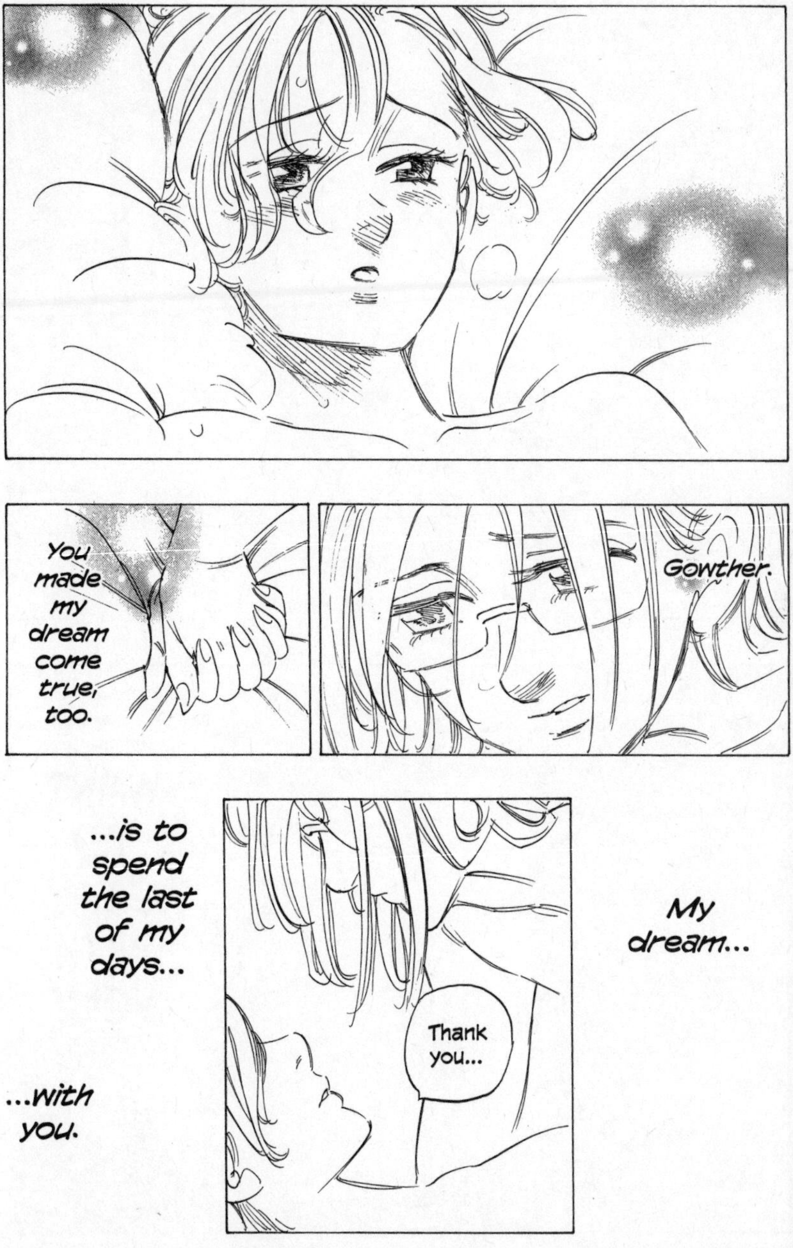
Gowther.
You made my dream come true, too.
My dream...
Thank you...
...is to spend the last of my days...
...with you.

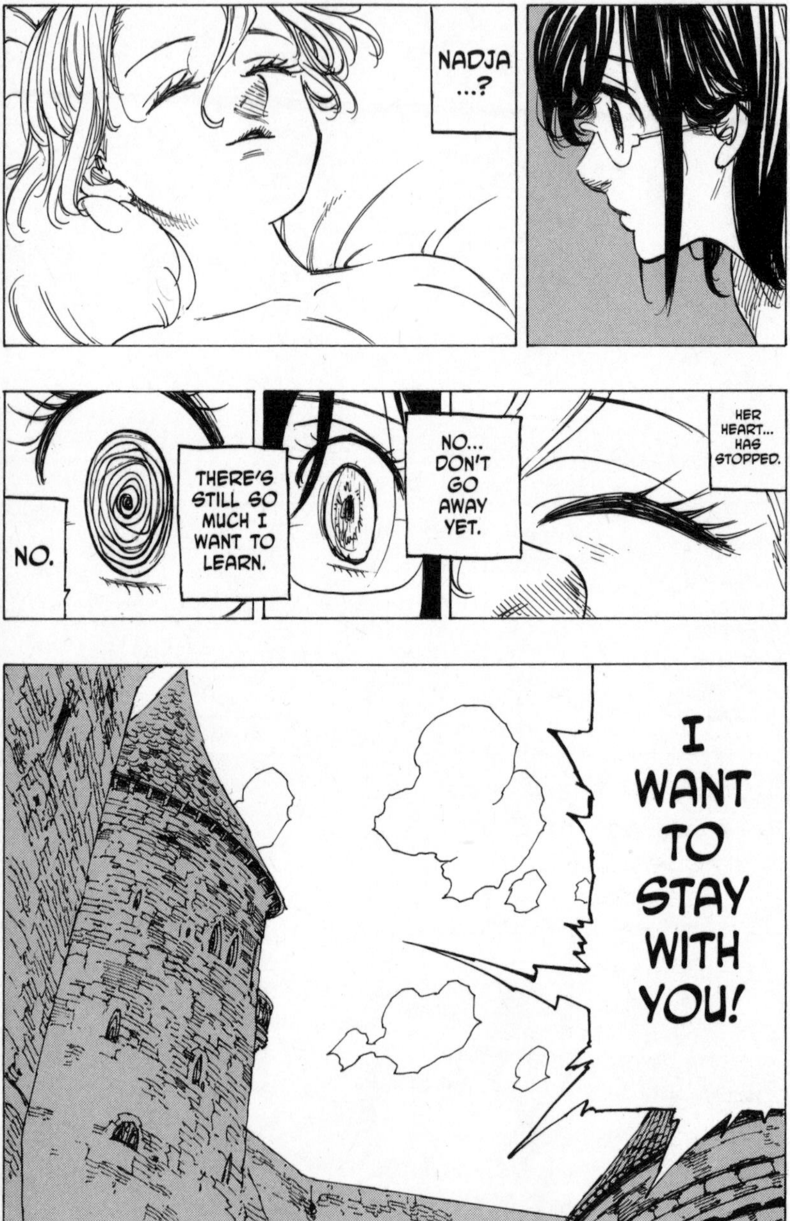
NADJA ...?
HER HEART... HAS STOPPED.
NO... DON'T GO AWAY YET.
THERE'S STILL SO MUCH I WANT TO LEARN.
NO.
I WANT TO STAY WITH YOU!

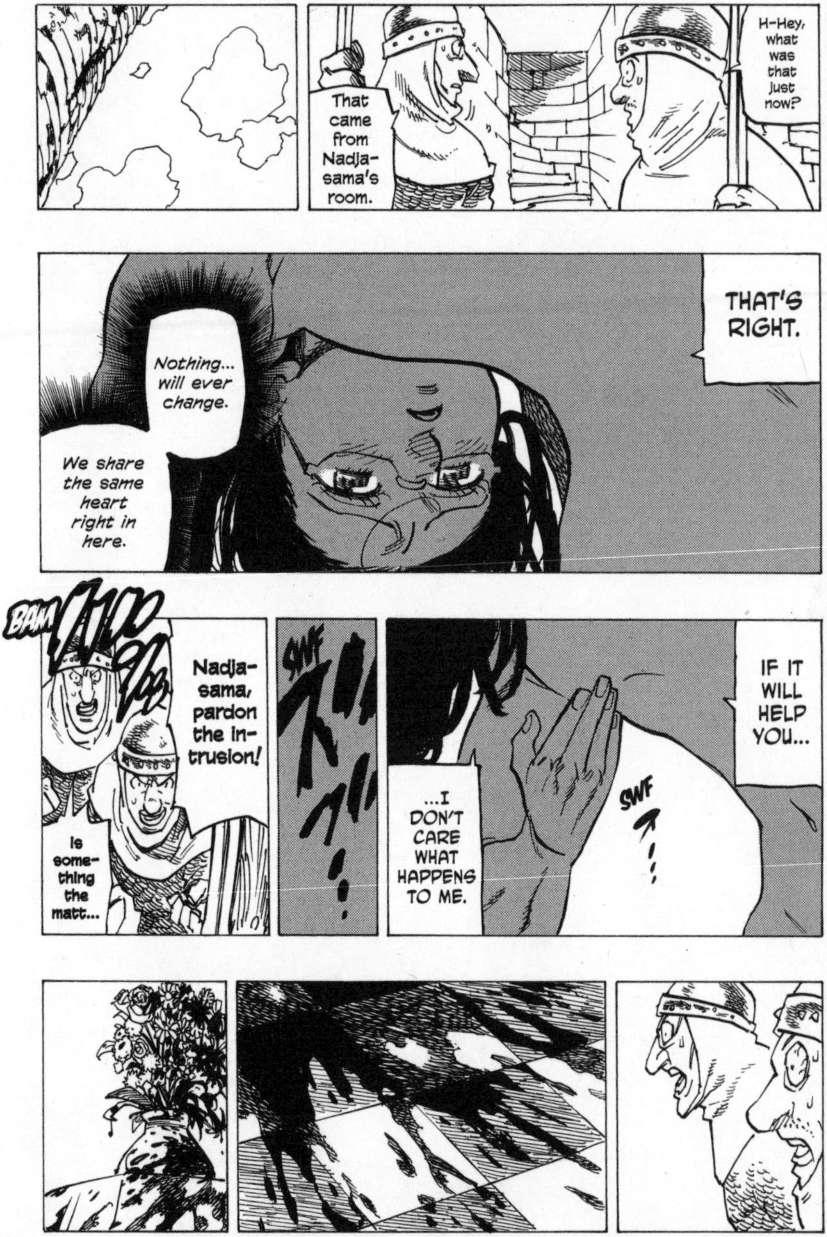
H-Hey, what was that just now?
That came from Nadja-sama's room.
THAT'S RIGHT.
Nothing... will ever change.
We share the same heart right in here.
IF IT WILL HELP YOU...
SWF
...I DON'T CARE WHAT HAPPENS TO ME.
SWF
BAM
Nadja-sama, pardon the intrusion!
Is something the matt...

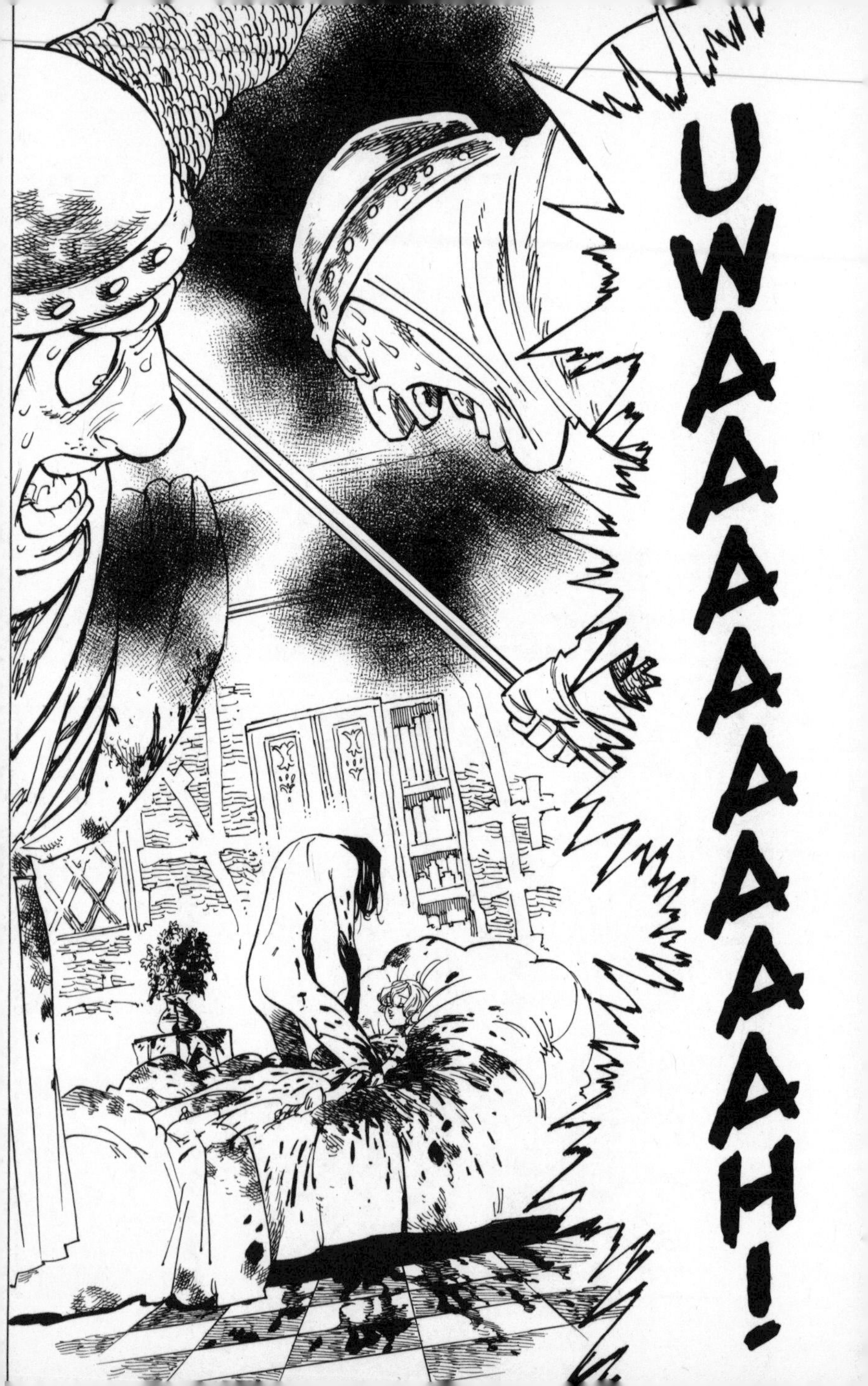
UWAAAAAAAH!

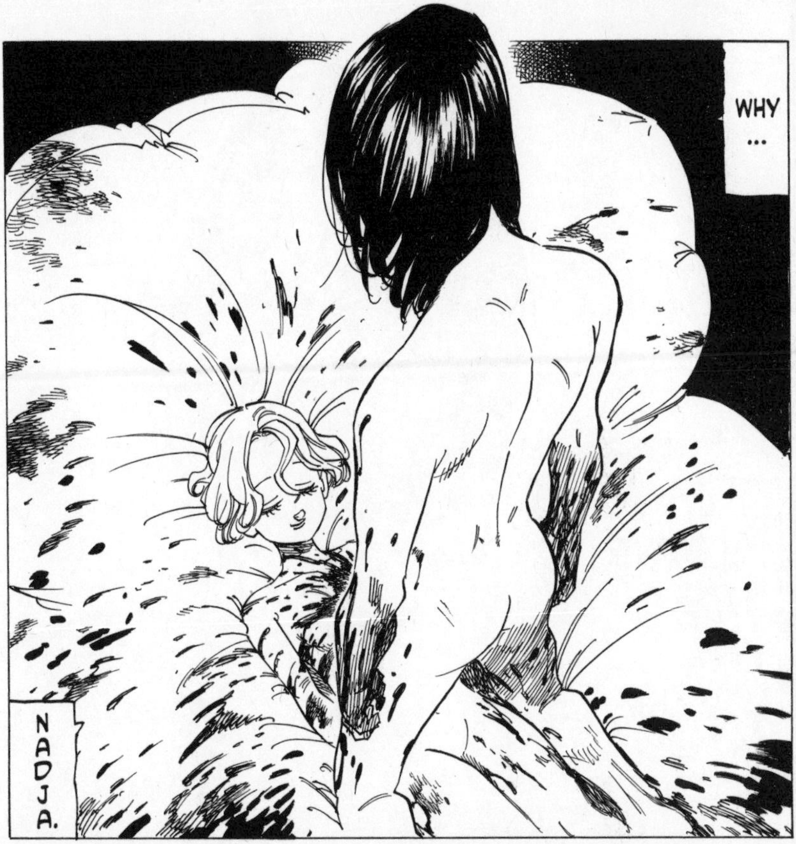
WHY ...
NADJA.
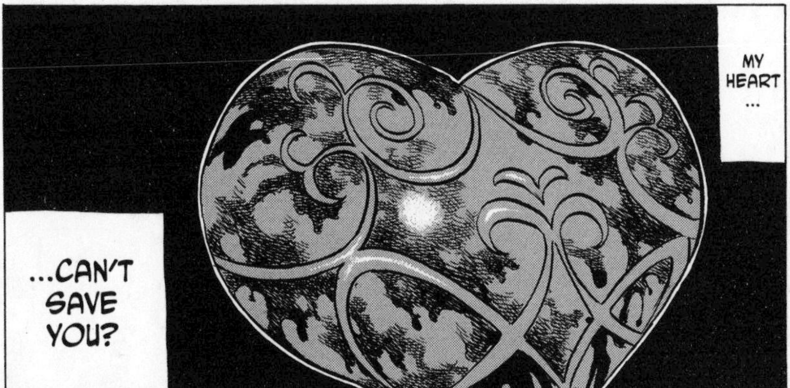
MY HEART ...
...CAN'T SAVE YOU?

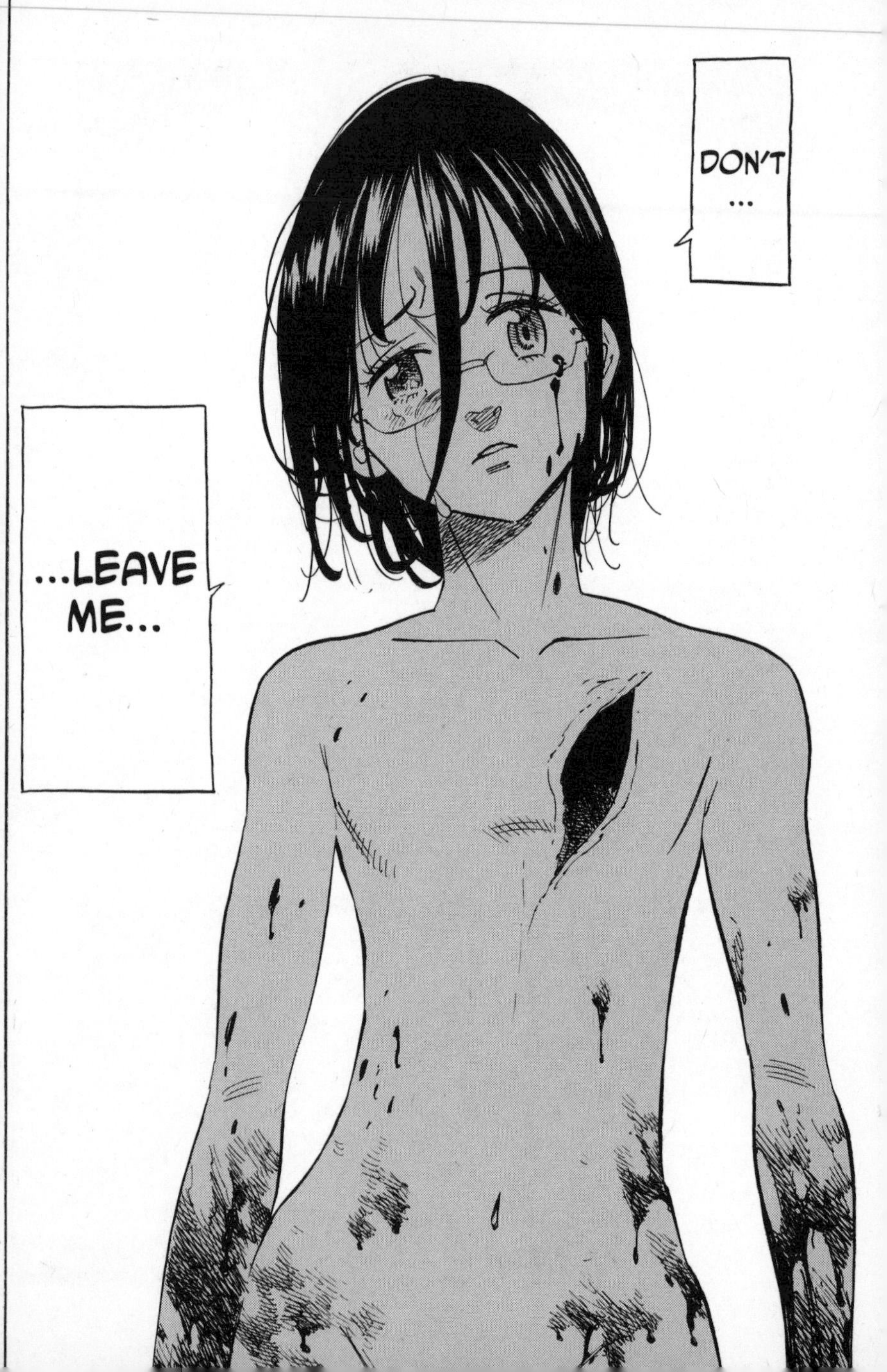
DON'T ...
...LEAVE ME...

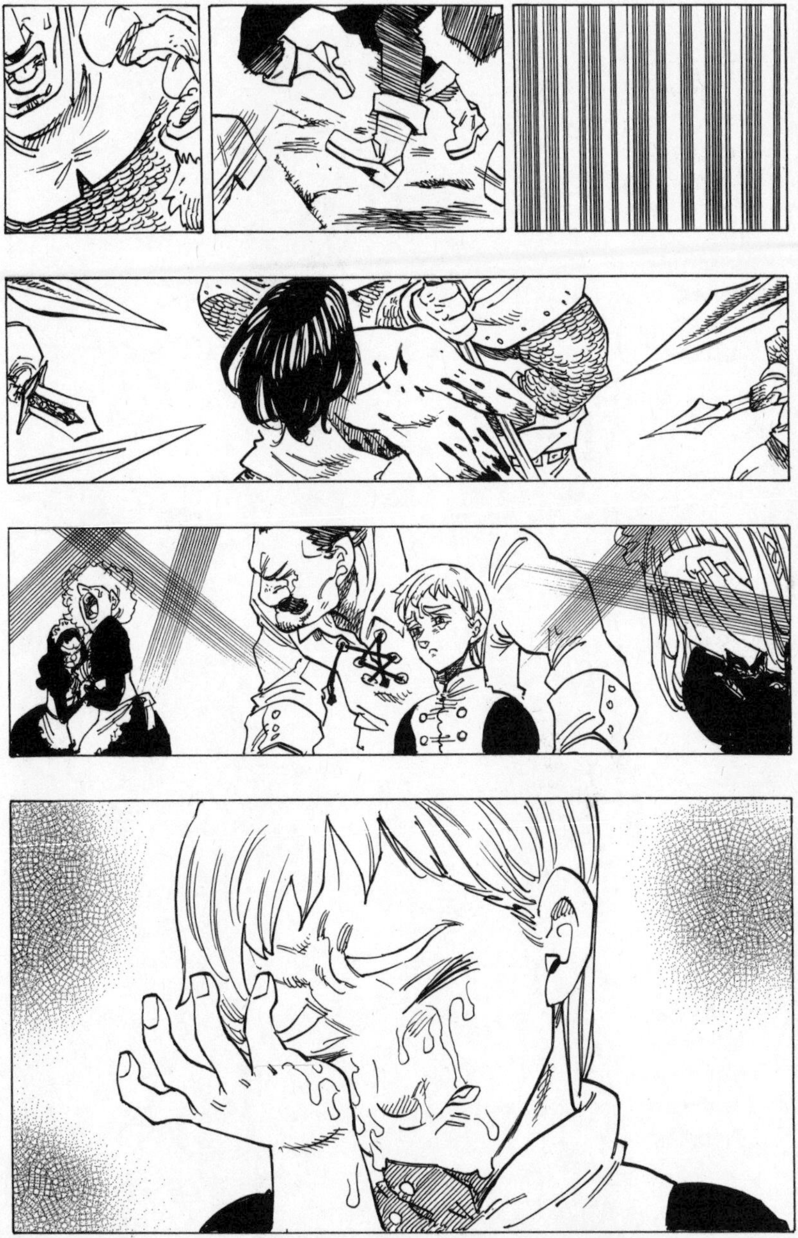

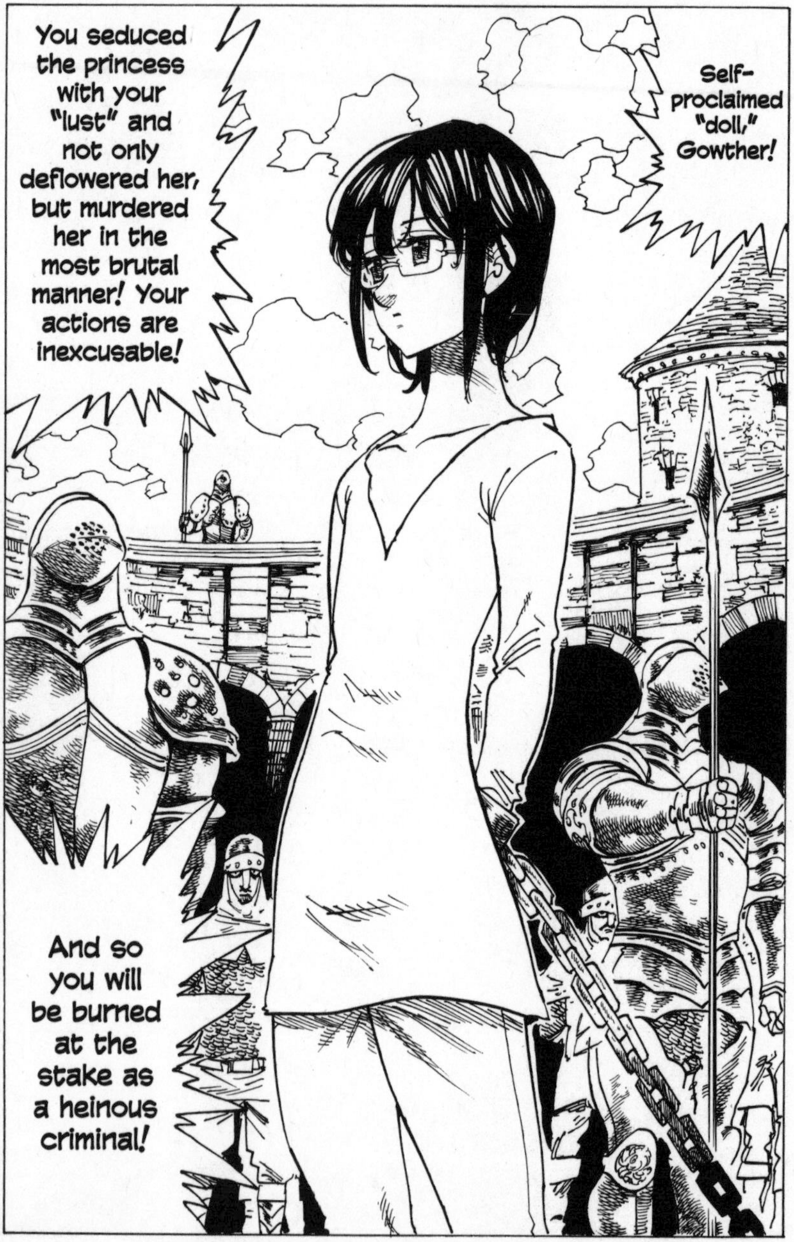
Self-proclaimed "doll," Gowther!
You seduced the princess with your "lust" and not only deflowered her, but murdered her in the most brutal manner! Your actions are inexcusable!
And so you will be burned at the stake as a heinous criminal!

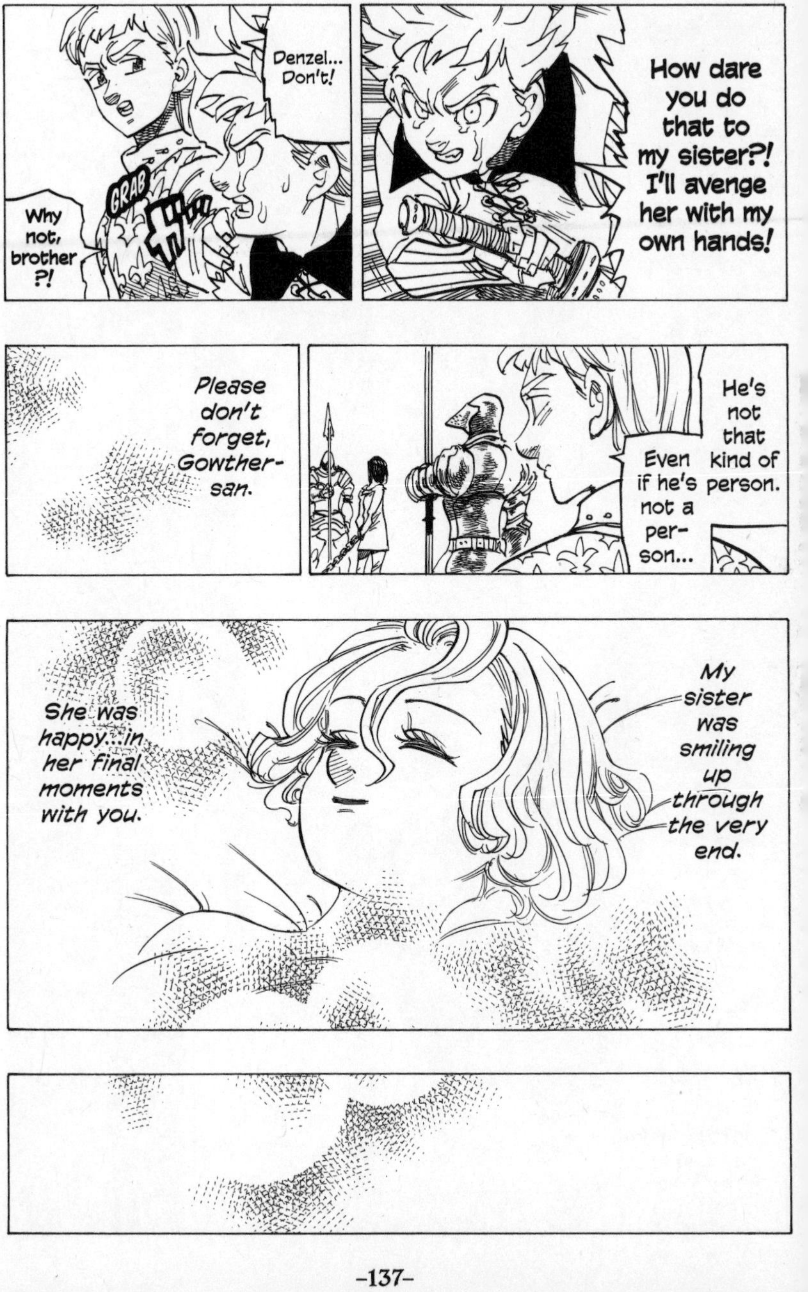
How dare you do that to my sister?! I'll avenge her with my own hands!
Denzel... Don't!
GRAB
Why not, brother?!
He's not that kind of person.
Even if he's not a per-son...
Please don't forget, Gowther-san.
My sister was smiling up through the very end.
She was happy...in her final moments with you.

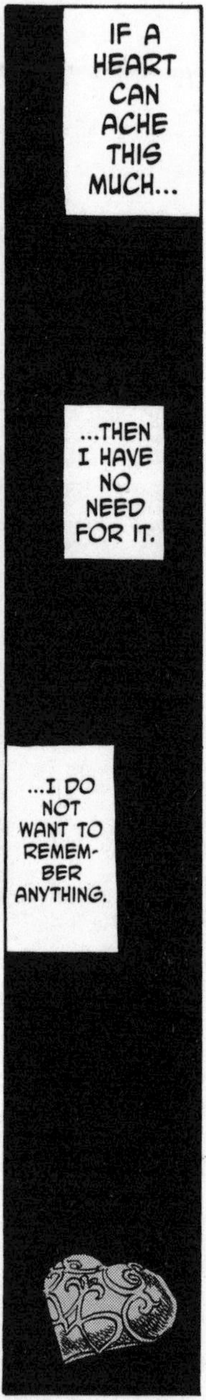
IF A HEART CAN ACHE THIS MUCH...
...THEN I HAVE NO NEED FOR IT.
...I DO NOT WANT TO REMEMBER ANYTHING.

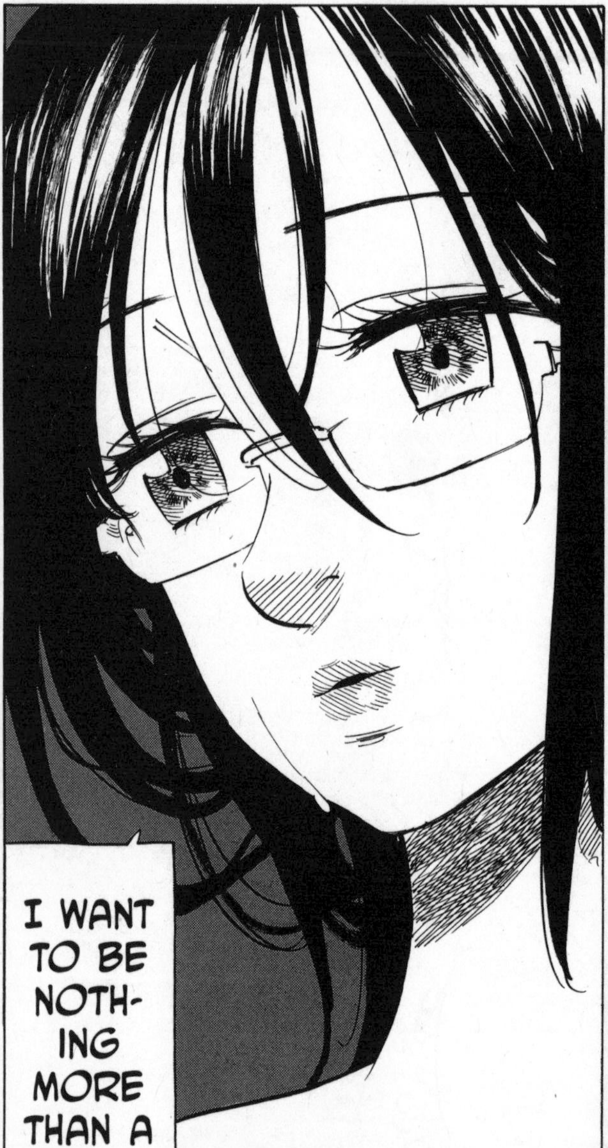
I WANT TO BE NOTHING MORE THAN A DOLL.

Chapter 212 - The Gift

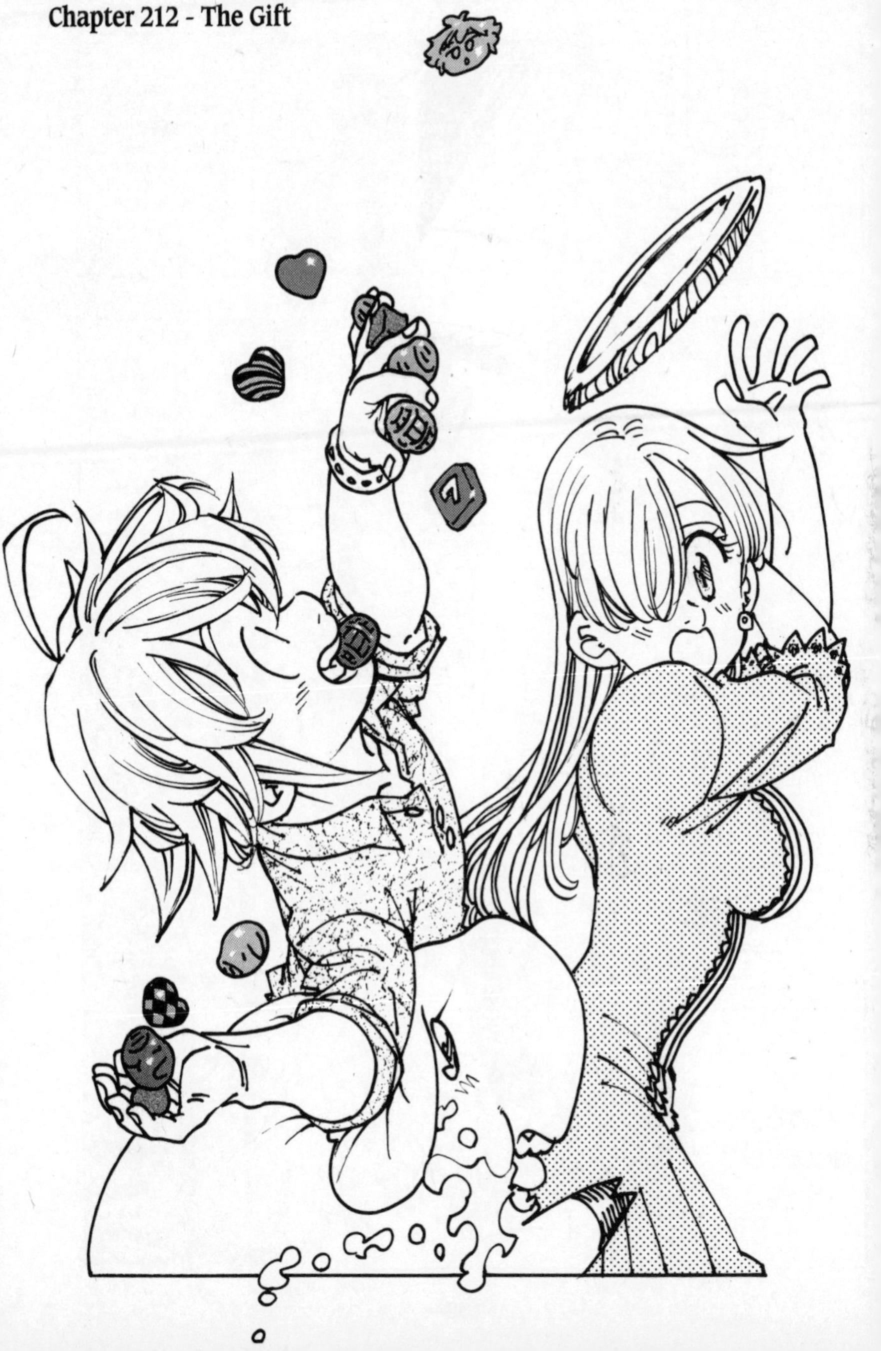

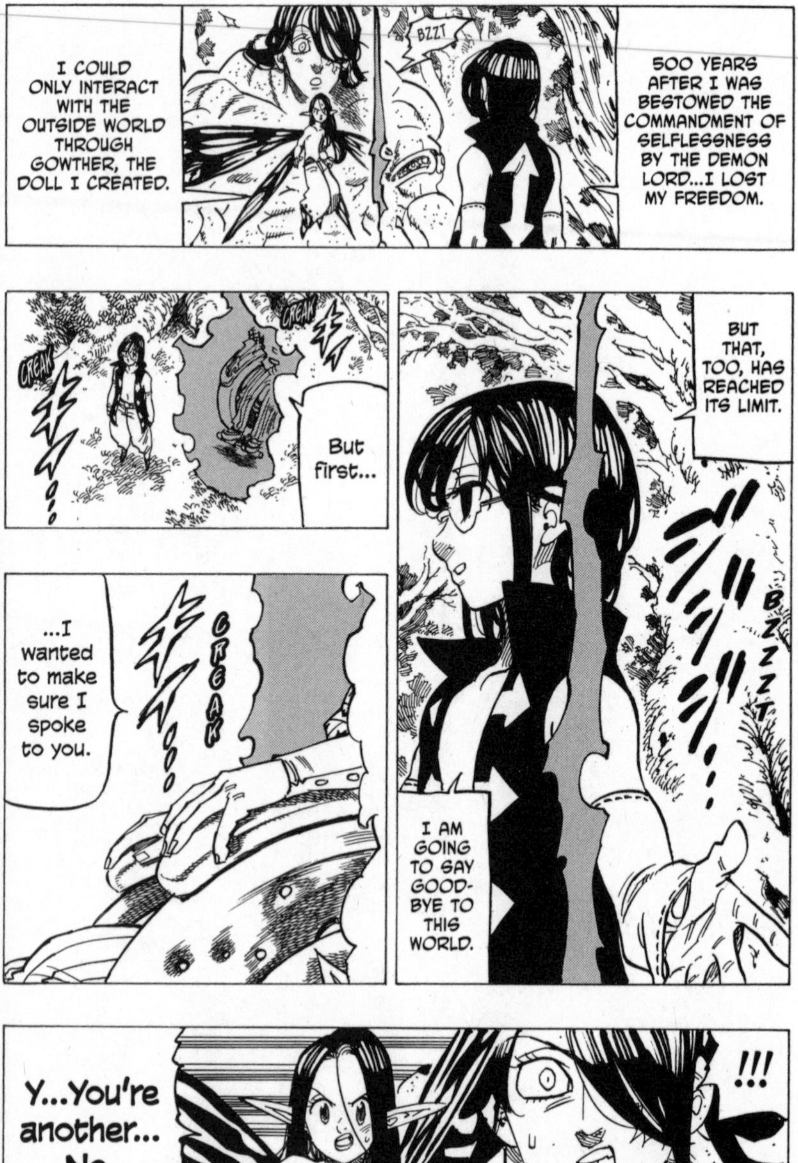
500 YEARS AFTER I WAS BESTOWED THE COMMANDMENT OF SELFLESSNESS BY THE DEMON LORD...I LOST MY FREEDOM.
BZZT
I COULD ONLY INTERACT WITH THE OUTSIDE WORLD THROUGH GOWTHER, THE DOLL I CREATED.
BUT THAT, TOO, HAS REACHED ITS LIMIT.
BZZZT
I AM GOING TO SAY GOOD-BYE TO THIS WORLD.
CREAK
CREAK
But first...
CREAK
...I wanted to make sure I spoke to you.
!!!
Y...You're another... No.

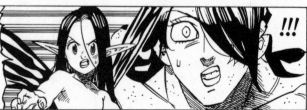

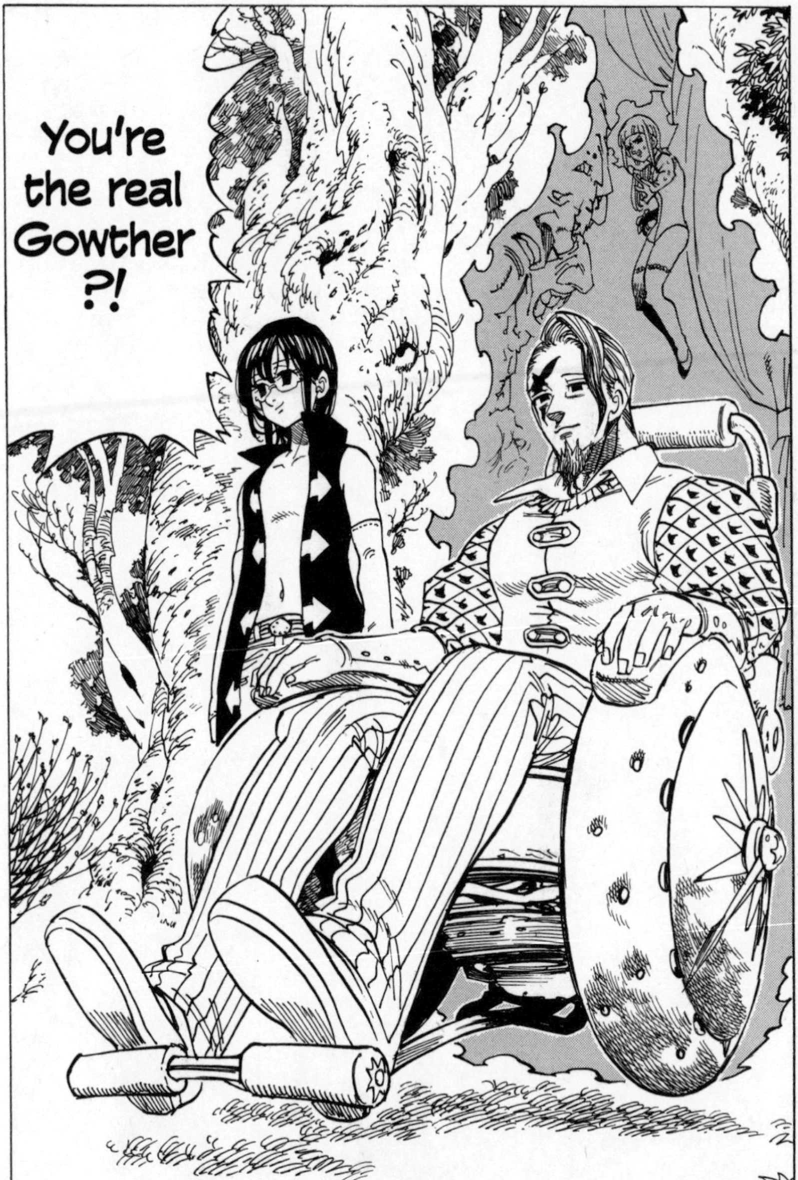
You're the real Gowther ?!

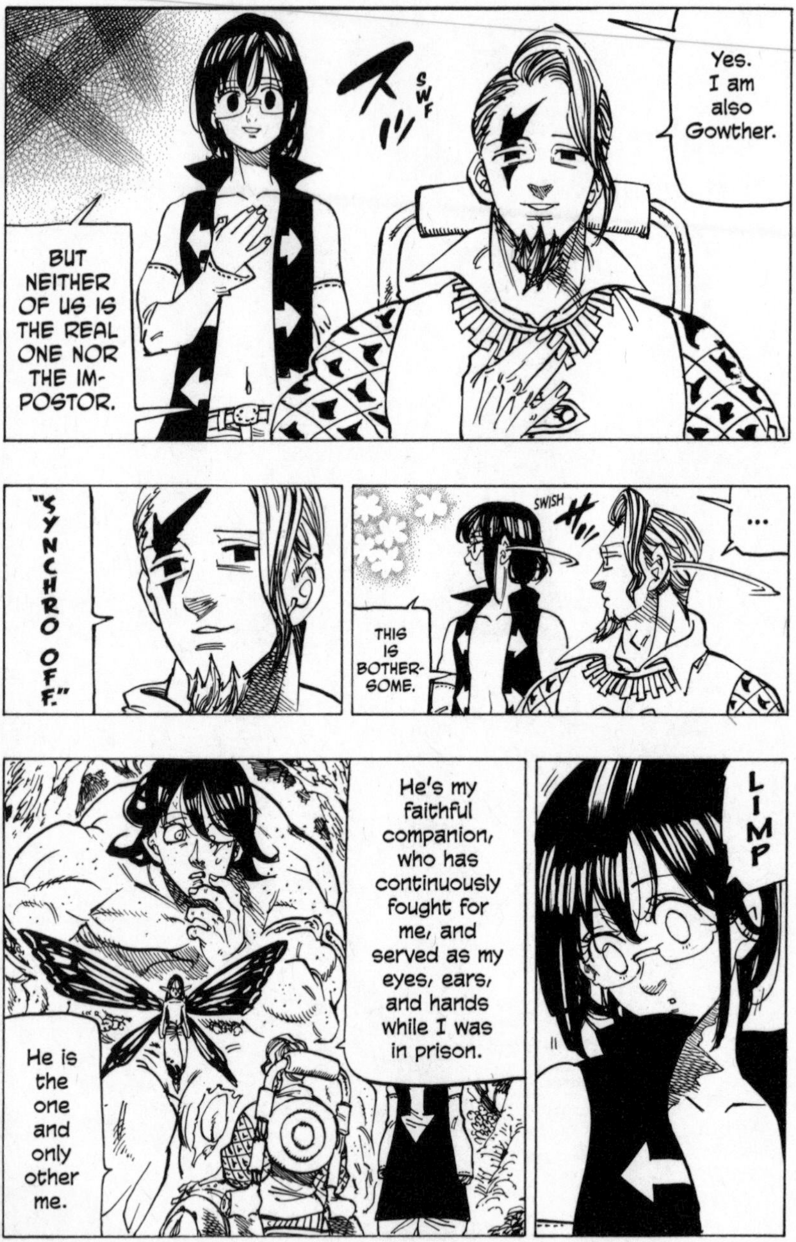
Yes. I am also Gowther.
SWF
BUT NEITHER OF US IS THE REAL ONE NOR THE IMPOSTOR.
...
SWISH
THIS IS BOTHERSOME.
"SYNCHRO OFF."
LIMP
He's my faithful companion, who has continuously fought for me, and served as my eyes, ears, and hands while I was in prison.
He is the one and only other me.

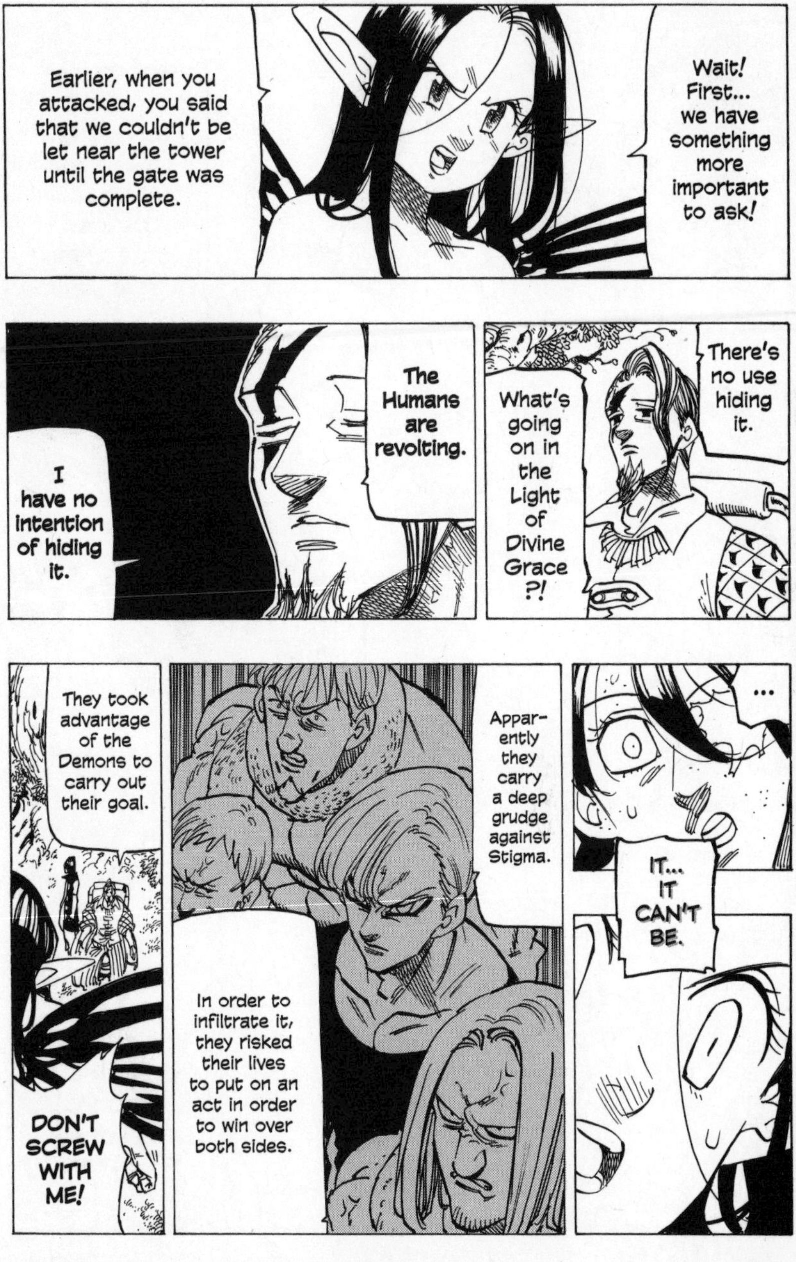
Wait! First... we have something more important to ask!
Earlier, when you attacked, you said that we couldn't be let near the tower until the gate was complete.
There's no use hiding it.
What's going on in the Light of Divine Grace?!
The Humans are revolting.
I have no intention of hiding it.
...
IT... IT CAN'T BE.
Apparently they carry a deep grudge against Stigma.
In order to infiltrate it, they risked their lives to put on an act in order to win over both sides.
They took advantage of the Demons to carry out their goal.
DON'T SCREW WITH ME!

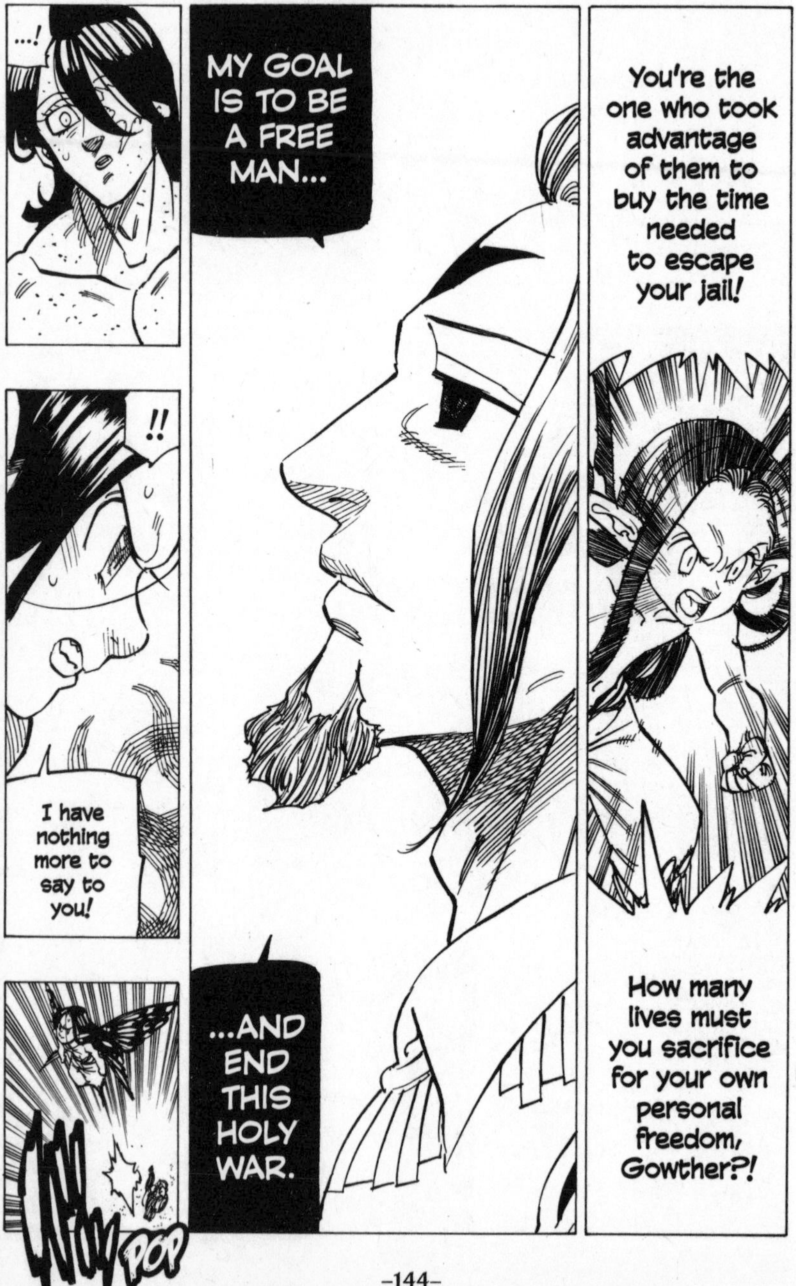
You're the one who took advantage of them to buy the time needed to escape your jail!
How many lives must you sacrifice for your own personal freedom, Gowther?!
MY GOAL IS TO BE A FREE MAN...
...AND END THIS HOLY WAR.
...!
!!
I have nothing more to say to you!
POP

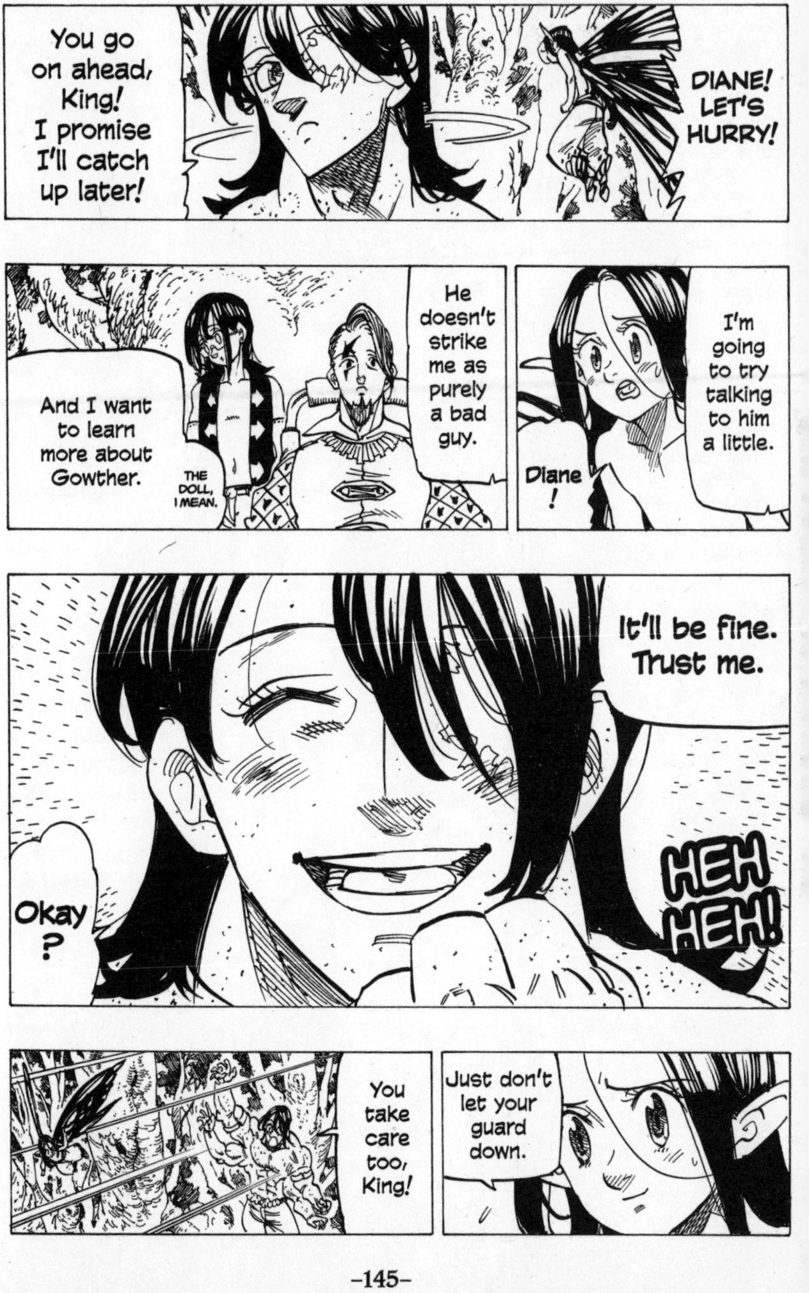
DIANE! LET'S HURRY!
You go on ahead, King! I promise I'll catch up later!
I'm going to try talking to him a little.
Diane!
He doesn't strike me as purely a bad guy.
And I want to learn more about Gowther.
THE DOLL, I MEAN.
It'll be fine. Trust me.
HEH HEH!
Okay?
Just don't let your guard down.
You take care too, King!

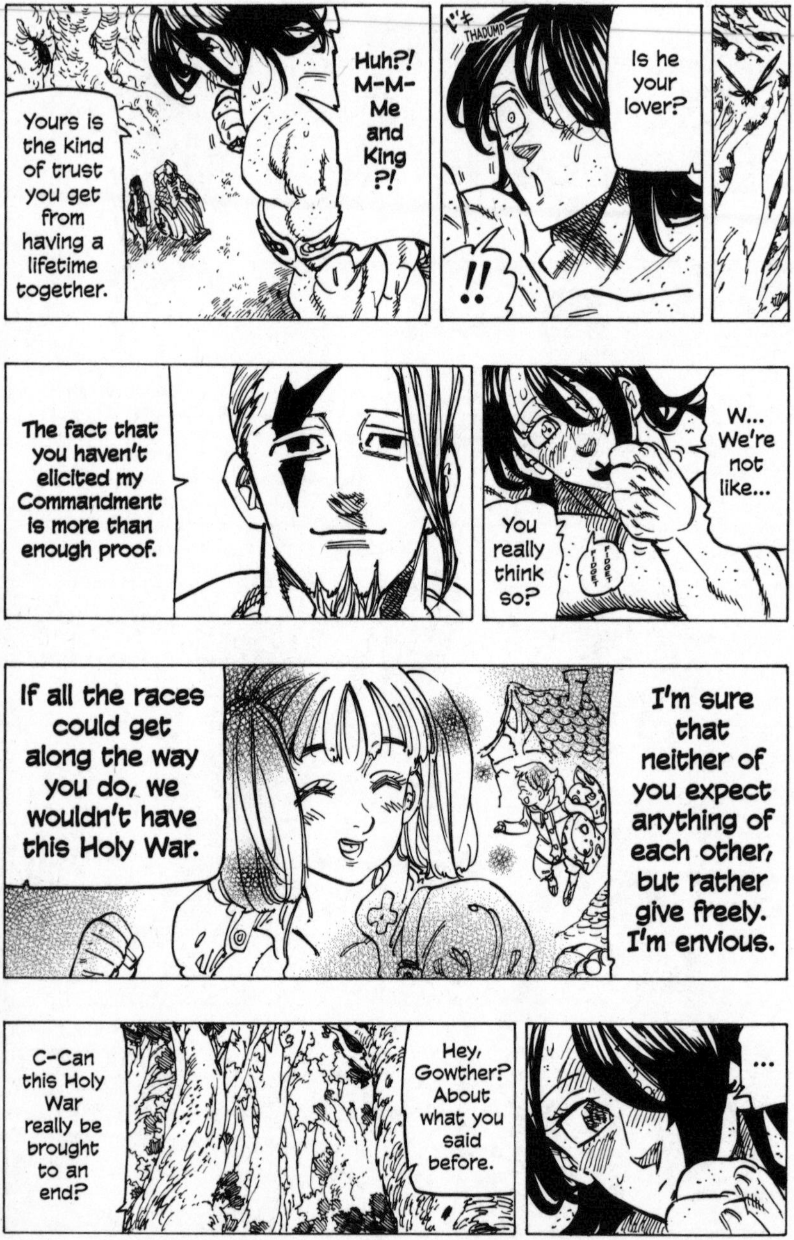
Is he your lover?
ドキ
THADUMP
!!
Huh?! M-M-Me and King?!
Yours is the kind of trust you get from having a lifetime together.
W... We're not like...
FIDGET FIDGET
You really think so?
The fact that you haven't elicited my Commandment is more than enough proof.
I'm sure that neither of you expect anything of each other, but rather give freely. I'm envious.
If all the races could get along the way you do, we wouldn't have this Holy War.
...
Hey, Gowther? About what you said before.
C-Can this Holy War really be brought to an end?

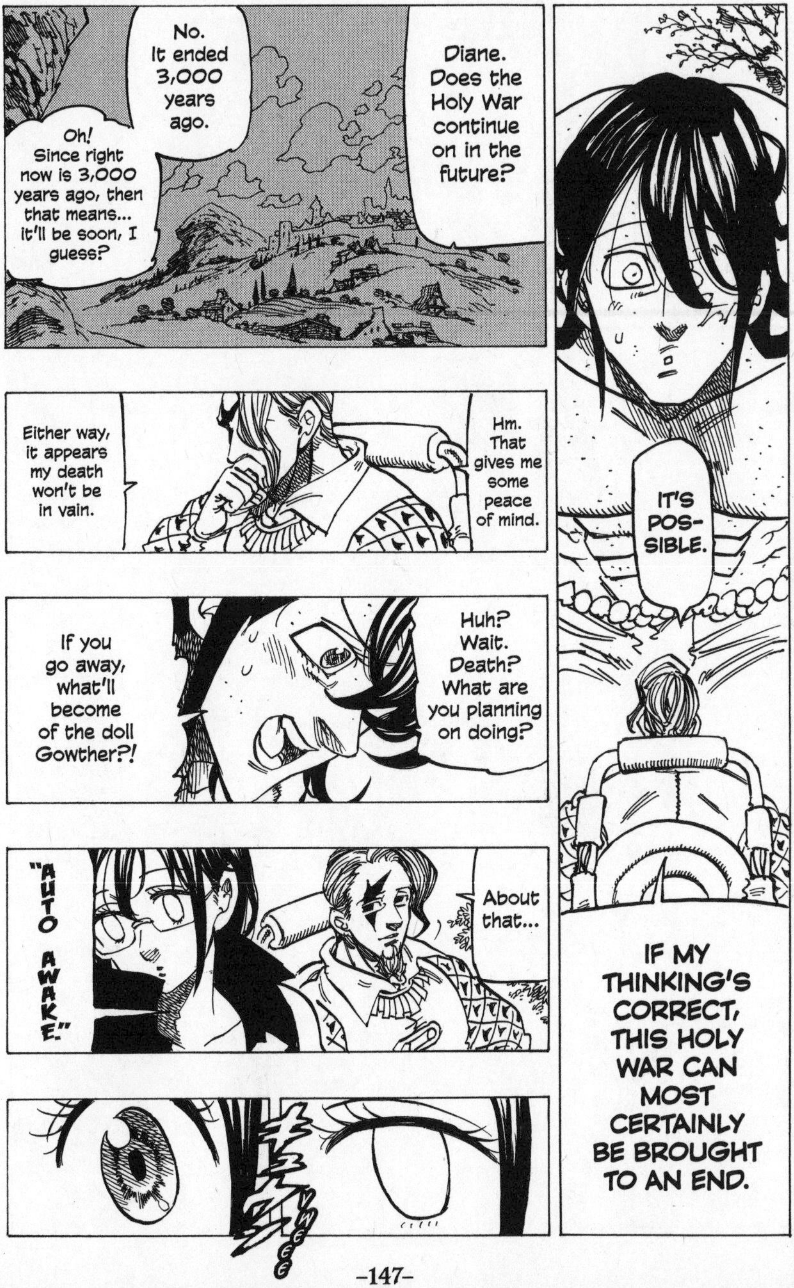
IT'S POSSIBLE.
IF MY THINKING'S CORRECT, THIS HOLY WAR CAN MOST CERTAINLY BE BROUGHT TO AN END.
Diane. Does the Holy War continue on in the future?
No. It ended 3,000 years ago.
Oh! Since right now is 3,000 years ago, then that means... it'll be soon, I guess?
Hm. That gives me some peace of mind.
Either way, it appears my death won't be in vain.
Huh? Wait. Death? What are you planning on doing?
If you go away, what'll become of the doll Gowther?!
About that...
"AUTO AWAKE."
VWEEE

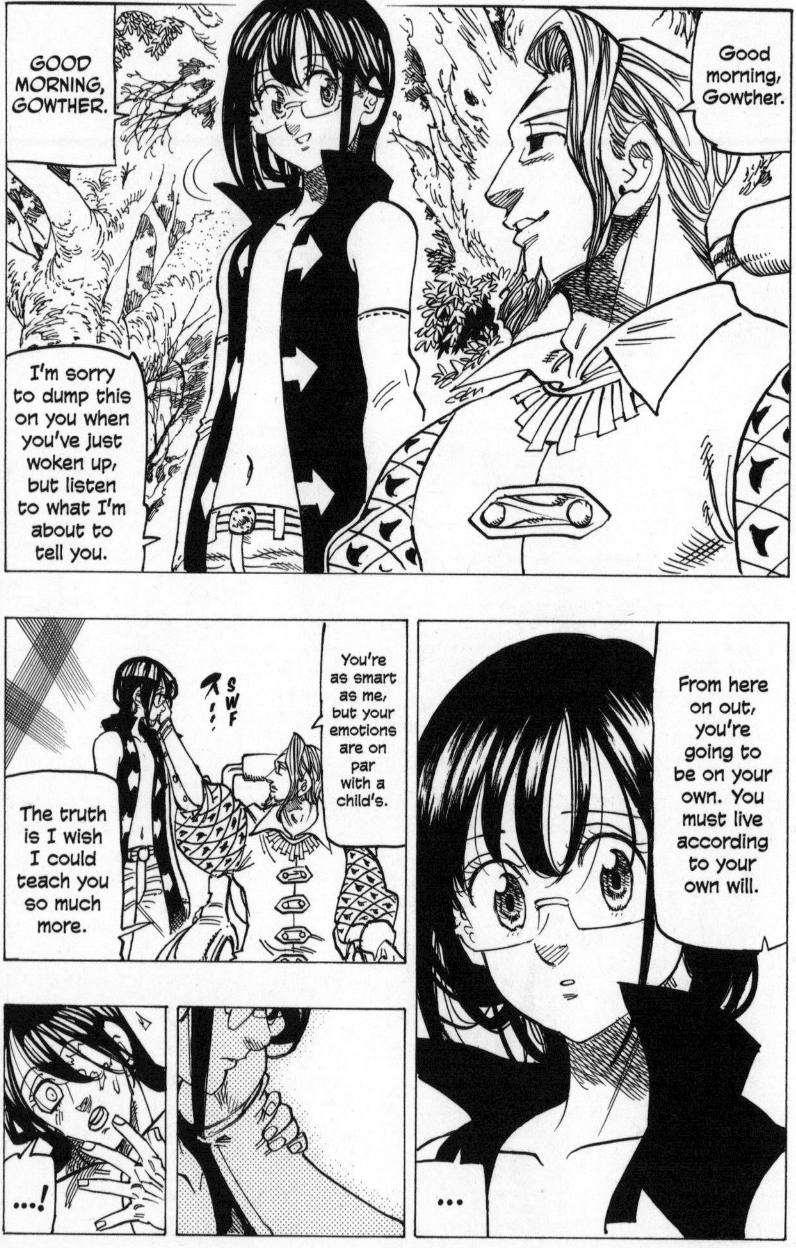
Good morning, Gowther.
GOOD MORNING, GOWTHER.
I'm sorry to dump this on you when you've just woken up, but listen to what I'm about to tell you.
From here on out, you're going to be on your own. You must live according to your own will.
...
You're as smart as me, but your emotions are on par with a child's.
SWF
The truth is I wish I could teach you so much more.
...!

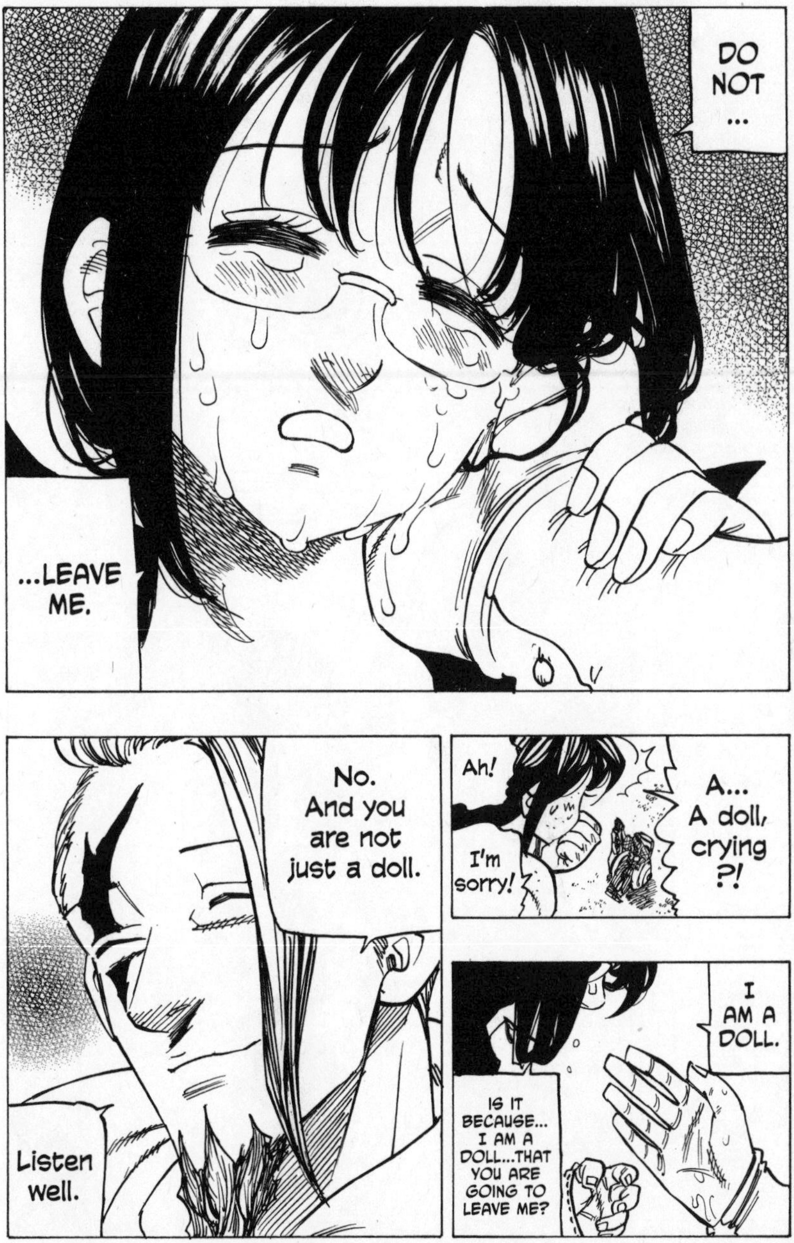
DO NOT ...
...LEAVE ME.
A... A doll, crying ?!
Ah!
I'm sorry!
I AM A DOLL.
IS IT BECAUSE... I AM A DOLL...THAT YOU ARE GOING TO LEAVE ME?
No. And you are not just a doll.
Listen well.

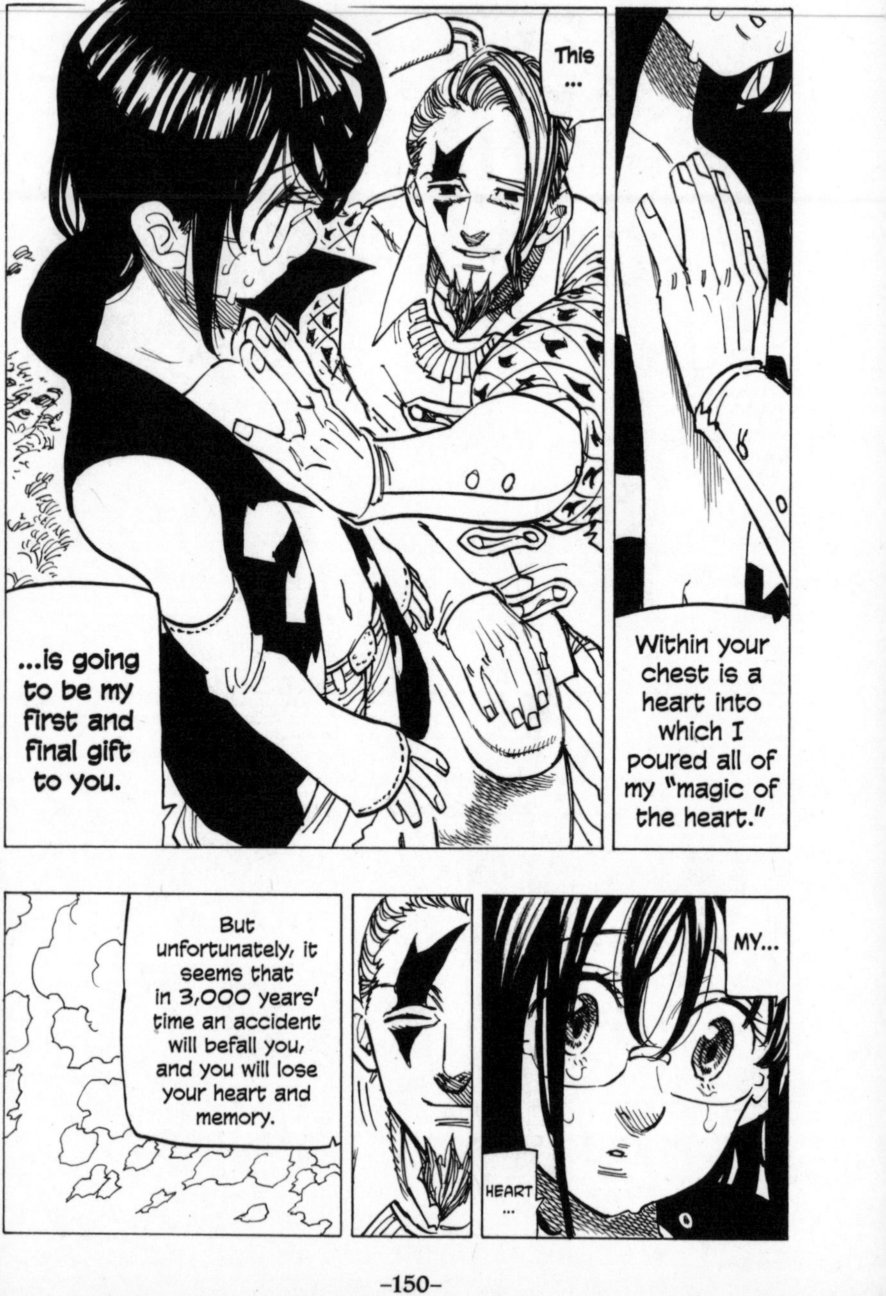
Within your chest is a heart into which I poured all of my "magic of the heart."
This ...
...is going to be my first and final gift to you.
MY...
HEART ...
But unfortunately, it seems that in 3,000 years' time an accident will befall you, and you will lose your heart and memory.

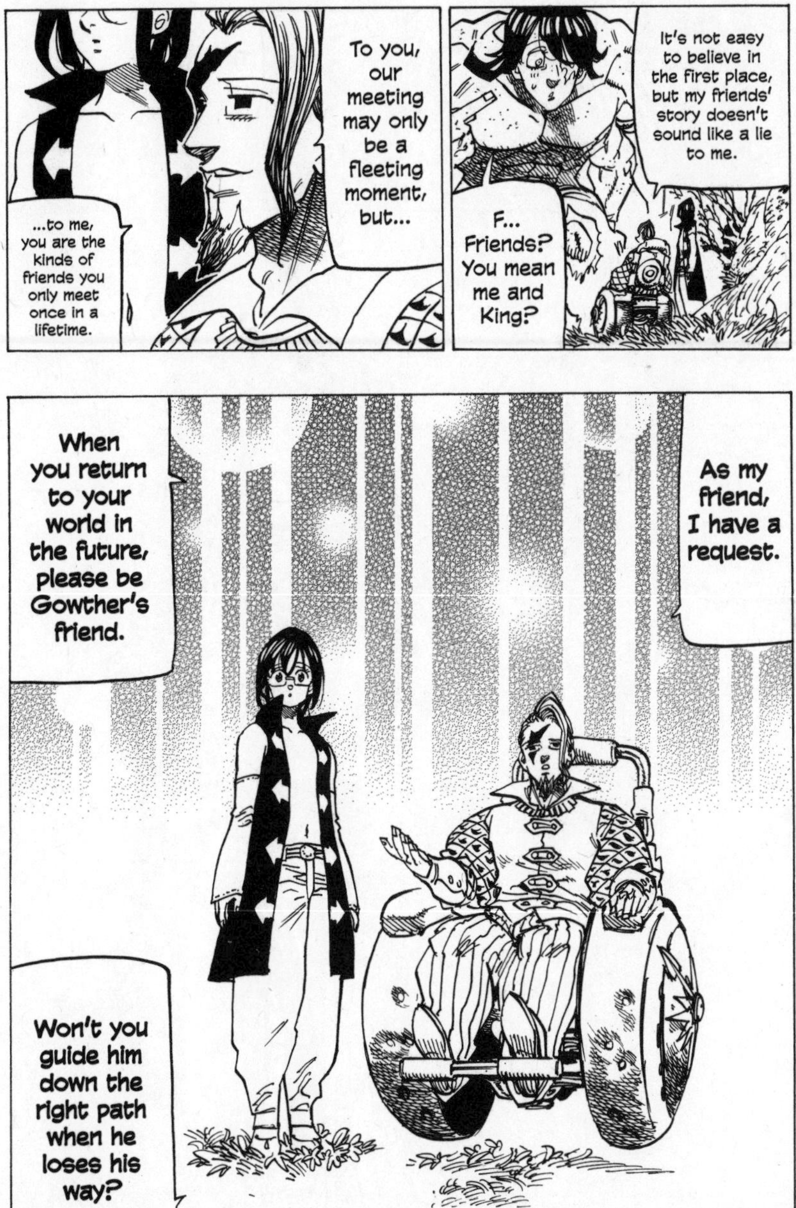

It's not easy to believe in the first place, but my friends' story doesn't sound like a lie to me.
F... Friends? You mean me and King?
To you, our meeting may only be a fleeting moment, but...
...to me, you are the kinds of friends you only meet once in a lifetime.
As my friend, I have a request.
When you return to your world in the future, please be Gowther's friend.
Won't you guide him down the right path when he loses his way?

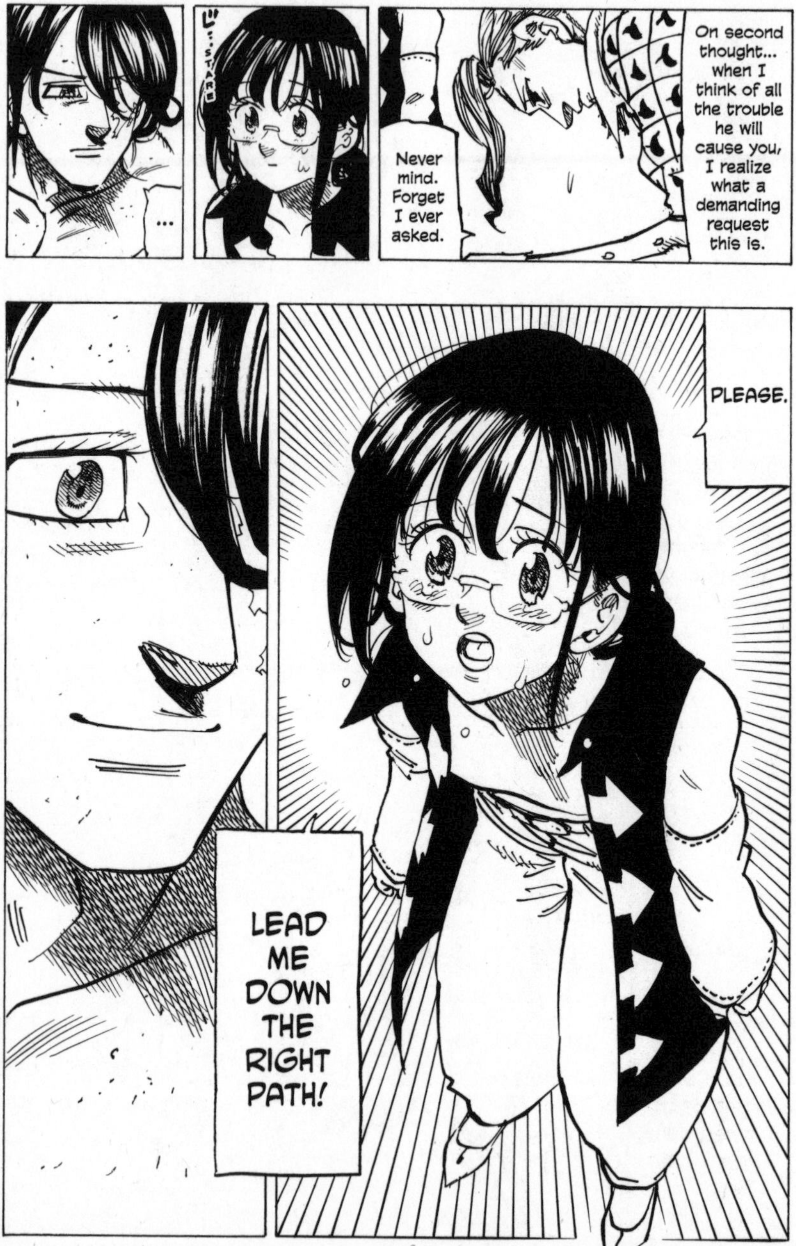
On second thought... when I think of all the trouble he will cause you, I realize what a demanding request this is.
Never mind. Forget I ever asked.
ジ…STARE
...
PLEASE.
LEAD ME DOWN THE RIGHT PATH!

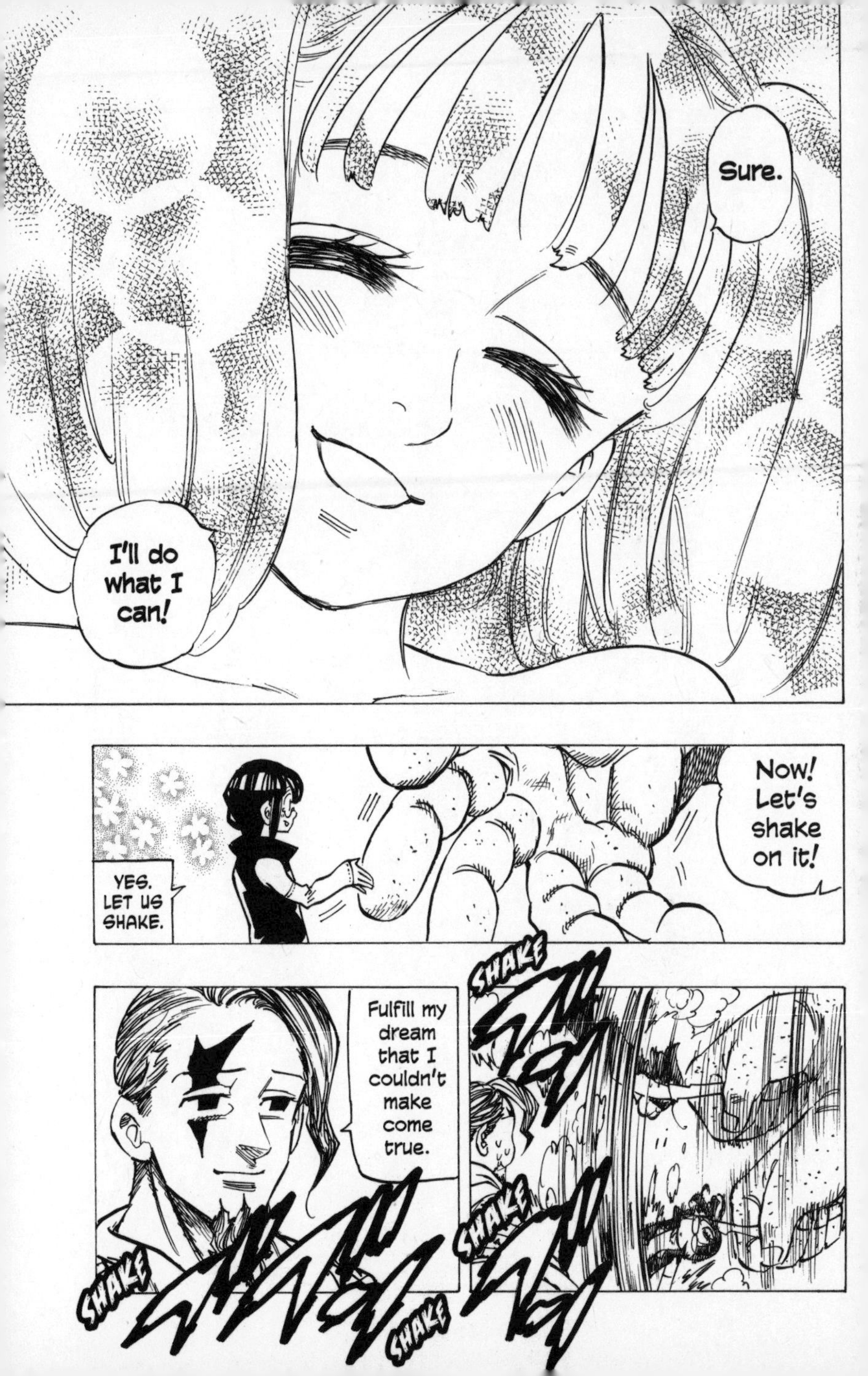
Sure.
I'll do what I can!
Now! Let's shake on it!
YES. LET US SHAKE.
SHAKE
SHAKE
SHAKE
Fulfill my dream that I couldn't make come true.
SHAKE

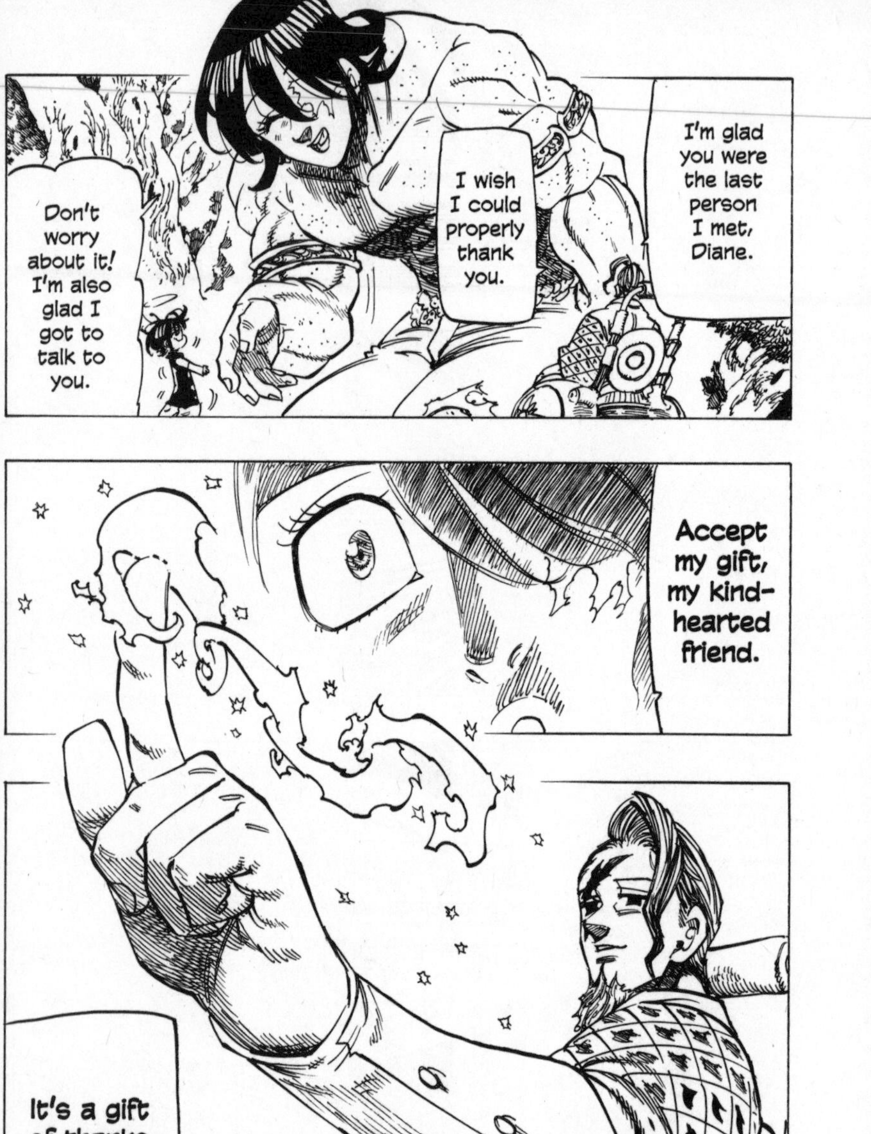
I'm glad you were the last person I met, Diane.
I wish I could properly thank you.
Don't worry about it! I'm also glad I got to talk to you.
Accept my gift, my kind-hearted friend.
It's a gift of thanks from both Gowthers.

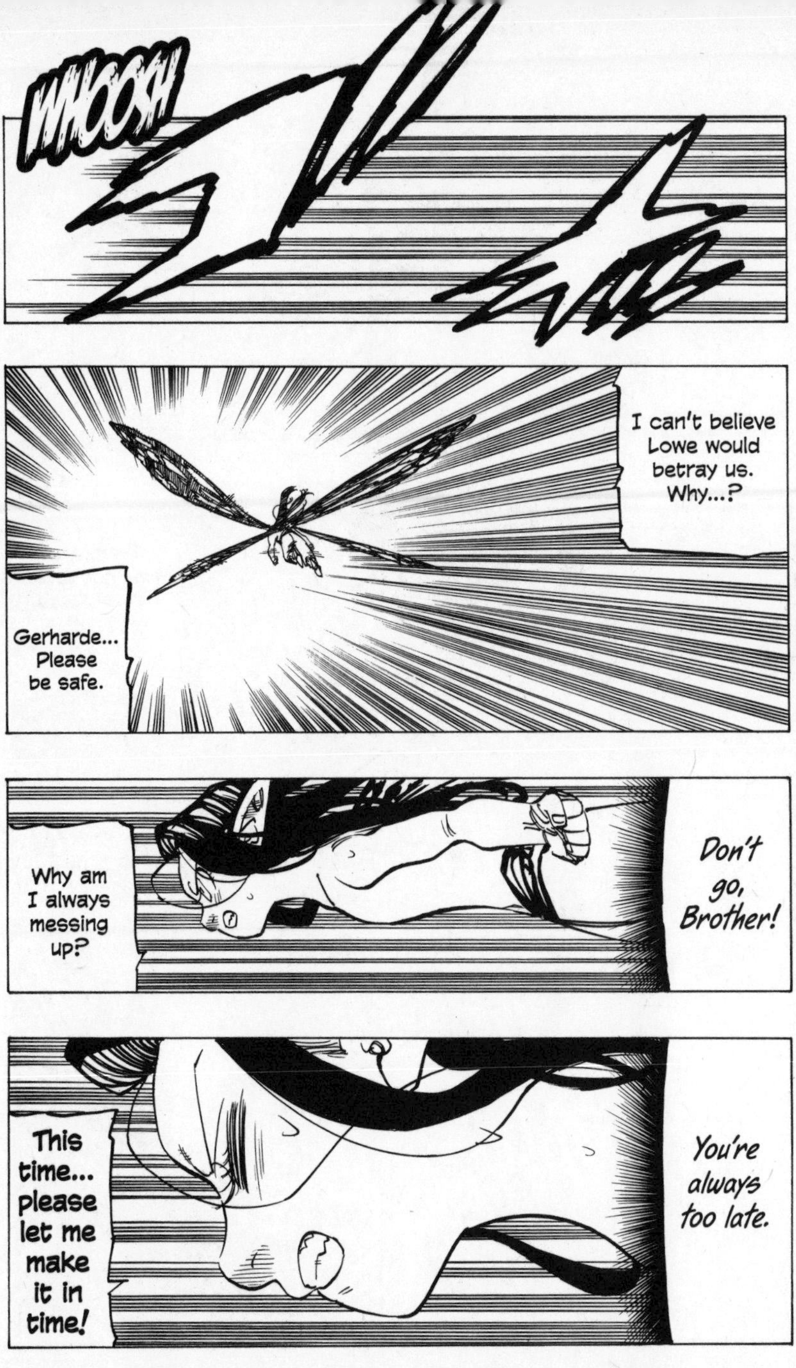
WHOOSH
I can't believe Lowe would betray us. Why...?
Gerharde... Please be safe.
Don't go, Brother!
Why am I always messing up?
You're always too late.
This time... please let me make it in time!

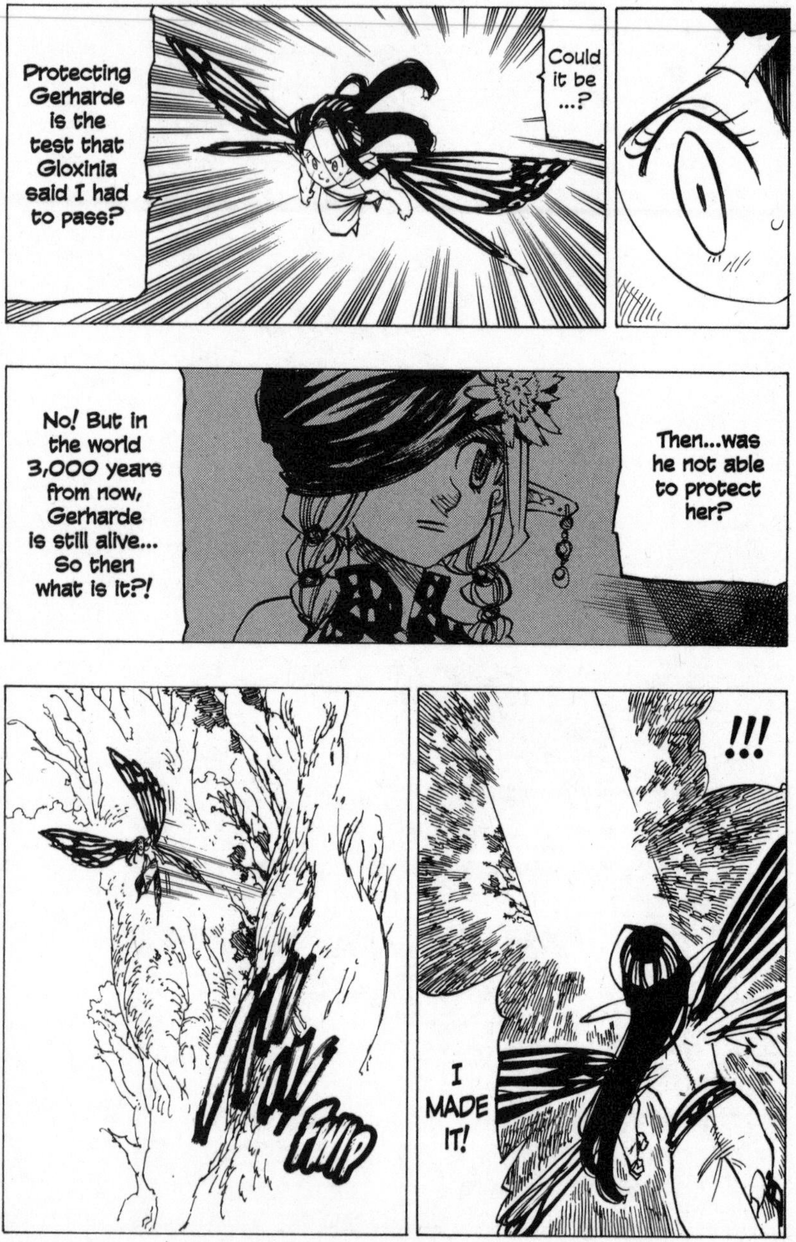
Could it be ...?
Protecting Gerharde is the test that Gloxinia said I had to pass?
Then...was he not able to protect her?
No! But in the world 3,000 years from now, Gerharde is still alive... So then what is it?!
!!!
I MADE IT!
FWIP

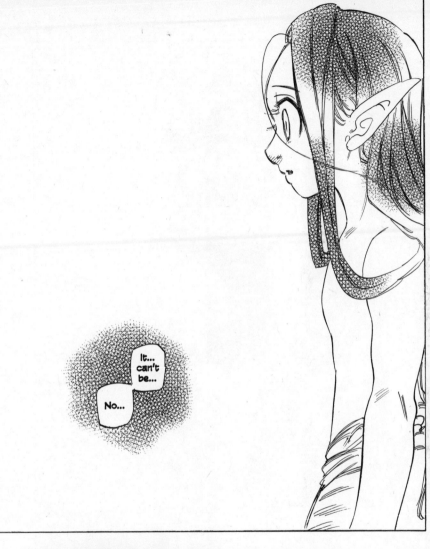

It...
can't
be...

No...

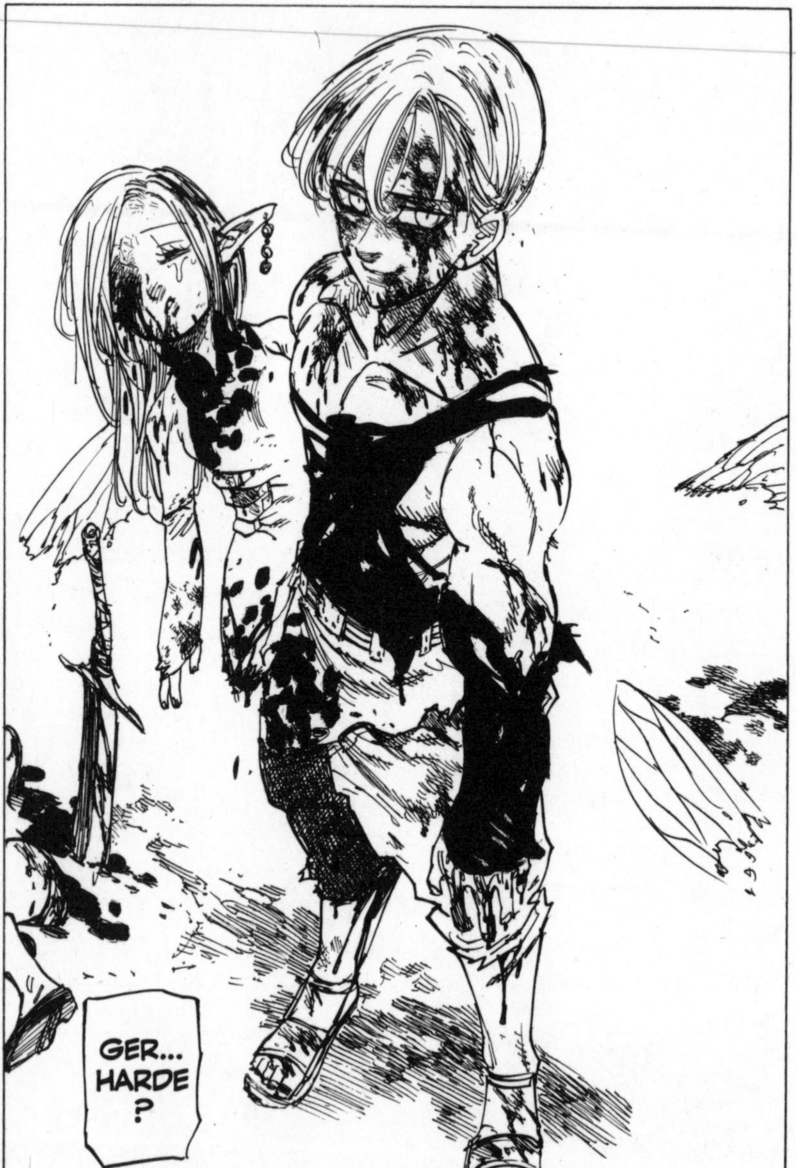
GER... HARDE ?

THE SEVEN DEADLY SINS

Chapter 213 - We Call That Love

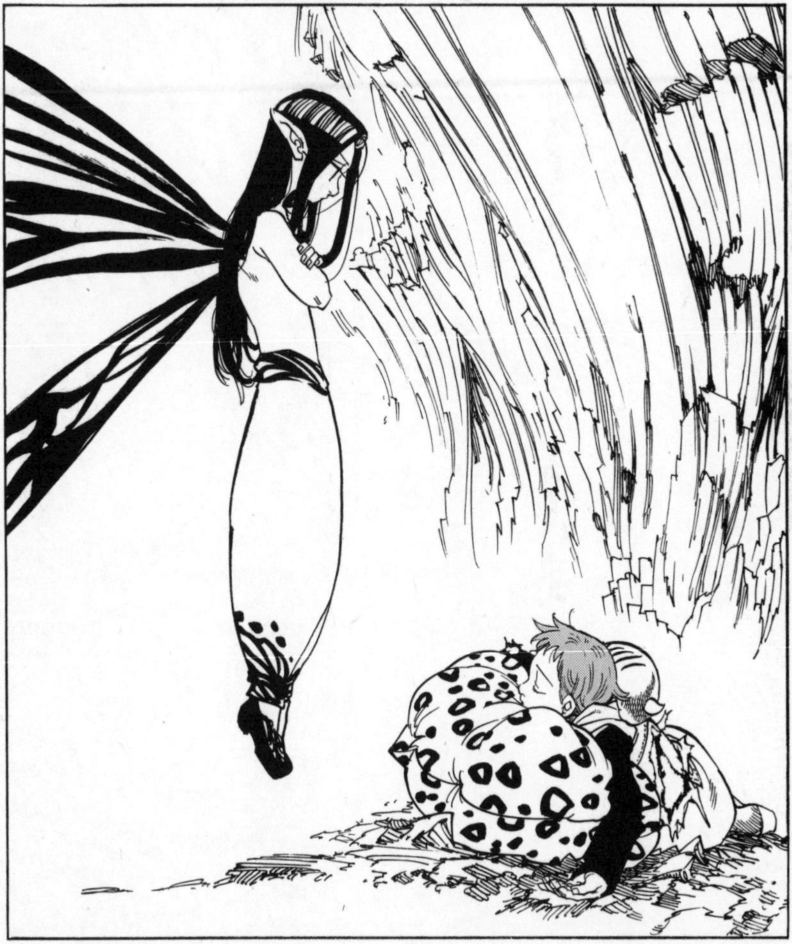

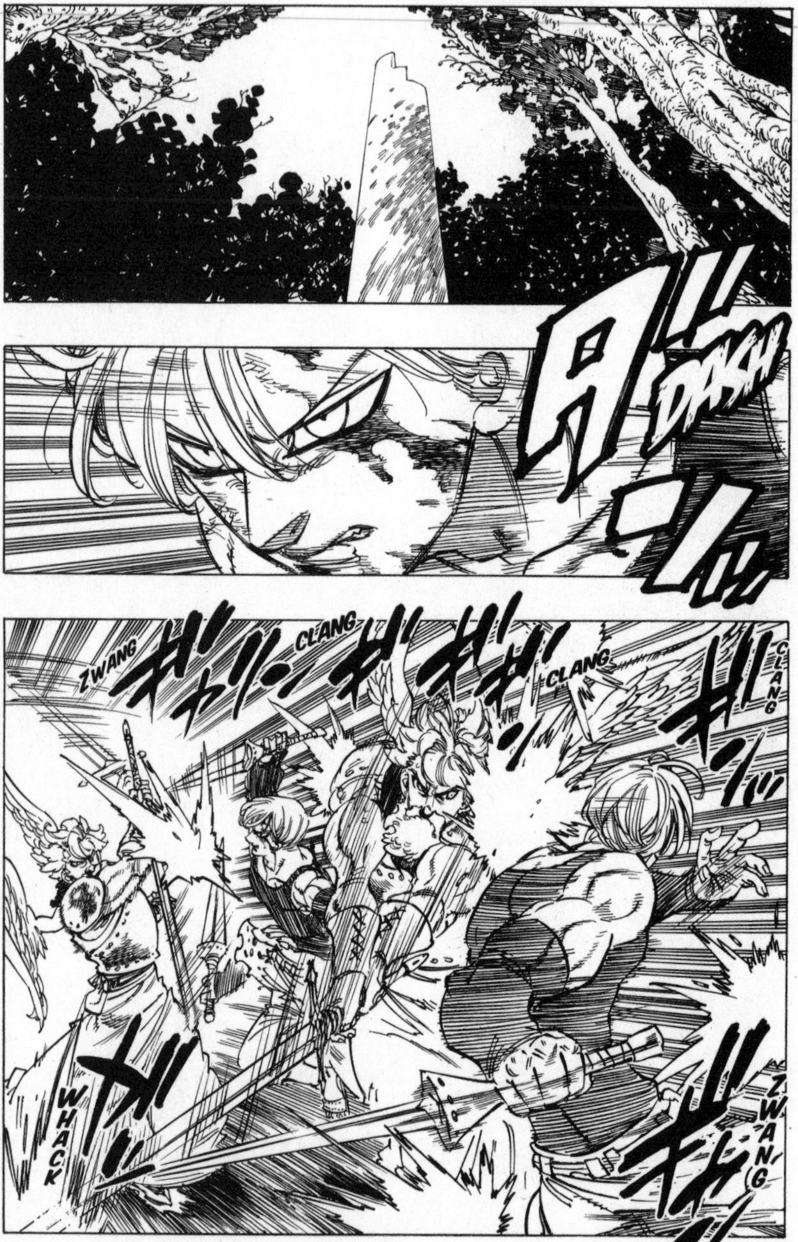
DASH
CLANG
CLANG
CLANG
ZWANG
ZWANG
WHACK

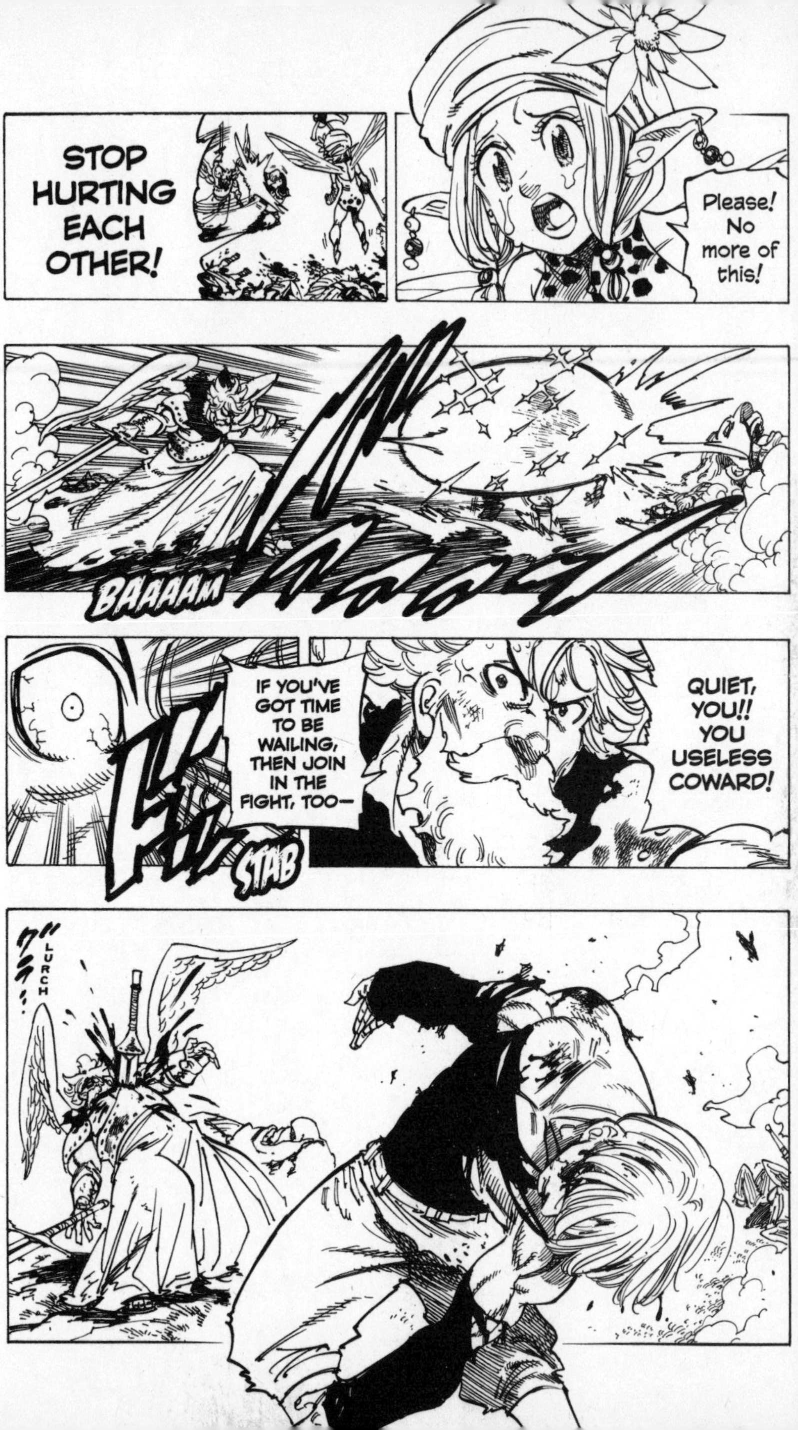
Please! No more of this!
STOP HURTING EACH OTHER!
BAAAAM
QUIET, YOU!! YOU USELESS COWARD!
IF YOU'VE GOT TIME TO BE WAILING, THEN JOIN IN THE FIGHT, TOO—
STAB
LURCH

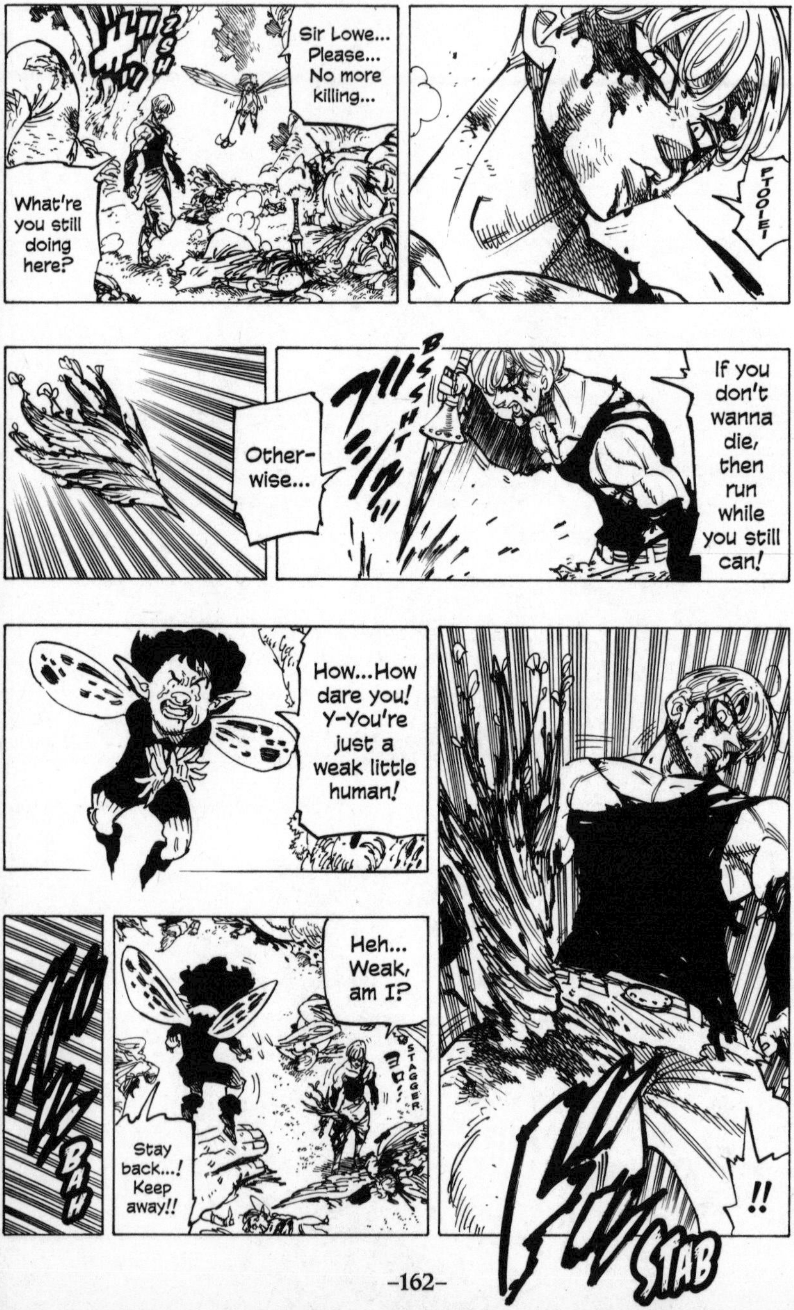
PTOOIE!
Sir Lowe... Please... No more killing...
ZSH
What're you still doing here?
If you don't wanna die, then run while you still can!
BSHT
Other-wise...
!!
STAB
How...How dare you! Y-You're just a weak little human!
Heh... Weak, am I?
STAGGER
Stay back...! Keep away!!
BAH

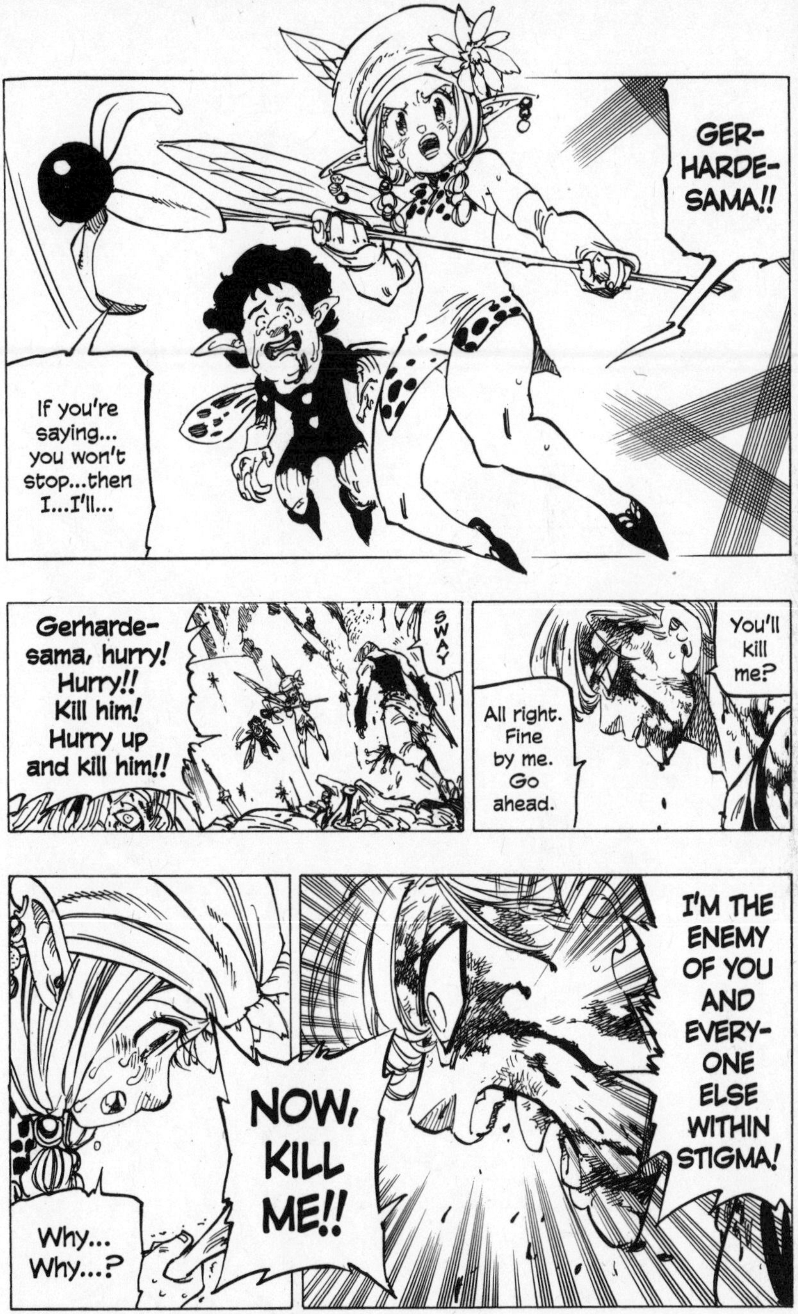
GER-HARDE-SAMA!!
If you're saying... you won't stop...then I...I'll...
You'll kill me?
All right. Fine by me. Go ahead.
SWAY
Gerharde-sama, hurry! Hurry!! Kill him! Hurry up and kill him!!
I'M THE ENEMY OF YOU AND EVERYONE ELSE WITHIN STIGMA!
NOW, KILL ME!!
Why... Why...?

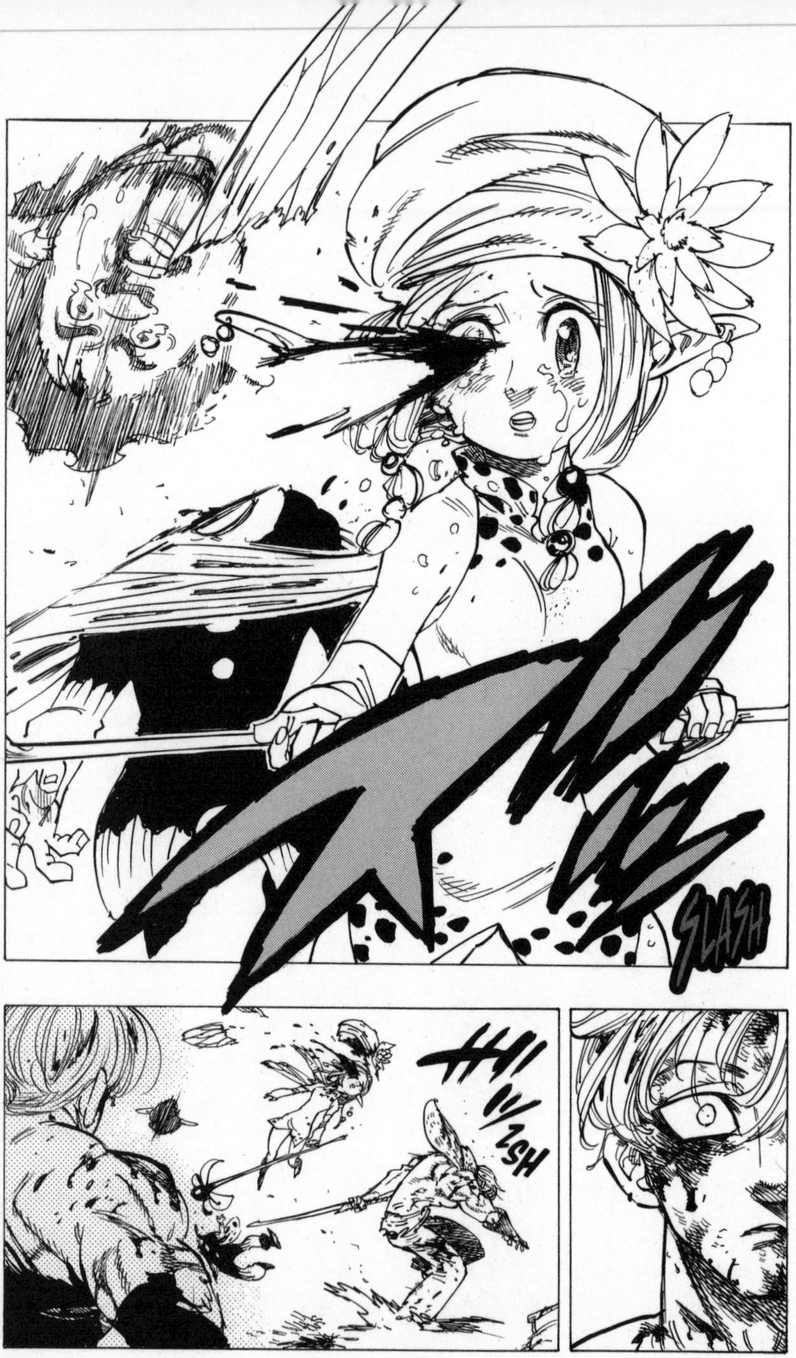
SLASH

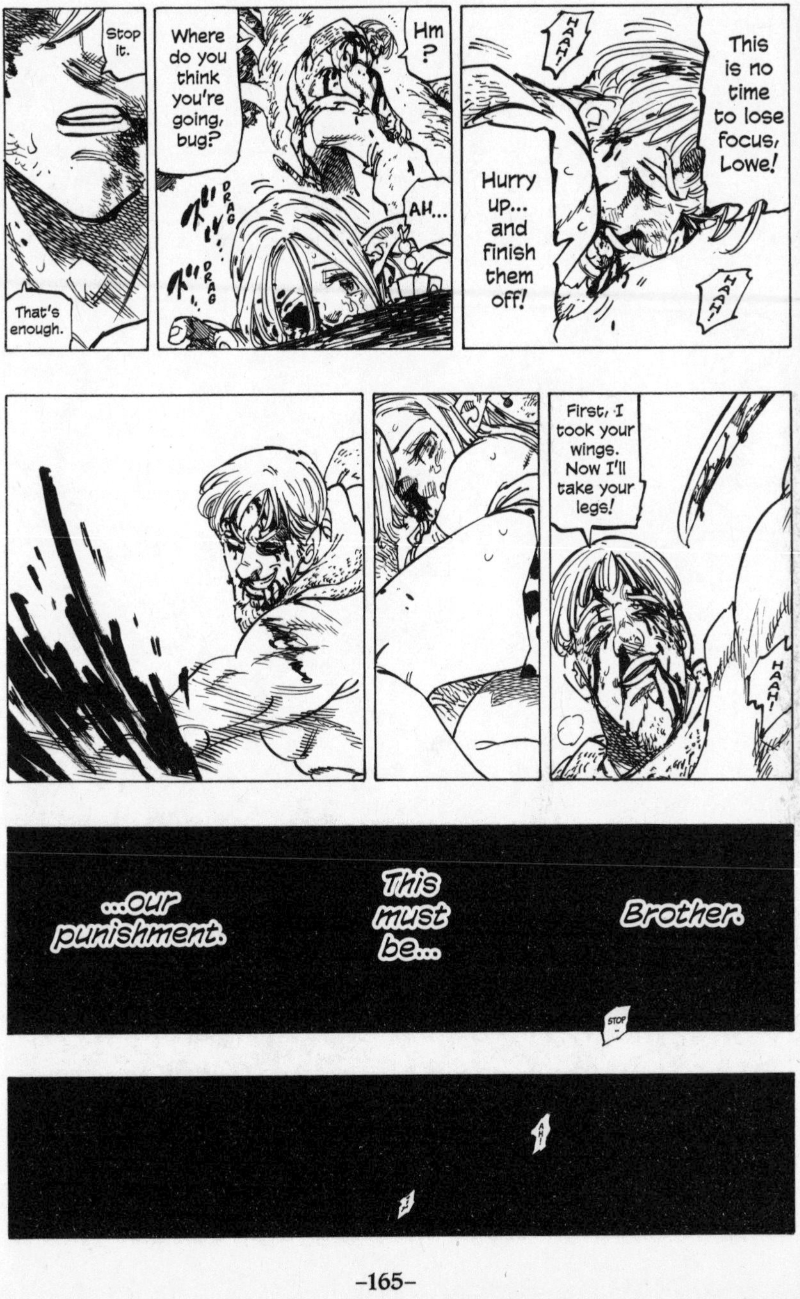
HAAH!
This is no time to lose focus, Lowe!
Hurry up... and finish them off!
HAAH!
Hm?
Where do you think you're going, bug?
AH...
DRAG
DRAG
Stop it.
That's enough.
First, I took your wings. Now I'll take your legs!
HAAH!
Brother.
This must be...
...our punishment.
STOP-
AH!

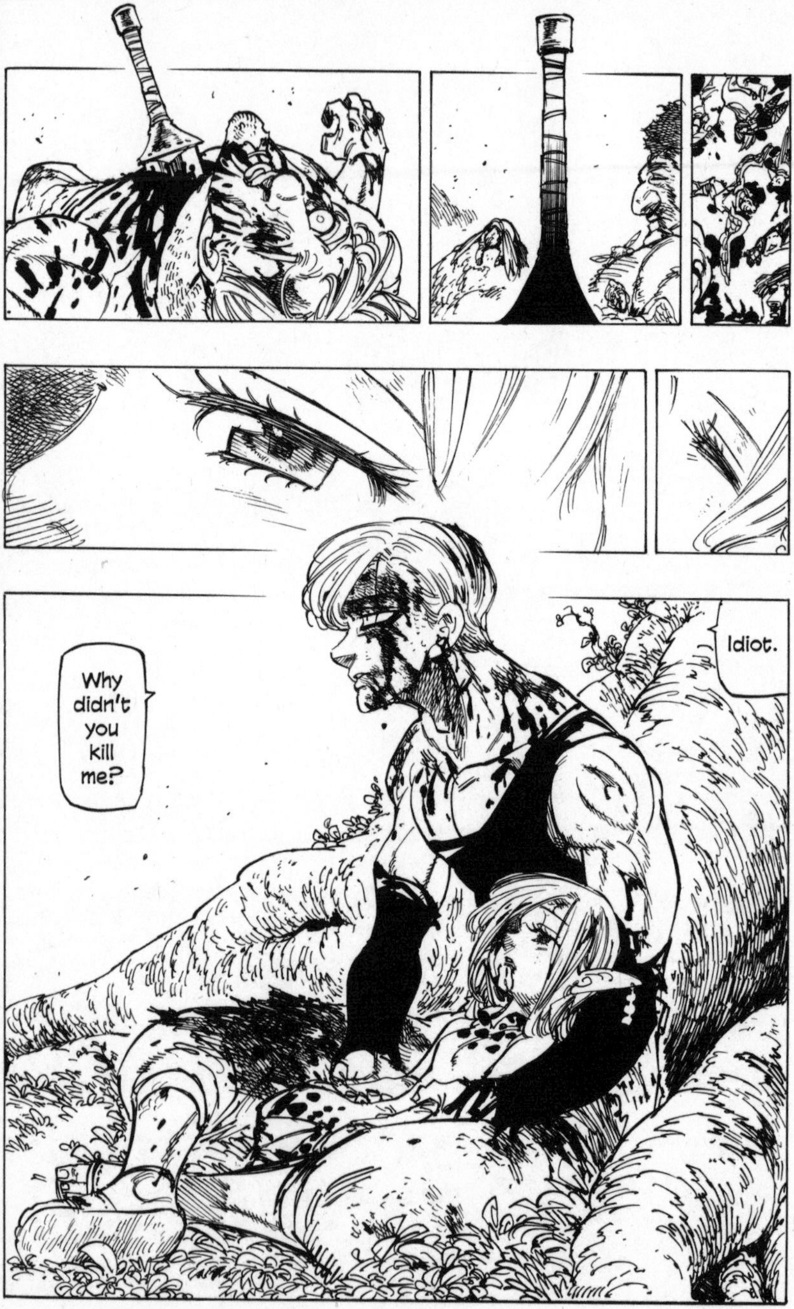
Idiot.
Why didn't you kill me?

When I spoke to you... about...my brother...

...I saw the anger...and sadness... that you were suppressing... and a face...

...the face... of a girl... very much like myself.

It was ...

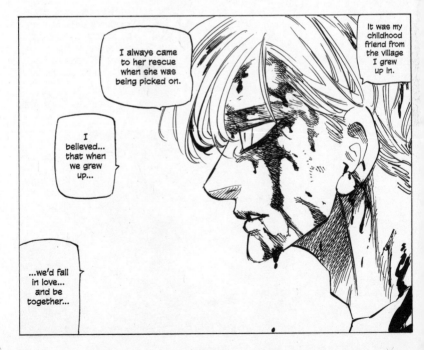

It was my childhood friend from the village I grew up in.

I always came to her rescue when she was being picked on.

I believed... that when we grew up...

...we'd fall in love... and be together...

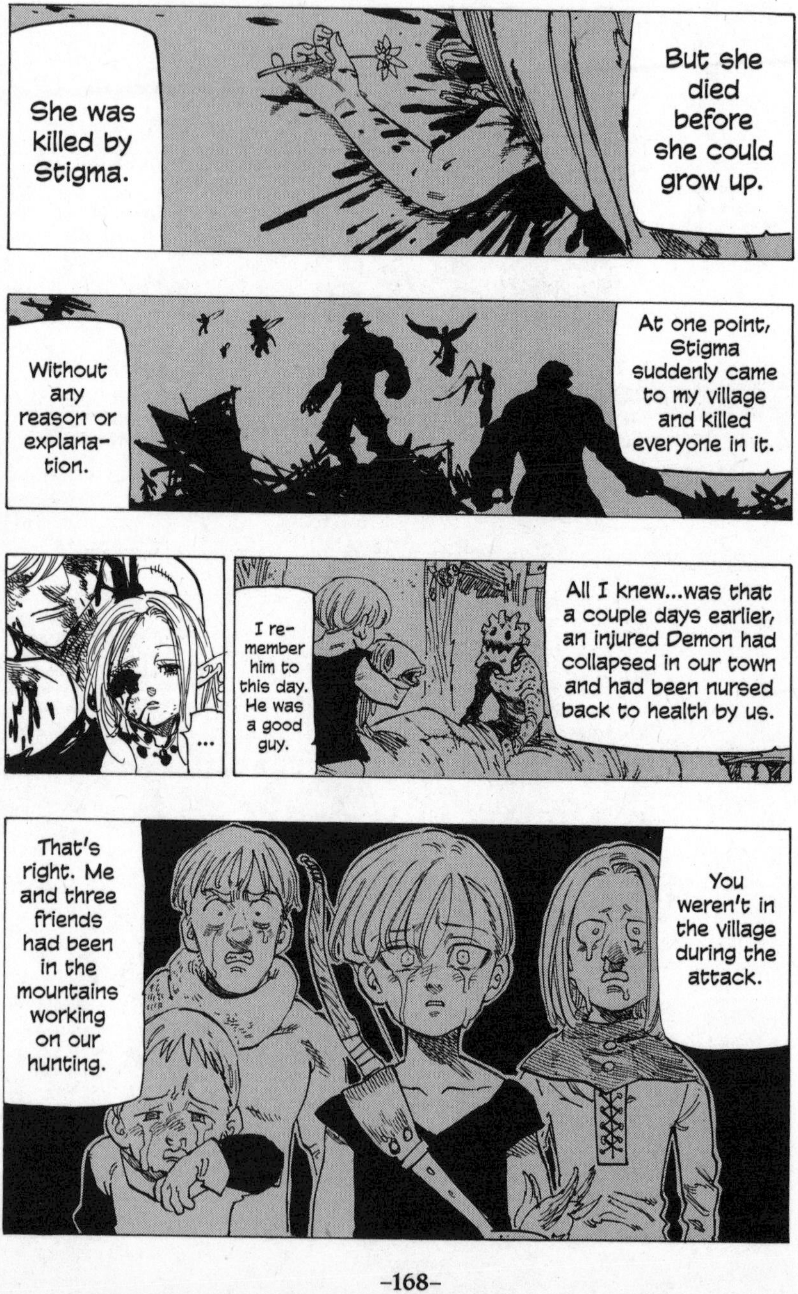
But she died before she could grow up.
She was killed by Stigma.
At one point, Stigma suddenly came to my village and killed everyone in it.
Without any reason or explana-tion.
All I knew...was that a couple days earlier, an injured Demon had collapsed in our town and had been nursed back to health by us.
I re-member him to this day. He was a good guy.
...
You weren't in the village during the attack.
That's right. Me and three friends had been in the mountains working on our hunting.

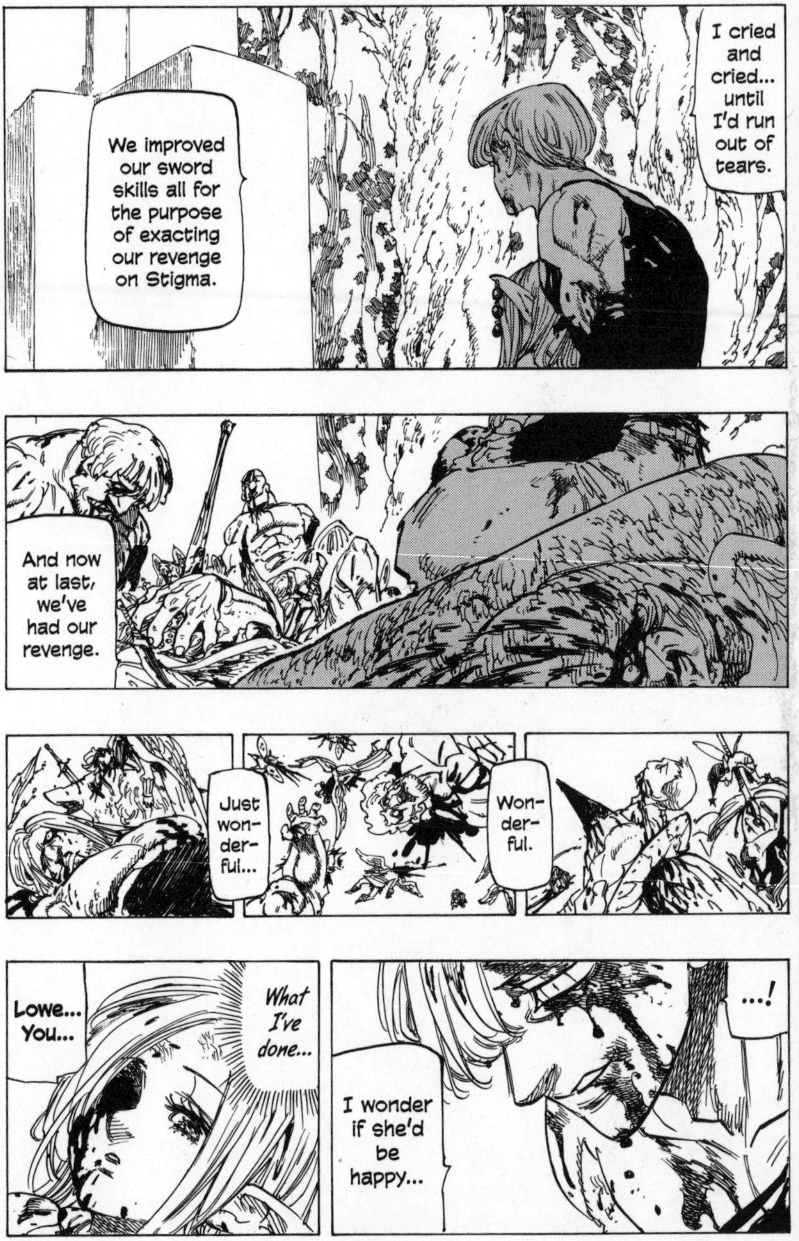
I cried and cried... until I'd run out of tears.
We improved our sword skills all for the purpose of exacting our revenge on Stigma.
And now at last, we've had our revenge.
Wonderful.
Just wonderful...
...!
I wonder if she'd be happy...
What I've done...
Lowe... You...

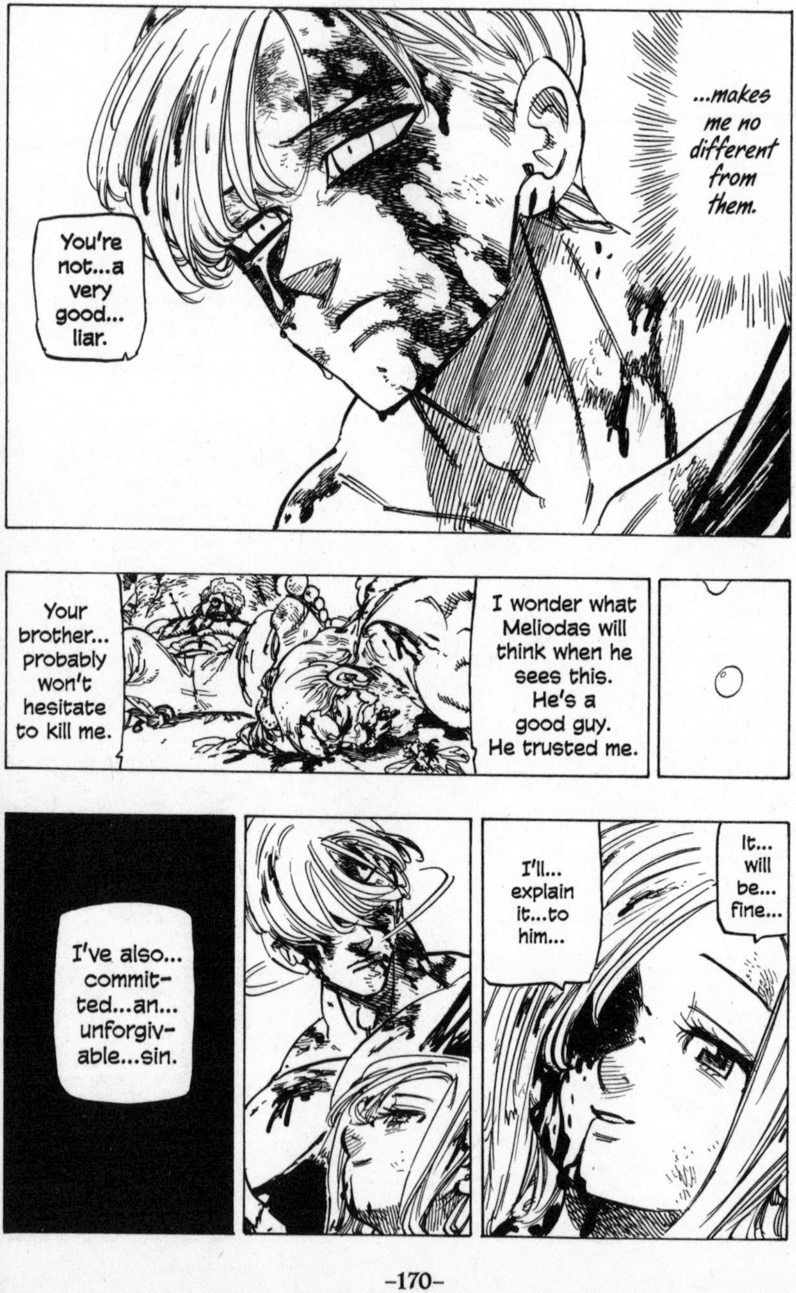
...makes me no different from them.
You're not...a very good... liar.
I wonder what Meliodas will think when he sees this. He's a good guy. He trusted me.
Your brother... probably won't hesitate to kill me.
It... will be... fine...
I'll... explain it...to him...
I've also... commit-ted...an... unforgiv-able...sin.

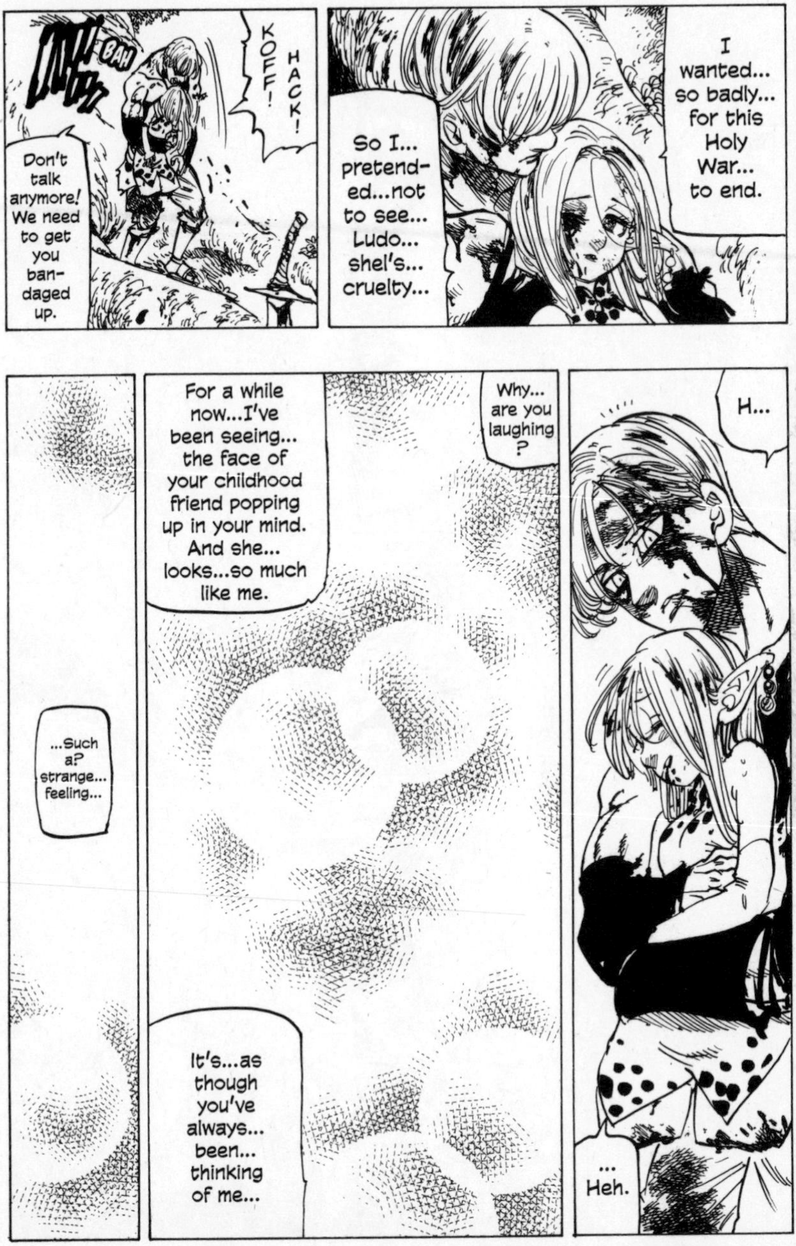
I wanted... so badly... for this Holy War... to end.
So I... pretended...not to see... Ludo... shel's... cruelty...
HACK!
KOFF!
BAH
Don't talk anymore! We need to get you bandaged up.
H...
...Heh.
Why... are you laughing?
For a while now...I've been seeing... the face of your childhood friend popping up in your mind. And she... looks...so much like me.
It's...as though you've always... been... thinking of me...
...Such a? strange... feeling...

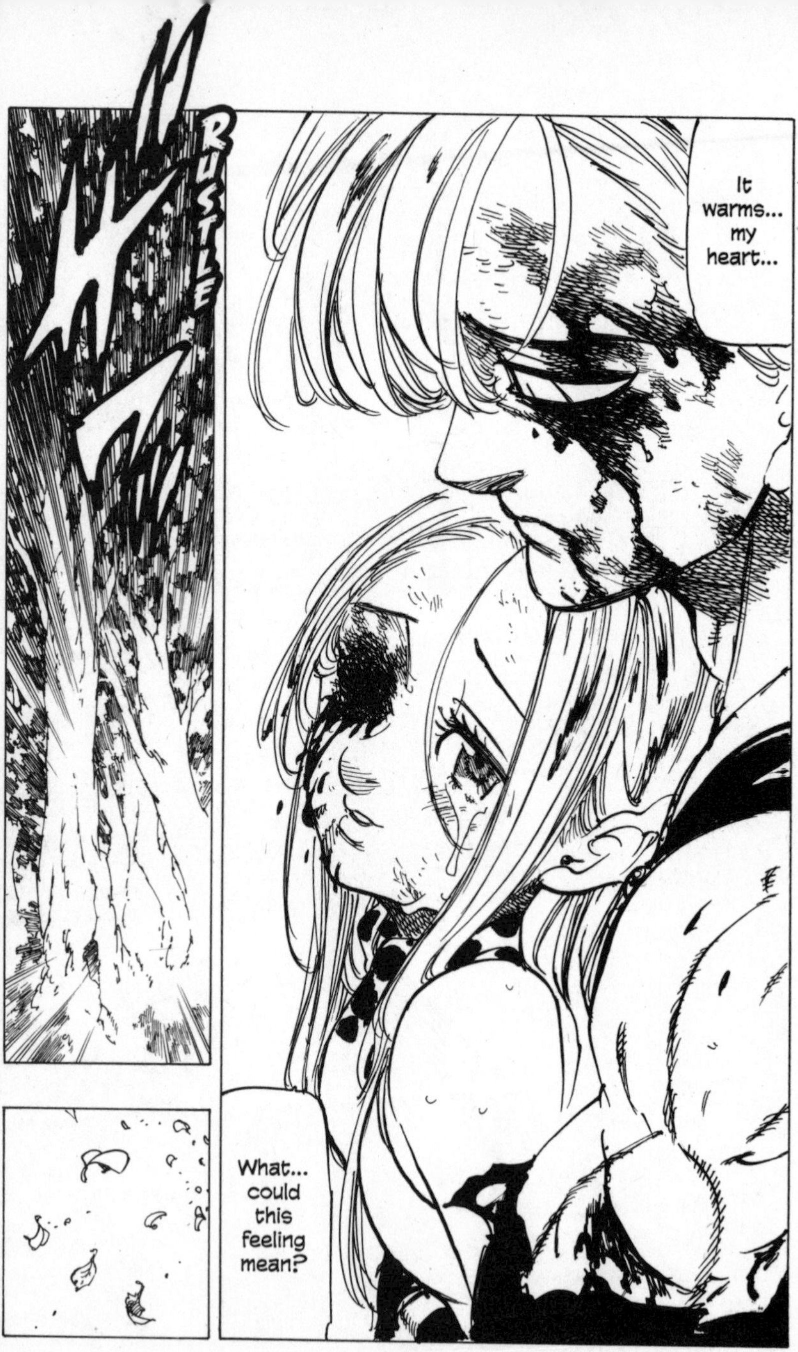
It warms... my heart...
What... could this feeling mean?
RUSTLE

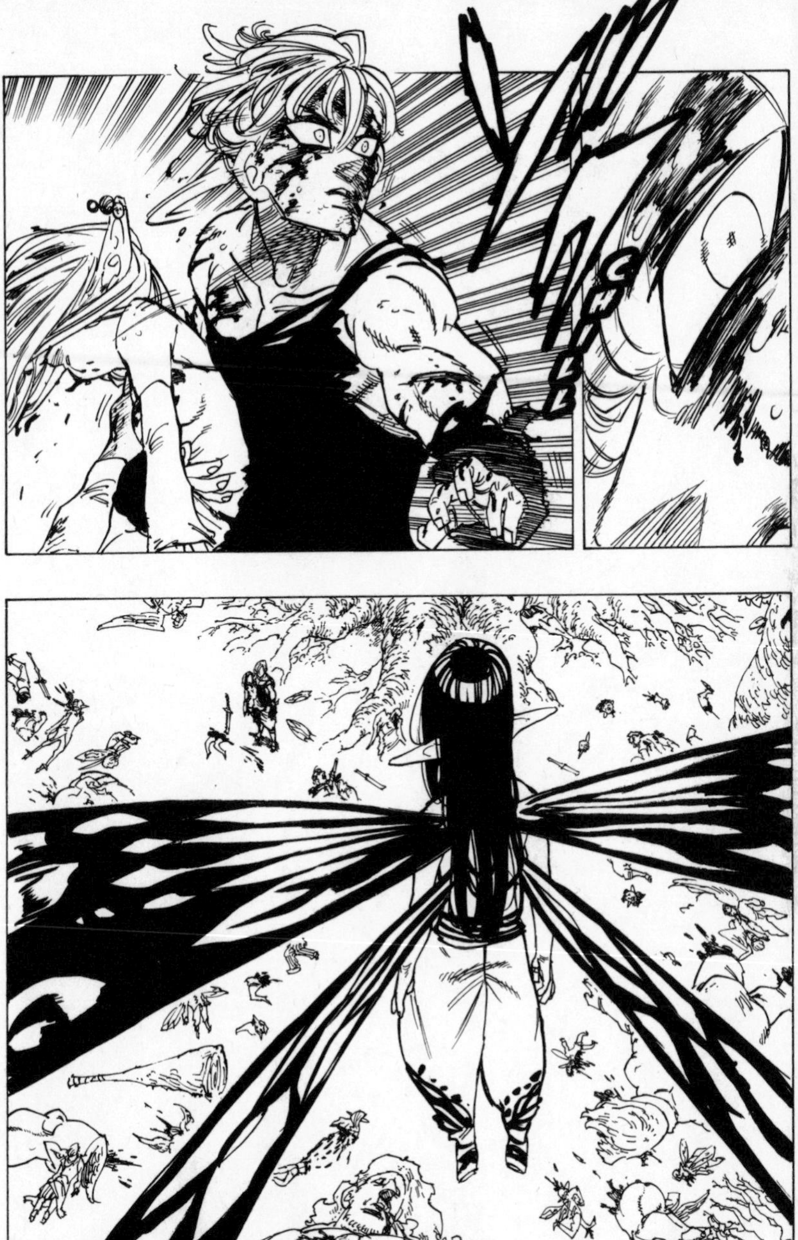
CHILL

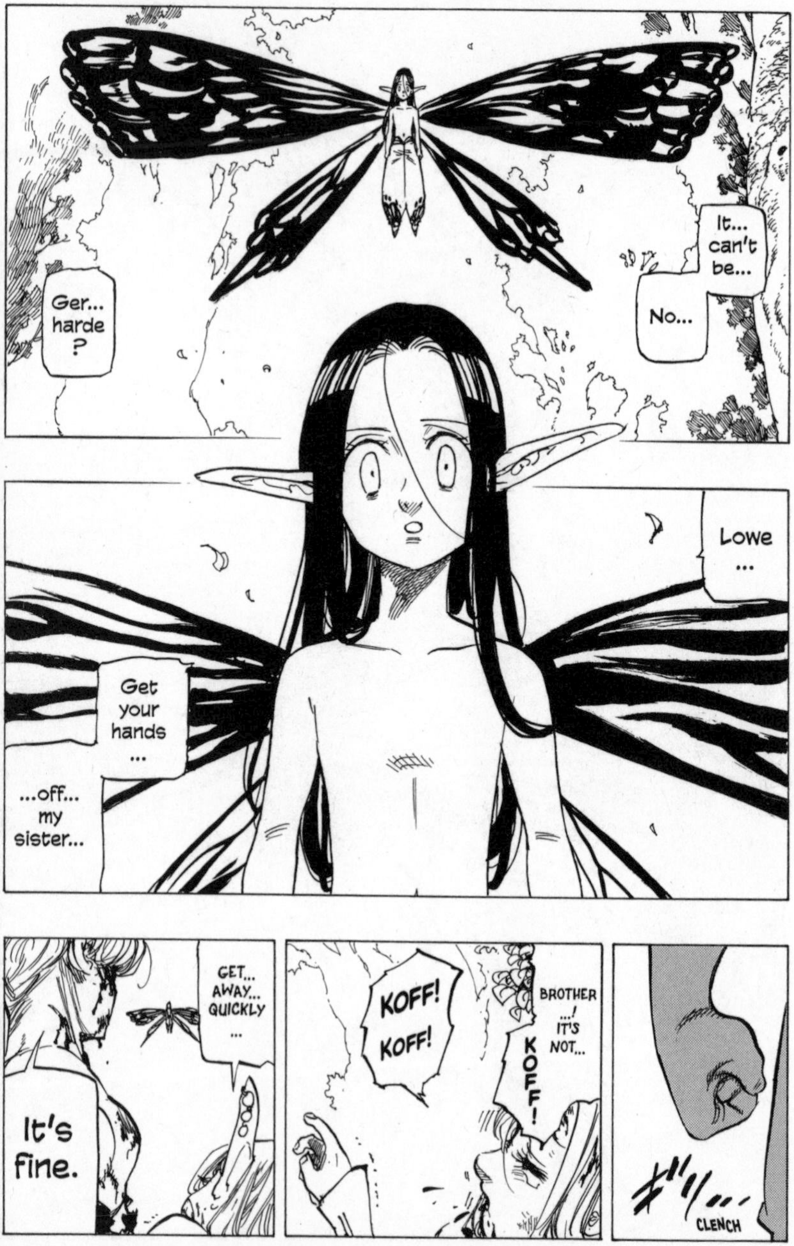
It... can't be...
No...
Ger... harde ?
Lowe ...
Get your hands ...
...off... my sister...
CLENCH
BROTHER ...! IT'S NOT...
KOFF!
KOFF! KOFF!
GET... AWAY... QUICKLY ...
It's fine.

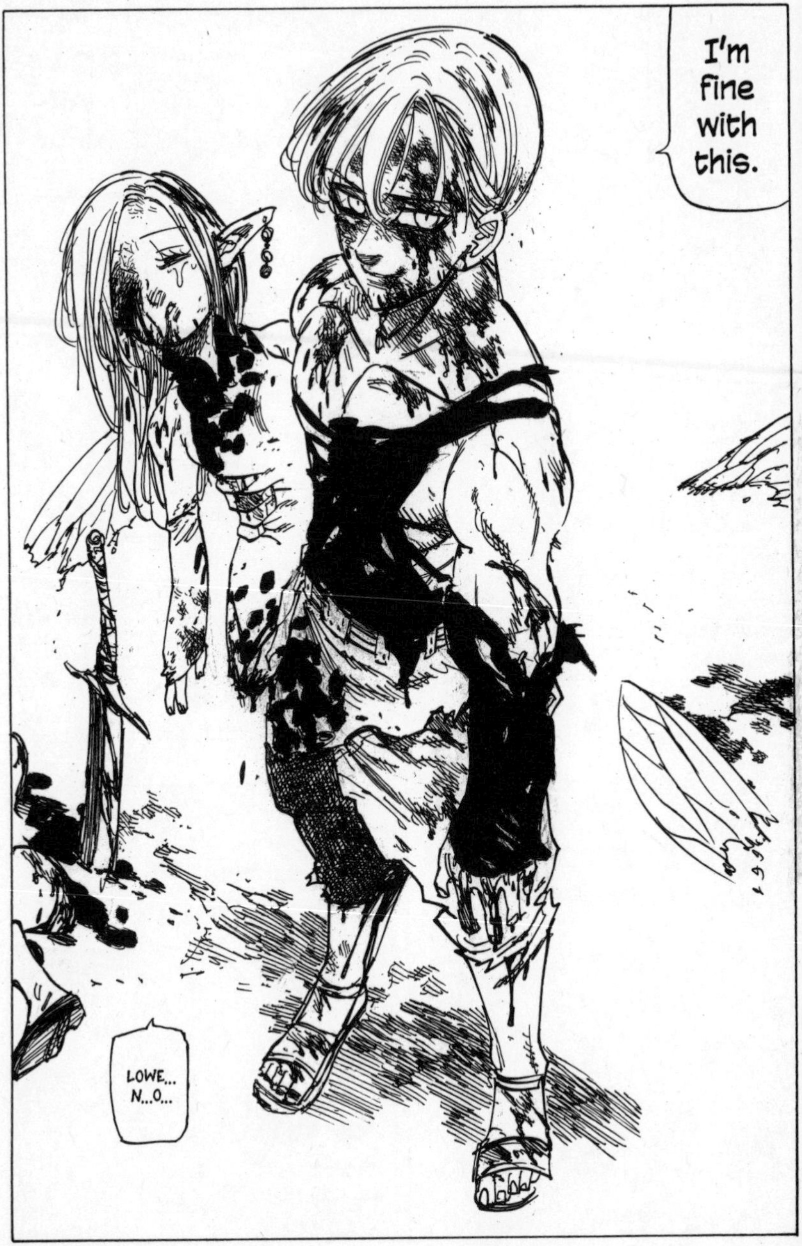
I'm fine with this.
LOWE... N...O...

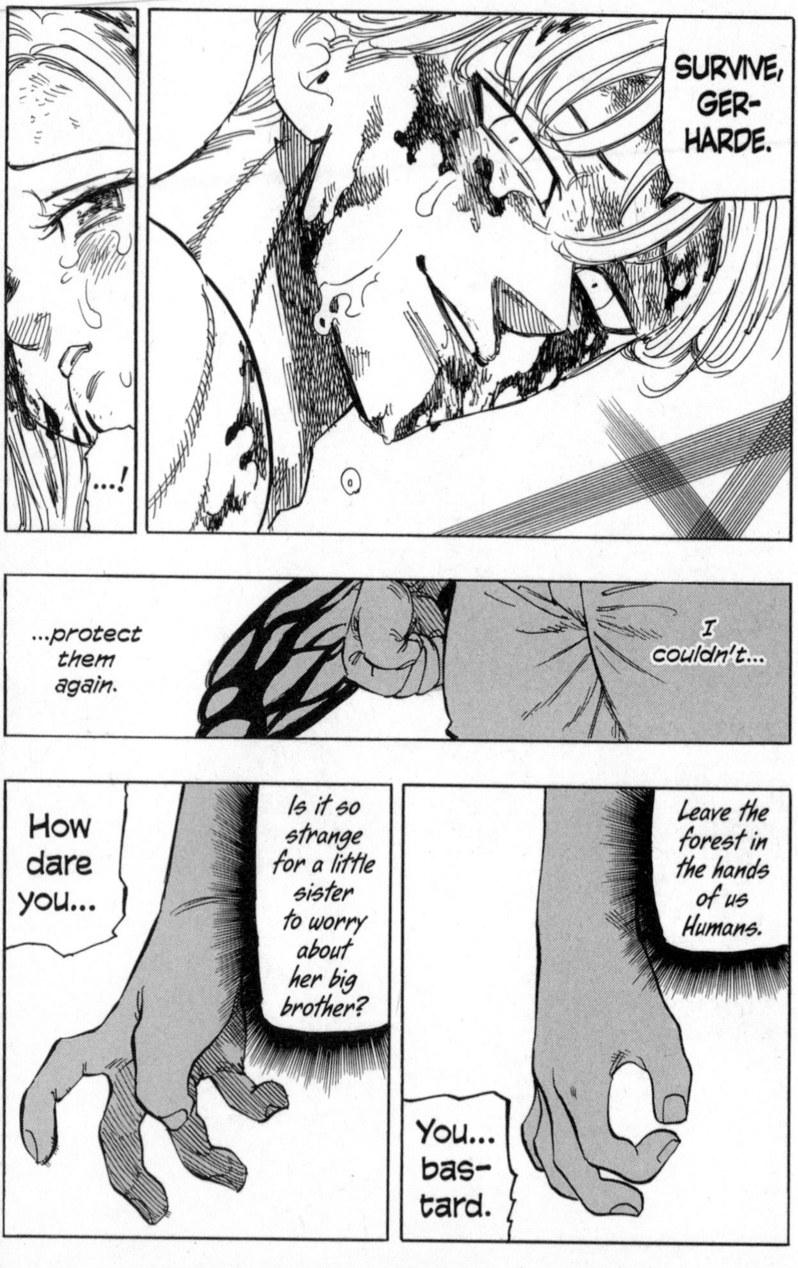
SURVIVE, GER-HARDE.
...!
I couldn't...
...protect them again.
Leave the forest in the hands of us Humans.
You... bas-tard.
Is it so strange for a little sister to worry about her big brother?
How dare you...!

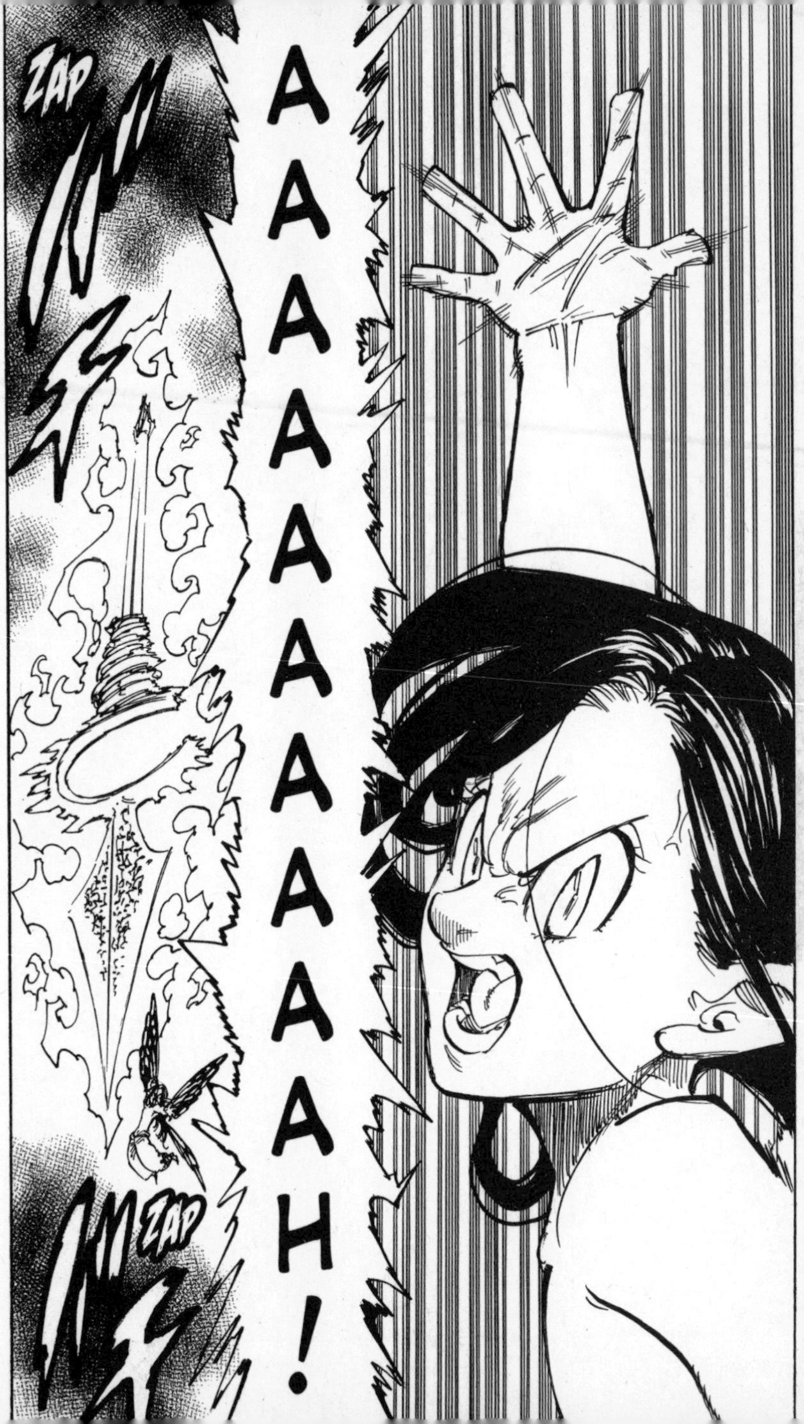
AAAAAAAAAH!
ZAP
ZAP

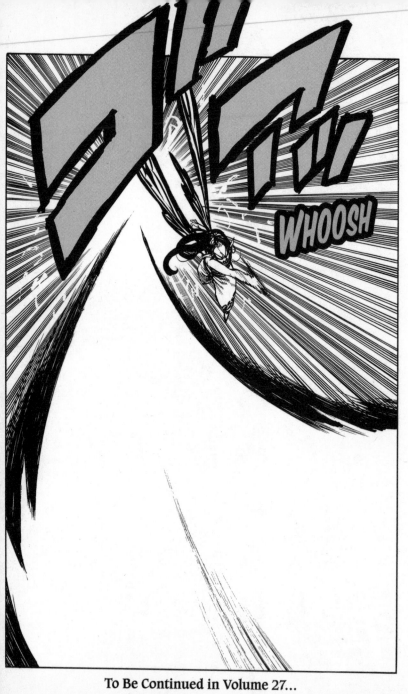

To Be Continued in Volume 27...

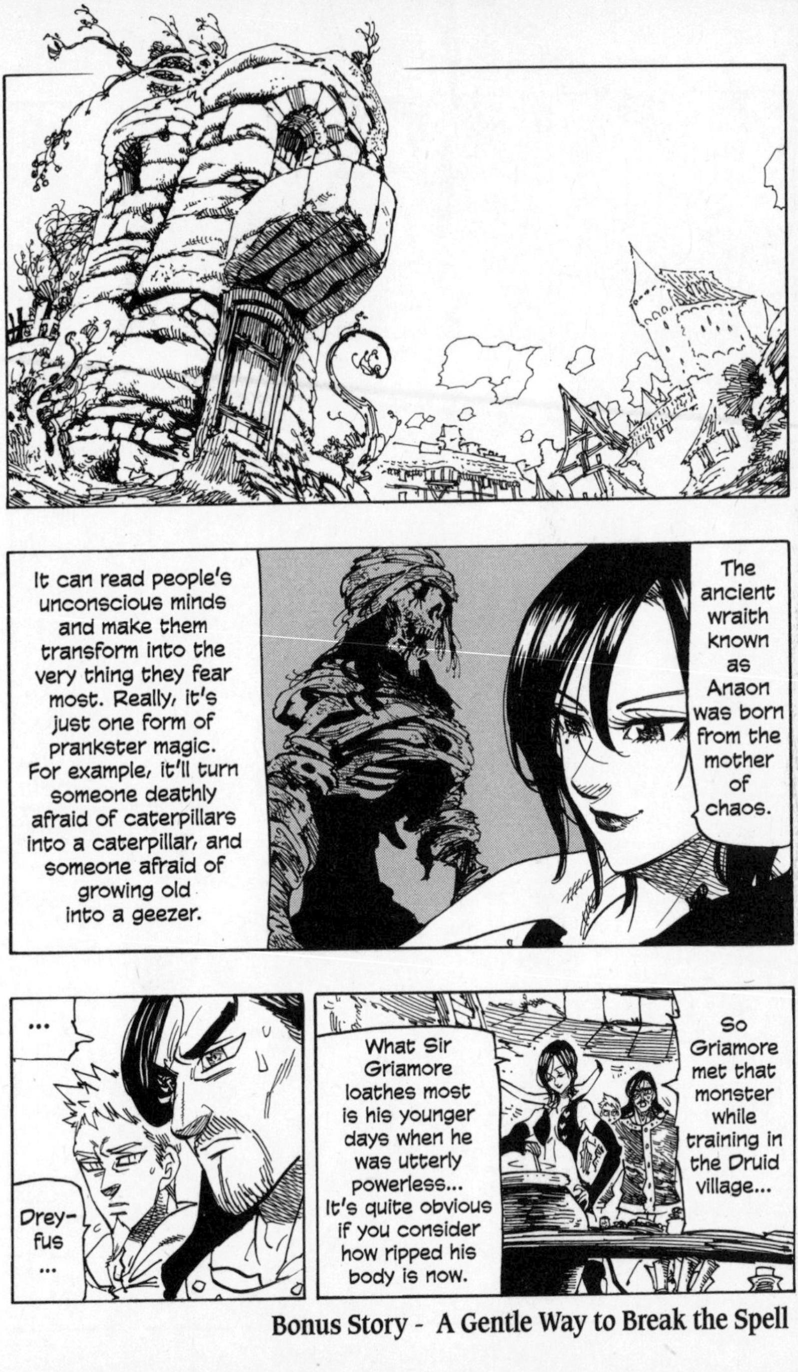
The ancient wraith known as Anaon was born from the mother of chaos.
It can read people's unconscious minds and make them transform into the very thing they fear most. Really, it's just one form of prankster magic. For example, it'll turn someone deathly afraid of caterpillars into a caterpillar, and someone afraid of growing old into a geezer.
So Griamore met that monster while training in the Druid village...
What Sir Griamore loathes most is his younger days when he was utterly powerless... It's quite obvious if you consider how ripped his body is now.
...
Drey-fus ...

Bonus Story - A Gentle Way to Break the Spell

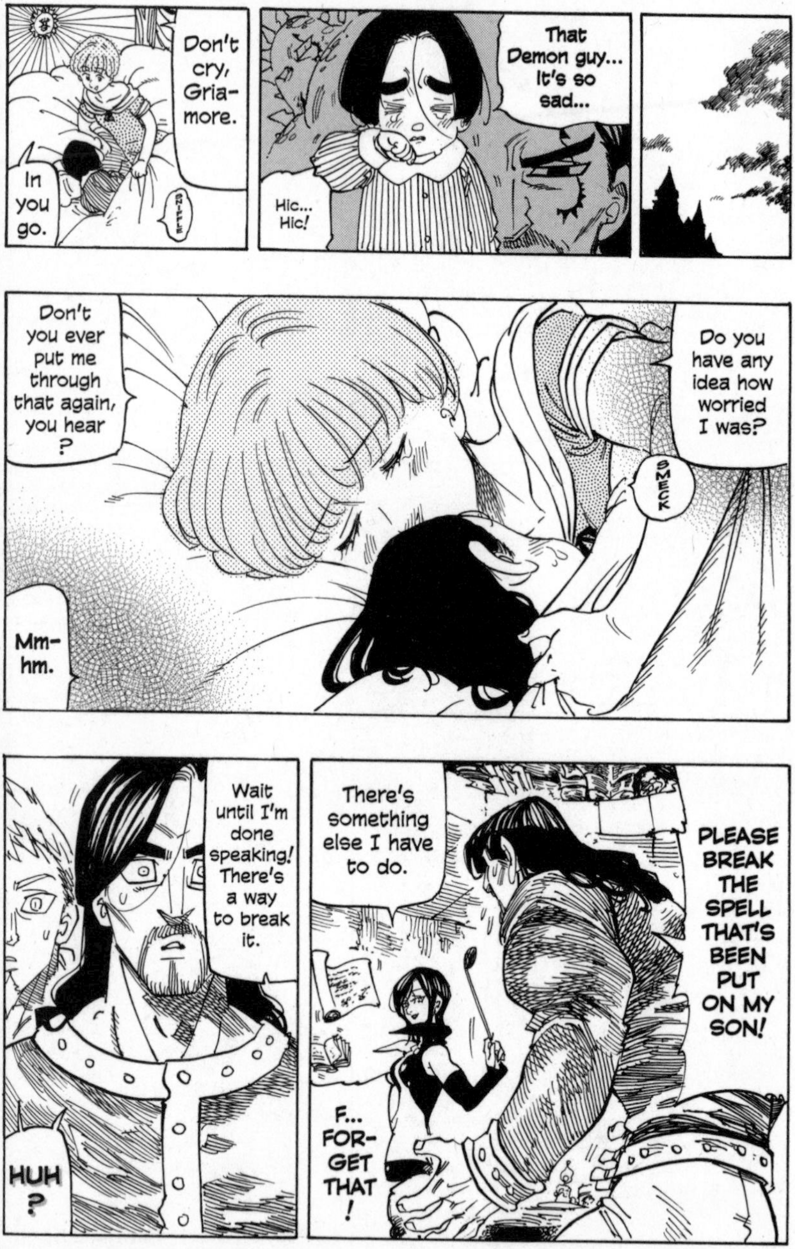
That Demon guy... It's so sad...
Hic... Hic!
Don't cry, Gria-more.
SNIFFLE
In you go.
Do you have any idea how worried I was?
SMECK
Don't you ever put me through that again, you hear?
Mm-hm.
PLEASE BREAK THE SPELL THAT'S BEEN PUT ON MY SON!
There's something else I have to do.
F... FOR-GET THAT!
Wait until I'm done speaking! There's a way to break it.
HUH?

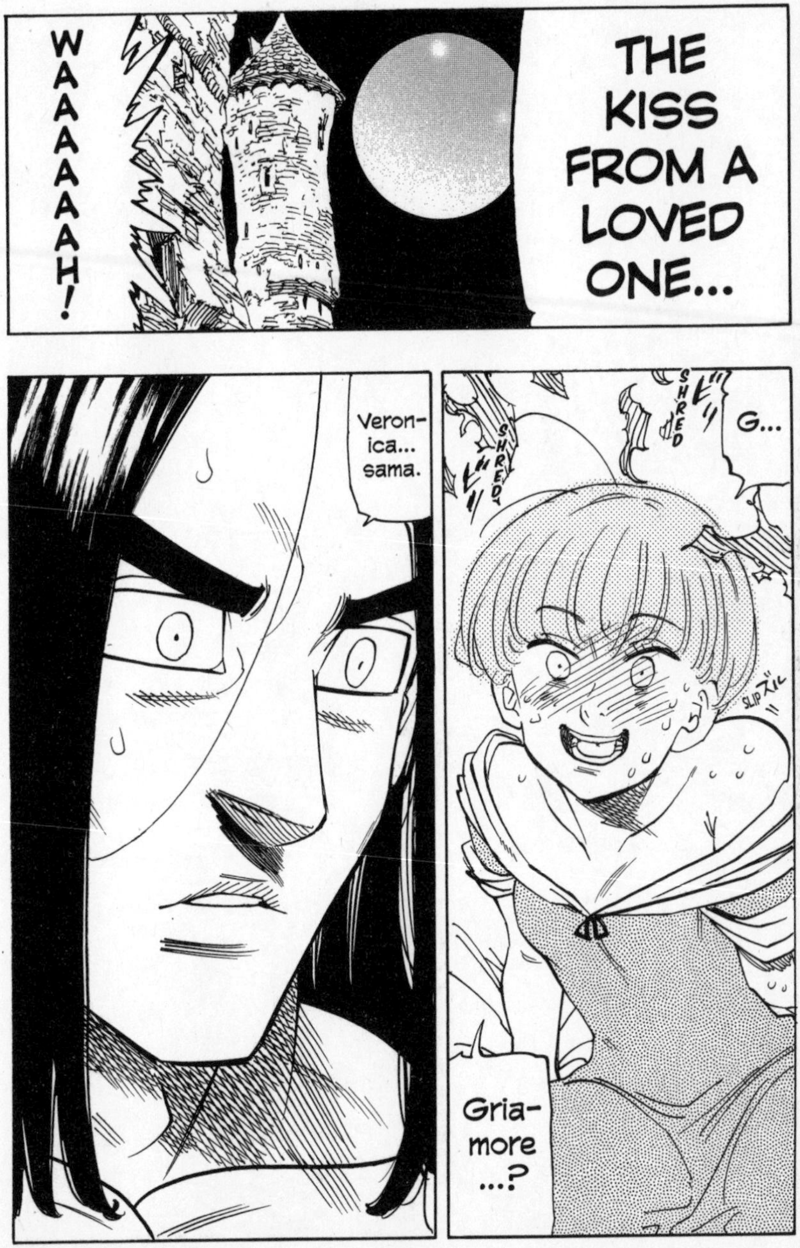
THE KISS FROM A LOVED ONE...
WAAAAAAAH!
SHRED
SHRED
G...
SLIP ズル
Gria-more ...?
Veron-ica... sama.

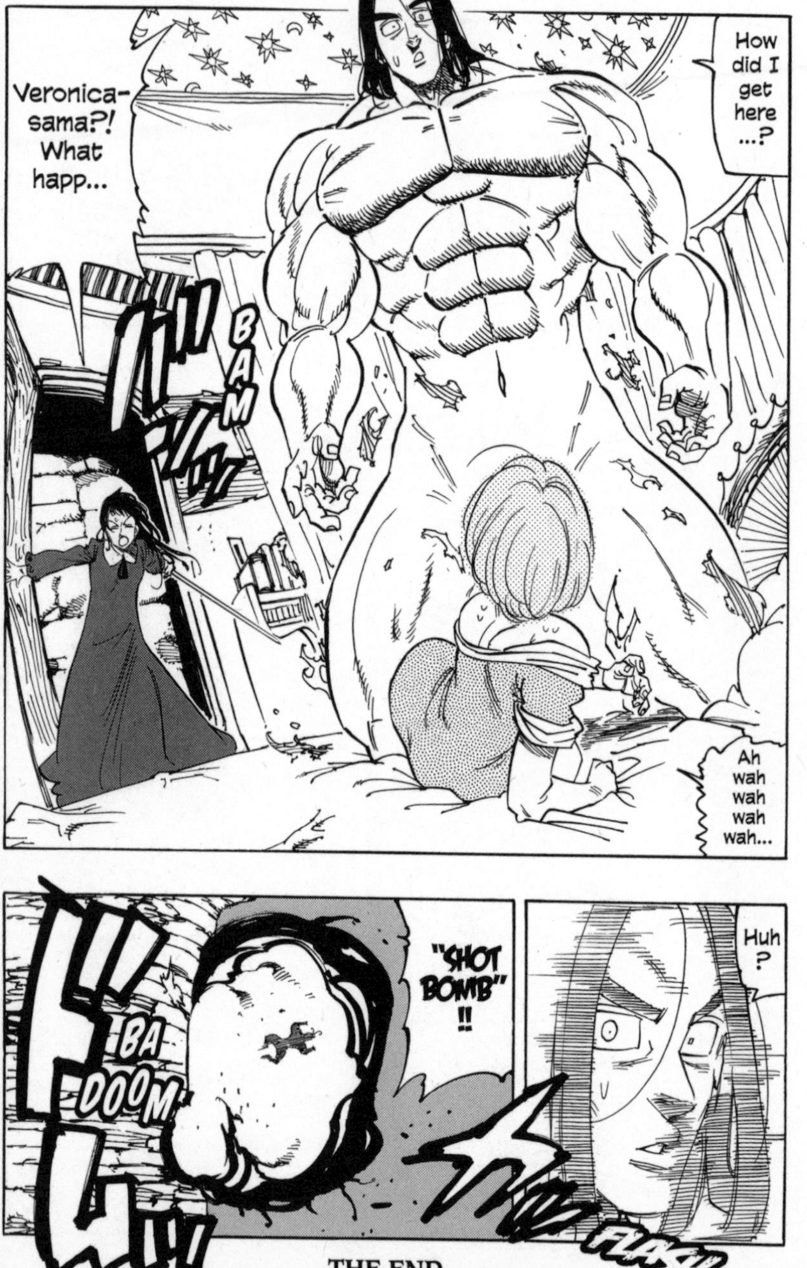
How did I get here ...?
Veronica-sama?! What happ...
BAM
Ah wah wah wah wah...
Huh?
FLASH
"SHOT BOMB" !!
BA DOOM

THE END

Bonus Story - What I Want to Tell You

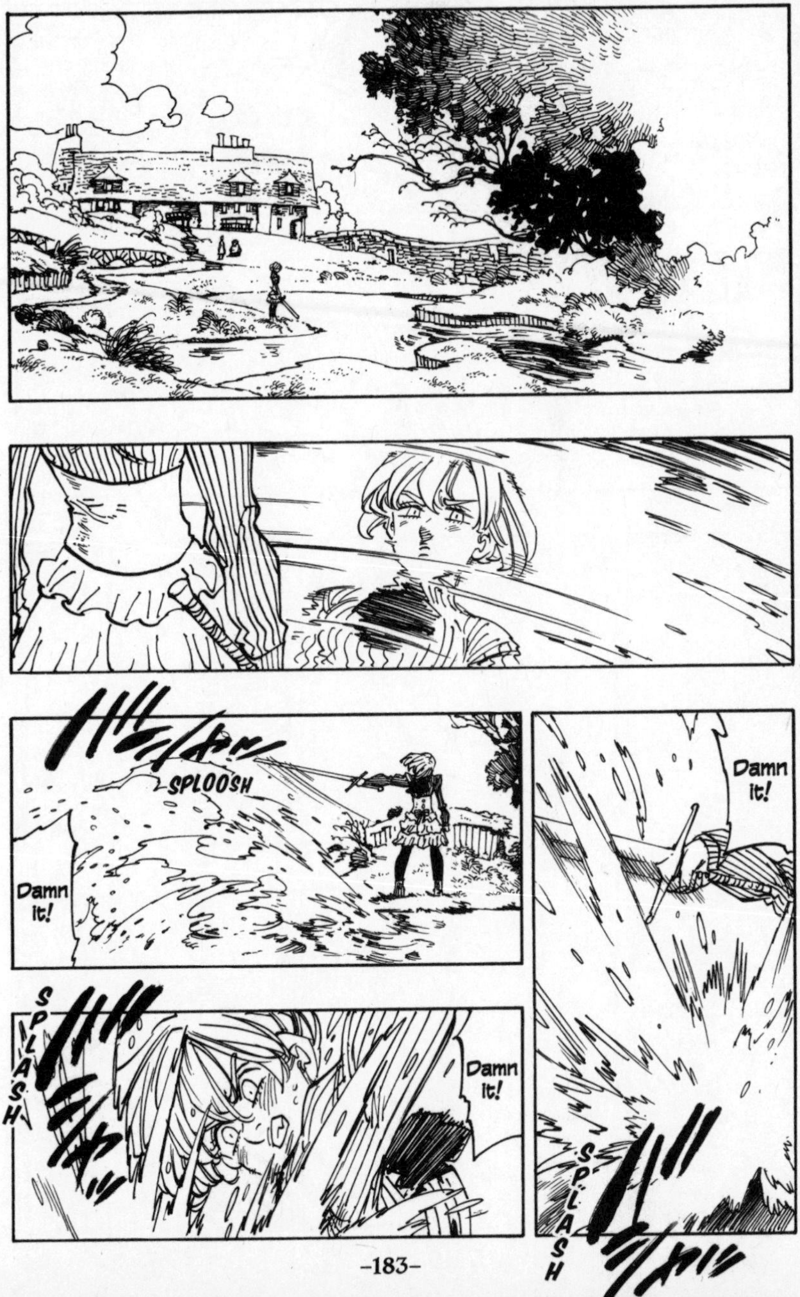
Damn it!
SPLASH
SPLOOSH
Damn it!
Damn it!
SPLASH

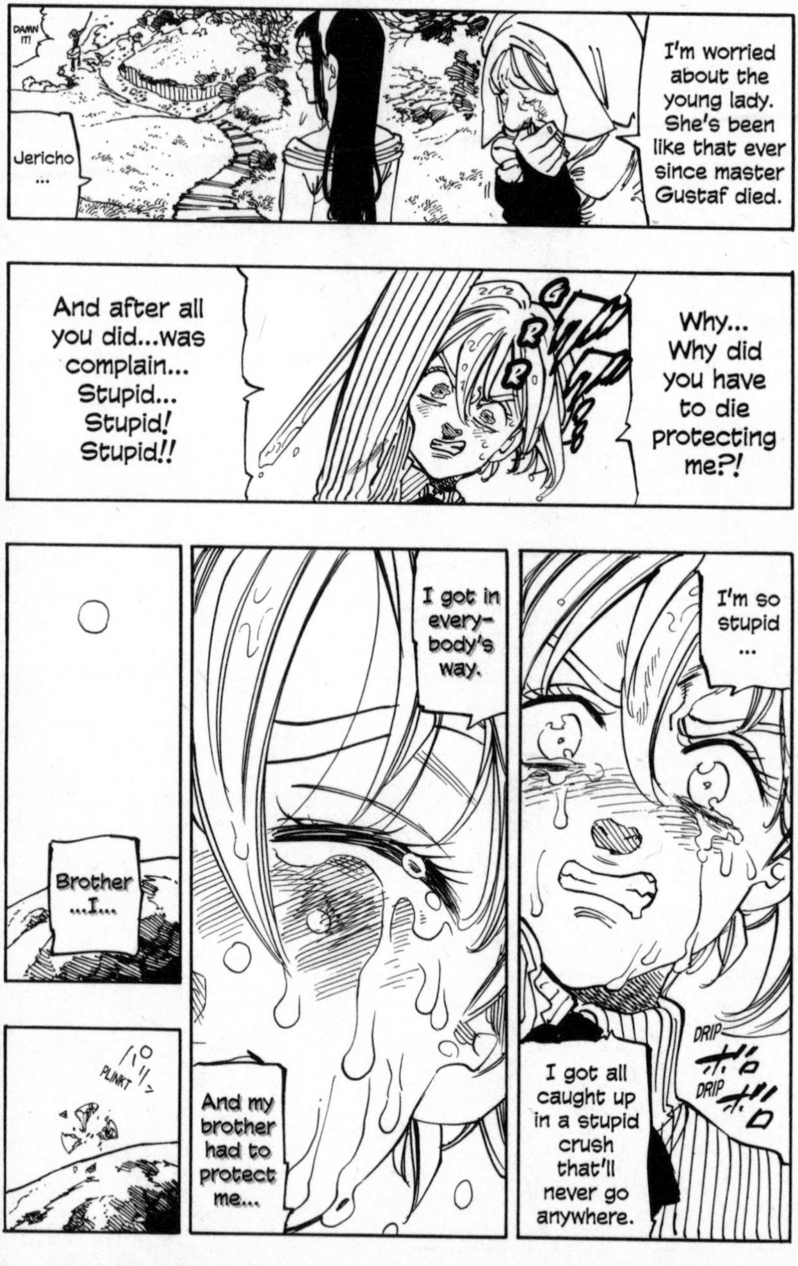
I'm worried about the young lady. She's been like that ever since master Gustaf died.
DAMN IT!
Jericho ...
Why... Why did you have to die protecting me?!
GRRR
And after all you did...was complain... Stupid... Stupid! Stupid!!
I'm so stupid ...
DRIP
DRIP
I got all caught up in a stupid crush that'll never go anywhere.
I got in every-body's way.
And my brother had to protect me...
Brother ...I...
PLINKT

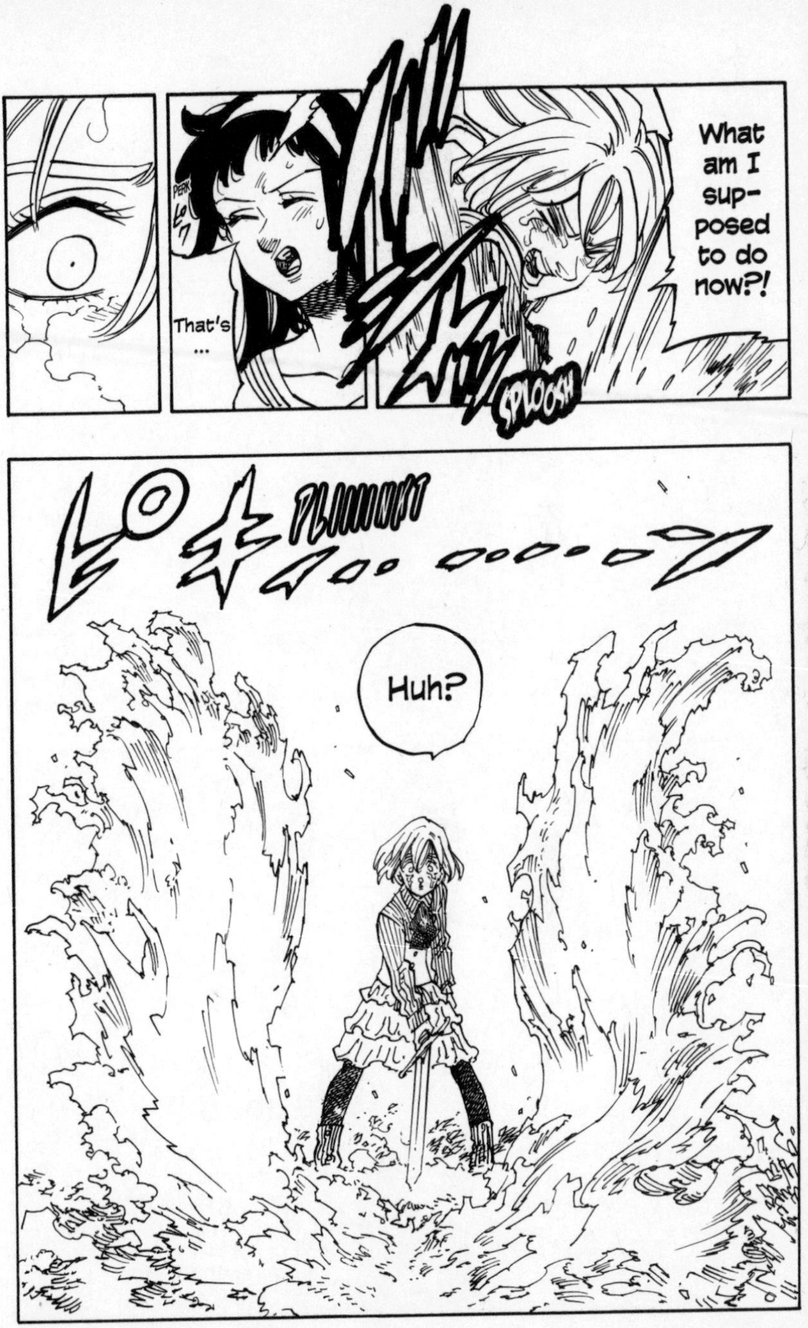
What am I sup-posed to do now?!
SPLOOSH
PERK
That's ...
Huh?

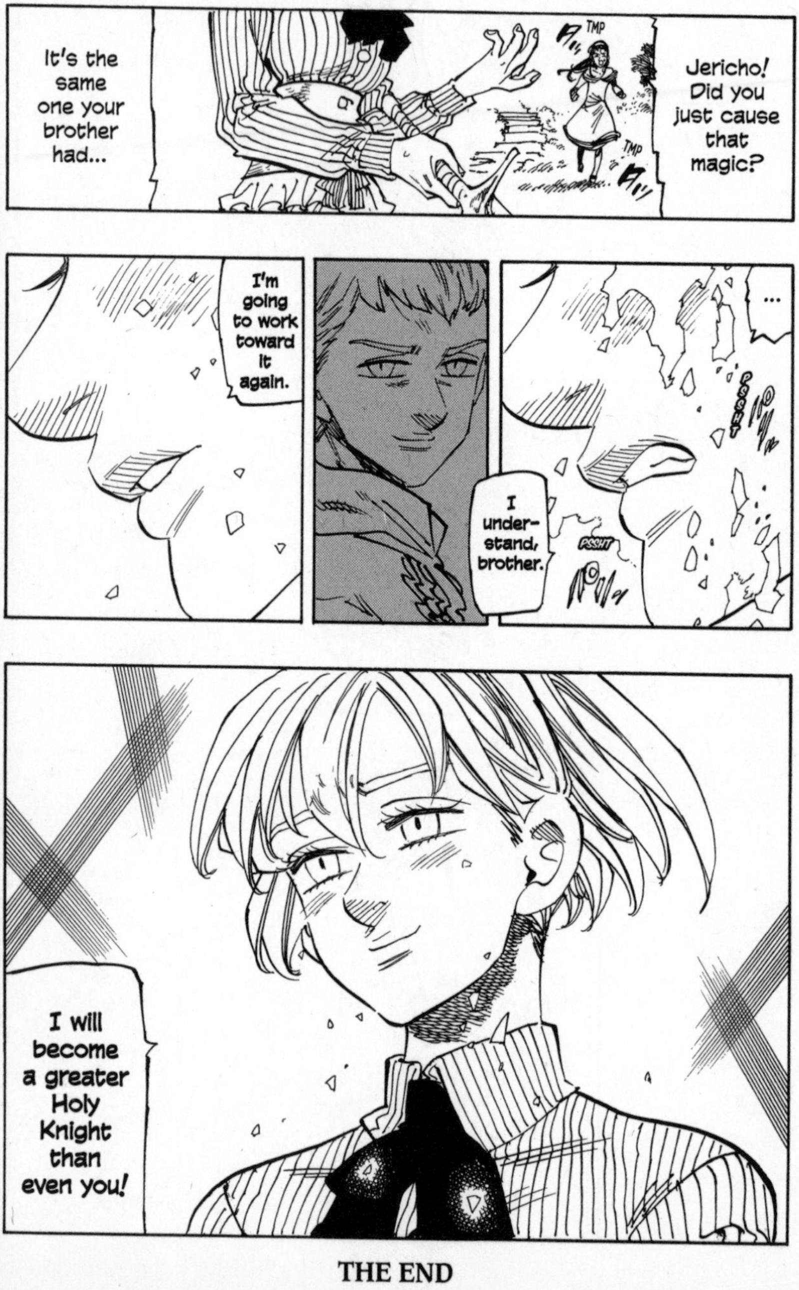
Jericho! Did you just cause that magic?
TMP
TMP
It's the same one your brother had...
...
PSSHT
PSSHT
I understand, brother.
I'm going to work toward it again.
I will become a greater Holy Knight than even you!

THE END

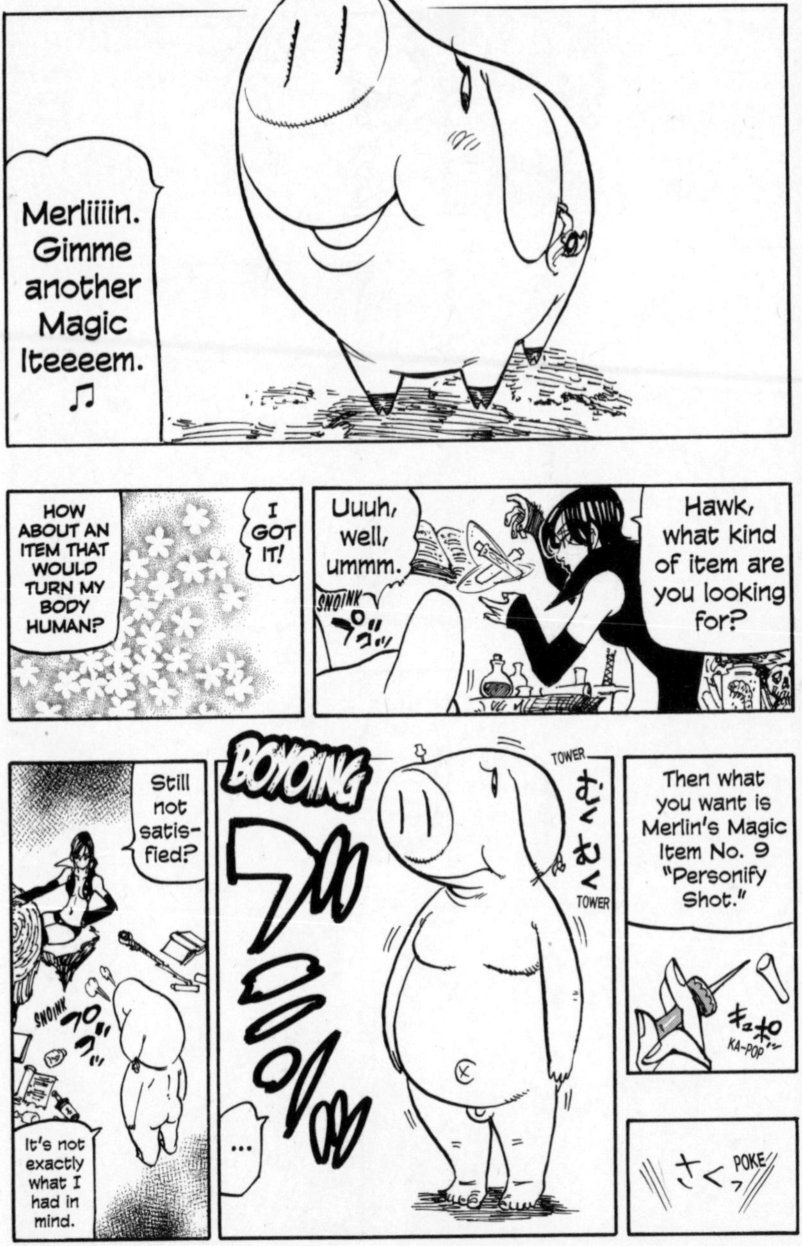
Merliiiin. Gimme another Magic Iteeeem. ♫
Hawk, what kind of item are you looking for?
Uuuh, well, ummm.
SNOINK
I GOT IT!
HOW ABOUT AN ITEM THAT WOULD TURN MY BODY HUMAN?
Then what you want is Merlin's Magic Item No. 9 "Personify Shot."
KA-POP
POKE
BOYOING
TOWER
TOWER
...
Still not satis-fied?
SNOINK
It's not exactly what I had in mind.

Bonus Story - Hawk the Materialist

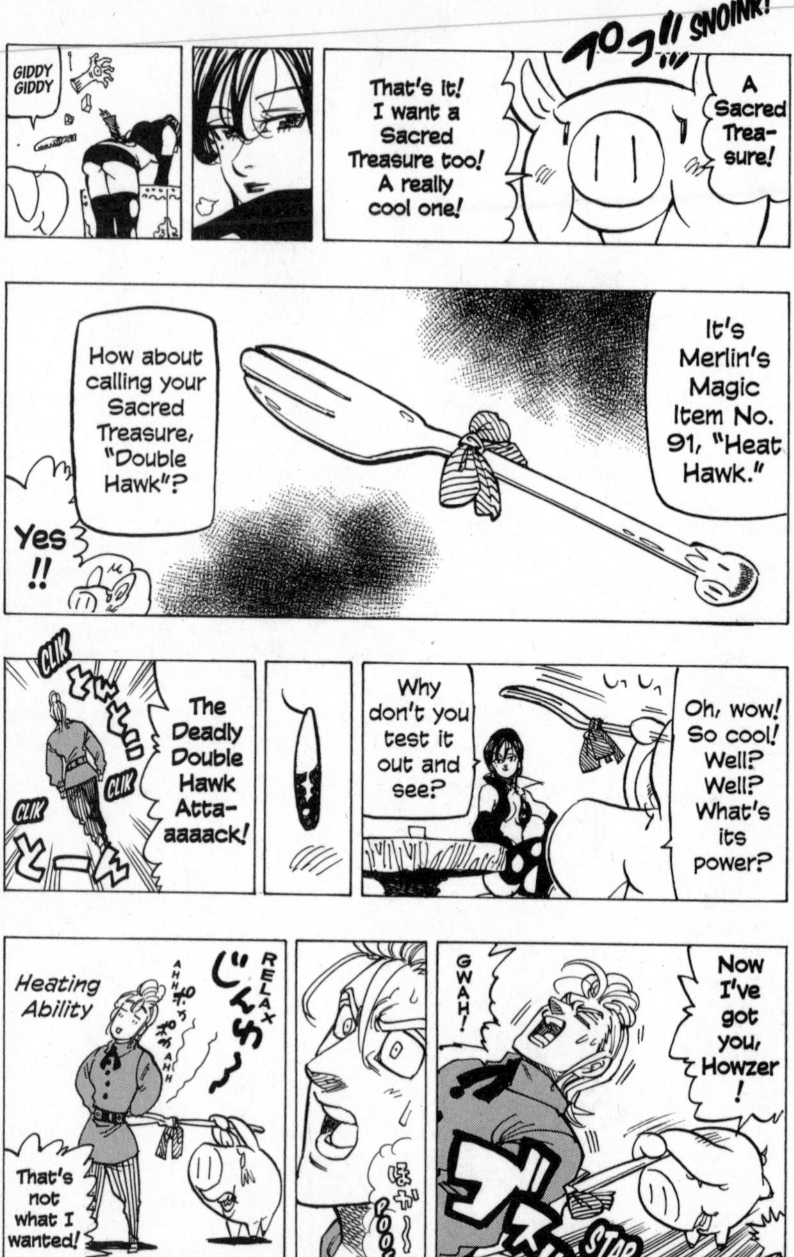
SNOINK!
A Sacred Treasure!
That's it! I want a Sacred Treasure too! A really cool one!
GIDDY GIDDY
It's Merlin's Magic Item No. 91, "Heat Hawk."
How about calling your Sacred Treasure, "Double Hawk"?
Yes!!
Oh, wow! So cool! Well? Well? What's its power?
Why don't you test it out and see?
CLIK
The Deadly Double Hawk Attaaaaack!
CLIK
CLIK
Now I've got you, Howzer!
GWAH!
STAB
POOF
RELAX
AHH
Heating Ability
That's not what I wanted!

THE END

She was the daughter of the tenth king of Liones, as well as the older sister of the former king Bartra and Captain Denzel of the The Pleaides of the Blue Sky.

She passed away at a mere 16 years old, though her last days were her most satisfying in all her life. Despite her heart giving her trouble, she still had a lively personality, and was enamored by adventure and romance. She also loved stories.

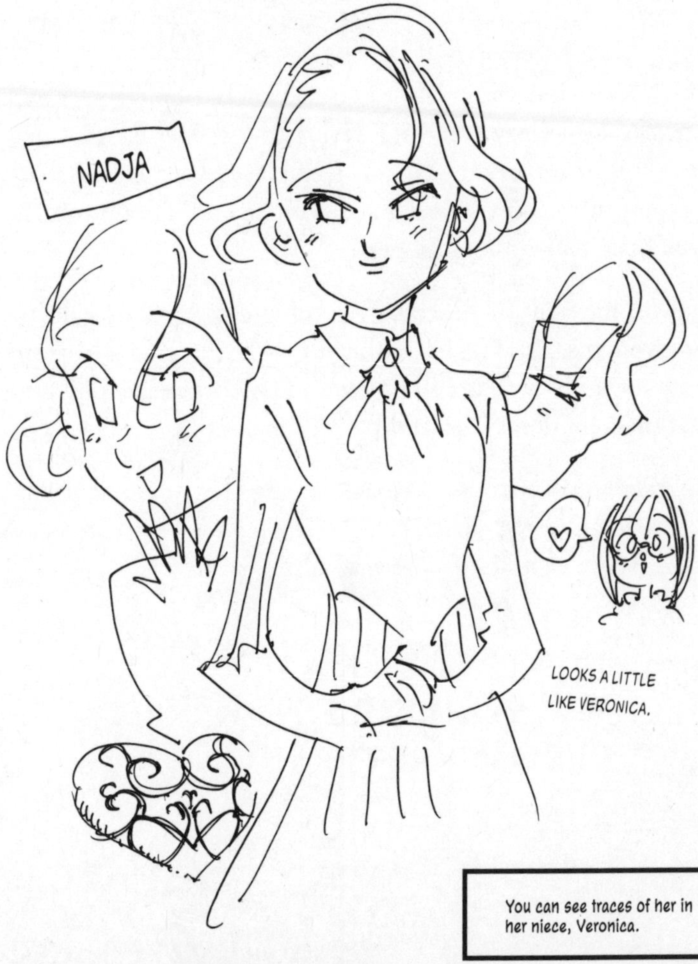
NADJA
LOOKS A LITTLE LIKE VERONICA.

You can see traces of her in her niece, Veronica.

Stories by Shuka Matsuda
Created by Nakaba Suzuki

Shaking the wide plains of Britannia, known only to a select few, is the legendary travelling tavern the BOAR HAT. Gathered in this tavern are the equally legendary Seven Deadly Sins, the proud order of knights that permits no disruption to the order of the Kingdom of Liones.

In a brief moment of peace before the great war that will test their strengths, the knights gather in the strange tavern to recall their rainbow-colored histories. The three episodes here reveal their hidden sweet and painful memories.

With original illustrations accompanying the stories collected here, *Seven-Colored Recollections* will continue to immerse readers in the rich, fantastic world of Britannia.

AVAILABLE NOW
FROM VERTICAL, INC.

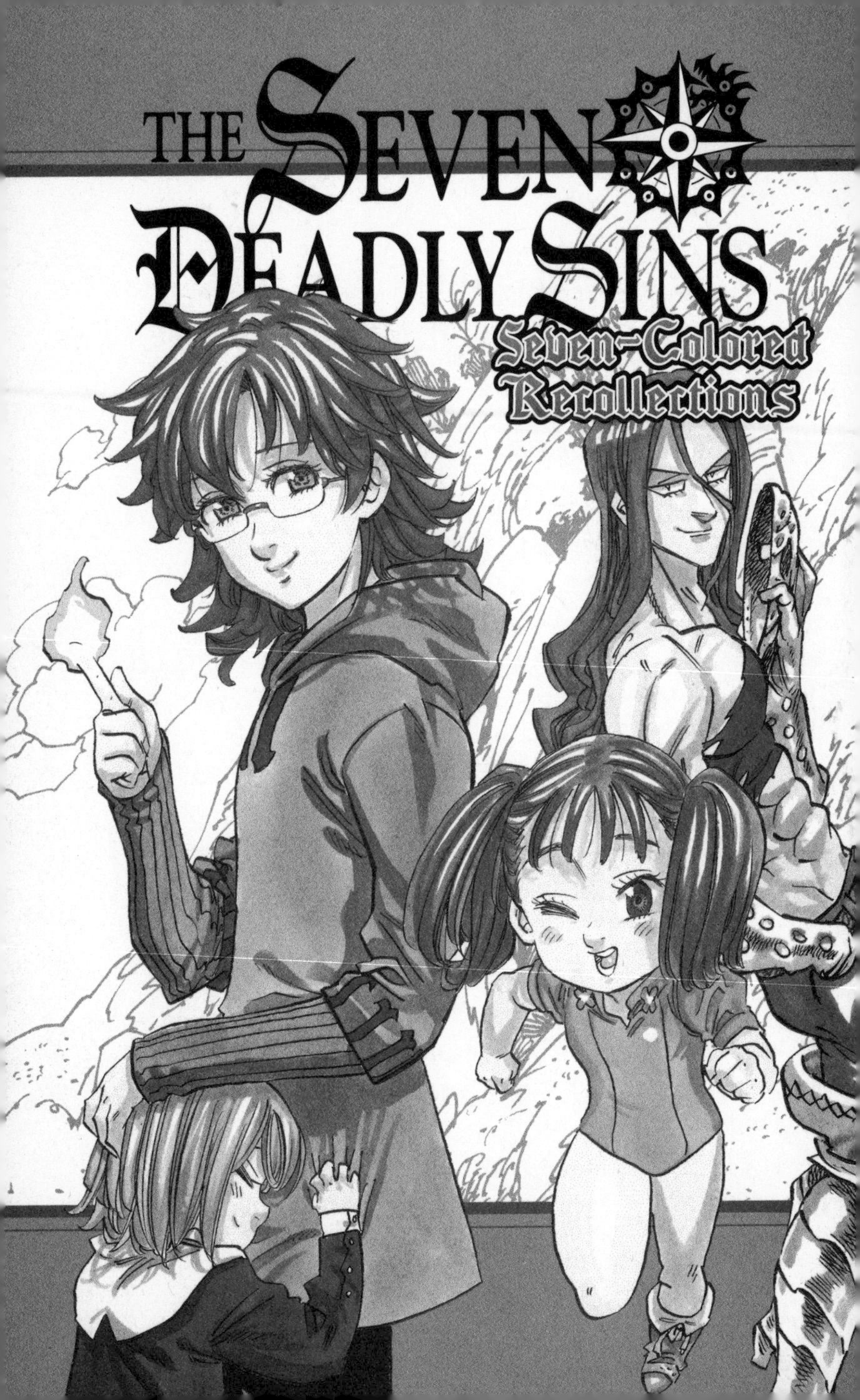
THE SEVEN DEADLY SINS
Seven-Colored Recollections

A Kodansha Comics Trade Paperback Original.

The Seven Deadly Sins volume 26 copyright © 2017 Nakaba Suzuki
English translation copyright © 2018 Nakaba Suzuki

Published in the United States by Kodansha Comics, an imprint of Kodansha USA Publishing, LLC, New York.

Publication rights for this English edition arranged through Kodansha Ltd., Tokyo.

First published in Japan in 2017 by Kodansha Ltd., Tokyo.

ISBN 978-1-63236-568-2

Printed in the United States of America.

www.kodanshacomics.com

9 8 7 6 5 4 3 2

Translation: Christine Dashiell
Lettering: James Dashiell
Editing: Lauren Scanlan
Kodansha Comics edition cover design: Phil Balsman